Business Grammar Builder

Macmillan Education
Between Towns Road, Oxford OX4 3PP
A division of Macmillan Publishers Limited
Companies and representatives throughout the world
ISBN 978-0-230-73252-0

Text © Paul Emmerson 2010
Design and illustration © Macmillan Publishers Limited 2010

First published 2002
This edition 2010

All rights reserved; no part of this publication may be reproduced, stored in a retrieval system, transmitted in any form, or by any means, electronic, mechanical, photocopying, recording, or otherwise, without the prior written permission of the publishers.

Designed by Carolyn Gibson
Cover design by Macmillan

Author's acknowledgements:
The author would like to thank Anna Cowper for commissioning the book, and for later content-editing it in a freelance capacity. Many thanks also to Darina Richter for overseeing everything in-house; to Nick Robinson for impeccable proofreading; and to Carolyn Gibson for design. Thanks are also due to my wife Estera, who, as a former Business English teacher, made numerous valuable and practical suggestions at proof stages. Finally, thanks to my beautiful baby Anna for not waking up too often while asleep in a sling on my tummy during much of the writing of the first half of the book.

The author and publishers would like to thank the following for permission to reproduce their photographs: Cartoonstock p171; The New Yorker Collection from Cartoonbank.com, all rights reserved pp11, 19, 27, 31, 35, 43, 55, 67, 75, 83, 91, 99, 107, 111, 119, 127, 135, 143, 179, 187, 199, 207.

These materials may contain links for third party websites. We have no control over, and are not responsible for, the contents of such third party websites. Please use care when accessing them.

Although we have tried to trace and contact copyright holders before publication, in some cases this has not been possible. If contacted we will be pleased to rectify any errors or omissions at the earliest opportunity.

Printed and bound in Thailand

2015 2014 2013 2012 2011
10 9 8 7 6 5 4 3 2

Paul Emmerson

Business Grammar Builder

2nd edition

Intermediate to Upper-intermediate

Clear explanations for real situations

Contents

TEST BANK (FOR DIAGNOSIS OR REVIEW)

APPENDICES

List of grammar terms

Active form	The **active form** of a verb is when the person or thing doing the action is the subject of the verb: ***I wrote*** *the report*. Compare with 'passive form' on page 9.
Adjective	An **adjective** helps to describe a noun or pronoun: *It's a* ***small, high-capacity*** *storage device*.
Adverb	An **adverb** adds information about *when*, *where* or *how* something happens: *I did it* ***yesterday****. I did it* ***quickly***.
Article	**Articles** are the word *the* (= the definite article) or *a/an* (= the indefinite article).
Auxiliary verb	An **auxiliary verb** (*be*, *do* and *have*) is used with other verbs to make tenses and passive forms: *He* ***is*** *working in Milan. Where* ***did*** *you go? Two hundred employees* ***have been*** *laid off.*
Clause	A **clause** is a group of words that contains a subject and a verb. It may be a sentence or only part of a sentence.
Conditional	A **conditional** is a sentence that includes *if*, *unless*, etc. and states something that must be true (the condition) before something else can be true or can happen (the result).
Continuous form	The **continuous** is the form of the verb that suggests that an activity is in progress. The continuous form ends in *-ing*.
Determiner	A **determiner** is a word like *the*, *some* and *every*. It is used before a noun or adjective to show which thing you mean.
Gerund	A **gerund** is an *-ing* form of a verb used like a noun: ***Smoking*** *is not allowed. My hobby is* ***sailing***.
Imperative	An **imperative** is when we tell people what to do. We use the base form of the verb: ***Come*** *here.* ***Switch*** *off the light.*
Infinitive	The **infinitive** is the base form of the verb (*work, go*, etc). It is used with or without *to*: *I hope* ***to see*** *you next week. I must* ***go*** *now.*
The *-ing* form	The ***-ing*** **form** is the form of the verb that ends in *-ing*. When it is used as a verb or adjective it is sometimes called a 'present participle': *I'm* ***leaving*** *tomorrow. A* ***boring*** *meeting.* When it is used as a noun it is sometimes called a 'gerund' (see above).
Intransitive verb	An **intransitive verb** is a verb that does not take an object. For example, the verb *arrive* is intransitive: *I* ***arrived*** *here last week*. In this sentence there is no object. Compare with 'transitive verb' on page 9.
Modal verb	A **modal verb** is a verb like *can, will, might* and *should*. It gives a meaning like ability, obligation, probability, permission, etc.
Noun	A **noun** is a word that is the name of an object, idea, place or person: *a* ***car****,* ***globalization****,* ***Singapore****,* ***Robert***.
Noun phrase	A **noun phrase** is a group of words, including a noun, which can act as a subject or object of a sentence: *investors* (noun), *some investors in emerging markets* (noun phrase).
Object	The **object** is the word that describes the person or thing that is affected by the verb: *I installed* ***some new software*** *on my PC.*

Passive form	The **passive form** is used to show how the subject of the verb is affected by the action of the verb: *The report* ***was written*** *by me*. Compare with the active form on page 8.
Past participle	A **past participle** is the form used in the perfect tense or passive structures. You can find it in the third column of tense tables. For example: *worked* is the past participle of *work* (this is a regular past participle), *gone* is the past participle of *go* (this is an irregular past participle).
Possessive	A **possessive** is a form that shows who or what something belongs to: *my/your* (possessive adjectives), *mine/yours* (possessive pronouns), etc. For example: *This is* ***my*** *car. This car is* ***mine***.
Phrasal verb	A **phrasal verb** is a verb with an adverb or preposition that has a different meaning from the verb used alone: *The plane* ***took off***.
Preposition	A **preposition** is a word like *at, behind, in, through, to, with* used before a noun or pronoun to show place, time, direction, etc.
Pronoun	A **pronoun** is a word like *it, me, you, him, her*, etc. that takes the place of a noun: *Have you been to Poland?* ***It*** *has changed a lot over recent years.*
Question tag	A **question tag** is a short question like *isn't it?* or *don't you?* that you add at the end of a sentence to check information or ask if someone agrees with you: *It's hot in here,* ***isn't it****?*
Reflexive pronoun	A **reflexive pronoun** is used to show that the person who does the action is also the person affected by it: ***She*** *introduced* ***herself*** *to me at the coffee break.*
Relative clause	A **relative clause** is used to identify someone or something, or give more information about them. It begins with *who, which, that*, etc: *The presentation* ***that I went to yesterday morning*** *was very interesting.*
The simple	The **simple** is the basic form of the verb: *I* ***agree*** *with you* (present simple), *He* ***agreed*** *with me* (past simple).
The subject	The **subject** is the word that shows who is doing the action of the verb: ***Jean*** *works here part time*. It usually comes before the verb.
Tense	A **tense** is the form of the verb. It helps us to know the time at which an action or event happened (past, present or future): *I* ***work*** *in the marketing area* (present simple tense), *I* ***worked*** *in the marketing area* (past simple tense). Academics sometimes have a more limited definition of the word 'tense', and they make a distinction between 'tense' and 'aspect'.
Transitive verb	A **transitive verb** is a verb that has an object. The verb *make* is transitive, and in this sentence *a mistake* is the object: *They've* ***made*** *a mistake*. Compare with 'intransitive verb' on page 8.
Verb	A **verb** expresses an action or state: *He* ***arrived*** *at 10.30. She* ***knows*** *the French market very well.*

1 Present time 1

A Present simple: form

The present simple is formed with the infinitive of the verb. We add *s* for *he/she/it*.

I/you/we/they ***work*** *here.*
He/she/it ***works*** *here.*

Negatives are formed with *do/does not*. In speech and informal writing we use contractions.

I/you/we/they ***do not (don't) work*** *here.*
He/she/it ***does not (doesn't) work*** *here.*

Questions are formed with the auxiliary verb *do/does* and the infinitive. Short answers to *yes/no* questions repeat the auxiliary.

A: ***Do*** *you* ***work*** *here?*
B: *Yes, I* ***do****./No, I* ***don't****.*
A: ***Does*** *she* ***work*** *here?*
B: *Yes, she* ***does****./No, she* ***doesn't****.*

B Present simple: uses

We use the present simple for permanent facts.

This machine ***cuts*** *the metal.*

We use the present simple for actions and situations that are generally true.

We ***offer*** *a full range of financial products.*

We use the present simple for actions which are repeated regularly over a long period of time, for example habits and routines.

Most of our customers ***invest*** *a regular amount every month.*

C Present simple: time expressions

We often use frequency adverbs with the present simple. Examples include: *always, often, usually, normally, sometimes, occasionally, rarely, hardly ever, never.*

Note the position of frequency adverbs:

Before the main verb.

I ***often use*** *my laptop on the train.*

After the verb *be*.

I'm usually *nervous before a presentation.*

Adverb phrases like *every day/year, once a week/quarter, most of the time, now and then* can come at the beginning or end of the sentence. If they come at the beginning there is more focus on the time phrase.

We use the present simple, not a future form, after these time expressions: *when, after, before, unless, in case, as soon as, until.*

I'll tell her when I see her.
(NOT I'll tell her when I ~~will~~ see her.)

D Present continuous: form

The present continuous is formed with the auxiliary verb *be* and the *-ing* form of the main verb. In speech and informal writing we use contractions.

I am (I'm) *work****ing*** *here.*
You are (you're) *work****ing*** *here.*
She is (she's) *work****ing*** *here.*
We are (we're) *work****ing*** *here.*
They are (they're) *work****ing*** *here.*

Negatives are formed with *be + not*.

I'm not *work****ing*** *here.*
You're not/You aren't *work****ing*** *here.*
She's not/She isn't *work****ing*** *here.*
We're not/We aren't *work****ing*** *here.*
They're not/They aren't *work****ing*** *here.*

Questions are formed by inverting the subject and the auxiliary *be*. Short answers to *yes/no* questions repeat the auxiliary.

A: ***Are you*** *working here?*
B: *Yes,* ***I am****./No,* ***I'm not****.*
A: ***Is he*** *working here?*
B: *Yes,* ***he is****./No,* ***he isn't****.*

E Present continuous: uses

We use the present continuous to talk about temporary actions and situations that are happening now.

The action or situation may be in progress now, at the moment of speaking.

Sorry, Mr Clark can't see you at the moment. ***He's talking*** *to a customer.*

The action or situation may be happening 'around now', even if it is not happening exactly at the moment of speaking.

Mr Clark is out of the office today. ***He's talking*** *at a conference in Stuttgart.*

The action or situation may be a current trend.

Workers all over the world ***are retiring*** *later in life.*

F Present continuous: time expressions

The present continuous is often used with these time expressions: *now, at the moment, nowadays, currently, these days, right now.*

See page 243 for an overview of the English verb tense system.

Exercises

Sections A, D

1.1 Underline the correct verb form.

1 *You often work/Do you often work* at the weekend?
2 *I don't know/I not know* why your invoice hasn't been paid. I'll try to find out.
3 Excuse me, *does you know/do you know* if this is the way to the IT seminar?
4 Sorry, that projector *don't work/doesn't work*. Use this one instead.
5 A: Do you know our new sales rep Marta?
B: *Yes, I do./Yes, I know.*
6 *I writing/I'm writing* the report at the moment. It should be ready tomorrow.
7 *They are replying not/They're not replying* to my emails. I'll have to phone them.
8 Why is there such a long delay? *What is happening?/What is happen?*
9 *You are enjoying/Are you enjoying* this conference?
10 A: Is Sara Lopez expecting me?
B: *Yes, she's expecting./Yes, she is.*

Sections B, E

1.2 Match uses a–e with sentences 1–5.

a) permanent facts
b) habits and repeated actions
c) temporary actions in progress at the moment of speaking
d) temporary actions happening 'around now', but not at this exact moment
e) current trends and changing situations

1 These days *we're selling* more and more of our products to Asia. [e]
2 Look over there! *They're selling* Adidas sportswear with 25% off! [ ]
3 *We're selling* a lot of this model – that's why we're out of stock right now. [ ]
4 *We* usually *sell* around 40% of our annual total at Christmas time. [ ]
5 *We sell* a full range of consumer electronics, from TVs to cameras. [ ]

Section C

1.3 Decide which word order is most usual, a) or b). Tick (✓) the correct answer.

1 a) I every day arrive at the office at about nine. [ ]
b) Every day I arrive at the office at about nine. [✓]

2 a) I always check my email before doing anything else. [ ]
b) Always I check my email before doing anything else. [ ]

3 a) This takes a lot of time usually, as I receive so many of them. [ ]
b) This usually takes a lot of time, as I receive so many of them. [ ]

4 a) Most of the time the emails are not very urgent. [ ]
b) The emails are most of the time not very urgent. [ ]

5 a) I quite often get junk email from companies I don't know. [ ]
b) I get quite often junk email from companies I don't know. [ ]

"I don't know how it started, either. All I know is that it's part of our corporate culture."

Exercises

Sections A, B **1.4 Denise introduces Claude to João in London. Put each of the verbs into the correct form of the present simple. Use contractions where possible.**

DENISE: Claude, [1] *Do you know* (you/know) João? João [2] ______ (work) in the oil industry, like you.
CLAUDE: Really! I [3] ______ (be) very pleased to meet you, João.
JOÃO: Pleased to meet you too, Claude.
CLAUDE: So what exactly [4] ______ (you/do)?
JOÃO: I [5] ______ (work) as a market analyst. My job [6] ______ (involve) studying market trends and giving advice on levels of production, but I [7] ______ (not/make) any real operational decisions myself. What about you?
CLAUDE: I work for a company that [8] ______ (supply) specialized equipment to the oil industry. We [9] ______ (be) one of the biggest companies in our market.
JOÃO: And [10] ______ (you/often/come) here to London?
CLAUDE: Yes, I normally [11] ______ (come) to London a couple of times a year. It [12] ______ (not/take) long to get here if you travel by Eurostar.

Sections D, E **1.5 Complete this newspaper article about trade between the Middle East and Asia with the words in the box in the present continuous.**

happen	increase	invest	look	try	become	~~boom~~	move

The New *Silk Road*

TRADE BETWEEN THE Middle East and Asia [1] *is booming* again – just like it did in ancient times, when caravans transported silk, spices and precious stones between the eastern Mediterranean and the heart of China.

Nowadays the trade is very different. Arab investors [2] ______ at Asia to find smart places to invest their petrodollars, while in the other direction Asian businesses [3] ______ to find reliable energy supplies, as well as markets for the goods that are mass-produced by their factories.

It's a phenomenon that [4] ______ right across the two regions. Chinese companies [5] ______ heavily in production facilities in Saudi Arabia, while in the opposite direction the Saudis [6] ______ the proportion of their oil exports that they send to China. And Kuala Lumpur, the capital of Malaysia, [7] ______ a centre for Islamic finance, channeling investments from the Middle East into the whole East Asia region.

Khaled Al-Muhairy is typical of the new breed of entrepreneur. His Abu Dhabi investment fund is focused on India. 'Power [8] ______ from West to East,' he says in an interview with *Business Week*, 'it is a huge opportunity.'

Tasks

Speaking: listen and repeat

1 01 **You are going to hear eight phrases. Listen and repeat.**

Translate

2 Translate these short texts taken from the Internet into your own language. Remember not to translate word for word, but rather to make it sound natural.

Computer games are getting better every year. The application of physics is making movement more realistic, and artificial intelligence is causing players to become more emotionally involved.

Economist website

A common sales technique is to generate a sense of urgency by setting a deadline: "offer ends June 30". It's terrible to feel you might miss out on something. But while you're worrying about missing a special deal, you're not worrying about whether you really need the item in question, or whether it's such a good deal. These tricks wouldn't be used so often if they didn't work. So beware the special offer.

Sydney Morning Herald website

Writing: personalized practice

3 Write questions using the words given, changing the form if necessary. Use the present simple for 1–4 and the present continuous for 5–8.

1 How/you/get to work? How long/it take?
How do you get to work? How long does it take?

2 What type of things/you do/when you first arrive at the office?

3 You have lunch/on your own or with colleagues? Where/eat?

4 How often/your boss check on your work/during the day/week?

5 What new product or service/you currently work on? You make good progress?

6 You have/any problems at work/right now? How you deal with them?

7 You do/any special work-related training/at the moment?

8 What/you do/outside work/to develop yourself at a personal level?

Now write your own answers to the same questions (on another piece of paper). Give a full, interesting answer, as if it was part of a conversation.

Rehearsal for the real world

4 Write a short text based on the ideas below.

1 Look again at how Claude and João describe their jobs in exercise 1.4. Notice the use of the present simple. Write a dialogue where someone you meet asks you about your job and you describe it.

2 Look again at the description of a current trend in the business world in exercise 1.5. Notice the use of the present continuous. Think of another current trend (in the business world, your company, or your personal life) and write a short text about it.

If you are working in class, read the dialogues or texts aloud and then discuss them.

2 Present time 2

A Present simple or continuous?

The present simple and present continuous are explained separately in unit 1. Now compare them:

Present simple	**Present continuous**
permanent	temporary
habits & routines	events in progress now
general situations	a particular situation

*I **live** in Budapest.*	(all the time)
*I'**m living** in Budapest.*	(for a few months)
*The plane **lands** at 10.25.*	(routine)
*Look! We'**re landing**.*	(in progress now)
*We **offer** IT solutions.*	(general situation)
*We'**re offering** you a special deal.*	(particular situation)

B Present continuous or present perfect continuous?

The present continuous is used for a temporary action happening now.
The present perfect continuous (unit 6) describes an action in progress from the past up to the present.

*Sue **is working** on the new design.*
(in progress now, and will continue)

*Sue **has been working** on the new design.*
(in progress up to now, and may or may not continue)

C Other uses of present tenses

PRESENT SIMPLE
The present simple can be used to refer to timetables and schedules, and here we are often thinking about the future.

*British Airways flight BA729 **leaves** Geneva at 16.40 and **arrives** in London at 17.20.*

The present simple can be used to make a story appear more immediate and interesting. This is common in journalism.

*Senior managers **walk** into the annual shareholders meeting through the back door. The steelworkers **throw** smoke bombs at the front. They **are not** happy about the job cuts.*

PRESENT CONTINUOUS
The present continuous can be used to describe a fixed future arrangement. There is usually a future time expression (unit 7).

*HSBC **are moving** to new premises next year.*

We can use *always* with the present continuous. This is often used for exaggerating or complaining. We emphasize *always* in speech in this case.

*This photocopier is **always** breaking down!*

D State verbs

Some verbs describe states, not actions; nothing 'happens'. Verbs like this are not normally used in the continuous form of any tense.

*I **notice** that you've changed the design.*
(NOT ~~I'm noticing~~)

*Let me help you – I **know** what to do.*
(NOT ~~I'm knowing~~)

*How much **does** it **cost**?*
(NOT ~~How much is it costing?~~)

*It **weighs** 4 kg with the packaging.*
(NOT ~~It is weighing~~)

The examples are in the present simple above, even though we are talking about temporary situations.

State verbs include:

the senses
appear, hear, look like, notice, see, seem, smell, sound, taste

feelings
dislike, fear, hate, like, love, prefer, want, wish

thinking
agree, believe, doubt, expect, feel, forget, imagine, know, realize, recognize, suppose, suspect, think

possession
belong to, contain, have, include, own, possess

being
be, consist of, exist

other verbs
cost, depend on, fit, involve, matter, measure, mean, need, satisfy, surprise, weigh

Many of the verbs in the previous list can have a 'state' meaning and an 'action' meaning.

*Our suppliers **are** usually very helpful.* (state)
*Our suppliers **are being** very helpful.* (action)
*I **feel** that the plan won't work.* (feel = think)
*I'**m feeling** cold – is the window open?* (feel ≠ think)
*I **have** two sisters.* (state)
*I'**m having** problems with this laptop.* (action)
*The manual **includes** cleaning instructions.* (state)
*I'**m including** you in the plans for dinner.* (action)
*I **think** you're right.* (state)
*I'**m thinking** about changing my job.* (action)
*I **weigh** 85 kg.* (state)
*I'**m weighing** the flour for your cake.* (action)

State verbs are not normally used in the imperative.

See page 243 for an overview of the English verb tense system.

Exercises

Section A

2.1 Underline the correct verb form.

1 A: What *do you do/are you doing*?
B: I'm an executive secretary.
2 A: What *do you do/are you doing*?
B: I'm looking for the invoice details on the computer.
3 A: Where *do you work/are you working*?
B: Paris this month, then Berlin the next.
4 A: Where *do you work/are you working*?
B: At our head office in Paris.
5 My name's Walter, and *I come/I'm coming* from Frankfurt.
6 *I come/I'm coming* home now – shall I buy something for dinner?
7 *I deal with/I'm dealing with* Andrew's clients while he's on vacation.
8 In my job *I deal with/I'm dealing with* a lot of routine paperwork.
9 Who *do you go/are you going* to the Trade Fair with this year?
10 Who *do you usually go/are you usually going* to the Trade Fair with?

Sections A, D

2.2 Put the verbs in brackets into the present simple or present continuous. Use contractions where possible.

1 I *'m looking at* (look at) your contact details on the screen right now.
2 I ________ (look at) the sales results in detail every month.
3 The production line ________ (not, work) at weekends.
4 The production line ________ (not, work) at the moment.
5 Yes, I agree. I ________ (think) it's a good idea.
6 I ________ (think) about it. I'll let you know tomorrow.
7 We ________ (take) a sample for testing once a day.
8 We ________ (take) a big risk if we go ahead with the project.
9 They ________ (not, be) usually very flexible in negotiations.
10 They ________ (not, be) very flexible in this negotiation.

Section D

2.3 Some of the following sentences are right and some are wrong. Put a tick (✓) next to the right ones, and correct the wrong ones.

1 Which wine are you drinking? ✓
2 Which wine are you preferring? *do you prefer*
3 I'm not believing it! ________
4 I'm not doing business with them again! ________
5 Yes, I'm making a note of all the key points. ________
6 Yes, I'm knowing exactly what you mean. ________
7 This building is containing all the printing machines. ________
8 This building is getting very old – we'll have to move. ________

Exercises

Sections A, D **2.4 Jennifer Elliot makes a call to try to get some new business. Complete the dialogue by putting the verbs into the correct form of the present simple or present continuous. Use contractions where possible.**

JENNIFER: This is Jennifer Elliot from Pritchard Evans. I [1] *'m calling* (call) to follow up a conversation I had recently with Kim Bryant.

SECRETARY: Oh, I'm sorry, Kim isn't here today. She [2] ________ (work) at home trying to finish an urgent report. I [3] ________ (think) she'll be back at her desk tomorrow. Perhaps I can help you?

JENNIFER: Thank you. I [4] ________ (work) for the corporate hospitality arm of Pritchard Evans. I [5] ________ (understand) from Kim that you [6] ________ (expect) a visit by a Korean trade delegation next month.

SECRETARY: Yes, I [7] ________ (believe) so.

JENNIFER: Well, Kim asked me to give her a call to discuss the services we [8] ________ (offer). For example, we can take your visitors to sporting or cultural events, and perhaps pick them up from their hotel in a limousine. It [9] ________ (depend on) what you [10] ________ (want).

SECRETARY: Yes, you really [11] ________ (need) to speak to Kim – she [12] ________ (deal) with this. Can you call back tomorrow?

JENNIFER: Of course. I'll call her tomorrow morning around 9.30.

Sections A, D **2.5 Complete this article about urbanization with the verbs in the box. Choose either the present simple or present continuous. On one occasion, both answers are possible.**

bring	focus	~~grow~~	have to	realize	spend

Cities & growth

Cities in the developing world [1] *are growing* at an alarming rate. The world's urban population has risen from 1.6 billion to 3.3 billion over the past 30 years, and is expected to reach 5.5 billion over the next 30 years. Internal migration on this scale inevitably [2] ________ massive social change, and nowadays urban planners [3] ________ deal with issues such as food supply, energy supply and the disposal of waste. Different countries are reacting in different ways. Saudi Arabia and Egypt [4] ________ billions on new super-cities to divert people away from Jeddah and Cairo, while China [5] ________ on developing its interior regions through spending on transport and infrastructure. These governments [6] ________ that urbanization is an inevitable process, and is necessary for economic progress. Manufacturing, business services, construction and retailing all develop together in cities in a way that they simply cannot do in remote rural areas.

Tasks

Speaking: listen and repeat

1 02 **You are going to hear eight phrases. Listen and repeat.**

Translate

2 **Translate these short texts taken from the Internet into your own language. Remember not to translate word for word, but rather to make it sound natural.**

There's a new trend that's sweeping the Web: Real-time. Everyone wants access to information as it happens instantaneously. Scoopler is a search engines that gives you live, real-time results across a variety of services. You enter a query and the page returns auto-updating results based on information coming in. It's a pretty nice view of what is happening on the web at any given moment. The problem is that Twitter dominates the results.

TechCrunch website

Unnoticed in the government's standard employment data, employers are begging for qualified applicants for certain occupations, even in hard times. Most of the jobs involve skills that take years to attain. Welder is one, critical care nurse is another. Civil engineers and special education teachers are also in demand.

New York Times website

Writing: personalized practice

3 **Write sentences using the words given. The first verb should be in the present simple and the second verb in the present continuous. Add or invent details where you see '…'.**

1 We operate in … and we set up new offices in …
We operate in France and Benelux, and we're setting up new offices in Spain.

2 I come from … but at the moment I live …

3 I usually enjoy my work at … but right now I have some problems with …

4 We normally do a lot of business with … but we take fewer orders from them these days because …

5 Traffic be a big problem in my city and the town council plan to …

6 I usually work from … to … each day but this week I work … because …

7 Every single day my boss tell me … and I become more and more …

8 I work as a … but I think of retraining to work as a … because …

Rehearsal for the real world

4 **Make a list of three activities that you do regularly (work or personal life). Then say what you are doing in connection with those activities at the moment. See the example below.**

Regular activities	**At the moment**
I do market research for various client companies.	I'm exploring various options for a foreign pharmaceutical company that wants to enter our market.

If you are working in class, read some texts aloud and then discuss them.

3 Past time 1

A Past simple: form

The past simple of regular verbs is formed by adding *-ed* to the infinitive. Verbs ending in *-e* simply add *-d*. Common irregular verbs are listed on page 240.

*check-check**ed***	*I check**ed** the figures.*
*like-lik**ed***	*They lik**ed** her idea.*

Irregular: *buy-**bought** do-**did** eat-**ate** drink-**drank** go-**went** sell-**sold** think-**thought***, etc.

Negatives are formed with *did not* and the infinitive. This is contracted to *didn't* in speech and informal writing.

*I **didn't go** to the meeting.*

Questions are formed with the auxiliary verb *did* and the infinitive. Short answers to *yes/no* questions repeat the auxiliary.

*A: **Did** you check the figures?*
*B: Yes, I **did**./No, I **didn't**.*

The verb *to be* is irregular and follows a different pattern. In negatives there is no *did*. In questions there is no *did* and the subject and verb are inverted.

*He **was** late.* *He **wasn't** late.* ***Was he** late?*

B Past simple: uses

We use the past simple to describe actions and states in a completed period of time. We know when the action happened, and this may be mentioned or clear from the situation.

*I **checked** the figures very carefully **yesterday**.*

The past simple is also used to describe habitual actions in the past.

*Every evening we **went out** and **ate** in a different restaurant.*

C Past simple: time expressions

Time expressions used with the past simple include:

at	*twelve o'clock/the end of the year*
in	*the morning/June/2008/the nineties*
on	*Friday/the second of April*
(no preposition)	*last week/yesterday/ago*

See unit 40 for more time expressions.

D Past continuous: form

The past continuous is formed with the past of *be* and the *-ing* form of the main verb. Negatives are formed with the verb *be + not*. In speech and informal writing we use contractions.

*He **was/wasn't** work**ing** yesterday.*

Questions are formed by inverting the subject and the auxiliary verb *be*. Short answers to *yes/no* questions repeat the auxiliary.

*A: **Was** he work**ing** yesterday?*
*B: Yes, he **was**./No, he **wasn't**.*

E Past continuous: uses

The past continuous is used to describe a situation in progress in the past.

*I **was waiting** in the departure lounge for more than two hours.*

There can be several situations in progress, happening at the same time.

*The company **was losing** its way and many employees **were leaving**.*

The past continuous is used to give information about the background situation. The separate, completed actions that happen during or after this period are in the past simple.

*I **was trying** to call you but my battery **died**.*

*I **came** into the company as it **was recovering** from the recession.*

If we do not mention the background situation, then the separate actions are in the past simple in the normal way.

*I **arrived** at the conference, **registered**, and **went** straight to the first presentation.*

F Past continuous: time expressions

We can use *when*, *while* or *as* with the past continuous to mean 'during the time that something was happening'.

***While/When** we **were developing** the software, we carried out a variety of simulations.*

But if we mean 'at the time that', then we only use *when* with the past simple.

He wasn't very happy when I told him the news.
(NOT ~~while I told him~~ ...)

G Past simple or continuous?

Sometimes the past simple or past continuous can be used. The past simple suggests a separate, complete action or event. The past continuous emphasizes the duration of the action.

*We **discussed** the report and agreed that direct marketing was a viable strategy.*

*We **were discussing** the report for over an hour. Eventually we came to some important decisions.*

See page 243 for an overview of the English verb tense system.

Exercises

Section A **3.1 Underline the correct words.**

1 A: Did you *get/got* the email I sent you yesterday?
  B: Yes, thanks, I *did/got*.
2 How *you felt/did you feel* when they *told you/did tell you* about the job cuts?
3 A: Did she *tell/told* you about the change of plans?
  B: Yes, she *told/did*.
4 I *didn't see/didn't saw* any reason for the delay, so I *got/did got* angry with them.

Section A **3.2 Complete the dialogue with the verbs in the box in the past simple. There is a mixture of affirmative, negative and question forms. Contractions count as one word.**

be (x2) buy have ~~make~~ sell take think

MARCO: Hi, Jill. How was the Milan Fashion Show?
JILL: Good. I 1 *made* a lot of good contacts as usual. But we 2 ____________ ____________ as many orders as last year. I'm not sure why. Our new range of shoes 3 ____________ very well at the Show, but we 4 ____________ so successful with some of our other lines, like handbags.
MARCO: Perhaps it was because of the current economic climate. 5 ____________ people ____________ our prices were too high?
JILL: Possibly. But unfortunately we 6 ____________ ____________ the authority to lower them. Maybe we should look at that for next year.
MARCO: But on the whole 7 ____________ it worth going?
JILL: Worth going? Of course! I 8 ____________ this great pair of Prada shoes.

Sections B, E **3.3 Underline the best continuation of the conversations.**

1 A: What happened after you launched the product?
  B: While we *marketed/were marketing* it, our main distributor suddenly *went/was going* bust.
2 A: I didn't see you in the office last week.
  B: No, I *worked/was working* at home for a few days.
3 A: How did Ana spend her holiday?
  B: I think that most days she *just went/was just going* to the beach.
4 A: What did Siga do when she saw the artwork for the advertising campaign?
  B: She *called/was calling* the designers and *said/was saying* it wasn't suitable.
5 A: Why did Renata take so long to get here?
  B: She said they *repaired/were repairing* the road in the city centre and the traffic *moved/was moving* very slowly.

"We structured the deal so it won't make any sense to you."

Exercises

Section A **3.4 Complete this article about Vivendi by putting the verbs into the past simple. Many are irregular (see Appendix 2 for a list of irregular forms).**

VIVENDI: Over 150 years of history

VIVENDI, the French media and telecommunications group, has a long history going back to 1853. The original company, Compagnie Générale des Eaux, [1] *supplied* (supply) water to farms, towns and cities in France. Their operations [2] ________ (grow) over the years and they [3] ________ (expand) to become the supplier of water to Venice, Constantinople and Oporto.

In the 1960s and 1970s CGE [4] ________ (begin) activities in the area of civil construction and [5] ________ (build) a large tower block in the La Défense business district of Paris. During the 1980s CGE [6] ________ (take) a controlling stake in the civil engineering giant SGE, and they [7] ________ (win) major construction contracts in the Asia Pacific region and in Latin America. They also [8] ________ (make) their first steps in the telecommunications business by helping to found Canal+, a pay TV channel.

In 1996 Jean-Marie Messier [9] ________ (become) CEO. He [10] ________ (sell off) the construction, water and waste divisions and [11] ________ (cut) the workforce. He [12] ________ (change) the name of the group to Vivendi and [13] ________ (transform) it into an international communications and entertainment company. However, in France he [14] ________ (be) a controversial figure and his expansion plans [15] ________ (be) overambitious. He [16] ________ (resign) in 2002, just before Vivendi [17] ________ (announce) a loss of €23 billion, the worst in French corporate history.

Vivendi then [18] ________ (go) through some difficult years while it restructured and [19] ________ (pay off) its debts. Now a successful company once again, a key moment in the turnaround was when it [20] ________ (buy) the American video game developer Blizzard, famous for creating the online game *World of Warcraft*.

Sections B, E **3.5 Put the verbs into the correct tense – either the past simple or past continuous.**

1 I *ate* (eat) some fantastic meals when I *went* (go) to Brussels.
2 While I *was negotiating* (negotiate) with them, our legal department *decided* (decide) to change the terms and conditions of the contract.
3 The last time something like this ________ (happen), she ________ (call) a press conference immediately.
4 Anne ________ (explain) her proposals when Pedro suddenly ________ (interrupt) her.
5 We never got the chance to discover his side of the story. While we ________ (investigate) the incident, he ________ (resign) from the company.
6 When he ________ (see) the article in the WSJ, he ________ (put) it on the notice board for everyone to see.
7 Everyone ________ (wait) for Hans when he ________ (call) to say that he was stuck in a traffic jam.
8 When I ________ (repair) the faulty part, I ________ (drop) it by mistake.
9 I ________ (find) the pdf file I ________ (look) for.
10 When Petra ________ (arrive), we ________ (tell) her what had happened.

Tasks

Speaking: listen and repeat

1 03 **You are going to hear eight phrases. Listen and repeat.**

Translate

2 Translate these short texts taken from the Internet into your own language. Remember not to translate word for word, but rather to make it sound natural.

European stocks rose for the first time in three days and oil rallied on speculation that the worst of the global recession is over. Russian shares led the advance after the country's central bank cut interest rates for the third time in six weeks.

Bloomberg website

'I came in to Oracle as it was recovering from the recession of the early 1990s. The business unit I joined had an ageing product line that was declining by 30 per cent a year in sales. Within a year we completely turned that unit around.'

Eurobusiness website

Writing: personalized practice

3 Complete the sentences with the past simple or the past continuous. Use whichever tense is not already used in the given words.

1 I looked out of the window. Someone *was trying to break into my car* .
2 My boss resigned last week. They found out that s/he ______________ .
3 While I was working at my desk this morning, ______________ .
4 We offered our sales agents a bigger discount because ______________ .
5 When I was working at my previous company, I ______________ .
6 The IT network crashed because of a virus. It happened just as ______________ .
7 While they were asking me questions in the interview, I suddenly ______________ .
8 Something really embarrassing happened – a new supplier offered me money under the table. It happened when I ______________ .

Rehearsal for the real world

4 Write two paragraphs about either your career or your company.

1 Write a history of your career. Include dates.
2 Write a history of your company. Include the major milestones and key events. Exact dates are not important.

If you are working in class, read some texts aloud and then discuss them.

4 Past time 2

A Past perfect: form

The past perfect is formed with the auxiliary *had* and the past participle. In speech and informal writing *had* is contracted to *'d*.

*We **had** (We**'d**) already **done** a lot of market research before we launched the product.*

Negatives are formed with *not* and contractions are used (*hadn't*). Questions are formed by inverting the subject and *had*.

*At that time we still **hadn't done** any research.*
***Had you** already **done** some market research?*

B Past perfect: uses

The past perfect is used to show clearly that one past event happened before another past event. We use the past perfect for the earlier event.

Compare these examples, which describe exactly the same situation:

1 Sue ***left*** at 2 pm. We ***arrived*** at her office at 2.15. (both verbs in past simple)
2 When we ***arrived*** at Sue's office, she ***had left***. (earlier action in past perfect)

In example 1 the two actions are separate in the mind of the speaker. In example 2 there is a stronger connection between the two actions and the past perfect emphasizes which one happened first.

It may not be necessary to use the past perfect if we use *before* or *after* to make the time sequence clear. In this case we use the past simple for both actions.

*Sue **left/had left** her office **before** we arrived.*
(both forms are possible)

The past perfect is often used with verbs of thinking, like *know, realize, remember, be sure, think.*

*When I got to their office, **I realized I'd left** all my papers behind.*
*Makan **was sure they hadn't received** the invoice, but he checked one more time.*

C Past perfect: time expressions

The time expressions *after, once, by, already, just, never, meanwhile* are often used with the past perfect. The word *still* is often used with negative forms.

*I **had** just **started** my presentation when the fire alarm rang.*
*It was Friday lunchtime and I still **hadn't finished** the report.*

D Past perfect continuous: form

The past perfect continuous is formed with the auxiliary phrase *had been* and the *-ing* form of the main verb.

***I'd been** work**ing** on the project for two months before they decided to cancel it.*

Negatives are formed with *had not been* and the *-ing* form of the main verb.

Questions are formed by inverting the subject and *had*.

*We **hadn't been doing** enough quality checks, and the number of defects was too high.*
***Had you been** work**ing** on the project for a long time before they cancelled it?*

E Past perfect continuous: uses

The past perfect continuous is used to describe a situation that was in progress up to a certain point in the past. It often emphasizes the duration of time.

***I'd been thinking** of changing my job for a long time before I finally made the decision.*

The past perfect and the past perfect continuous both look back from a point in the past. The past perfect looks back at an earlier event. The past perfect continuous looks back at a situation in progress.

*The economy was improving. The central bank **had lowered** interest rates because inflation **had been falling** steadily for several years.*

F *Used to / would* + infinitive

Used to describes a habit, state or repeated action in the past. *Used to* normally suggests that the action or situation is no longer true and so makes a contrast with the present.

*We **used to do** a big sales promotion every summer.*
(= but now we don't)

*I **used to work** in marketing.*
(= but now I work in another area)

With negatives and questions *used to* becomes *use to.*

***Did you use to** work in marketing?*
***I didn't use to** spend so much time on reports.*

Would is used in the same way as *used to*, but it only describes repeated actions in the past, not states. It is slightly more formal.

*In the old days we **used to archive/would archive** every single email.*
Our company used to belong to an American multinational.
(NOT ~~would belong~~)

See page 243 for an overview of the English verb tense system.

Exercises

Sections A, B, F, unit 3

4.1 Underline the correct verb form. This exercise includes some verb forms from unit 3.

1 While I *looked for/was looking for* the USB stick with my presentation on it, I suddenly remembered I *left/had left* it at home.
2 In those days the unions *used to/did used to* go on strike whenever there *was/was being* a problem.
3 After the private equity group *were buying/had bought* the company, they *started/were starting* to sell the assets and lay off a lot of people.
4 Dieter *used to have/was having* a PC, but then he *used to change/changed* to an Apple.
5 I asked about my package in reception, but they *said/were saying* that it still *hadn't arrived/wasn't arriving*.
6 I was sure that I *used to turn off/had turned off* my laptop, but it *was/had been* still on and the battery was nearly dead.
7 I'm sure that the winters *used to be/had been* colder when I was a child. I remember that we *used to walk/were walking* to school in the snow.
8 We wanted to register a patent on the new invention, but *found/were finding* that someone *already did/had already done* it for a very similar idea.
9 When Jorge saw Diana at the seminar, he *knew/was knowing* that he *met/had met* her somewhere before.
10 While I *had/was having* breakfast I had a look at my favourite financial website. I *saw/was seeing* that my original investment *grew/had grown* by over 40%.

Sections A, B, unit 3

4.2 In each sentence put one verb into the past simple and the other into the past perfect.

1 After she *had made* (make) a few notes, she *started* (start) writing the introduction to the Annual Report.
2 I ____________ (be sure) that I ____________ (set) the security alarm before leaving the office.
3 I ____________ (call) my wife on my mobile because the meeting ____________ (still not finish).
4 I ____________ (not see) the figures before the meeting, so it ____________ (put) me at a disadvantage during the discussion.
5 After Jill ____________ (give) her presentation, she ____________ (feel) much more relaxed and started to enjoy the conference.
6 Before Edite ____________ (become) Michael Edward's personal assistant, she ____________ (already be) in the company for two years.
7 The rain ____________ (stop) by the time I ____________ (arrive).
8 I ____________ (be) surprised to find that she ____________ (already sign) the contract without showing it to the legal department first.

Exercises

Sections A, B, unit 3

4.3 Complete what Vincent says about his last job with the best form of the verb in brackets. Choose between the past simple, past continuous or past perfect.

"It was January and I [1] *had graduated* (graduate) from university the previous summer. I was really fed up being unemployed – I [2]________ (just/sit) at home doing nothing. To be honest, I [3]________ (nearly/give up) hope. Then a friend told me about a graduate recruitment fair. I still [4]________ (not/decide) what kind of job I wanted to do, and I [5]________ (think) the fair would be interesting. While I [6]________ (look) at some information on one of the stands, a recruiter came up to me and [7]________ (tell) me about openings in a well-known company – an accountancy firm. I thought it would be a good opportunity for me, as I [8]________ (already/take) some accountancy exams as part of my business degree and I did well in them. I've always been good with figures. So I [9]________ (complete) an application form and gave it to the recruiter. They [10]________ (interview) me the following week and I got the job. In the end I was there for three years. You want to know why I left? Well, the situation was like this. I [11]________ (work) for a person who was very demanding and gave me very little space to take initiatives on my own. Also, I [12]________ (not have) a salary increase since I [13]________ (start). They [14]________ (really/exploit) me. Then, on top of that, the job [15]________ (become) quite repetitive after three years and I really wanted to do something different. So I [16]________ (resign). I [17]________ (not/have) another job to go to, but I just knew I [18]________ (have) to make a change. It was a pity because I [19]________ (put) a lot of effort into that job and I [20]________ (always want) to work for an international company like that, but it was the only thing to do."

Sections D, E

4.4 Underline the correct verb form.

1 When the company went public, they *had produced/had been producing* wind-powered generators for over ten years.

2 Sorry it took so long. I needed to go to the store room – the photocopier *had run out of/had been running out of* paper.

3 I was under a lot of stress at the time and I *hadn't slept/hadn't been sleeping* well.

4 I thought we *had already chosen/had already been choosing* the name for the new product.

Section F

4.5 Complete the sentences with *used to* alone, or *used to/would* (meaning that both are possible).

1 With my old boss we ________ have meetings several times a week.

2 I ________ own a BMW, but now I have a Lexus.

3 Before they built the motorway it ________ take me an hour to get to work.

4 I ________ think I wanted to work for a large organization with lots of opportunity for promotion. Now I want to be self-employed.

Tasks

Speaking: listen and repeat

1 04 **You are going to hear eight phrases. Listen and repeat.**

Translate

2 **Translate these short texts taken from the Internet into your own language. Remember not to translate word for word, but rather to make it sound natural.**

The origins of SAP were in the 1970s. IBM had grown fat and arrogant and had started dictating to its customers. The decisive moment came in 1972 when some of its European staff saw an opportunity to leave and set up their own company.

Eurobusiness website

Rocker Morrissey regularly bans all food "that used to have a face" from concert halls. The ardent vegetarian – whose second album with his former group The Smiths was titled 'Meat Is Murder' – demanded the Webster Hall venue be a meat-free zone before, during and immediately after his performance on Wednesday night. Apparently, Morrissey also prohibits his staff from eating meat and will fire anyone on the spot if caught doing so.

Ecorazzi website

Writing: personalized practice

3 **Complete the sentences in your own way with the past perfect (simple or continuous). Add another sentence or two to make a complete paragraph.**

1 My flight was delayed until the following morning because *it had been snowing all night and they said it wasn't safe for planes to take off. I had to sleep at the airport and all I could find was some hard plastic chairs* .

2 I got a lot of work done yesterday morning. By lunchtime I ______________________ .

3 My boss was in a good mood because ______________________ .

4 At first the project seemed to be going very well. But after some time we realized that ______________________ .

5 The negotiations with the new suppliers broke down because ______________________ .

6 I checked that everything was turned off, locked the front door, and got into the taxi. It was only when I arrived at the airport that I remembered ______________________ .

Rehearsal for the real world

4 **Look again at exercise 4.3, where Vincent describes his last job, what he did there, why he left, etc. Notice the use of the different verb tenses. Now write a short text where you describe your own last job.**

If you are working in class, read some texts aloud and then discuss them.

5 Connecting past and present 1

A Present perfect: form

The present perfect is formed with the present tense of the auxiliary verb *have* and the past participle. In speech and informal writing we use contractions (*'ve* and *'s*).

I/you/we/they ***have ('ve) gone***.
He/she/it ***has ('s) gone***.

Negatives are formed with *not*.

I/you/we/they ***have not (haven't) gone***.
He/she/it ***has not (hasn't) gone***.

Questions are formed by inverting the subject and the auxiliary verb *have*. Short answers to *yes/no* questions repeat the auxiliary.

A: ***Have they*** *gone?*
B: *Yes,* ***they have***.*/No,* ***they haven't***.
A: ***Has he*** *gone?*
B: *Yes,* ***he has***.*/No,* ***he hasn't***.

B Present perfect: uses

In general we use the present perfect to talk about a present situation which is connected to the past.

There may be a present situation that started in the past.

I've lived *here for about ten years.*

There may be a series of actions that happened in our life up to now.

I've been *to Singapore many times.*

There may be a result in the present of a past event.

I think ***I've set up*** *the spreadsheet incorrectly – I hope I don't have to enter all the data again.*

In this last case we are explaining the current importance of a past event. When it happened is not important and is not mentioned.

C Present perfect: time expressions

We use *ever* and *never* to ask and talk about our general life experience.

Have *you* ***ever spoken*** *to a large audience?*
I've never used *this software before.*

If the answer to the question is *Yes* then we continue to give more information about the specific events by using verbs in the past simple.

A: ***Have*** *you ever* ***spoken*** *to a large audience?*
B: *Yes, I* ***have***. *Last year I* ***went*** *to a sales conference in Berne and I* ***gave*** *a presentation to about 100 people.*

The present perfect is often used with *already* and *yet*. *Already* is normally used in affirmative sentences.

We ***have already made*** *75% of our planned investment.*

Yet is used in questions and negatives, and suggests that although something has not happened, we do expect it to happen.

Have *you* ***finished*** *the report* ***yet****?*
We ***haven't had*** *any delays with the project –* ***yet****!*

We use *just* to describe something that happened a short time ago.

I've just spoken *to her on the phone.*

The present perfect is often used with time expressions that refer to unfinished time. In other words, the time period includes the present. Common expressions like this are: *this morning, today, this month, so far, up to now, recently, lately, over the last few years,* etc.

Growth in the Asia-Pacific region ***has exceeded*** *5% annually* ***over the past few years***.

We use *for* and *since* with the present perfect to refer to periods of time.

A: *How long* ***has*** *Wolfgang* ***worked*** *here?*
B: *He****'s worked*** *here* ***for*** *three months.*

OR

B: ***He's worked*** *here* ***since*** *May.*

For describes the length of the time period. *Since* describes the point when the time period started. (Unit 40C).

Frequency adverbs that are used with the present simple (unit 1C) can also be used with the present perfect.

Our lawyers ***have often given*** *us good advice.*

Some time expressions can be used with the present perfect or the past simple, depending on when you are speaking.

Have *you* ***spoken*** *to Sue* ***this morning****?*
(It is now 11 am; the morning has not finished.)

Did *you* ***speak*** *to Sue* ***this morning****?*
(It is now 3 pm; the morning has finished.)

D *been (to)* and *gone (to)*

If we *have been to* a place, we went there and have now returned. If we *have gone to* a place, we went there but have not yet returned.

She's been to *Head Office. Everything is sorted out now.*
(she has come back)

She's gone to *Head Office. I hope everything will be sorted out.*
(she is still there)

See page 243 for an overview of the English verb tense system.

Exercises

Section A, C **5.1 Put the verbs into the present perfect. Use contractions where possible.**

1 Are you sure it isn't working? *Have you tried* (you/try) restarting it?
2 I ________________ (never see) such a boring presentation in my life.
3 We ________________ (already/spend) a lot of money on this project.
4 ________________ (they/reply) to your last email?
5 I ________________ (not/get) the figures to hand – can I call you back later?
6 I'm sorry, she's not here. She ________________ (just/leave).
7 Their shares ________________ (go up) by 5% since the merger.
8 ________________ (you/ever/take) the TGV to Toulouse? It's really fast.

Section B **5.2 Look at the paired sentences below. Match each one with situation a) or b).**

1 Inflation has fallen by 1%. [*b*] 2 Inflation fell by 1%. [*a*]
a) Three years ago it was 4%. Two years ago it was 3%.
b) Last month it was 4%. This month it is 3%.

3 I think I've lost the file. [ ] 4 Sorry, I lost the file. [ ]
a) I can't find the file. I wonder where I put it?
b) The file has gone and I'll never find it.

5 Has Jane called this morning? [ ] 6 Did Jane call this morning? [ ]
a) Jane promised to call this morning. It's 11 am.
b) Jane promised to call this morning. It's 2 pm.

7 Sales improved. [ ] 8 Sales have improved. [ ]
a) Last year sales were poor. This year they are better.
b) Sales were poor initially. A year later they were better.

9 How long have you worked here? [ ] 10 When did you start working here? [ ]
a) In 2005.
b) Since 2005.

Section C **5.3 Complete the sentences with the time expressions in the box.**

~~already~~	yet	ever	never	just	for	since	always

1 The goods will be with you soon. They've *already* left our warehouse.
2 I've ____________ had an idea – why don't we restyle the packaging for a new, younger target market?
3 We've known each other ____________ more than twenty years.
4 I've ____________ used my credit card on the Internet. I don't think it's safe.
5 I haven't spoken to Magda ____________, but I'm sure she'll agree.
6 I've ____________ worked in insurance, ever since leaving University.
7 She's had no time to deal with this. She's been in a meeting ____________ nine.
8 Have you ____________ been to São Paolo? It's completely different to Rio.

"We've done a computer simulation of your projected performance in five years. You're fired."

Exercises

Section B **5.4 Match the uses of the present perfect 1–3 with examples a–c.**

1 a present situation that started in the past ☐
2 a series of actions that happened in our life up to now ☐
3 a result in the present of a past event ☐

a) **I've seen** a lot of changes since I started working here.
b) The marketing campaign started last month and sales **have** already **gone up** 8% year-on-year.
c) He**'s run** the company since his father retired.

Sections C, D **5.5 Read this email from Patrick, the Purchasing Manager of an Irish manufacturer, who is in Poland on a business trip. Complete the email by choosing the correct alternative from A,B,C or D below.**

Send | To... Edward Kelly
Subject: Poland trip – Katowice

Ed – sorry I haven't contacted you [1] _B_ last week, but I've been very busy. I've [2]____ to Katowice in the south-west of Poland [3]____ a few days, and I've [4]____ returned to my hotel in Warsaw, where I'm sending this email from.

I visited several firms when I was in Katowice, and one of them looks quite promising as a future supplier for us. I've [5]____ had a few discussions with the people there, and I've got some product samples to show you. Unfortunately I haven't met the guy in charge [6]____ . He wasn't there – he's [7]____ to Gdansk and should be back next week.

So, the trip has been quite successful [8]____ . Have you [9]____ been to Poland? They really are shaping up to be a major player in Europe – the people have a real entrepreneurial spirit and I've [10]____ seen so much construction work going on. Not even in Ireland in the boom years after 2000!

Anyway, I'll email you again later in the week – after I've been to Poznan – to give you an update on everything.

Regards

Patrick

	A	B	C	D
1	A for	B since	C just	D so far
2	A going	B gone	C being	D been
3	A for	B since	C already	D so far
4	A now	B been	C just	D so far
5	A yet	B already	C been	D gone
6	A just	B already	C now	D yet
7	A going	B gone	C being	D been
8	A so far	B yet	C just	D now
9	A yet	B since	C ever	D never
10	A yet	B since	C ever	D never

Tasks

Speaking: listen and repeat

1 05 **You are going to hear eight phrases. Listen and repeat.**

Translate

2 Translate these short texts taken from the Internet into your own language. Remember not to translate word for word, but rather to make it sound natural.

Cosmetics giant Revlon has launched a social media campaign as part of its biggest ever product launch. The two-month campaign aims to drive awareness of its new lipstick brand and engage customers across social media sites such as YouTube, Facebook and Twitter.

NewMediaAge website

Squeezing more out of your IT budget isn't easy. You've outsourced, you've consolidated data centers, you've decided that the usual three-year PC refresh cycle can be stretched to four years. All well and good, but what else can you do?

CFO website

Writing: personalized practice

3 Write a sentence (statement or question) using the time expression in brackets. You can see examples in exercise 5.3. Write something that you might say in real life, in a professional or personal context.

1 (already) *There's no need to prepare the room for the training seminar – I've already done it.*
2 (yet) ____________________
3 (ever) ____________________
4 (never) ____________________
5 (just) ____________________
6 (for) ____________________
7 (since) ____________________
8 (always) ____________________

Now take another piece of paper. For each sentence above write the name of a person who you might be speaking to at the time, and write what they say in reply.

Rehearsal for the real world

4 Look again at the email in exercise 5.5 and notice how Patrick uses the present perfect to give news. Now imagine you arrived in a foreign country a few days ago (either for business or for pleasure). Write an email to a colleague or friend. Give news about what has happened and what you have done.

If you are working in class, put all the emails on the desks or on the walls. Go round the room and read the emails. Return to your seats and say which email you liked best and why.

6 Connecting past and present 2

A Past simple or present perfect?

The past simple is used to describe actions in a completed time period.

The present perfect is used when the time period includes the present.

*I **lived** in Milan many years ago.*
(completed: now I live in another place)

*I've **lived** in Milan since 2008.*
(a situation that started in the past and continues in the present: I still live there)

***I've been** to Milan several times.*
(life experience)

*My boss **has agreed** to your proposal.*
(present result of a past action)

Time phrases used with the past simple (unit 3C) refer to a particular point in the past: *yesterday, last month.*

Time phrases used with the present perfect (unit 5C) link the past to the present: *since, never, this month.*

The choice of tense often depends on the situation and where our attention is.

*Good news! We**'ve won** the contract!*
(recent news: the event is present in my mind)

*So, we **won** the contract, and then ...*
(telling a story: the event feels distant in my mind)

B Present simple or present perfect?

The present simple is used for permanent facts and states, and regular habits.

The present perfect makes a connection between past and present.

*I **work** here.*
(a permanent state: I work here every day)

***I've worked** here for two years.*
(I started two years ago and still work here now)

C Present perfect continuous: form

The present perfect continuous is formed with the present perfect of *be*, and the *-ing* form of the verb. Negatives are formed with *not*.

***I've been (haven't been)** wait**ing** here for more than an hour.*
*She**'s been (hasn't been)** wait**ing** here for ages.*

Questions are formed by inverting the subject and *have*.

***Have you** been wait**ing** long?*
***Has she** been wait**ing** long?*

D Present perfect continuous: uses

The present perfect continuous describes an action or situation in progress from the past up to the present.

*Production at this site **has been increasing** steadily since we started here five years ago.*

The present perfect continuous often emphasizes the length of time of the action.

***I've been working on** this report all week.*

The present perfect continuous can be used for repeated actions.

***I've been calling** her all afternoon, but she's always in a meeting.*

The action may be finished or continuing; we only know by the situation.

*You're late! **I've been waiting** here for ages!*
(the waiting is finished now)

***I've been waiting** for ages. Where is she?*
(I will continue waiting)

E Present perfect continuous: time expressions

Typical time expressions used with the present perfect continuous include: *all day, for months, for ages, recently, over the last few years, since, for.*

F Present perfect or present perfect continuous?

Sometimes there is no difference in meaning between the present perfect and present perfect continuous.

*I've **worked/been working** here for two years.*

The choice of tense often depends on where our attention is. We use the present perfect if our attention is on the present result.

***I've written** the report. Here it is.*
(the finished report is in my mind)

We use the present perfect continuous if our attention is on the action in progress.

***I've been writing** the report. I'm exhausted.*
(the act of writing is in my mind)

If we give details of how many or how much, we do not use a continuous form.

***I've written** three reports this week.*
***I've done** a lot of research on this company.*

See page 243 for an overview of the English verb tense system.

Exercises

Sections A, B

6.1 Underline the correct words.

1 Yesterday *I phoned/I've phoned* the bank about our overdraft.
2 *I work/I have worked* here since the end of last year.
3 *I work/I have worked* from home one day a week.
4 I'm enjoying the conference. *I made/I have made* a lot of useful contacts.
5 *I saw/I've seen* Hugh Hopper a few days ago – he sends his regards.
6 *We went/We have been* to an interesting seminar last week.
7 Today *has been/was* really busy – and it's only lunchtime!
8 Today *has been/was* really busy. It's 7 pm – I'm going home.
9 I'm sorry but Patricia *left/has left* the office an hour ago.
10 Patricia? No, she isn't here right now. She *left/has left* the office.

Sections A, B

6.2 Put the verbs in brackets into either the present simple, past simple or present perfect.

1 The company is doing very well. Last year sales *went up* (go up) 15%, and so far this year they *have gone up* (go up) another 12%.
2 We ______ (operate) all over Latin America. Recently we ______ (set up) branches in Peru and Colombia.
3 ______ (you/see) my laptop? I'm sure I ______ (leave) it here earlier.
4 This ______ (not look) like the right block. Are you sure we ______ (come) to the right address?
5 I ______ (never/speak) to him, but I ______ (speak) to his assistant on the phone yesterday.
6 I ______ (work) for WorldCom since last year, but now I ______ (want) to change jobs. ______ (you/hear) of anyone taking on new staff?

Sections C, D, F

6.3 In each mini-dialogue put one verb into the present perfect simple and the other into the present perfect continuous. Use contractions where possible.

1 A: What's the matter? You look worried!
B: Yes, I am. I *'ve been looking at* (look at) the contract in detail, and I *'ve noticed* (notice) a lot of potential problems.
2 A: I ______ (call) Carol all day, but it goes straight to voicemail.
B: I expect she ______ (go) to Head Office.
3 A: 'Tosca' is coming to the Opera House. ______ (you see) it?
B: Not yet, but I ______ (look forward) to it for ages. Shall we go together?
4 A: How long ______ (you produce) cars at this site?
B: About four years. We ______ (invest) around twenty million dollars in plant and machinery.

"Oh, and your feelings have been trying to get in touch with you."

Exercises

Section A **6.4 Put the verbs into the correct form of the past simple or present perfect simple. Use contractions where possible.**

VICTORIA: Hi, Sue. I [1] *haven't seen* (not/see) you for ages!
SUE: Hi, Victoria, nice to see you again. No, you're right, I [2] ______ (not/be) in touch with anyone recently.
VICTORIA: So what have you been up to?
SUE: You know I [3] ______ (leave) my job in January so that I could go freelance as a graphic designer?
VICTORIA: Yes, I remember you [4] ______ (talk) a lot about that last year.
SUE: Well, it [5] ______ (be) a really difficult year so far. I [6] ______ (never/do) anything like this before and it's much harder than I [7] ______ (imagine). [8] ______ (you/ever/be) self-employed?
VICTORIA: No, never, although I [9] ______ (often/think) about it. So why [10] ______ (it/be) so difficult?
SUE: There's a lot of insecurity. At the beginning I [11] ______ (have) two or three good clients. These are people that I [12] ______ (know) for many years. They're still with me. But apart from that nothing really.
VICTORIA: What about advertising in the specialist magazines?
SUE: Yes, I [13] ______ (already/do) that. I [14] ______ (put) an advert in *Design Monthly* a couple of months ago but there were only a few replies. But I have a new website and I'm quite optimistic about using it to generate business. I [15] ______ (finish) it just last week. It's optimized for search engines so that people can find me more easily. I [16] ______ (have) quite a few hits already, so things might improve soon.

Section A **6.5 Complete the text about technology stocks by putting the verbs into the correct form of the past simple or present perfect.**

MARKET REPORT a rocky road for tech stocks

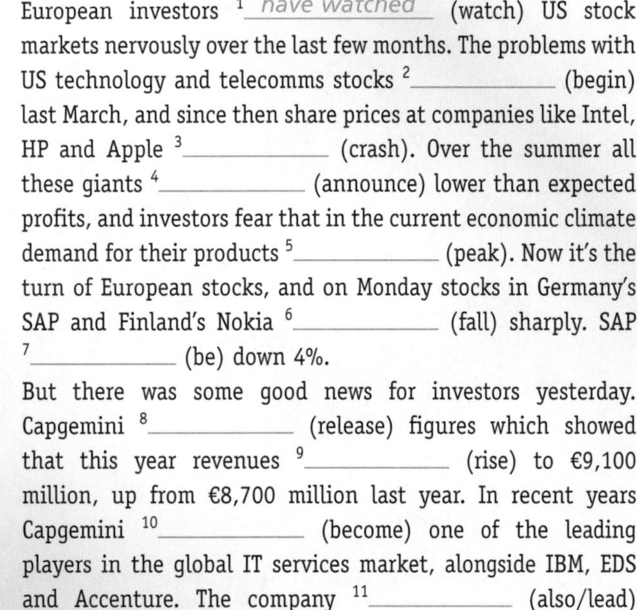

European investors [1] *have watched* (watch) US stock markets nervously over the last few months. The problems with US technology and telecomms stocks [2] ______ (begin) last March, and since then share prices at companies like Intel, HP and Apple [3] ______ (crash). Over the summer all these giants [4] ______ (announce) lower than expected profits, and investors fear that in the current economic climate demand for their products [5] ______ (peak). Now it's the turn of European stocks, and on Monday stocks in Germany's SAP and Finland's Nokia [6] ______ (fall) sharply. SAP [7] ______ (be) down 4%.

But there was some good news for investors yesterday. Capgemini [8] ______ (release) figures which showed that this year revenues [9] ______ (rise) to €9,100 million, up from €8,700 million last year. In recent years Capgemini [10] ______ (become) one of the leading players in the global IT services market, alongside IBM, EDS and Accenture. The company [11] ______ (also/lead)

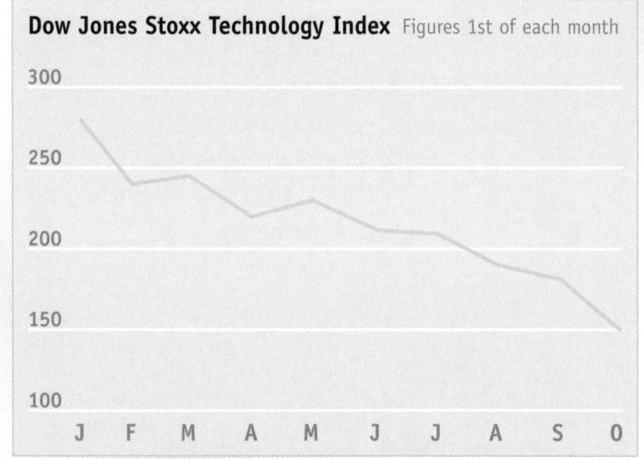

the way in the use of offshoring, often transferring work to countries such as India and Poland. This [12] ______ (improve) profitability as well as providing a wider range of options in the event of a sudden change in the market.

Tasks

Speaking: listen and repeat

1 06 **You are going to hear eight phrases. Listen and repeat.**

Translate

2 Translate these short texts taken from the Internet into your own language. Remember not to translate word for word, but rather to make it sound natural.

The technology-heavy Nasdaq index has been falling for three weeks, and is now 34% lower than its March peak. Shares of companies announcing poor results have fallen by a third or a half after profits warnings.

Washington Post website

Since completing a consolidation phase three years ago, ThyssenKrupp has been following a sustained and profitable course of growth. The company has raised its earnings forecast for the current fiscal year to over €3.2 billion before taxes.

business-magazine.de website

Writing: personalized practice

3 Think about your life in the last year. Write answers to these questions using the past simple, present perfect simple and present perfect continuous.

1 How have you tried to keep fit and healthy?
I've joined a health club. I went a few times after joining, but since then I haven't been at all. Also I've been trying to eat more healthy food. I don't really have much time for cooking, but I've learned a few new recipes.

2 How have you spent your money?

3 What have you done to keep up with new ideas in your professional field?

4 Have you been anywhere interesting?

5 What haven't you done that you would like to have done? Why?

Rehearsal for the real world

4 Look again at the dialogue in exercise 6.4 and notice how the speakers use the past simple and the present perfect. Now write a similar dialogue between yourself and a friend or colleague who you meet after not being in contact for some time. Start like this:

Friend (give their name): Hi! I haven't seen you for ages!
Me: Hi, nice to see you again.

If you are working in class, read some dialogues aloud.

7 Future 1

A *will*

We can use *will* + the infinitive (without *to*) to refer to the future. *Will* is usually shortened in speech and informal writing to *'ll*. The negative of *will* is *won't*.

We use *will* to make predictions and to state facts about future events.

Over the next decade there ***will*** *be a big increase in the use of nuclear power.*
In June we ***will*** *bring out two new models.*

We can add *perhaps/maybe* or *probably*.

Maybe I'll *join you later in the bar.*

Notice that *probably* comes after *will* but before *won't*.

*He'**ll probably*** *agree with you.*
He ***probably won't*** *agree with you.*

We can use *will* with an introductory phrase to give other meanings. For example, a personal opinion (*I think*), a hope (*I hope*) or an expectation (*I expect*).

I think *we'**ll probably*** *open an office in Taipei next year.*

Will can be used for instant decisions and thoughts that come into our head at the moment of speaking.

I'll *wait for you outside.*
I'll *call you tomorrow.*

See unit 11D for more uses of *will*.

B *be going to*

We use the verb *be* + *going to* + the infinitive to make a connection between the present and the future.

We use *be going to* for plans and intentions. These are things we have already decided to do.

I'm going to email *her this afternoon.*
The ECB ***is going to monitor*** *inflation closely.*

We use *be going to* to make predictions when there is evidence in the present situation (we already know or can see something).

*Be careful! It'**s going to*** *fall.*
(I can see it on the edge of the table)

Note that *be going to* can refer to near or distant time. For example, we can say '*the world is going to end in 8 billion years*' because scientists have evidence now.

C Present continuous

We can use the present continuous to talk about things we have arranged to do. There is nearly always a future time expression.

HSBC ***are moving*** *to new premises* ***next year***.

The arrangements are often social arrangements or appointments.

I'm busy on Tuesday afternoon. ***I'm seeing*** *Jack at two, and after that* ***I'm meeting*** *my bank manager.*

See also units 1E and 2C for the present continuous.

D *will* or *be going to*?

There are many occasions when we can use either form.

In my presentation ***I'll talk/I'm going to talk*** *about three main areas. First, ...*

Here the speaker could see it as a fact (*will*) or an intention (*going to*).

Will and *be going to* are both used for decisions. *Will* is used for instant decisions; *be going to* is used for decisions already made (i.e. plans and intentions).

Great idea! ***I'll do*** *it tomorrow.*
(an instant decision)

Yes, I know. ***I'm going to do*** *it tomorrow.*
(a plan or intention)

Will and *be going to* are both used for predictions. *Will* is used for general beliefs about the future; *be going to* is used when there is some present evidence.

*I'm sure they'**ll like*** *the new design.*
(general belief or opinion)

*We'**re going to make*** *a loss on this product line.*
(I have the figures in front of me)

Will is more usual in writing. *'ll* and *be going to* are more usual in speech.

E *be going to* or present continuous?

For plans and arrangements there is often little difference in meaning. However, *be going to* can suggest that the details of the arrangement are still open, while the present continuous can suggest that the arrangement is more fixed.

I'm going to meet *her next week.*
(just a plan – time and place are still unknown)

I'm meeting *her at ten in my office.*
(a definite arrangement with a time and place)

F Time expressions

Common time expressions for the future include: *tomorrow, the day after tomorrow, on Friday, at the weekend, next week/year, in a few days' time, in the next five minutes/months.*

See page 243 for an overview of the English verb tense system.

Exercises

Sections A, B, C

7.1 Match the forms in italics below with their uses a–f.

a) future fact
b) belief or opinion
c) instant decision
d) future plan or intention
e) prediction with evidence in the present situation
f) future arrangement

1 I*'m going to ask* my boss for a pay rise next week. [d]
2 I'm sorry to hear that. I*'ll find out* what the problem is right now. [ ]
3 I'm sorry, but I *won't be* here tomorrow. I*'ll be* in Paris. [ ]
4 I*'m meeting* Angela for lunch. Do you want to join us? [ ]
5 Their share price *will probably rise* when the market recovers. [ ]
6 With so much competition it*'s going to be* difficult to increase sales. [ ]

Sections D, E

7.2 Underline the correct words in each mini-dialogue.

1 A: Are you free next Tuesday morning?
B: Sorry, *I'll have/I'm having* a meeting with Sue.
2 A: What are your plans for next year?
B: *We'll open/We're going to open* a new factory in Hungary.
3 A: What do you think of their new marketing campaign?
B: I think *it'll probably do well/it's probably doing well.*
4 A: What about tomorrow after work – say, six thirty?
B: OK, *I'll see you/I'm seeing you* then.
5 A: As you can see, I've been thinking quite a lot about this issue.
B: Yes, I see. So *what are you going to do/what are you doing*?
6 A: It would be nice to see you next week.
B: Yes. *Are you doing anything/Will you do anything* on Wednesday?

Sections A, B, C, D, E

7.3 Put the verbs in brackets into the most appropriate future form. Choose between *will, be going to* and the present continuous.

1 Have you heard the news? BHP Billiton _is going to buy_ (buy) Rio Tinto.
2 I __________ (meet) Andrea at the airport at 9 am next Thursday.
3 Do we need more paper? I __________ (get) some.
4 Richard's just called – he __________ (be) late.
5 Next year __________ (be) the company's centenary year.
6 This taxi driver is terrible. He __________ (have) an accident.
7 In the future, web conferences __________ (probably replace) many international meetings.
8 We __________ (test) the prototype sometime next week.
9 Would you mind waiting for a moment? I __________ (not be) long.
10 Look at those clouds! I think it __________ (rain).

CBarsotti

"No, Hoskins, you're not going to do it just because I'm telling you to do it. You're going to do it because you believe in it."

Exercises

Sections A, B, D **7.4 Maria has asked Sebastien to come to her office. Complete the dialogue by putting the verbs into a future form. Choose between *will* and *be going to*. Often either answer is possible, but decide which form is the most natural. Use contractions where possible.**

MARIA: Come in, have a seat. Would you like a drink? Coffee? Mineral water?

SEBASTIEN: I [1] *'ll have* (have) a coffee, please. White, no sugar.

MARIA: Here you are. Well, thanks for coming this morning. I [2] ______ (tell) you why I asked you here. As you know, there [3] ______ (be) some big changes in the company. In fact, we [4] ______ (restructure) the whole department.

SEBASTIEN: Yes, I heard something about that. Is my job at risk?

MARIA: Not necessarily, but there may be some changes. The new structure [5] ______ (be) in place by the summer, and we want you to be a part of it. We value your work very highly. We've decided we [6] ______ (offer) you a new job.

SEBASTIEN: Really! And what exactly [7] ______ (the new job/involve)?

MARIA: Well, we [8] ______ (expand) the whole customer services area. If you accept the job, you [9] ______ (be) responsible for leading the new team. You [10] ______ (have) more responsibility, and the salary [11] ______ (be) much better. But it would mean relocating to Hamburg – we [12] ______ (move) most business functions there and close down the office here. What do you think?

SEBASTIEN: Well, it sounds like a great opportunity. Of course I [13] ______ (have to) speak to my wife and family about it.

MARIA: No problem. We [14] ______ (talk) again soon.

Sections A, C **7.5 Complete this email from a PA to her boss by putting the verbs into a future form. Choose between *will* and the present continuous. Use contractions where possible.**

Send | To... Pierre Gaudard, Technical Director
Subject: Visit to Slovenia

I've booked your flight to Slovenia. You [1] *'re leaving* (leave) on Tuesday 3rd at 8.45 in the morning, so you [2] ______ (arrive) in Ljubljana before lunch. Someone [3] ______ (be) at the airport to meet you. Your first appointment is with Aleksander Presekar, and you [4] ______ (meet) him at 1 pm at our local office. He [5] ______ (probably/take) you out to lunch. After lunch you [6] ______ (not/do) anything until 4 pm, so you [7] ______ (have) time to go to the hotel. You [8] ______ (stay) at the Intercontinental, which is in a very central location.

I [9] ______ (ask) our travel agent to forward the e-ticket to you, and you [10] ______ (have) it by the end of the week.

Tasks

Speaking: listen and repeat

1 07 **You are going to hear eight phrases. Listen and repeat.**

Translate

2 **Translate these short texts taken from the Internet into your own language. Remember not to translate word for word, but rather to make it sound natural.**

In the future, companies will need to search the world for the best intellectual capital, then create the kinds of challenging environments that will allow talented people to develop and be successful.

BusinessWeek website

My favorite line from *Jaws* comes when the police chief at last sees the shark: 'You are going to need a bigger boat.' We are at last seeing the shape of this current economic downturn – and we are going to need a bigger stimulus. We might get lucky: maybe four months from now we will think that what we have collectively done to stabilize the world economy is appropriate. More likely not.

Seeking Alpha website

Writing: personalized practice

3 **Answer these questions.**

1 What are your personal plans for next weekend?
I'm going to do some shopping on Saturday morning, and clean my flat. In the afternoon I'll probably meet up with some friends. On Sunday my parents are coming to visit, so I'll be busy – I have to prepare some food before they arrive.

2 What are your personal plans for the next few years?

3 What predictions can you make about your company two years from now?

4 What predictions can you make about mobile communications ten years from now?

5 What predictions can you make about *one* of these countries twenty years from now: China, Brazil, India, Russia?

Rehearsal for the real world

4 **Look again at the dialogue in exercise 7.4 and notice how the speakers use *will* and *be going to*. Your own boss (or Head of Department if you are a student) calls you in to their office to tell you about some important plans for the future and how they affect you. Write the dialogue.**

Boss: Come in, have a seat. We've been doing some thinking about future plans and there are a few things I'd like to discuss with you.
Me: Of course. Tell me more.

If you are working in class, read some dialogues aloud.

8 Future 2

A Using *when, after, until,* etc.

We use the present simple or present perfect (not *will*) to refer to the future after these words: *when, after, before, unless, in case, as soon as, until, by the time, the next time.*

***When** I **see** her, I'll pass on your message.*
*We'll discuss it again **after** you **get back**.*
***As soon as I've** finished, I'll tell you.*

Notice that *will* can be used in the other part of the sentence.

B Fixed timetables

We often use the present simple (or present continuous) when we talk about events in the future based on a fixed timetable, program or calendar.

*Jim's plane **leaves** (**is leaving**) at 12.20.*
*Our boss **retires** (**is retiring**) next year.*

C Future continuous

The future continuous is formed with *will* + *be* + the *-ing* form of the verb.

***I'll be seeing** Konstantin this afternoon.*
***Where will you be working** next month?*

The future continuous describes an activity in progress in the future. We often use it when we compare activities now and in the future. There is nearly always a time expression.

*Next year **I'll be working** in our São Paolo office.*

The future continuous is often used to say that something will definitely happen.

***We'll be holding** a meeting soon, so we can make a decision then.*

D Future perfect

The future perfect is formed with *will* + *have* + past participle.

*By the time I retire, **I'll have been** in banking for over thirty years.*
*By the time the contract expires, **what will we have paid** in total?*

We use the future perfect to look back from one point in the future to an earlier event or period of time. We often use *by* or *by the time* with the future perfect.

***By** the end of the year **we'll have sold** around 20,000 units.*
***By the time** our supplier ships this order **we'll have run out** of inventory in the warehouse.*

It is common to use a simple *will* form in place of the future perfect.

*By the end of the year **we'll sell** around 20,000 units.*

We use the continuous form of the future perfect to look back from one point in the future at an activity in progress.

*Next year **we'll have been manufacturing** the same model, without a facelift, for four years.*

E *was going to*

Was/were going to is not a future form. We use it to talk about plans or intentions in the past that didn't actually happen.

*I'm sorry, I **was going to call** this morning, but we had an urgent quality control issue that I had to deal with.*

F Other ways to talk about the future

We use the verbs *expect, hope, intend, would like, plan, want* followed by an infinitive to refer to the future.

*We **hope to get** the contract.*
***I'd like to discuss** this in more detail when we meet.*
*We **plan to extend** our sales network next year.*

Notice the different negative forms:

*I expect/hope I **won't** ...*
*I **wouldn't** like to ...*
*We **don't** intend/plan/want to ...*

We often use the verb *think* followed by *'ll*:

*I **think I'll** change my mobile network.*

We can use *be due to* for things that we expect to happen soon.

*He **is due to** name his replacement as CEO within the next few days.*

We can use *be about to* for things that will (or will not) happen very soon.

*The pace of development in new technology **is not about to** slow.*

Shall is used as a simple future like *will* only in very formal contexts, for example legal documents and contracts. Normally *Shall I/we ... ?* are used to make suggestions (about the present or the future).

***Shall I** open the window?*
***Shall we** meet again next week?*

G Future probability

We can use modals and other phrases to talk about the probability that something will happen in the future. The table below gives an overview which is developed in unit 13 (page 58) and not practised here.

100%	certainty	*will, be certain to*
95–100%	deduction	*must, can't*
80%	expectation	*should, shouldn't, ought to, ought not to, be likely to, be unlikely to*
30–70%	uncertainty	*may, may not, might, might not, could*
0%	certainty	*won't*

See page 243 for an overview of the English verb tense system.

Exercises

Sections A, B, C, D, E, F

8.1 Underline the correct or most likely words.

1 Don't forget to turn off the lights before *you will leave/you leave.*
2 Tomorrow *I'll interview/I'll be interviewing* candidates all morning.
3 By the end of the year I think the building work *will have finished/will be finishing,* and we'll be working normally again.
4 Our visitors are *due to arrive/due arriving* at 10.30.
5 You can wait here until *she comes back/she will come back.*
6 *I was going to mention it/I was mentioning it* at the meeting, but I forgot.
7 *I hope/I will hope* to be able to speak at the press conference myself.
8 We *will be repaying/will have repaid* the bank loan by December.
9 When the contract *is/will be* ready, I'll let you know.
10 *Will we/Shall we* break for coffee now?
11 We can't send the goods until *we've received/we will receive* a firm order.
12 I can't do it right now – *I'll nearly have/I'm about to have* a meeting.

Sections A, C, D

8.2 Match each sentence 1–8 with an ending a–h.

1 They won't accept our order as it is, so
2 They won't accept our order unless
3 Helen wants to see you before
4 You won't see Helen. By the time she arrives
5 By the time I leave the office today I'll
6 While the baby is still small I'll
7 I'm on vacation next week. I'll
8 Next time we meet I'll have a suntan! I'll

a) you leave.
b) you'll have left.
c) we'll give them a bank guarantee.
d) we give them a bank guarantee.
e) have been here for twelve hours.
f) be working part-time.
g) have just come back from Malta.
h) be relaxing by the pool in Malta.

Sections A, B, C, D

8.3 Put the verbs into the right tense. Choose between the present simple (*I do*), future continuous (*I'll be doing*) and future perfect (*I'll have done*).

1 By the time all the legal documents are ready, the deadline for the proposal *will have passed* (pass).
2 The flight ________ (leave) at 1 pm and ________ (arrive) at 3.45 local time.
3 When I ________ (see) him, I'll ask him.
4 I ________ (see) Nick tomorrow, so I can give him your message.
5 This traffic is terrible. By the time we get to their office the meeting ________ (finish).
6 This time next year I ________ (do) my part-time MBA.
7 I won't do anything until I ________ (hear) from you.
8 Hurry up! By the time we arrive the concert ________ (start).
9 What ________ (you/learn) by the end of your course?
10 ________ (you/use) the conference room next Tuesday morning?

Exercises

Sections A, C, D, F

8.4 An economist has prepared a report about his country next year. Complete the Executive Summary by choosing the correct alternative from A, B, C or D below.

Executive Summary: 12-month economic forecast

The Central Bank [1] *C* keep interest rates low next year in order to stimulate economic growth, and so we [2]____ the economy to continue growing at about 4%. This means that unemployment [3]____ in most sectors of the economy next year. Exchange rates are very difficult to predict, but the currency [4]____ remain relatively stable against the dollar. This is important as 40% of our revenue is in dollars.

Some important events are [5]____ take place in the political field. The president [6]____ call elections within the next twelve months, and so by the middle of next year the election campaign [7]____ . The government [8]____ on a platform of honesty and competence, and it [9]____ introduce reforms to the legal system so that judges can investigate the misuse of public funds more easily. When that [10]____ , international investor confidence should increase rapidly.

1	A is wanting to	B is liking to	C would like to	D due to
2	A predict	B expect	C believe	D hope
3	A will be fallen	B will been falling	C will falling	D will fall
4	A probably will	B will probably	C probably is	D is probably
5	A about to	B soon	C being	D expecting
6	A dues to	B due to	C is due to	D is duing to
7	A will have begun	B will be begun	C has begun	D will begin
8	A will be fought	B will be fighting	C will fighting	D will have fight
9	A is planning	B planning to	C is planned to	D is planning to
10	A happening	B will happen	C happens	D happen

Sections A, C, D, E

8.5 It is January and an HR Director is explaining the performance review process to a group of new employees. Put the verbs into the right tense. Choose between the present simple (*I do*), future continuous (*I'll be doing*), future perfect (*I'll have done*) and *was going to*. Use contractions where possible.

"Your first performance review [1] *is* (be) at the end of April. It [2]____ (be) earlier but we decided to change it. By the end of April we [3]____ (collect) all the information we need, and we will call you for an interview. In the interview we [4]____ (discuss) your performance during the first few months and any issues relating to your future needs, such as training. By the end of that meeting I hope that we [5]____ (agree) on your personal objectives for the next six months in terms of key performance indicators and professional development. Of course there is always some flexibility in any targets we set, in case anything [6]____ (happen) that we cannot predict. Then, after April, the next time that you and I [7]____ (meet) formally will not be until November, although of course behind the scenes I [8]____ (talk) to your line managers and monitoring your progress. OK? Well, unless you [9]____ (have) any questions, I think that's all."

Tasks

Speaking: listen and repeat

1 08 **You are going to hear eight phrases. Listen and repeat.**

Translate

2 Translate these short texts taken from the Internet into your own language. Remember not to translate word for word, but rather to make it sound natural.

Innovation is an important contributor to long-term growth in an economy. Should we be concerned that as the world enters a recession, firms will be investing less in developing new products and processes? The answer to this question is not obvious. During a recession the cost of investing in innovation is lower than in times of expansion. Labour and other inputs will be less in demand, and thus are likely to be cheaper.

ESRC website

By the year 2030 the volume of goods produced by traditional manufacturing worldwide will probably be at least twice what it is today. But in the US, the share of manufacturing in GDP, which is still around 12% or so, will have shrunk to 5%.

IndustryWeek website

Writing: personalized practice

3 Complete the sentences with the future continuous or future perfect as shown in the brackets. Add a few more sentences each time.

1 (f. cont.) This time tomorrow *I'll be sitting in the budget meeting. The Finance Director will proabably have finished his overview of the current situation and everyone will be feeling nervous about allocation of resources for next year. Everyone wants sufficient resources for their own plans and projects, but of course some people will be disappointed* .

2 (f. cont.) There's an important meeting next week. In the meeting we __________ .

3 (f. cont.) This time next year I expect that I __________ .

4 (f. perf.) I'm going to be very busy. By the next time we meet I __________ .

5 (f. perf.) By the end of the year our company __________ .

6 (f. perf.) By the end of this English course I hope that I __________ .

Rehearsal for the real world

4 Look again at the Executive Summary in exercise 8.4. Now write a short report on one of the topics below, using real or invented information:

Twelve-month economic forecast for my country
Two-year business development plan for my company
Ten-year tourism development plan for my city/town

If you are working in class, read some texts aloud and then discuss them.

9 Passive 1

A Form

To make the passive we use *to be* and a past participle. Compare the Active (A) and Passive (P) for different tenses:

A: *Intel* ***produces*** *millions of chips every year.*
P: *Millions of chips* ***are produced*** *every year.*

A: *Our supplier is* ***shipping*** *the goods next week.*
P: *The goods* ***are being shipped*** *next week.*

A: *The ECB* ***raised*** *interest rates by 0.25%.*
P: *Interest rates* ***were raised*** *by 0.25%.*

A: *He* ***was asking*** *me some difficult questions.*
P: *I* ***was being asked*** *some difficult questions.*

A: *They* ***have chosen*** *the new design.*
P: *The new design* ***has been chosen****.*

A: *Rosa* ***will give*** *a briefing tomorrow.*
P: *A briefing* ***will be given*** *tomorrow.*

A: *They* ***can arrange*** *a loan within three days.*
P: *A loan* ***can be arranged*** *within three days.*

A: *We* ***may produce*** *some new sales targets.*
P: *Some new sales targets* ***may be produced****.*

The object in the active sentence (*millions of chips/interest rates*) moves to the front in the passive sentence and becomes the new subject.

We form negatives and questions in the same way as in active sentences.

The new design ***hasn't been*** *chosen.*
Has *the new design* ***been*** *chosen?*

B Uses: focus on important information

In the active sentences above the person or organization who does the action (*Intel/The ECB/Rosa*) is important.

In the passive sentences above the person or organization who does the action is not mentioned. It might be:

- unimportant
- clear from the situation
- unknown

Instead, the important information is either the actions (*raised/chosen*) or the things affected by the action (*Millions of chips/The goods/A briefing*).

C Uses: systems and processes

We often use the passive to talk about systems, processes and procedures. Language is often specialized and technical, as in this example adapted from the Dewar's Scotch Whisky website.

Malt whisky ***is made*** *exclusively from barley. In August the barley* ***is harvested*** *and then* ***left*** *to rest for a couple of months. The next step is 'malting', where the grain* ***is soaked*** *in water to germinate, and then* ***heated****. This causes the grain to produce starches, which* ***are*** *later* ***converted*** *to sugars and then alcohol. The malted barley* ***is placed*** *into huge vessels and* ***mixed*** *with water to make a 'wort'. The wort* ***is cooled****, then* ***run*** *into another vessel. After that yeast* ***is added****, and fermentation begins. When fermentation is complete, a liquid called 'the wash' remains. This liquid is ready for distilling. In distilling, the liquid* ***is heated*** *until the spirit turns to vapour, which* ***is*** *then* ***condensed*** *back into liquid. Repeated distillation produces whisky. The final stage is maturing, and by law Scotch whisky* ***must be aged*** *for at least three years in oak barrels.*

To show a sequence in a process we use linking words like: *Firstly/First of all, Then, The next step is, Next, After that, Later, Finally, The final stage is.* There are some examples in the text above.

D Saying who does the action: *by*

In the passive examples in section A the person or organization that does the action is not mentioned. If we want to say who does the action, we use *by*.

The goods are being shipped next week ***by our supplier in China****.*
A briefing will be given tomorrow ***by our Information Officer, Rosa Mendoza****.*

E Transitive and intransitive verbs

Verbs which usually take objects are called transitive verbs, while verbs which do not are called intransitive verbs. Dictionaries show this information with T or I, and some verbs can be both. Only transitive verbs can be made passive.

Raise (T)	*Taxes were raised last year.* possible
Increase (T/I)	*Taxes were increased last year.* possible
Go up (I)	*Taxes ~~were gone up~~ last year.* not possible

Exercises

Section A

9.1 Complete the sentences with a passive verb. You may need a negative form.

1 Somebody damaged the goods in transit.
The goods *were damaged* in transit.
2 Millions of people see this ad every day.
This ad ________________ by millions of people every day.
3 They will not finish the project by the end of the month.
The project ________________ by the end of the month.
4 They have closed twenty retail outlets over the last year.
Twenty retail outlets ________________ over the last year.
5 We are reviewing all of our IT systems.
All of our IT systems________________ .
6 We cannot ship your order until we receive payment in full.
Your order ________________ until we receive payment in full.

Sections B, D

9.2 Decide if it is necessary to say who does the action. If it is not necessary, cross it out. If it is necessary, put a tick (✓).

1 I don't think your proposal will be accepted ~~by people~~.
2 The company was founded by the father of the present Chairman. ✓
3 Our machines are serviced by highly trained technicians.
4 This machine was repaired yesterday by a technician, and now it isn't working.
5 The conference was opened by someone from the London Business School.
6 You'll be shown round the factory by someone, and then you'll meet the sales team.

Sections A, B, D, E

9.3 Rewrite these sentences using the passive if it is possible. You may need a negative form. If it is not possible to make a passive, put a cross (✗).

1 Our R & D department have discovered a promising new drug.
A promising new drug has been discovered by our R&D department.
2 The rate of inflation went up by around 1% last quarter.
____
3 One of our best young designers created this line.
____
4 I'm sorry, we can't do that.
____
5 Something very interesting happened to me last week.
____
6 The Accounts Department may not authorize this payment.
____
7 I worked as a consultant for four years after my MBA.
____
____
8 They were asking me all sorts of highly technical questions.
____
____

"I see myself in a position where mediocrity is rewarded."

Exercises

Sections A, B, C, D **9.4 A manager is writing a training manual for new employees. Complete the text by putting the verbs in the box into the present simple passive.**

complete	~~design~~	offer	print out	put	outsource	analyze

The use of questionnaires in market research

This company makes extensive use of questionnaires in market research. The process is standard. First, we carefully select a sample of people to ask; these may be existing or potential customers. Then the questions 1 *are designed* by a small, specialized team. The questions 2 ________ into sequence and grouped together by topic. After that, we distribute the questionnaire; either we send a link by email and it 3 ________ by the customer online, or it 4 ________ as hard copy and distributed through the mail with a covering letter. Our response rate needs to be above 25% for the process to be statistically significant, and we usually achieve this. Sometimes a small gift 5 ________ to people who complete the questionnaire, as an incentive. Finally we enter all the results onto a spreadsheet, and the information 6 ________ . If the questionnaire involves a face-to-face interview with members of the public, then the work 7 ________ to an external company to ensure objectivity in the responses and results.

Sections A, B **9.5 Helen is starting her own business. Here is an extract from her notes.**

Contact bank to arrange loan ✓
Find office space ✓
Decorate office – finish end of month
Order equipment – in progress
Quotation for leaflets ✓
Part-time staff ?

Helen is writing a letter to a business advisory service. Put the verbs into either the present perfect passive (*has/have been done*), present continuous passive (*is/are being done*), or the passive form of a modal (*might/should/will be done*).

Dear Sir or Madam,

I am writing to arrange an interview with one of your small business advisors to discuss my business start-up. Your advice and detailed comments would be very useful. I have attached a copy of my business plan, and I can give you a few details of my progress so far:

- I've had several meetings with my bank, and a loan 1 *has been arranged* (arrange).
- I've found some office space in a good location, although some work 2 ________ (will/need) there before I can move in. I've employed some contractors and the work 3 ________ (should/finish) by the end of the month.
- I will need some specialized equipment, and this 4 ________ (order) at the moment.
- I know that the initial marketing of my business will be very important. I'm going to use flyers distributed door-to-door, and I 5 ________ (offer) a good deal on printing and distribution by a specialist leaflet distribution firm.
- One thing that I'm unsure of is how to employ part-time staff. Extra staff 6 ________ (might/need) over the Christmas period.

I look forward to hearing from you soon.

Yours faithfully,

Helen Chapman

Tasks

Speaking: listen and repeat

1 09 **You are going to hear eight phrases. Listen and repeat.**

Translate

2 Translate these short texts taken from the Internet into your own language. Remember not to translate word for word, but rather to make it sound natural.

Motorola estimates that a specific type of bar code called the Universal Product Code is used more than 10 billion times a day in applications that service 25 industries, including packaged goods, food services and medicine. Nowadays bar codes can be transmitted to cell phones to be read by a scanner directly from the phone – for example, for admittance to a baseball game – and they have evolved to the point where they can be read by cameras instead of lasers.

The Industry Standard website

Some of the regulations that discourage foreign investment in Japan have been removed. A start has been made on dealing with the huge government spending deficit.

BusinessWeek website

Writing: personalized practice

3 Look again at the malt whisky text in section C on page 42, and the text about questionnaires in exercise 9.4. Write a short text describing a system, process or procedure you know well. Examples of possible processes you could use are:

- a business-related process (production/how advertisements are designed and placed/the preparation of accounts/finding, interviewing and selecting new employees)
- a process in your personal life (cooking your favourite meal/feeding a baby or changing its nappy)
- a process from everyday life (check-in and security procedures at an airport).

Rehearsal for the real world

4 Look again at the letter in exercise 9.5. Notice how the writer talks about what *has been done*, what *is being done*, and what *will/should/might be done*.

Your boss has asked you to organize the office Christmas party at a local restaurant. Write an email to him/her about your progress with the planning. Examples of possible topics to include are:

- contacting colleagues (to estimate numbers of people going)
- researching some local restaurants (menus, prices, atmosphere) and finalizing the booking with one particular restaurant
- establishing the cost (company pays for everybody? individuals pay one fixed amount per head? everyone orders what they want and pays separately?)
- meeting place/time (option to meet first at a nearby bar for a drink? go straight to restaurant?)
- organizing a few 'extras' (decorations? small gift for everyone?)
- option for the boss to 'say a few words' at some point, or for toasting, and if so at what point during the evening?
- decision about bringing spouses/partners/children.

If you are working in class, put all the emails on the desks or on the walls. Go round the room and read the emails. Return to your seats and say which email you liked best, and why.

10 Passive 2

A Uses: maintaining the focus

A passive can be used to keep the focus of a paragraph. The second sentence starts with a word that relates to the subject of the first sentence.

Hasso Plattner is a German entrepreneur. ***He founded*** *SAP in 1972 after working for IBM.*
(Hasso Plattner continues to be the focus)

SAP is a world leader in business software. ***It was founded*** *by Hasso Plattner in 1972, after he left IBM.*
(SAP continues to be the focus)

Both of the above are good style. Compare with this version, which is poor style:

SAP is a world leader in business software. ~~Hasso Plattner founded it~~ in 1972 after he left IBM.

Here the two sentences begin with a different subject, and it is unclear whether the focus of the paragraph is going to be SAP or Hasso Plattner.

B Uses: being formal and impersonal

Passives are frequent in formal writing generally, for example in reports and legal documents. Try to find a balance between active and passive forms, as too many passive forms can make the text difficult to understand.

A typical context for formal/impersonal language is a complaint. Compare:

ACTIVE
We ordered *20 filter units from you on the 16th March and* ***the courier delivered*** *them yesterday. Unfortunately, when* ***we opened*** *the package,* ***someone had damaged*** *two of the units.* ***Our production department needs*** *these items urgently.*

PASSIVE (more formal and serious)
20 filter units were ordered *from you on the 16th March and* ***they were delivered*** *yesterday. Unfortunately, when* ***the package was opened, two of the units had been damaged*** *in transit.* ***These items are needed*** *urgently by our production department.*

Passives are used in phrases with *It* to report formally what people believe or said.

It was agreed/claimed/suggested that …

A typical context for this is a summary of a meeting, written after it has finished (unit 27C).

C Passive + infinitive

The verbs *believe, expect, know, report, say, think, suppose, understand* are often used in the present simple passive followed by an infinitive (*to do*). This use is common in news reports.

The Hungarian economy ***is expected to expand*** *6% over the next two years.*

To refer to the past we use the same verbs with *to have done.*

Credit card companies ***are believed to have suffered*** *significantly reduced profits.*

To refer to an activity in progress at the moment, we use the same verbs with *to be doing.*

Pfizer ***is known to be looking at*** *the possibility of acquiring some biotech start-ups.*

D Verbs with two objects

Some verbs have two objects (unit 21D). We can:

give/lend/offer/promise/sell/send/take **something** *to* **somebody**.
book/buy/keep/make/prepare/save **something** *for* **somebody**.

In active sentences we can use these verbs in two ways.

ABB ***gave us*** *a large order last year.*
ABB ***gave*** *a large order* ***to us*** *last year.*

The first form, without *to*, is more usual.

Each way can be made passive. One of the objects becomes the subject of the passive sentence, the other stays as an object.

We ***were given*** *a large order by ABB last year.*
A large order ***was given*** *to us by ABB last year.*

The first form, without *to*, is more usual.

E *have something done*

When a professional person, for example a builder or an accountant, does some work for us we can use *have something done.*

We ***have*** *our accounts* ***audited*** *by KPMG.*
We're ***going to have*** *a new air conditioning system* ***installed.***

We can use *get* in place of *have* in most cases. This is more informal.

We ***got*** *the contract* ***checked*** *by our lawyers.*

F *to be born*

To be born is a passive form but does not have an obvious passive meaning.

I ***was born*** *in a little town in Austria.*

Exercises

Section A

10.1 Read the first sentence, then choose which sentence a) or b) should follow. Put a tick (✓) by the correct answer.

1 Optimo and Primus are going to merge via a $36 billion offer by Optimo.
  a) Senior executives first discussed it over a year ago. ☐
  b) It was first discussed by senior executives over a year ago. ☑
2 Joaquín Almunia is the EU commissioner for economic and monetary affairs.
  a) He is directing the difficult process of economic union. ☐
  b) The difficult process of economic union is being directed by him. ☐
3 The process of EU enlargement is progressing slowly.
  a) A commissioner from Finland called Olli Rehn is directing it. ☐
  b) It is being directed by Olli Rehn, a commissioner from Finland. ☐
4 Novartis shares rose by three Swiss francs in Zurich yesterday.
  a) They are going to launch a new cardiovascular drug later this year. ☐
  b) A new cardiovascular drug is going to be launched by them later this year. ☐

Sections C, E, F

10.2 Underline the correct words.

1 I had my car *be repaired/repaired* yesterday.
2 Profits are expected *grow/to grow* by 10% in the next quarter.
3 I *born/was born* in a village just outside Dijon.
4 We're getting the machines *cleaned/to be cleaned* tomorrow.
5 The Board is thought *to be demanded/to have demanded* his resignation.
6 We have the components *assembling/assembled* in Vietnam.
7 Where exactly *were you born/did you born*?
8 She is supposed *to been looking/to be looking* for a new job.

Section D

10.3 Complete the second sentence so it has a similar meaning to the first sentence.

1 David from Marketing lent me this book.
  I was lent this book by David from Marketing.
2 This sample was given to me at the trade fair.
  ____________ this sample at the trade fair.
3 They promised us delivery within two weeks of our order.
  ____________ delivery within two weeks of our order.
4 A textile firm near Milan made this fabric for us.
  ____________ for us by a textile firm near Milan.
5 This order was sent to us through our website.
  ____________ this order through our website.
6 My secretary booked the flight for me.
  ____________ for me by my secretary.

Exercises

Section B **10.4 Complete this report by putting the verbs in brackets into either the present perfect active (*has done*) or passive (*has been done*).**

Investment opportunities: Brazil

Brazil 1 *has been transformed* (transform) from an economy based on sugar and coffee into a leading industrial power, and this 2 ________ (happen) over a relatively short time period. The Government 3 ________ (privatize) many state-owned companies, and they 4 ________ (also/invest) a lot of money in infrastructure. Inflation 5 ________ (bring) under control, and foreign direct investment 6 ________ (encourage). No one pretends that all the old problems 7 ________ (solve), but Brazil is finally taking its place on the world stage.

Section B **10.5 The two emails below are similar, but the second is more formal. Complete it by using verbs from the first email in the correct form of the passive.**

Thank you for your order, which you made online. Our fulfillment team is dealing with your order, and we expect that we will deliver the package to you within ten working days.

I attach a list of special promotions – you may need to click on the link below to download Adobe Acrobat if you cannot open the file. Please note we guarantee these prices only until the end of this month.

Thank you for your order, which 1 *was made* online. Your order 2 ________ by our fulfillment team, and we expect that the package 3 ________ to you within ten working days.

A list of special promotions 4 ________ – you may need to click on the link below to download Adobe Acrobat if the file 5 ________. Please note that these prices 6 ________ only until the end of this month.

Section C **10.6 Complete the article about LG by putting the reporting verbs into the present simple passive (*is known, is said*) and the main verb into a suitable form of the infinitive (*to do, to be doing* or *to have done*).**

LG: a Korean conglomerate with a global vision

LG, the Korean consumer electronics company, is pushing to become a truly global company. The company 1 *is known to have made* (know/make) many difficult decisions along the way. For example, many senior managers are now non-Koreans, and the company 2 ________ (say/be) keen to move away from its Asian 'face-saving' culture. Dermot Boden, the Chief Marketing Officer, is an Irishman. At an early meeting he argued a lot, and afterwards asked the CEO if his behaviour was appropriate. The CEO, Nam Yong, 3 ________ (report/reply), 'Why don't we argue more often?'. The foreigners are being asked to standardize LG's complex mixture of systems and processes. Didier Chenneveau, the Chief Supply-chain Officer, is a Swiss who used to work at HP. At the moment he 4 ________ (believe/try) to merge all the warehousing and transportation operations into a single global system.

Tasks

Speaking: listen and repeat

1 10 **You are going to hear eight phrases. Listen and repeat.**

Translate

2 Translate these short texts taken from the Internet into your own language. Remember not to translate word for word, but rather to make it sound natural.

The best way to rapidly develop a disruptive product or service – and get it out into the market – is to set up a heavyweight team, give it operational autonomy, and task it with complete responsibility for the project. The team should be backed by explicit senior management support recognized throughout the organization. It must be given the freedom to write its own rules, and conservative forces within the company who say 'Oh, we don't do that' must be short-circuited.

Forbes website

A 28-year-old man who is believed to be China's youngest city mayor admitted yesterday that he understood the reasons for the heated debate on the Internet over his youth and alleged inexperience. 'The concerns about my inexperience are reasonable,' acknowledged Zhou Senfeng, 'I lag far behind senior officials in experience, but what young officials need is a stage where they can perform and develop.'

ShanghaiDaily website

Writing: personalized practice

3 Look again at section E. Now write a sentence or two about what you *have done*, *had done* or *are going to have done* by the people/places below. Use real or invented information.

1 (hair stylist) *I have my hair done at my favourite stylist about once a month. They offer manicure as well, and I'm going to have my nails done there the next time I go.*

2 (spa/health farm) ______________________________

3 (garage) ______________________________

4 (external company auditors) ______________________________

5 (outsourcing firm that your company works with) ______________________________

6 (local building contractor) ______________________________

Rehearsal for the real world

4 Look again at section C on page 46 and exercise 10.6. Notice how news articles often have reporting verbs in the present simple passive + the main verb in the infinitive.

Now write a short news article about one of the following: your company, your university, your favourite sports team, a well-known celebrity.

If you are working in class, read some articles aloud and then discuss them.

11 Modals, etc. 1

A Modal verbs: form

Units 11–14 deal with modal verbs. Modal verbs are *can, could, will, would, may, might, shall, should* and *must*.

Modal verbs are auxiliary verbs – they are used with other main verbs. The verb that follows is an infinitive without *to*.

Sorry, I must go now. (NOT I must ~~to go~~ now)

Two modal verbs cannot be put together.

Modal verbs have only one form, so there is no *-s* in the third person singular and no form with *-ing*, *-ed*, etc.

The modal verbs *can* and *must* have very similar alternatives: *be able to* (for *can*) and *have to* (for *must*). In these expressions the rules of the previous three paragraphs do not apply, as *be* and *have* are used in the usual way (e.g. they can be combined with another modal, used with a past form, etc.).

I'm sorry I ***won't be able to*** *come.*
I ***had to*** *cancel my original flight.*

Questions are made by putting the modal in front of the subject. Negatives are made by putting *not* immediately after the modal (often shortened to *-n't* in spoken English and informal written English).

QUESTIONS	NEGATIVES
Can I …?	*I cannot (can't)*
Could you …?	*You could not (couldn't)*
Will I …?	*I will not (won't)*
Would he …?	*He would not (wouldn't)*
May I …?	*I may not*
Might they …?	*They might not*
Shall I …?	*I shall not (shan't)*
Should we …?	*We should not (shouldn't)*
Must she …?	*She must not (mustn't)*

Modal verbs show the speaker's attitude or feelings about a situation; for example, how probable something is, or that the speaker is requesting something.

Modal verbs can be used in different ways with different meanings. You only know the meaning from the context. For example, *could:*

I ***could*** *get to work in 30 minutes in my last job.*
(ability: past time)

Could *you pass the salt, please?*
(request: present time)

That ***could*** *be difficult.*
(uncertainty: future time)

B Ability

To talk about ability we use *can* and *can't* (or *cannot* in formal writing).

Can *you deliver in two weeks? – No, we* ***can't****.*

Can't is used for all things that we are not able to do.

I ***can't*** *speak German.*

For the special case of things that we are not able to do because of rules or laws, we can also use *mustn't* (unit 12B).

I'm sorry, you ***can't/mustn't*** *park here.*

We sometimes use *be able/unable to* instead of *can/can't*. This is common in writing.

We ***are*** *now* ***able to*** *track goods in transit.*

C Past ability

To talk about general past ability (not limited to one occasion) we use *could/could not*.

In my twenties I ***could*** *play tennis quite well.*

To talk about one specific past action it is less common to use *could*. Instead we use *was/were able to, managed to* and *succeeded in* (+ *-ing*).

I ***was able to/managed to*** *install the new software quite easily.*

Could can be used with a specific past action where there is a verb of the senses (*see, feel, hear, understand*).

I ***could/managed to*** *understand most of what he said.*

In questions and negative sentences we can use *could, was/were able to* and *managed to*.

Could *you/****Were*** *you* ***able to/Did*** *you* ***manage to*** *speak to your boss today?*
Sorry, I ***couldn't/wasn't able to/didn't manage to*** *do it today – I was very busy.*

D *will*

Will is used as a future form (unit 7A). But *will* also has modal uses.

I think ***I'll*** *go home now.*
(a spontaneous decision)

I'll *give you a lift to the station.*
(an offer of help)

I'll *give you my full support in the meeting.*
(a promise)

The engine ***won't*** *start.*
(certainty about something working/not working)

Will *you hold the elevator for me, please?*
(a request)

Will *you have some more coffee?*
(offering something)

Further uses of *will* include probability in the past (unit 13E) and conditionals (unit 17C).

Exercises

Section A

11.1 Underline the correct words.

1 *Do you can come/Can you come* to the training seminar next week?
2 *I can come/I can to come* to the training seminar next week.
3 Sorry that *I didn't could come/I couldn't come* to the training seminar last week.
4 What *we can do/can we do*?
5 I hope *to can/to be able to* fly directly to Munich.
6 *I must speak/I must to speak* with Mr Reiner as soon as possible.
7 *I managed to speak/I could speak* to Mr Reiner yesterday.
8 The hotel was OK, but *I managed to hear/I could hear* a lot of noise from the street.

Sections A, B, C

11.2 Complete the sentences with *can, can't, could, couldn't* or *be able to*.

1 I'm sorry, I *can't* help you right now. Ask me again in an hour or so.
2 I don't think I'll ______________ come to the conference.
3 The negotiations broke down because we ______________ agree on the quality standard.
4 I ______________ see you were talking to a client, so I didn't interrupt.
5 If you ______________ make a firm order today, we should ______________ ship by Friday.
6 I ______________ understand Portuguese, but I ______________ speak it.
7 Sorry. I ______________ see you next week, but I might ______________ make the week after.
8 I'm sorry I ______________ come to your talk yesterday. I had to sort out a problem.
9 I ______________ ski really well when I was in my twenties, but now I'm out of practice.

Section D, unit 7

11.3 Match sentences 1–8 with the uses of *will* a–h. This exercise includes revision of unit 7.

a) future fact
b) belief or opinion about the future
c) instant decision
d) certainty about something (not) working (used with *work/start/open*, etc.)
e) promise
f) request
g) offering something
h) offer of help

1 I think sales *will* probably improve in the spring. [*b*]
2 I'*ll* give you a hand with your bags. [ ]
3 *Will* you give me a hand with these bags? [ ]
4 OK, I'*ll* call her right now. [ ]
5 I'*ll* be there at six o'clock. Don't worry, I *won't* be late. [ ]
6 In January we'*ll* have two new products ready to launch. [ ]
7 *Will* you have another glass of wine? [ ]
8 The software *will* work now. I've reinstalled it. [ ]

Exercises

Sections B, D, unit 7

11.4 Make phrases for a telephone conversation by using one item from each column. Then use the phrases to complete the dialogue below.

Could I	repeat	through
Could you	you	this number
I'll just go and	back	to someone
I'll put	speak	that, please
I'll get	on	a look
I'll be	have	to you

JON: Good morning, the Tech Store, this is Jon speaking.
SARA: [1] *Could I speak to someone* in Customer Services, please?
JON: Yes, of course, [2] ________ .
MARK: Customer Services, Mark speaking, how can I help you?
SARA: I'm calling about the new Samsung home theater system, model number HT-BQ8ST. Do you have it in stock?
MARK: [3] ________ . Hold the line please. (*silence*) Hello? I can't see it on the shelves. I need to check the order status on the computer. Can I call you back?
SARA: Certainly. My name is Sara Hall, and my number is 01682 829193.
MARK: Sorry, [4] ________ ?
SARA: It's Sara Hall, and my number is 01682 829193. [5] ________ all morning.
MARK: OK, Sara, [6] ________ as soon as I have the information.

Sections A, B, D

11.5 This exercise introduces the full range of modal verbs. Some are covered in later units. Match each sentence 1–16 with a meaning a–p.

1	I *should* do it.	*d*	a) Sorry, it's impossible.
2	I *shouldn't* do it.		b) I have the ability to do it.
3	I *can* do it.		c) It's a bad idea.
4	I *can't* do it.		d) It's a good idea.
5	I *mustn't* do it.		e) I'm making a suggestion.
6	*Shall* we do it?		f) It's forbidden (prohibited).
7	I *have to* do it.		g) I have a choice whether to do it.
8	I *don't have to* do it.		h) It's necessary to do it.
9	I*'ll* do it.		i) I'm asking you to do it.
10	*May* I do it?		j) I'm asking permission to do it myself.
11	I *might* do it.		k) Perhaps I will do it.
12	*Would* you do it, please?		l) I promise.
13	I *couldn't* do it.		m) I'm reporting a decision (made using *will*)
14	*Could* you do it, please?		n) I expect that I can do it.
15	I said I *would* never do it.		o) I was unable to do it.
16	I *should* be able to do it.		p) I'm requesting that you do it.

Tasks

Speaking: listen and repeat

1 11 **You are going to hear eight phrases. Listen and repeat.**

Translate

2 **Translate these short texts taken from the Internet into your own language. Remember not to translate word for word, but rather to make it sound natural.**

'We're seeing many situations where smaller companies have projects in an advanced stage of development that they cannot carry forward at this point. They just don't have the capital or the resources to do so. I think we will be able to acquire some of those projects.'

Business News Americas website

I always wondered how people managed to lose their life's savings in the stock market. Then it hit me. Some people read a little bit on the Internet, assume the rest, and then just click to buy a stock using their online broker. People can overhear something at a cocktail party and just buy shares of a business they don't understand. What is it? Intellectual laziness? A failure of schools to teach critical thinking?

About website

Writing: personalized practice

3 **Look again at exercise 11.3 and the different uses of *will*. Now write eight sentences of your own to match the different uses. Remember to use contractions where appropriate.**

1 (future fact about your career/life) *I'll be 40 next year. I guess it's time to do something with my life.*

2 (belief or opinion about the future of technology) ______

3 (instant decision after finishing a call with a customer) ______

4 (certainty about something working/not working) ______

5 (promise you make your boss/teacher) ______

6 (request made to a colleague in your office) ______

7 (offering something in the restaurant) ______

8 (offer of help to a team member before a deadline) ______

Rehearsal for the real world

4 **Look again at sections B and C on page 50. Now write a few sentences about the things in the following list, using details from your personal or professional life.**

Two things you could do when you were younger but can't do now.
Two things you couldn't do when you were younger but can do now.
Two things you'd like to be able to do in the future.
Two things you managed to do yesterday.
Two things you didn't manage to do yesterday.

If you are working in class, choose some sentences to read aloud. Ask and answer questions.

12 Modals, etc. 2

A Obligation (necessity)

To say that something is necessary we use *have to* and *must*.

*We **must** finish the meeting by 11 at the latest. I **have to** get to the airport.*

The two forms have the same meaning in writing. In speech there is a small difference. With *have to* the situation makes something necessary, while with *must* the speaker personally feels something is necessary.

*You **have to** pay the invoice within sixty days.*
(that's the company rule)

*You **must** stop working so hard.*
(I'm telling you – it's my strong advice)

To make a question we normally use *have to*. If we use *must* we can sound annoyed, particularly if we stress *must* in speech.

***Do you have to** work this evening?*
***Must you** work this evening? It's our wedding anniversary today.*

Have got to and *will have to* are also used for necessity. They are more informal.

***I've got to** finish this report today.*
***You'll have to** contact them immediately.*

Need to has the same meaning as *have to* and can be used in its place (see this section and sections B and C).

*You **have to/need to** sign this form in two places, here and here.*

Need to has two possible negative forms.

*You **don't need to/needn't** wait for me – I'll come along later.*

B No obligation; permission; prohibition

When something is not necessary we use *don't have to*.

*You **don't have to** go. Helmut can go instead.*
(you are free to choose)

When something is permitted we use *can* and *be allowed to*.

*You **can** park on the street after 6 pm*

When something is prohibited we use *can't, be not allowed to* and *mustn't*.

*You**'re not allowed** to park on a yellow line.*
(that's the law)

*You **mustn't** talk about politics at dinner tonight.*
(You shouldn't – it's forbidden socially.)

Notice that *have to* and *must* have similar meanings in their affirmative forms (section A above), but different meanings in their negative forms (this section).

*I **have to/must** leave now.*	(it's necessary)
*I **don't have to** leave now.*	(I have a choice)
*I **mustn't** leave now.*	(I shouldn't)

C Past forms

To talk about obligation in the past, we use *had to*. There is no past form of *must*.

*Sorry I'm late – I **had to** send some figures to the financial controller.*

To talk about no obligation in the past, we use *didn't have to*.

*You **didn't have to** take a taxi. There's a very good train service from the airport.*

To talk about permission in the past, we use *could, was allowed to*.

*In my last job I **was allowed to** leave early on Fridays.*

To talk about prohibition in the past, we use *couldn't, wasn't allowed to*.

*In the old days we **weren't allowed to** meet clients unless we had a suit and tie.*

D Opinions and advice

To give an opinion about what is the best or most sensible thing to do we use *should, should not (shouldn't), ought to* and *ought not to (oughtn't to)*.

*We **should** invest more heavily in marketing.*

When we speak to someone else our opinion becomes advice.

*You have no social life. You **should** get out more.*

Note the relation between advice and necessity:

*You **should/ought to** go to the doctor.*
(advice: it's the best thing to do)

*You **must/have to** go to the doctor.*
(strong advice: it's really necessary)

Had better (not) is used for strong opinions. *Had* is usually contracted.

***I'd better not** interrupt him just now.*

E Past criticism

When we use *should* and *ought to* in the past (+ *have* + past participle), we mean that we didn't do the right thing and now we are making a criticism.

*We **ought to have seen** the danger signs a long time ago.*
*We **shouldn't have spent** so much money on top-of-the-range company cars.*

Exercises

Sections A, B, C, D, E

12.1 Match each sentence 1–12 with a meaning a–l.

1 I can do it. [c]
2 I mustn't do it. [ ]
3 I don't have to do it. [ ]
4 I have to do it. [ ]

5 I couldn't do it. [ ]
6 I didn't have to do it. [ ]
7 I had to do it. [ ]
8 I could do it. [ ]

9 I should have done it. [ ]
10 I shouldn't have done it. [ ]
11 I shouldn't do it. [ ]
12 I should do it. [ ]

a) It's necessary.
b) It's not necessary.
c) It's allowed.
d) It's not allowed.

e) It was necessary.
f) It wasn't necessary.
g) It was allowed.
h) It wasn't allowed.

i) Doing it would be a good idea.
j) Doing it would be a bad idea.
k) I did it, unfortunately.
l) I didn't do it, unfortunately.

Section A

12.2 Complete the sentences with *must* or *have to*. Both are possible each time, but one is slightly more natural in a spoken context.

1 I *must* remember to email Steve and thank him for all his help.
2 You ____________ fill in this application form and return it to the HR department.
3 You ____________ try to be more diplomatic when you're speaking to Tania.
4 I ____________ go the dentist next Friday morning, so I'll be a little late.

Sections A, B, C, D

12.3 Look at the pairs of sentences. If the meaning is the same or similar, write *S*. If the meaning is different, write *D*.

1 You must be here before 8.30. / You have to be here before 8.30. [S]
2 We don't have to decide yet. / We don't need to decide yet. [ ]
3 You can't park here. / You're not allowed to park here. [ ]
4 We don't have to cut the budget. / We mustn't cut the budget. [ ]
5 You didn't have to give a tip. / You didn't need to give a tip. [ ]
6 I have to speak to my boss. / I'll have to speak to my boss. [ ]
7 We have to hurry. / We've got to hurry. [ ]
8 I couldn't contact her. / I didn't need to contact her. [ ]
9 We ought to sign the contract. / We should sign the contract. [ ]
10 You shouldn't worry so much. / You ought not to worry so much. [ ]
11 I should finish this spreadsheet. / I'd better finish this spreadsheet. [ ]
12 We ought not to raise our prices. / We can't raise our prices. [ ]

"What do you think . . . should we get started on that motivation research or not?"

Exercises

Sections A, B, D **12.4 An HR manager is explaining company rules to a group of new employees. Complete the text with *have to, don't have to, can, can't, should* or *shouldn't*.**
Study the context carefully to choose the best answer, using each item once.

> I'd like to take this opportunity to explain some of the procedures that we have here. First of all, vacation time. All employees get twenty days paid leave per year. You [1] *don't have to* take all the days in one calendar year – it's quite OK to carry days forward to the next year, up to a maximum of ten days. We try to be flexible and give you the days you want, and the only real restriction is that you [2] __________ keep having two weeks in August year after year – someone has to be here over the summer to keep the business running. Next, fire drills. Government regulations state that we [3] __________ organize a fire drill once a month at random times and with no warning to staff. When you hear the bells, don't ignore them. You [4] __________ leave the building immediately, using the emergency fire exits. These are clearly signed in the rooms and corridors. If you are away from your desk, you [5] __________ go back to collect personal belongings – this would be very risky in the event of a real fire. And finally, trade union membership. This is entirely your own choice. You [6] __________ join the union if you want to, but it's not compulsory. About 60% of our employees belong to a union, and we work closely with the union representatives on matters such as pay and health and safety. OK, I think that covers everything. Does anyone have any questions?

Sections C, E **12.5 A businessman is describing a recent flight. Complete the text with *had to, didn't have to, couldn't, should have* or *shouldn't have*.**
Study the context carefully to choose the best answer, using each item twice.

> I [1] *should have* caught the 10 am flight, but it was overbooked. I checked in quite late and so I was one of the unlucky people who lost their seat – it meant I [2] __________ catch a later flight. Also they told me at the check-in desk that I [3] __________ take both my bags on board with me as hand luggage, and I [4] __________ put one of them in the hold. Of course that delayed me at the other end at baggage reclaim. When I got on the plane I wanted to use my laptop, but of course I [5] __________ do so until after takeoff. The flight attendant told me to turn it off and said that I [6] __________ known not to use it. To be honest I'd just completely forgotten, and he [7] __________ been so rude. Anyway, I arrived at my destination much later than planned, so it was lucky I [8] __________ go to any meetings that afternoon. Of course in retrospect I can see that I [9] __________ traveled with that airline – after all, they are well known for their overbooking policy. It was my fault really. I [10] __________ fly with them – my company would have been happy to pay for a more expensive ticket with a better airline.

Tasks

Speaking: listen and repeat

1 12 **You are going to hear eight phrases. Listen and repeat.**

Translate

2 Translate these short texts taken from the Internet into your own language. Remember not to translate word for word, but rather to make it sound natural.

To really work, pay TV online or for mobile platforms will have to be accessible through every major video portal, including Hulu and YouTube. Both the TV networks and the distributors should provide high-quality, consumer-friendly sites for viewing TV content – with easy authentication.

Reuters website

The storms on Wall Street seem never ending. Regardless of who did what or why, one thing is clear: shareholders were not given any sympathy amid the emergency rescue operations that helped support our financial system when it was on the brink of collapse. Some may say that the ends justify the means. But I still believe that it should have been possible to bail out the banks without treating the shareholders so unfairly.

TheStreet website

Writing: personalized practice

3 Look again at exercise 12.4 and notice how the HR manager uses the different modal forms. Now write a paragraph for each of the following situations, explaining the rules and procedures. Use a good variety of modal forms.

1 (on a flight) *You have to fasten your seatbelt before take-off, although you can take it off later. You should follow the safety demonstration given by the cabin crew. You shouldn't complain when a baby cries all through the flight – one day it might be your baby doing the same thing. And finally, you don't have to eat the horrible food they give you – you can bring your own sandwiches if you think of it before leaving home.*

2 (on a first date with a boyfriend/girlfriend) ______

3 (entertaining foreign guests at a restaurant) ______

4 (in my company or in my educational institution) ______

Rehearsal for the real world

4 Look again at exercise 12.5 and notice how the businessman uses the different modal forms in the past. Now write a short text where you tell a story (real or invented) about a business trip or holiday where a lot of things went wrong.

If you are working in class, read some stories aloud.

13 Modals, etc. 3

A Degrees of probability

We can use modals and other phrases to talk about the probability that something will happen in the future. The table below gives an overview which is developed in the following sections.

100%	certainty	*will, be certain to*
95–100%	deduction	*must, can't*
80%	expectation	*should, shouldn't, ought to, ought not to, be likely to, be unlikely to*
30–70%	uncertainty	*may, may not, might, might not, could*
0%	certainty	*won't*

B Certainty and deduction

When we are certain something will happen we use *will* and *be certain to.*

*Toyota **will** present their all-electric city car at the Paris Motor Show.*

When we are certain something will not happen we use *won't.*

*I'm sorry, Christiane is on vacation. She **won't** be back until the 14th.*

We can use *probably* and *definitely* with *will* and *won't.* Note the word order.

*She**'ll probably** be at the meeting.*
*She **probably won't** be at the meeting.*

We use *must* and *can't* to show that something is certain because it is logical from the evidence. This is called 'deduction'.

*There's no answer from her phone. She **must** be in a meeting.*
*Both the meeting rooms are empty. She **can't** be in a meeting.*

Note that *can't*, not *mustn't*, is used in this last example.

C Expectation

When we expect that something will happen we use *should, ought to* or *be likely to.*

*They **should** arrive around 10.30.*
*Our profits **are likely to** improve next year.*

When we expect that something will not happen we use *shouldn't, ought not to* or *be unlikely to.*

*I have all the information I need now. There **shouldn't** be any problem.*

D Uncertainty

When we are uncertain we use *may, might* or *could.* The meaning is 'perhaps'.

*I **might** have more news for you next week.*
*It **could** take a long time to arrange the finance for this deal.*

There is no real difference between these three modals in this context.

The negative forms are *may not* and *might not.*

*I have a suggestion. You **might not** agree, but listen to what I'm going to say.*

Note that *could not* is not used with this meaning (unit 11C for *could not*).

E Probability in the past

For different degrees of probability in the past we use modal verb + *have* + past participle. See the table below.

CERTAINTY
*You**'ll have seen** our new model, I'm sure. It's in all the shops.*

DEDUCTION
*There was no answer from her phone. She **must have been** in a meeting.*
*Both the meeting rooms were empty. She **can't have been** in a meeting.*

EXPECTATION
*They **should have arrived** by now. I hope they haven't got lost.*

UNCERTAINTY
*We're only five minutes late. The talk **might not have started** yet.*

CERTAINTY
*You **won't have seen** our new model. It's not in the shops yet.*

This language area is sometimes called 'speculating about the past'. In this context, 'certainty' is really 'assumption' (you think something is true, although you have no proof).

F 'Possibility'

Be careful with the idea of 'possibility', because it refers to two different things: uncertainty (section D above) and ability (unit 11B).

***It's possible** they will go bankrupt.*
(uncertainty: *they **might** go bankrupt*)

***It's possible** to make this in a larger size.*
(ability: *we **can** make this in a larger size*)

Exercises

Sections A, B, C, D

13.1 <u>Underline</u> the correct words.

1 Look at those clouds. I think it *can/might/must* rain.
2 That's impossible. It *can't be/mustn't be/may not be* true.
3 Well done! You *may be/must be/might be* very pleased.
4 I'm not sure. I *must not be/may not be/won't be* able to get there in time.
5 That *can't be/mustn't be/may not be* Dana. She's away at a conference.
6 Lisa isn't at home. She *can be/must be/mustn't be* on her way here.
7 Lisa hasn't arrived yet, but she *should be/can be/can't be* here soon.
8 A: Who's that man over there?
B: I don't know. It *can be/might be/mustn't be* the new Sales Director.
9 I'm not sure where Sue is. She *could be/must be/can be* at lunch.
10 I've looked everywhere for Sue. She *could be/must be/can be* at lunch.

Sections A, B, C, D

13.2 Match each sentence 1–7 with a similar sentence a–g.

1 They're likely to do it.	a) I'm sure that they'll do it.
2 They might/could do it.	b) I'm nearly sure that they'll do it.
3 They're almost certain to do it.	c) They'll probably do it.
4 They'll definitely do it.	d) Maybe they'll do it.
5 They're unlikely to do it.	e) I'm sure they won't do it.
6 They're very unlikely to do it.	f) They probably won't do it.
7 They definitely won't do it.	g) They almost certainly won't do it.

Sections A, B, D

13.3 Complete the second sentence so it has a similar meaning to the first sentence. Use *can't, might, must* or *should.*

1 Deliver by the end of the month? Yes, I expect we can do that.
Deliver by the end of the month? Yes, we *should* be able to do that.
2 It's possible that we will lose this client unless we're careful.
We ________ lose this client unless we're careful.
3 I'm sure this isn't the right road.
This ________ be the right road.
4 I'm sure you're tired after your flight – I'll let you get back to the hotel.
You ________ be tired after your flight – I'll let you get back to the hotel.
5 It's possible that I'll be coming to Paris with Jack, but I don't really know.
I ________ be coming to Paris with Jack, but I don't really know.
6 It's likely that we'll make our sales targets this quarter.
We ________ make our sales targets this quarter.
7 From what I know about computers, that isn't the problem.
From what I know about computers, that ________ be the problem.
8 I suppose you're Kate Perry. Pleased to meet you.
You ________ be Kate Perry. Pleased to meet you.

Exercises

Section E

13.4 Match each sentence 1–8 with its meaning a–d.

1 He won't have arrived yet. [d]
2 He'll have arrived by now. [ ]
3 He can't have arrived yet. [ ]
4 He might have arrived by now. [ ]
5 He could have arrived by now. [ ]
6 He should have arrived by now. [ ]
7 He must have arrived by now. [ ]
8 He couldn't have arrived yet. [ ]

a) 95–100% probability of his arrival.
b) 80% probability of his arrival.
c) 30–70% probability of his arrival.
d) 0% probability of his arrival.

Sections A, B, C, D

13.5 Complete this article about the economy with the words and phrases in the box. The graphs and ideas in the text will help you.

will definitely	is almost certain to	~~is likely to~~	might	are unlikely to	definitely won't

Since the beginning of this year unemployment has fallen from 2.5 million to 1.8 million, and [1] *is likely to* drop below 1.5 million by the end of the year. Unemployment is a key political issue in the country at the moment, and so this [2] ________ be good news for the government. In two years' time, when the next election is due, it [3] ________ even fall below 1 million. On the other hand inflation is going up rapidly, and it [4] ________ reach 6% by the end of the year. Opposition parties [5] ________ let this issue drop out of sight. However, inflation is a worldwide phenomenon, and targeting inflation is the responsibility of the Central Bank. The Bank is fiercely independent and [6] ________ be influenced by government pressure. In fact, this is good news for the government – they have someone else to blame.

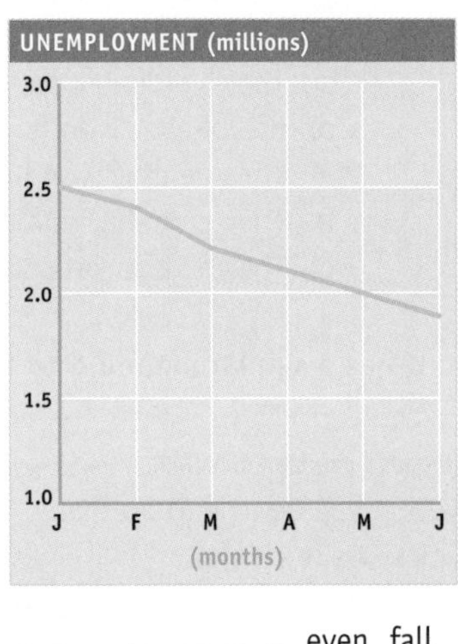

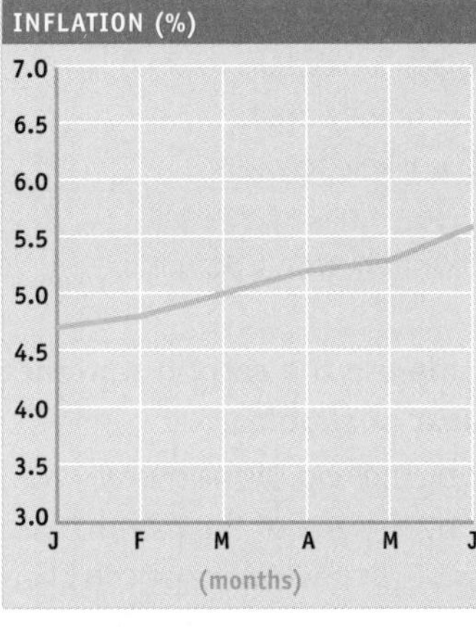

Sections A, B, D, E

13.6 Martin and Anne have arrived at check-in at Heathrow airport. Complete their dialogue with *must, must have, might, might have, can't* or *can't have*.

MARTIN: Oh, no. I can't find my passport.
ANNE: You're kidding.
MARTIN: No, really. It's not in my briefcase.
ANNE: Well, it [1] *must* be in your other bag. Have a look.
MARTIN: It's not there. Where on earth is it?
ANNE: I don't know. Do you think you [2] ________ left it at home?
MARTIN: That's impossible. I [3] ________ done. I made sure I had it with me before I left the house.
ANNE: OK, calm down. What about checking your coat pockets? You never know, it [4] ________ be there.
MARTIN: Let me see. No, no luck. This is ridiculous, we're going to miss our flight.
ANNE: You [5] ________ be looking in the right place. I'm sure you'll realize in a moment where it is. Just sit down and think about it.
CHECK-IN AGENT: Excuse me, sir. Is that your passport there on the ground?
MARTIN: Oh, yes, so it is. I [6] ________ dropped it when I was looking for the tickets. Silly me!

Tasks

Speaking: listen and repeat

1 13 **You are going to hear eight phrases. Listen and repeat.**

Translate

2 Translate these short texts taken from the Internet into your own language. Remember not to translate word for word, but rather to make it sound natural.

The report said that 62% of over 50s worry that their pensions and savings are unlikely to see them through retirement. And it warned that the pension crisis would bring further misery to the Sandwich Generation – defined as those who support both their children and their parents. 71% of adults fear their parents' shortage in retirement funding could cause severe problems for their own financial futures.

Telegraph website

It struck me that while Esperanto may be dead, the language of food may have replaced it as one that transcends borders and can be universally understood. A Tokyo resident probably doesn't have to be proficient in English to know what's in the McPork sandwich at the local McDonald's. And Americans, who are terrible at learning Japanese, have learned something from the sushi bars that now dot the US landscape.

Newsweek website

Writing: personalized practice

3 Look again at sections A–D on page 58 and the variety of ways to express future probability. Now write sentences on each of the following topics. Discuss possible consequences and/or guess what is going to happen.

1 (lack of sleep) *Missing one night's sleep, for example because of a very early flight or a long journey, shouldn't be too much of a problem. In fact, during the next day you might feel completely normal. However, by the time evening comes you'll probably be quite tired.*

2 (doing regular exercise) ______________________________

3 (house prices in my country) ______________________________

4 (product development in my company) ______________________________

5 (worldwide use of nuclear power) ______________________________

Rehearsal for the real world

4 Look again at exercise 13.6 and notice the use of modals to express probability in the past. Now think of a disaster in the real world that has recently happened, either business related or a national or international news event. Write a short text describing what happened and consider a variety of reasons for what went wrong. Use *must have*, *might have* and *can't have*.

If you are working in class, read some texts aloud and then discuss them.

14 Modals, etc. 4

A Direct / indirect language

Language can be direct or indirect depending on the situation. Direct language is typical of work conversations between colleagues or people of the same status. Indirect language is typical of situations where we have to be a little more formal or polite. In general:

- present forms (*can, will*) are more direct than past forms (*could, would*)
- short forms (*Can you*) are more direct than long forms (*I wonder if you could*).

B Requests

To make a request (ask someone to do something) we use *can, could, will, would*. We can add the word *possibly* to make the request very polite.

Could we (possibly) *take a short break now?*
Would you *give me a hand with these suitcases?*

We can use an indirect question (unit 16A) to make the request more polite.

Do you think *we could take a short break?*

We reply by agreeing or refusing.

Agreeing: *Sure, no problem. / Yes, of course.*
Refusing: *Actually, it's a bit inconvenient right now. / Sorry, that's not possible.*

C Requests with *mind*

We can make a polite request with *Would you mind* followed by an *-ing* form.

Would you mind *repeat**ing** that?*

Questions with *mind* mean *Is it a problem for you?* So, to agree to a request with *mind* we say 'no'.

A: ***Would you mind*** *opening the window?*
B: ***No****, of course not.*

To refuse we use a phrase like *Well, Actually, To be honest* and then give a reason.

B: ***Actually****, I think it's quite cold in here.*

D Permission

To ask if we can do something ourselves we use *can, could, may*.

Can I *change my ticket?*

We can use an indirect question (unit 16A) to ask for permission.

I'd like to know *if I can change my ticket.*
Is it all right *if I change my ticket?*

We can ask for permission with *Do you mind if I …?* or *Would you mind if I …?* In the examples below notice the forms in bold. They follow the normal rules for first and second conditionals (unit 17).

Do *you mind if I* ***open*** *the window?*
Would *you mind if I* ***opened*** *the window?*

E Offers and invitations

To offer help we use *Can / Could / Shall I, Would you like me to, I'll* and *Let me*.

Shall I *make a copy for you?*
Would you like me to *give you a lift?*
I'll *give you a hand.*

To offer things we use *Would you like* or short phrases with choices.

A: ***Would you like*** *tea or coffee?*
B: *I'll have coffee, please. White, no sugar.*
A: *Anything to drink? Tea or coffee?*
B: *I'd rather have water, if you don't mind.*

To invite somebody to do something we use *Would you like to*.

Would you like to *come to the restaurant with us tonight?*

We reply by accepting or rejecting.

Accepting: *Thanks. That's very kind of you. / Thank you. / That sounds great.*
Rejecting: *That's very kind of you, but … / Thanks, but I can manage.*

F Suggestions

To make a suggestion we use *Could, Shall, What / How about* and *Let's*. Notice the different forms:

We could / Let's *have a short break now.*
(statement)

What about *hav**ing** a short break now?*
(question + verb with *-ing*)

Shall we have *a short break now?*
(question)

We often use a negative question.

Couldn't we / Why don't we / Why not *try to renegotiate this part of the contract?*

We reply by accepting or rejecting.

Accepting: *Yes, I think we should do that. / That's a good idea. / Yes, let's do that.*
Rejecting: *I'm not really sure about that. / That sounds like a good idea, but … / Are you sure?*

Exercises

Sections B, C, D, E, F

14.1 Underline the correct words.

1 Would you mind *to give/giving* me a hand?
2 We're getting nowhere. How about *talking/to talk* to another supplier?
3 Are you having problems? *Would I/Shall I* help you?
4 *Would you/May you* help me carry these boxes, please?
5 *Would I/May I* ask you a personal question?
6 I think *you should/you can* spend less time playing golf and more time in the office.
7 Excuse me, *could you/may you* tell me the way to the station?
8 *Do you like/Would you like* some more soup?
9 *Would I/Could I* borrow your copy of The Economist?
10 We're not getting anywhere. Do you think *could we/we could* try another approach?
11 Do you mind if *I give/I gave* you a decision next week?
12 Would you mind if *I give/I gave* you a decision next week?

Section E

14.2 Match the forms 1–3 with the uses a–c.

1 Would you like a/some ...	a) offering help
2 Would you like to ...	b) offering something
3 Would you like me to ...	c) inviting somebody to do something

Sections B, D, E, F

14.3 Read the questions a–f and the replies i–vi.

a) Would you like a coffee?
b) Would you like me to carry your coffee for you?
c) Would you like to come with us for a coffee?
d) Could you get me a coffee from Starbucks when you go out?
e) Shall we break for coffee now?
f) Is it all right if I help myself to coffee?

i Yes, of course. Go right ahead.
ii Actually, I'd rather have water if you don't mind.
iii To be honest, I don't think I'll have time.
iv Yes, let's do that.
v Thanks, that's very kind of you.
vi Thanks, but I can manage.

Now match the questions and replies to the situations below.

1 Making a request + refusing a request *d* + *iii*
2 Asking for permission + replying with a 'yes' ☐ + ☐
3 Offering help + rejecting an offer of help ☐ + ☐
4 Offering something + replying with a preference ☐ + ☐
5 Inviting somebody + accepting an invitation ☐ + ☐
6 Making a suggestion + accepting a suggestion ☐ + ☐

Exercises

Sections C, D, E, F

14.4 George is visiting Sergio in São Paolo. Complete the dialogue with the phrases in the box.

shall we	thanks, that sounds great	of course	of course not
~~would you like~~	would you like to	would you like me to	
do you mind	would you mind	I don't mind	

SERGIO: Please, come in. Let me take your coat. It's good to see you!

GEORGE: *(after sitting down)* It's very nice to be here in São Paolo. Thank you so much for your invitation to come and see you.

SERGIO: Not at all. It's my pleasure. [1] *Would you like* something to drink?

GEORGE: Mineral water, please.

SERGIO: Still or sparkling?

GEORGE: Oh, [2]__________. Either would be fine. [3]__________ if I just make a quick call before we start? The number was busy before.

SERGIO: [4]__________. Go right ahead.

GEORGE: Still busy – no problem. You have a wonderful building here.

SERGIO: It's designed by one of our most famous architects, César Pelli. There's a restaurant on the top floor. [5]__________ take you there later?

GEORGE: [6]__________.

SERGIO: Now then, [7]__________ get down to business? [8]__________ telling me a little about your company and your long-term objectives here in Brazil?

GEORGE: I have a short presentation prepared on my laptop. It explains everything. [9]__________ see it?

SERGIO: [10]__________. Let me make some space here on the desk.

Sections B, C, D, E

14.5 Read the following impolite dialogue between a hotel receptionist and a guest.

Receptionist	Guest
1 Give me your name.	2 It's Jessop.
3 Spell it.	4 J-E-S-S-O-P.
5 Give me your passport.	6 Here it is. I want an early morning call.
7 Of course.	8 And I must leave a message for a colleague.
9 Do you want a pen?	10 Thank you. Are there any nightclubs nearby?
11 Yes, one or two.	12 Good. I can walk back at 3.00 a.m. in the morning.
13 Don't do that.	

Now rewrite the following lines from the dialogue using the words in brackets.

1 (May/have/name/please) *May I have your name, please?*

3 (Could/spell/that/me/please) __________

5 (Would you/leaving/passport) __________

6 (Do/think/have/early morning call) __________

8 (Would/mind if I/message/colleague) __________

9 (Would/like me/lend/pen) __________

13 (don't think/ought/that) __________

Tasks

Speaking: listen and repeat

1 14 **You are going to hear eight phrases. Listen and repeat.**

Translate

2 Translate these short texts taken from the Internet into your own language. Remember not to translate word for word, but rather to make it sound natural.

Q: Would you mind providing our readers with a brief overview of Elitra Pharmaceuticals?
A: Elitra's business is to develop novel antibiotic drugs. This is one of the largest therapeutic markets with over $30 billion in annual sales. Increasing bacterial resistance is making existing drugs less effective in their treatment of infections.
Q: Would you say there will always be a need to create a new class of antibiotics just because of this resistance problem?

The Wall Street Transcript website

The IPPR has just published a report, "Shall We Stay or Shall We Go?". The report sets out to quantify and analyse re-migration from the United Kingdom – in other words, the emigration of immigrants. International competition for highly-skilled migrants is intensifying, and it makes no sense for the UK to succeed in attracting such migrants only to lose them quickly because of re-migration. The report uses a wide range of original qualitative research undertaken in a number of countries, and involves a comprehensive analysis of all the data relating to re-migration.

Institute for Public Policy Research website

Writing: personalized practice

3 Look at the two following situations and complete the sentences below.

Situation: Your boss has invited you to dinner at their private home. You want to show that you are polite and can be trusted with important clients in social situations. Write sentences that might be said during the evening, either by you or your boss.

1 Do you think you could *pass me the water* ?
2 Would you mind ______ ?
3 Do you mind if I ______ ?
4 Would you like to ______ ?
5 Why don't we ______ ?

Situation: Your office is being renovated and you have to move out temporarily and share with a colleague from another department who you don't know. Write sentences that might be said on your first morning in your new office, either by you or your colleague.

6 Is it all right if I *put a photograph of my family on this shelf* ?
7 I'll ______ .
8 I wonder if you could ______ ?
9 Would you like me to ______ ?
10 Shall we ______ ?

Now write possible replies to the ten sentences above, using the same situations.

Rehearsal for the real world

4 You have been given an assistant to help you in your job. It is your assistant's first day in the job; they are keen to find out what to do, and you have lots of tasks that need doing. Now write three short pieces of dialogue between you and your assistant at different points during the day.

If you are working in class, read some dialogues aloud.

15 Questions 1

A *Yes / No* questions and answers

Questions with the answer *yes* or *no* are formed with an auxiliary verb + subject + main verb. The auxiliary can be *do, be, have* or a modal verb like *can, will, would*. Short answers repeat the auxiliary.

A: ***Do*** *you* ***speak*** *French?*
B: *Yes, I* ***do****./No, I* ***don't****.*

A: ***Are*** *you* ***staying*** *at the Hilton?*
B: *Yes, I* ***am****./No, I****'m not****.*

A: ***Did*** *you* ***check*** *all the invoices?*
B: *Yes, I* ***did****./No, I* ***didn't****.*

A: ***Were*** *you* ***living*** *in Paris at the time?*
B: *Yes, I* ***was****./No, I* ***wasn't****.*

A: ***Had*** *you already* ***left*** *when I phoned?*
B: *Yes, I* ***had****./No, I* ***hadn't****.*

A: ***Have*** *you* ***seen*** *these figures?*
B: *Yes, I* ***have****./No, I* ***haven't****.*

A: ***Will*** *you* ***be*** *back before lunch?*
B: *Yes, I* ***will****./No, I* ***won't****.*

A: ***Can*** *you* ***speak*** *French?*
B: *Yes, I* ***can****./No, I* ***can't****.*

When the main verb is *be*, the form of *be* comes before the subject in a question.

Is it *time?* ***Are you*** *ready?* ***Was it*** *useful?*

B Question words

Question words are: *what, when, where, which, who, whose, why* and *how*.

After the question word we use the same structure as a *yes/no* question: auxiliary verb + subject + main verb.

When do *you* ***service*** *the machines?*
Which *project* ***are*** *you* ***working on****?*
Whose *car* ***did*** *you* ***use****?*
Where were *you* ***working*** *at the time?*
How have *you* ***been doing?***
Why have *you* ***cut*** *the advertising budget?*
When will *you* ***be*** *back?*
Who can *we* ***ask*** *for help on this matter?*

C Question phrases

We often start a question using *what* or *which* + noun. *What* is more usual for things and when there are many possible answers. *Which* is more usual for people and organizations, and when there is a limited number of possible answers.

What time *are you arriving?*
What areas *do we need to cover in the meeting?*
Which customer service representative *were you speaking to?*
Which way *is it?*

We can use *which of* or *which one*.

Which of the proposals *did you accept?*
Which one *did you accept?*

We cannot use *what* in this way.

We can make phrases with *how*: *how many, how much, how old, how far, how often, how long, how fast*.

How much *will the economy grow next year?*
How much *research had you done beforehand?*
How often *do you travel abroad on business?*
How long *will the meeting last?*

D Question words as the subject

Sometimes the question word is the subject.

Who did you meet *at the conference?*
('you' is the subject of *meet*)

Who met *you at the airport?*
('who' is the subject of *meet*)

When a question word is the subject, like in the second example above, we do not use *do/does/did*.

Who works *here?*
(NOT ~~Who does work here?~~)

What happened*?*
(NOT ~~What did happen?~~)

Note that auxiliaries other than *do/does/did* can be used.

Who will *meet you?*
What was *happening?*

Note that there is no subject pronoun, as the question word is already the subject.

What *has happened?*
(NOT ~~What it has happened?~~)

E Negative questions

We use negative questions to disagree politely.

Don't you think *that the costs are too high?*
But ***isn't there*** *a limit to what we can do?*

We use negative questions when we expect the answer to be 'no'. Notice in the second example below how B's reply sounds more polite because the 'no' answer is expected by the negative question.

A: ***Do you like*** *Japanese food?*
B: *No, not really.* (the answer is very strong)
A: ***Don't you like*** *Japanese food?*
B: *No, not really.* (the answer is not so strong)

We use negative questions to show surprise.

Don't you accept *American Express?*

Exercises

Sections A, B, D **15.1** **Underline the correct words.**

1 *Did you spoke/Did you speak* to Lara yesterday?
2 What *did Lara say/did Lara said* when you spoke to her?
3 A: Do you like Scotch whiskey?
B: *Yes, I like./Yes, I do.*
4 How *works this machine?/does this machine work?*
5 Who *started the company?/did start the company?*
6 When *started the company?/did the company start?*
7 Who *did call me/called me* this morning?
8 Who *you called/did you call* this morning?

Section A **15.2** **Expand the *And you?* questions to make full *Yes/No* questions.**

1 I've seen the news today. And you? *Have you seen the news today?*
2 I work from home. And you? ____________
3 I can understand German. And you? ____________
4 I've already had lunch. And you? ____________
5 I'll be back in time for lunch. And you? ____________
6 I'm enjoying the conference. And you? ____________
7 I agreed with her. And you? ____________
8 I've never spoken to Pierre. And you? ____________

Section B **15.3** **Expand the *And you?* questions to make questions with question words.**

1 I know Jim from University. And you? How *do you know Jim* ?
2 I've invited Manuela. And you? Who ____________ ?
3 I'm going on Monday. And you? When ____________ ?
4 I parked at the front. And you? Where ____________ ?
5 I'm here for the IT seminar. And you? Why ____________ ?
6 I'll have the steak. And you? What ____________ ?

Section B **15.4** **Write a question for each answer.**

1 *When do you get to work?*
Get to work? At about 8.30 usually.
2 ____________
Done! I haven't done anything!
3 ____________
The report? I put it over there.
4 ____________
Here? I stay here because the pay is good.
5 ____________
Yesterday? I was feeling awful.
6 ____________
Staying? I'm staying at the Ritz.
7 ____________
Report to? I report to Mike Taylor.
8 ____________
This bag? I think it's Helena's.

"Hey, this is brilliant! Where do you get my ideas?"

Exercises

Sections A, B

15.5 Rearrange the words in each group in the box to make questions. Then match them to the answers below to make a complete dialogue.

~~you business here are on~~	you did do what before
are how long you staying for	like what's it
been how have long that you doing	you what do do
to is first this Lyon your visit	staying you where are
involve traveling job does much your	arrive did when you

A: 1 *Are you here on business?*
B: Yes, I'm here on a sales trip.
A: 2 ______
B: I work for a small biotech start-up.
A: 3 ______
B: About three years, I suppose.
A: 4 ______
B: I worked for a large drug company.
A: 5 ______
B: Yes, quite a lot. All over Europe.

A: 6 ______
B: No, I've been here once before.
A: 7 ______
B: A couple of days ago.
A: 8 ______
B: Just until Friday.
A: 9 ______
B: At the Marriott.
A: 10 ______
B: Oh, it's very comfortable.

Sections B, C, E

15.6 Complete the dialogue with the question words and phrases in the box.

how far	how long	how many	how much	~~what kind of~~	what	which	whose

EVA: So, tell me about your new job. 1 *What kind of* work is it?
JOE: It's in sales, like my last job, but it's working for a bigger company.
EVA: Really? 2 ______ people work there?
JOE: I suppose there's about sixty people in our office, but it's a worldwide organization.
EVA: And 3 ______ holiday time do they give you?
JOE: Twenty days plus public holidays.
EVA: That's not too bad. 4 ______ is it from your home?
JOE: Quite near. And I can drive there without going through the city centre.
EVA: That's good. 5 ______ does it take you?
JOE: About twenty minutes.
EVA: It sounds perfect.
JOE: The only problem is that sometimes I have to work weekends as well.
EVA: 6 ______ idea was that?
JOE: I don't know. It's just something you have to do. But they're going to give me a company car – a VW.
EVA: 7 ______ model?
JOE: A Golf, I think.
EVA: And 8 ______ colour?
JOE: I can choose. I'm thinking of dark blue.
EVA: Well, congratulations. I'm sure you'll do really well.

Tasks

Speaking: listen and repeat

1 15 **You are going to hear eight phrases. Listen and repeat.**

Translate

2 Translate these short texts taken from the Internet into your own language. Remember not to translate word for word, but rather to make it sound natural.

Generally speaking, aren't all generalizations false? Did you ever think that the glass is neither half empty nor half full but maybe it's just twice as large as it needs to be? Is it certain that everything is uncertain? Why are fools and fanatics always so certain of themselves, but wiser people so full of doubts? Isn't it true that you can get everything you want in life, if you just help enough other people get what they want?

Gadzillionthings website

The price of oil reflects many, many factors. Has an oil field shut down? Has a cold spell hit northern Europe? What is the International Energy Agency forecasting? What are the major oil producers forecasting in terms of production?

Gulf Business Magazine website

Writing: personalized practice

3 Complete the questions with the words in brackets.

1 (Whereabouts you from originally? And where based now?)
Whereabouts are you from originally? And where are you based now?

2 (What do for a living? How long you doing that?)

3 (What you do before? Why you leave?)

4 (The company where you work now, how large?)

5 (And what main products?)

6 (well known in the market? How long been in business?)

7 (What pay like? many opportunities for promotion?)

8 (think you stay there?)

9 (What do in your free time?)

10 (you any children? How old? What name/s? got a photograph?)

Now write your own answers to the questions.

Rehearsal for the real world

4 Think of a friend, family member or colleague from a previous job who you haven't seen for some time. Now write the dialogue for the next time you meet this person. You ask each other questions about your lives and give full, friendly replies.

If you are working in class, read some dialogues aloud.

16 Questions 2

A Indirect questions

An indirect question allows us to be more polite or tentative. Typical phrases are:

Do you know …?	*Could you tell me …?*
Could I ask …?	*Could you tell me if …?*
I'd like to know …	*I was wondering whether …*

The word order of an indirect question is like a normal statement.

Statement: ***You are*** *thirty years old.*
Direct question: *How old* ***are you****?*
Indirect question: *Could I ask how old* ***you are****?*

We often use *if* or *whether* in an indirect question.

Direct: ***Does*** *Jane still* ***work*** *here?*
Indirect: ***Do you know if*** *Jane still* ***works*** *here?*

B Prepositions in questions

The preposition comes in the same place as in a statement, following the main verb, and this is often at the end.

Where do you come ***from****?*
What were they talking ***about*** *in the meeting?*

C *What is it for?* and *What was it like?*

We use *What ... for?* to ask about a purpose. The meaning is 'why'.

What *is this switch* ***for****?* (= Why is it here?)
What *did you do that* ***for****?* (= Why did you do it?)

We use *What ... like?* to ask if something is good or bad. The meaning is 'how'.

What *was the conference* ***like****?* (= How was it?)

This structure is common with verbs of the senses.

What *does it look/feel/sound/taste* ***like****?*

D Question tags: form

A question tag is a short phrase at the end of a statement that turns it into a question.

Question tags are formed using auxiliaries (*do, be, have* or a modal). An affirmative statement has a negative tag and vice-versa.

You went *to the conference,* ***didn't you****?*
You didn't *go to the conference,* ***did you****?*
He's *here,* ***isn't he****?*
He isn't *here,* ***is he****?*

Tags are used in the UK, Ireland, Canada, Australia, etc., but they are rare in America. In America people often just say *Right?*

E Question tags: use

Here are four possible uses of question tags presented in a dialogue:

A: ***You haven't*** *got the sales figures yet,* ***have you****?* (request for information)
B: ***They don't*** *have to be ready till Friday,* ***do they****?* (confirmation)
A: ***You're not*** *going to leave it until the last minute again,* ***are you****?* (attack)
B: *Well,* ***I haven't*** *had any time,* ***have I****?* (defence)

If we use a negative statement with an affirmative tag, we usually expect the answer to be *no*. Compare:

You went *to the conference,* ***didn't you****?*
(I think you did – I just want confirmation.)

You didn't go *to the conference,* ***did you****?*
(I think you didn't – but I'm asking just in case.)

Note that a negative statement with an affirmative tag makes it easier for the other person to reply with a *no*, since this is the expected answer.

A: *Someone will have to meet him at the airport.*
B: *Of course.* ***You can't*** *go,* ***can you****?*
A: *No, sorry, I can't.*

F Question tags: other points

If the main verb in the statement is *have*, you make a tag with *do*.

You ***had*** *a meeting this morning,* ***didn't*** *you?*

If the auxiliary verb is *have*, the tag is with *have* as normal.

*You****'ve*** *just been to Austria,* ***haven't*** *you?*

The tag with *I am* is *aren't*.

I'm *a fool,* ***aren't*** *I?*

The tag with *Let's* is *shall*.

Let's *break for coffee now,* ***shall*** *we?*

G Reply questions

We can use a short question to reply to what someone says. We do this to show interest, surprise or uncertainty. The meaning is like *Really?* or *Is that true?*

A: *I went to Head Office last week.*
B: ***Did you?*** (interest)
A: *I can't install the new software.*
B: ***Can't you?*** (surprise)
A: *I think they're arriving at ten.*
B: ***Are they?*** (uncertainty)

The reply question uses an auxiliary verb like in a question tag, but there is no change of affirmative to negative.

Exercises

Section A

16.1 Underline the correct words.

1 Could you tell me *what are your terms of payment/what your terms of payment are*?
2 Do you know *where the marketing seminar is/where is the marketing seminar*?
3 I'd like to know *how can we/how we can* finance this project.
4 Could I ask you *why you left/why did you leave* your last job?
5 I was wondering *whether you could/whether could you* give me a hand.

Sections D, F

16.2 Add a question tag to each sentence.

1 We're nearly there, aren't we ?
2 You know the Brazilian market, ________ ?
3 You went to Brazil in March, ________ ?
4 You haven't been to Brazil, ________ ?
5 She's never been to Brazil, ________ ?
6 You won't be late, ________ ?
7 Harry isn't going to retire yet, ________ ?
8 We had a good meal last night, ________ ?
9 I'm late, ________ ? Sorry about that.
10 Let's meet again soon, ________ ?

Section E

16.3 Choose the most likely reply in each situation. Put a tick (✓).

1 If I go to Portugal, I'm going to have problems with the language.
a) Of course. You speak Portuguese, don't you? ☐
b) Of course. You don't speak Portuguese, do you? ✓
2 In the meeting you said that our competitors had a better product than us.
a) What! I said that, didn't I? ☐
b) What! I didn't say that, did I? ☐
3 I haven't seen Ann for ages. I think she's working abroad.
a) Yes, that's right. She's got a job in Spain, hasn't she? ☐
b) Yes, that's right. She hasn't got a job in Spain, has she? ☐
4 The deadline for the project is Friday and there's still so much work to do.
a) It's not looking good. We're going to make the deadline, aren't we? ☐
b) It's not looking good. We're not going to make the deadline, are we? ☐
5 Do you mind if I help myself to some more couscous?
a) No, of course not. You like Moroccan food, don't you? ☐
b) No, of course not. You don't like Moroccan food, do you? ☐
6 I'll meet you at the airport two hours before departure.
a) You will be late, won't you? ☐
b) You won't be late, will you? ☐

Exercises

Sections B, C **16.4 Rearrange the words to make questions.**

1 to where are going you *Where are you going to?*
2 from where did get you that information ______
3 in which funds do invest you ______
4 does what on it depend ______
5 where are you traveling on to Friday ______
6 who you did go on with the sales trip ______
7 for what is this piece of equipment ______
8 like what the weather was in Sweden ______

Section E **16.5 Make a question with a question tag.**

1 Ask a colleague if he sent the invoice. You expect the answer to be 'no'.
You *didn't send the invoice, did you* ?
2 Ask a colleague if he sent the invoice. You expect the answer to be 'yes'.
You ______ ?
3 Ask a stranger at the airport if his name is Mr Peters. You're not sure.
Your name ______ ?
4 You recognize someone. You are sure his name is Mr Peters.
Your name ______ ?
5 You guess that Biotec have canceled their order.
Biotec ______ ?
6 You are very surprised that Biotec have canceled their order.
Biotec ______ ?

Sections D, E, F **16.6 Complete this dialogue during a conference coffee break with question tags.**

SERGE: That last talk on netbooks was interesting, 1 *wasn't it* ?
NICOLE: Yes, very interesting. You know our company is selling more netbooks than PCs right now. They're small and fun and cheap.
SERGE: That cuts into your profit margins, 2 ______ ?
NICOLE: Only if they replace a PC. But we find that many people buy them as a third machine, as well as a PC and a laptop.
SERGE: Right. Hey, look at the time. We should go back to the main hall now, 3 ______ ?
NICOLE: Actually I'm not going to join you. I've decided to miss the next session. You don't mind, 4 ______ ?
SERGE: No, of course not. I hope it doesn't go on for too long. It shouldn't finish later than about five, 5 ______ ?
NICOLE: No, I don't think so. Anyway, at some point I'd like to continue that conversation we were having earlier about outsourcing. We're thinking of switching some of our production from China to Vietnam.
SERGE: OK. How about meeting up for lunch tomorrow?
NICOLE: Yes, let's do that 6 ______ ? I'll meet you here at twelve.

Tasks

Speaking: listen and repeat

1 16 **You are going to hear eight phrases. Listen and repeat.**

Translate

2 Translate these short texts taken from the Internet into your own language. Remember not to translate word for word, but rather to make it sound natural.

Q: I am wondering whether offering free postage and packing is of benefit to an e-commerce site, or do you think that reasonable postage charges are a better way to go?

A: If you can build free delivery (and free returns) into your business plan, do it. But make sure you promote it so it's visible on all pages of your website. This is because free delivery is one of those things that tips the balance towards a purchase with an undecided customer.

Drapers website

'E-commerce is like mail order, isn't it? If you need to change an item because it's wrong, it is quite time-consuming – although I would possibly buy a scarf online from Hermes.'
– shopper in Bond Street

FT website

Writing: personalized practice

3 Make questions for the given answers, using the underlined verb and the preposition in bold from the answer.

1 Which bag *did you put it in* ?
→ I don't know, I thought I put it **in** this bag.

2 Which station ______________________________ ?
→ I'm getting off **at** Köln, and then changing to another train.

3 What ______________________________ ?
→ He was accused **of** accepting a bribe, but they never proved anything.

4 Which of our ______________________________ ?
→ I know **about** your wealth management service, but not your tax planning service.

5 Who ______________________________ ?
→ I report directly **to** the Regional Sales Director.

6 Which exit ______________________________ ?
→ I think we should leave **by** the exit over there – there are fewer people.

7 Which areas of English ______________________________ ?
→ You need to work **on** your pronunciation, but your knowledge of specialized vocabulary is very good.

8 Thanks for the wine. What a lovely present! What type of food ______________________________ ?
→ It will go **with** any red meat or strong cheese.

Rehearsal for the real world

4 Think of a real person who you don't know very well, but would like to get to know better. You are sitting next to them at a meal. Now write down some questions that you would like to ask them, using both direct and indirect question forms (see section A on page 70).

If you are working in class, read some of the questions aloud. Try to imagine some possible answers.

17 Conditionals 1

A Conditions and results

Compare these sentences. The '*If* ...' clause is the condition, and the other part of the sentence is the result.

1 ***If*** *sales* ***increase*** *(generally), we* ***make*** *more profit.*
2 ***If*** *sales* ***increase*** *(next quarter), we****'ll make*** *more profit.*
3 ***If*** *sales* ***increased*** *(next quarter), we****'d make*** *more profit.*

Sentence 1 is about something that is always true. This is often called a 'zero' conditional. See section B below.

Sentence 2 is about something that is likely to happen in the future. This is often called a 'first' conditional. See section C.

Sentence 3 is about something that is imaginary or unlikely in the future. This is often called a 'second' conditional. See section D.

With all types of conditional, the *If* clause can come second.

*We****'ll make*** *more profit* ***if*** *sales* ***increase****.*

B Zero conditional (any/all time)

When we talk about things that are always or generally true, we use:

condition	result
IF/WHEN + present,	present or imperative

If *you* ***don't get*** *the best people into the company, your reputation* ***suffers****.*

In this type of conditional we are not referring to one specific event.

In the condition clause there can be a variety of present forms.

When *you* ***fly*** *business class, you get much more legroom.*
(present simple)
If *interest rates* ***are rising****, bank loans become more expensive.*
(present continuous)
When *you****'ve finished*** *the course, they give you a certificate.*
(present perfect)

In the result clause there can be a present simple (previous examples) or an imperative.

Keep trying. If you fail, ***try*** *again.*

We can use either *if* or *when* in every case with no difference in meaning.

C First conditional (likely future)

When we talk about future events that will happen, or are likely to happen, we use:

condition	result
IF + present,	future or imperative

If *the product* ***is*** *successful in China, we* ***will introduce*** *it into other Asian markets.*

In the condition clause there can be a variety of present forms.

If *you* ***increase*** *your order, we'll give you a bigger discount.*
(present simple)
If *you****'re meeting*** *her at three, I'll join you later at about four.*
(present continuous)
If *I****'ve made*** *any mistakes, I'll correct them later.*
(present perfect)

In the result clause *'ll* is very common (previous examples). We can also use other future forms or an imperative.

If anyone from Head Office calls, ***say*** *I'm in a meeting.*
(imperative)

The examples above are about two actions in the future. If the result clause refers to the present, we use a present tense.

*If you need me, I****'m working*** *in my room.*

D Second conditional (imaginary future)

When we talk about future events that are imaginary, unlikely or impossible, we use:

condition	result
IF + past,	*would/could/might* + infinitive

If *I* ***worked*** *for AMC, I****'d get*** *a better salary.*
If *you* ***were*** *still* ***working*** *for AMC, you* ***could help*** *me with my application form.*
If *I* ***was*** *more organized,* ***I'd create*** *folders and subfolders for all my Word docs.*

Note that in the condition clause we use a past form to refer to the future.

We can use *If I were* in place of *If I was* in imaginary futures, particularly when we give advice with the phrase *If I were you.*

If I were you*, I'd wait until tomorrow.*
I'd be more careful, ***if I were you****.*

E *Unless*

Unless means the same as *If ... not*. Compare these sentences, which have the same meaning:

If *he does****n't*** *arrive soon, he'll miss the flight.*
Unless *he arrives soon, he'll miss the flight.*

F Other modals

Many examples of conditionals are given with *will* and *would*. But we can use all other modals (*can, should, must,* etc.) with their normal meanings (unit 18E).

Exercises

Sections B, C, D, E

17.1 Underline the correct words.

1 If *we're/we would be* late, *they'll start/they'd* start the meeting without us.
2 If *we would take/we took* a taxi, *we'll arrive/we'd arrive* at their offices sooner.
3 When inflation *goes up/will go up*, there *would be/is* pressure to raise salaries.
4 If *we don't act/we won't act* soon, *we'll miss/we would miss* the deadline for the tender.
5 If *you change/you will change* your mind, *give me/you will give me* a call.
6 Unless *you click/you don't click* on that icon, *it won't work/it didn't work*.
7 When *you order/you will order* goods on our website, we always *send/will send* an email confirmation.
8 If *you signed/you will sign* today, *we'd ship/we ship* the goods by Friday.
9 If *you hear/you heard* anything in the next few days, *let me/you'd let me* know.
10 *I wouldn't/I won't* worry if *I am/I were* you.

Sections C, D

17.2 Read these sentences and decide if the events are likely or unlikely. Then put the verbs in brackets into either the present simple + *will* or the past simple + *would*. Use contracted forms where possible.

1 If you *follow* (follow) this road, you *'ll come* (come) to the station.
2 If I ______ (be) on the Board of this company, I ______ (argue) against the merger.
3 If you ______ (have) any questions, I ______ (deal) with them at the end of my presentation.
4 A: I have no idea what the other side are going to say in the negotiation.
B: Neither do I. If I ______ (know), I ______ (tell) you.
5 It only takes ten minutes to the station by taxi. If you ______ (leave) now, you ______ (catch) your train.
6 A: Is that the time? I really should be going.
B: If you ______ (wait) a moment, I ______ (give) you a lift.
7 I'm sorry, I can't help you right now. I'm really busy. If I ______ (have) more time, I ______ (be) happy to.

Sections B, C, D

17.3 Complete the sentences with two correct forms from a, b, c or d.

1 If the bank lends us the money, *a/d* it in new machinery.
a) we'll invest b) we'd invest c) we were investing d) we're going to invest
2 When ______ a lot of orders, we always employ extra staff in the factory.
a) we'll have b) we have
c) we've had d) we had
3 If ______ this project again, I think I'd do it differently.
a) I'll start b) I was starting
c) I've started d) I started
4 If you have a computer problem, ______ someone from IT services.
a) call b) you'll have to call
c) you called d) you are calling

"If they don't like our proposal I'll show them the kittens. Everybody likes kittens."

Exercises

Sections B, C, D, E

17.4 Paula, the Marketing Director of a car manufacturing company, is talking to her colleague Frank, a Production Manager. Complete their conversation with the words in the box.

~~will~~	will	won't	won't	would	would	wouldn't
unless	unless	be	is	is going to be	don't	didn't

PAULA: Aren't you worried? If the workers in the factory go on strike, we [1] *will* lose a lot of production. If we lose production, we [2] ________ be able to supply all our customers. If we [3] ________ supply our customers, they'll probably buy other makes of car. If that happens, our market share [4] ________ go down. It's not looking good. Also, in my experience, when workers go on strike, there [5] ________ a bad atmosphere for months afterwards. So [6] ________ you can come to an agreement with the workers soon, there [7] ________ a lot of trouble ahead. If you want my advice, [8] ________ very careful.

FRANK: Don't worry. The workers know that the success of the company depends on this new model. [9] ________ they're stupid, they [10] ________ go on strike. Just imagine – if this model sold really well, the whole financial situation of the company [11] ________ improve. If that happened, we [12] ________ need to go ahead with the planned job cuts. And if we [13] ________ have plans to cut jobs, the workers [14] ________ be much happier.

Sections B, C, D

17.5 You are talking to a friend about your new job. Look at your thoughts in italics and write the words that you say. Put the verbs in brackets into either the present simple, past simple, imperative, *will* + infinitive or *would* + infinitive.

You think: *People say hard work usually results in promotion in my new company.*
You say: [1]They say if you *work* (work) hard, you *get* (get) promoted.

You think: *I want to show that I'm good at my job – I need some job security.*
You say: [2]I hope that if I ________ (do) my best, they ________ (give) me a permanent contract after a few months.

You think: *I sometimes arrive late. I wish I could work at their other site.*
You say: [3]I have been late once or twice. They have another site nearer my home – if I ________ (work) there, it ________ (not be) such a problem.

You think: *I had a health problem a few years ago. But it's very unlikely to reoccur.*
You say: [4]One thing worries me. I wonder what ________ (happen) if my health problem ________ (reoccur)?

You think: *Maybe it's not a problem. In general they seem to be very reasonable about illness.*
You say: [5]Actually, if you ________ (miss) one or two days because of illness, they ________ (not seem) to mind.

You think: *OK, that's all. I hope I'll see you again soon.*
You say: [6]If you ________ (fancy) a drink one evening, just ________ (give) me a call.

Tasks

Speaking: listen and repeat

1 17 **You are going to hear eight phrases. Listen and repeat.**

Translate

2 Translate these short texts taken from the Internet into your own language. Remember not to translate word for word, but rather to make it sound natural.

On a website you should ask people for their email addresses at a time and for a reason that makes sense to them. If you ask for an email address out of context, people will say, 'What's in it for me? Why do you need my email?' If you cannot overcome those two barriers, you are not going to be successful.

DMNews website

Now that labour forces are starting to contract and the number of pensioners is rising, pension schemes are rapidly becoming unsustainable. If nothing is done, the cost of state pensions in developed countries will probably rise from an average of 7.7% of GDP now to around 15% by 2050. In Japan and some western European countries (Germany, Italy, France) it could rise to well above 20%.

The Economist website

Writing: personalized practice

3 Write answers to these questions using your own ideas. Begin as shown.

1 What do you do if you get hiccups?
If I *get hiccups, I hold my breath for as long as possible* .
2 What do you do if you can't get to sleep at night?
If I ______ .
3 What do you do if your boss is in a bad mood?
If my ______ .
4 What will you do if you have some free time this evening?
If I ______ .
5 What will you do if this quarter's sales figures are a disaster?
If this quarter's ______ .
6 What will your company do if the economy stays in (goes into) recession?
If the economy ______ .
7 What would you do if you won €1m on the 'Euro Lotto'.
If I ______ .
8 What would your company do if your main supplier started having serious quality issues?
If our main supplier ______ .
9 Where would you like to be right now if you could be anywhere in the world?
If I ______ .

Rehearsal for the real world

4 Look again at exercise 17.4 and see how the speakers talk about a 'chain of events', where one scenario leads to another. Now write a similar 'chain of events', starting with the following sentences.

1 If I do an MBA in the next few years, …
2 If I stay in my current company, …
3 If I was a billionaire, …
4 If my budget for current projects was halved, …
5 If my budget for current projects was doubled, …
6 If the weather is bad at the weekend, …

If you are working in class, choose some 'chain of events' to read aloud. Ask and answer questions.

18 Conditionals 2

A Third conditional (imaginary past)

When we talk about past events that are different to what really happened, we use:

condition	result
IF + past perfect,	*would* + *have* + past participle

If *sales* ***had increased*** *last quarter, my boss* ***would have been*** *happier.*

This is called a 'third' conditional.

There is often a suggestion of criticism or regret.

If the economic situation ***had been*** *better, we* ***wouldn't have lost*** *so many customers.*

A contracted *'d* in speech can be *had* in the condition or *would* in the result.

*If I'****d*** *done an MBA, I think I'****d*** *have had more opportunities in my career.*

The examples above are about two actions in the past. If the result clause refers to the present, we use *would* + infinitive.

If I ***had done*** *an MBA, I* ***would be*** *on a higher salary now.*

B Conditional (possible past)

When we talk about past events which possibly happened, we just use the normal, appropriate tenses. There are no special rules.

If *you* ***missed*** *the TV programme last night, you* ***can borrow*** *the DVD I made.*
If *you* ***were listening*** *to the radio in your car, you probably* ***heard*** *the news.*

This type of conditional has no name.

C Conditionals without *if*

We use *if* for something that might happen in the future. We use *when* for something that we know will happen.

I'll *call you* ***if*** *I get a chance.* (maybe)
I'll *call you* ***when*** *I arrive.* (definitely)

We can use *if, when* or *whenever* where the meaning is 'every time'.

If/Whenever *I dial her number, it goes straight to voicemail.*

In informal speech we sometimes use *imagine* or *supposing* in place of *if.*

Imagine *you* ***had*** *a million dollars. How* ***would*** *you invest it?*

We can use *provided that, providing, on condition that, as long as* and *so long as* for emphasis. The meaning is 'if and only if'.

As long as *you're happy with all the clauses, I'll send you a pdf of the final contract.*

We can use *in case* to talk about doing something to avoid a possible problem later. The result clause usually comes first and often uses *going to.*

I'm going to *give you my Skype name* ***in case*** *we need to have a web conference.*

We use *Unless* to mean *If not* (unit 17E).

D Forms with *wish*

We use *I wish* to express regret or dissatisfaction. This is like a conditional because we can replace *I wish* with *If only.*

I wish *I* ***was*** *eighteen again.*
If only *I* ***was*** *eighteen again.*

For the present and future, use *I wish* followed by the past simple or continuous.

I wish *we* ***didn't have*** *so many meetings.*
I wish *I* ***was playing*** *golf this afternoon.*

For the past, use *I wish* followed by the past perfect.

I wish *we* ***had done*** *more direct marketing.*
I wish *I* ***hadn't eaten*** *the oysters.*

If the wish is for something good or positive, use *I hope* followed by the present simple or *will.*

I hope *your presentation* ***goes*** *well.*
I hope *the merger* ***will be*** *a success.*

If the wish is about doing something that is difficult or impossible, use *I wish I could.*

I wish I could *contact my daughter. She's backpacking in India.*

E Modal verbs in conditionals

Many examples of conditionals are given with *will* and *would.* But other modal verbs like *can, could, may, might, must* and *should* are common in conditional sentences and have their usual meanings.

If *you* ***deal with*** *the Middle East, you* ***must be*** *available on Saturdays and Sundays.*

We often use *will* and *can* with first conditionals, and *would* and *could* with second conditionals. However, look at this typical example:

If we ***improve*** *productivity, we* ***could have*** *a bigger share of the market.*

An improvement in productivity is likely, so we start with a first conditional form. We expect *will* or *can* in the result clause, but neither one gives the intended meaning of uncertainty about the market share. *Could* does give this meaning and is used in a normal way.

Exercises

Sections A, B, E, unit 17

18.1 Underline the correct words. This exercise includes revision of second conditionals (unit 17).

1 If you *called/had called* me yesterday, I *had told/would have told* you.
2 If you *took/would have taken* more exercise, you *might feel/will feel* better.
3 If Edi *would have listened/had listened* more carefully, he *wouldn't have made/didn't make* that mistake.
4 It took us a long time to move. If *we'd found/we found* suitable premises, *we'd have moved/we had moved* earlier.
5 If people *kept/had kept* their offices tidier, it *might present/must present* a better image to our visitors.
6 If *I'd known/I would know* about their financial problems, I *wouldn't invest/wouldn't have invested* in their company.
7 In the end we didn't get the contract. But if our side *had been/was* better prepared, I'm sure we *succeeded/could have succeeded* in the negotiations.
8 Were you at the meeting yesterday? If you *had gone/went*, you *must know/can know* more than I do.

Section C

18.2 Complete the sentences with the words in the box. Each word is used twice.

when	as long as	in case	unless

1 I'll speak to you again *when* I've looked at the contract in detail.
2 Leave your return flight open ________ the negotiations take an extra day.
3 We can start the project next week ________ everyone agrees.
4 We can start the project next week ________ anyone disagrees.
5 The Board will be happy ________ our share price remains high.
6 Keep your receipt ________ you need to return the goods.
7 The new stock will arrive ________ the Christmas sales are finished.
8 We'll probably make a loss this year ________ sales improve significantly in the remaining few months.

Section D

18.3 Underline the correct words.

1 I wish I *hadn't drunk/didn't drink* so many whiskies last night.
2 There's so little space in here. I wish I *have/had* a bigger office.
3 I don't feel well. I wish I *could stay/will stay* in bed this morning.
4 I must get in touch with Angela. If only I *know/knew* her number!
5 I've been waiting thirty minutes for the bus. I wish I *took/had taken* a taxi.
6 I wish Jim *didn't interrupt/doesn't interrupt* so often in meetings.
7 I have to finish this report by tomorrow. If only I *had/would have* more time.
8 That presentation was a disaster! I wish I *could do/would do* it all again!
9 Enjoy your holiday. I hope you *have/could have* a good time.
10 I'm disappointed with this camera. I wish I *didn't buy/hadn't bought* it.

Exercises

Sections A, C, E

18.4 Patrick and Dieter are discussing a negotiation that went wrong. Complete the dialogue with the words in the box (notice the contractions that are used in speech).

~~if~~	as long as	in case	unless		
'll	'd	'd	've	'd have	wouldn't've

PATRICK: Dieter, [1] *if* you've got a moment, can I have a word with you?
DIETER: Sure, [2] __________ it doesn't take too long. I have a meeting in five minutes. Is it about that contract that we lost?
PATRICK: Yes. What went wrong? Do you think we [3] __________ got the deal if we [4] __________ offered a better price? Maybe we [5] __________ lost the business. It's a pity – we need some new clients.
DIETER: No, I don't think the problem was the price.
PATRICK: No? So was it a problem with our shipping dates? If we [6] __________ given them a quicker shipping time, would it [7] __________ made a difference?
DIETER: No, the shipping time was OK.
PATRICK: How strange. The thing is, we should find out what went wrong [8] __________ a similar situation happens in the future. [9] __________ we learn from our mistakes, we [10] __________ lose more orders.
DIETER: Well, I did hear something. Apparently they didn't think much of our negotiating team.
PATRICK: Oh, I see. I was the head of that team.

Sections A, E, unit 17

18.5 A supplier is thinking about a future negotiation. Match his thoughts in italics 1–4 with his words a–d. This exercise includes revision of second conditionals (unit 17).

1 *We'll probably offer a lower price. If we do, success is possible.* [b]
2 *We'll probably offer a lower price. If we do, success is certain.* [ ]
3 *Maybe we'll offer a lower price. If we do, success is possible.* [ ]
4 *Maybe we'll offer a lower price. If we do, success is certain.* [ ]

a) If we offer a lower price, we'll get the contract.
b) If we offer a lower price, we might get the contract.
c) If we offered a lower price, we'd get the contract.
d) If we offered a lower price, we might get the contract.

The same supplier is thinking about a past negotiation. Match his thoughts in italics 5–8 with his words e–h.

5 *We offered a lower price. That's why we succeeded.* [ ]
6 *We offered a lower price. That's probably why we succeeded.* [ ]
7 *We didn't offer a lower price. That's why we failed.* [ ]
8 *We didn't offer a lower price. That's probably why we failed.* [ ]

e) If we'd offered a lower price, we'd have got the contract.
f) If we'd offered a lower price, we might have got the contract.
g) If we hadn't offered a lower price, we'd have lost the contract.
h) If we hadn't offered a lower price, we might have lost the contract.

Tasks

Speaking: listen and repeat

1 18 **You are going to hear eight phrases. Listen and repeat.**

Translate

2 **Translate these short texts taken from the Internet into your own language. Remember not to translate word for word, but rather to make it sound natural.**

Raven Industries, Earnings Call Transcript:
Q: Can you talk about what percentage of sales came from new products? It would be helpful if you could provide us with a metric.
A: It's not a huge percentage. But the interesting thing is that the construction industry today is more receptive to our new products than they were three years ago. If we had introduced those same products three years ago, nobody would have wanted to talk to us because they had more business than they could handle; they had a backlog of work to do. But today they're hungry, they're looking for ways to differentiate themselves from the competition.

BNET website

The gold price slid downhill today. It closed just 50 cents below the psychologically important $1,000 mark, down $8.50 for the day. The range was fairly tight, from a $1,009 high to a $998 low. Tomorrow the battle will take place around $995 and $990. My view has not changed: as long as gold doesn't close below $985, it's in an uptrend.

Goldprice website

Writing: personalized practice

3 **Complete the sentences with your own ideas.**

1 If I'd known she was vegetarian, *I'd have prepared something special* .
2 We wouldn't have been late if ______ .
3 If I'd remembered to water that plant, ______ .
4 She would have married Eric if ______ .
5 If I hadn't acted immediately, ______ .
6 I wouldn't have spent so long preparing the presentation if ______ .
7 If we'd done more market research beforehand, ______ .
8 We'd have cancelled the project sooner if ______ .
9 Imagine I hadn't checked the figures – what ______ ?
10 We ______ , as long as nothing unexpected happens.
11 I ______ , provided that our legal department checks everything first and gives the go-ahead.
12 I ______ , in case the people at the back can't see the screen.
13 Unless we make progress with the negotiations soon, ______ .
14 I ______ , unless you'd prefer to do it yourself.

Rehearsal for the real world

4 **Think about something you regret. Now write a short paragraph explaining what happened, what the consequences were, and how life might have been different if you'd done the opposite. Here are some ideas:**

something you didn't do
somewhere you didn't go
something you said to someone
an interesting idea you didn't follow up

If you are working in class, read some texts aloud. Ask and answer questions.

19 Verb + *-ing* or infinitive 1

A Verb + *-ing*

Some verbs are followed by an *-ing* form.

*Have you **considered postponing** the product launch?*
*Do you **mind waiting** a moment?*
*We'll **keep on cutting** costs until the company is profitable again.*

saying and thinking
admit, consider*, deny*, describe, imagine*, mention*, suggest**

liking and disliking
dislike, enjoy, fancy, (not) mind, resent*

phrasal verbs
carry on, give up, keep on, put off

phrases with *can't*
can't bear, can't help, can't resist, can't face, can't stand

other common verbs
avoid, delay, finish, involve, keep, miss, postpone, practise, risk

common phrases
spend/waste time …
spend/waste money …
It's not worth …
It's no use/good …
There's no point (in) …

*The meaning of the asterisk * is explained in section E.*

Most of the verbs in the list above can also be followed by a noun or pronoun.

*The purchasing manager **admitted taking** a bribe.*
*The purchasing manager **admitted** his **mistake**.*

Go and *come* plus an *-ing* form are often used for sports and outdoor activities.

*I often **go skiing** in the winter.*
*Do you want to **come shopping** with me?*

Some verbs and verb phrases have *to* as a preposition. These include: *look forward to, object to, be used to, get used to, respond to*. Prepositions are always followed by the *-ing* form.

*I **look forward to** see**ing** you next week.*
(NOT ~~look forward to see~~)

*I **got used to** wak**ing** up early in the morning.*
(NOT ~~got used to wake up~~)

B Verb + *to* + infinitive

Some verbs are followed by *to* + infinitive.

*They have stated that they **wish to become** the biggest telecoms company in Asia.*
*We're **managing to improve** our supply chain one step at a time.*

plans and decisions
aim, arrange, choose, decide, intend, plan*, prepare*

expectations
demand, deserve, expect*, hope*, want, wish*, would like*

promises and refusals
fail, guarantee, offer, promise, refuse, threaten*

other common verbs
can/can't afford, agree, learn*, manage, pretend*, seem*, tend, train, wait*

Most of the verbs in the list can also be followed by a noun or pronoun.

*We must **prepare to take** action.*
*We must **prepare** a **plan**.*

Note that 'verb + *to* + infinitive' is also used in these cases:

1 To explain why we do something – the 'infinitive of purpose' (unit 42C).

*I'm calling **to find out** if you stock spare parts.*
(NOT ~~for to find out~~)

2 After a question word.

*Can you show me **how to use** this software?*

3 With *used to, be going to, be able to, be allowed to, have to, need to* and *ought to*.

C Verb + object + *to* + infinitive

Some verbs are followed by an object + *to* + infinitive.

*They **told us to wait** here.*
*He **persuaded the bank to lend** him €4 million.*

advise, allow, ask, cause, encourage, expect, force, help, invite, order, pay, prefer, persuade, remind*, teach*, tell*, train, want, warn**

D *make* and *let*

After *make* and *let* we use the bare infinitive without *to*.

*I **made** them **check** all the figures again.*
(NOT ~~made them to check~~)

*They **let** us **keep** all these free samples.*
(NOT ~~let us to keep~~)

E Verb + *that* clause

The verbs marked with an asterisk* in sections A, B and C can also be followed by a *that* clause. In everyday speech we can leave out the word *that*.

*We **decided to cancel** the meeting.*
*We **decided (that) we would cancel** the meeting.*

Exercises

Sections A, B

19.1 Underline the correct words.

1 We can't afford *to miss/missing* this opportunity.
2 It's not worth *to spend/spending* any more time on this.
3 We decided *to close down/closing down* the plant in Slovakia.
4 You promised *to deliver/delivering* by the end of April.
5 I considered *to call/calling* him, but I decided it was better to send an email.
6 If we don't decide soon, we risk *to lose/losing* the whole contract.
7 She agreed *to prepare/preparing* some figures before the next meeting.
8 Is Mr Messier busy? OK, I don't mind *to wait/waiting* for a few minutes.
9 May I suggest *to postpone/postponing* the meeting until next week?
10 He refused *to sign/signing* the contract until he'd spoken to his boss.

Sections A, B

19.2 Complete the sentences with the verbs in the box. Choose either the *-ing* form or *to* + infinitive.

advertise	employ	fly	~~give~~	help	make	receive	speak	think	write

1 They agreed *to give* us thirty more days to pay the invoice.
2 There's no point __________ this brand on TV. It would cost too much.
3 I suggested __________ another sales rep, but no-one agreed.
4 We're expecting __________ some more stock early next week.
5 I'll join you later. I need to finish __________ this report.
6 I learned __________ Portuguese while I was working in Brazil.
7 I work in PR. My job involves __________ contact with the media.
8 I can't help __________ that something is going to go wrong.
9 I can't afford __________ business class all the time.
10 I can't promise __________ you with this problem, but I'll do my best.

Section C

19.3 Complete the sentences with the verbs in the box. Include an object in every case. One solution uses each verb once.

~~advise~~	encourage	expect	invite	force	persuade	prefer	remind

1 I'm sorry I missed work yesterday. The doctor *advised me to* stay in bed.
2 I tried to __________ come with us tonight, but he said he was busy.
3 Could you __________ call Head Office later? I might forget.
4 She hasn't called yet, but I __________ contact me some time today.
5 I didn't feel very confident, but she __________ apply for the job.
6 The fall in demand has __________ lay off some of our workers.
7 I'm renovating my house, and the builder __________ pay him in cash.
8 I'd like to __________ join us for dinner this evening.

"I hereby empower you, Ambrose T. Wilkins, to water my plants. And let's hear no more talk about how I never delegate authority."

Exercises

Sections A, B

19.4 Complete this mini-dialogue between two colleagues by putting the verbs in brackets in the correct form, either *-ing* or *to* + infinitive.

VIKTOR: My line manager has asked me [1] *to meet* (meet) with her next week for my first performance review. I keep [2] ________ (wonder) what I should say.

ISABEL: Well, since you started working here your performance has been excellent. You deserve [3] ________ (be) rewarded for all your work.

VIKTOR: Thanks. I considered [4] ________ (ask) them [5] ________ (raise) my salary at the review meeting, but Anna advised me [6] ________ (wait) a little longer before asking for a rise. Instead I might ask for some training. I'd like to learn [7] ________ (use) our SAP software better.

ISABEL: It's a good idea – there's no point [8] ________ (try) to learn just by watching other people. The software is quite complex, and really we should all be trained [9] ________ (use) it.

VIKTOR: Exactly. I don't want to risk [10] ________ (lose) any information by entering data in the wrong way. Sometimes I think I might even cause the whole system [11] ________ (crash) by doing something stupid. I'm new in this job and I can't afford [12] ________ (take) risks like that.

ISABEL: You're right. I think you'll manage [13] ________ (persuade) them [14] ________ (send) you on the course without any difficulty.

Sections A, B, E

19.5 Complete this email, which circulated inside a mobile phone manufacturer. Choose a verb from the box and use the correct form, either *-ing* or *to* + infinitive.

be	~~interview~~	pay	pretend	receive	show	take	talk	use	worry

Send

To... Senior management team

Subject: Visit by journalist next week

A journalist from the *Daily Planet* wants [1] *to interview* someone about the safety risks of using hands-free phones in cars. It will involve [2] ________ to him over lunch one day next week. He's offered [3] ________ . Any volunteers?

In my opinion it's not worth [4] ________ too much about this, as any changes in this area depend on government legislation, not on the phone manufacturers. However, it's no good [5] ________ we have no responsibility at all for this issue. For example, in our advertising we use images of people using our phones hands-free while driving, and common sense does suggest that [6] ________ a phone in this way might distract the driver's attention. We need [7] ________ careful, and point out the similarities between using a hands-free phone and just having a normal conversation with a passenger.

Anyway, he's kindly agreed [8] ________ us the article before it's published, and he's promised [9] ________ a balanced view and not refer to individual phone manufacturers by name.

I look forward to [10] ________ your comments on this matter asap.

Peter Halonen

Tasks

Speaking: listen and repeat

1 19 **You are going to hear eight phrases. Listen and repeat.**

Translate

2 Translate these short texts taken from the Internet into your own language. Remember not to translate word for word, but rather to make it sound natural.

Virtual market research allows companies to test how their products perform in a virtual store in cyberspace. Chicago-based In Context Solutions writes the software that creates the store and analyzes the data on shoppers' behavior. Their aim, according to their founder, is to provide companies with 'data-driven analytics to help them make key decisions on product placement, pricing, promotion, branding, display design and store layout.'

Forbes website

Ford Motor Co. and Nissan Motor Co. will get loans from the Obama administration to retool their plants for electric vehicle production. President Barack Obama said the loans 'will create good jobs and help the auto industry to meet and even exceed the tough fuel economy standards we've set, while helping us to regain our competitive edge in the world market.'

Freep website

Writing: personalized practice

3 Complete the sentences with an *-ing* form or *to* + infinitive. Use your own ideas.

1 Next summer I hope *to go backpacking in New Zealand* .
2 When questioned by journalists, the CEO denied ______ .
3 The warranty on this product is very good. They guarantee ______ .
4 I'm the sort of person who can't resist ______ .
5 I'm a very busy person and I really can't afford ______ .
6 When it comes to ideas for new products, my company tends ______ .
7 When I'm away from home I miss ______ .
8 We have a very ambitious two-year marketing plan. We aim ______ .
9 One of my colleagues is really annoying. He keeps on ______ .
10 Basically, my job involves ______ .
11 I didn't have much time, but I did manage ______ .
12 The project is behind schedule and I think we should consider ______ .
13 The negotiations are not going well. The other side refuses ______ .
14 This year I've spent a lot of time ______ .
15 This year I've wasted a lot of time ______ .
16 This year I've spent a lot of money ______ .

4 Complete the sentences with an object + *to* + infinitive.

17 My company allows *us to dress 'smart casual' as long as we are not meeting clients* .
18 Last week my boss asked ______ .
19 My colleague was wonderful. S/he really encouraged ______ .
20 Changes in the market have forced ______ .
21 His memory is getting worse. Yesterday I needed to remind ______ .
22 I went on a really useful course recently. They trained ______ .
23 I said to him, 'Listen very carefully, I want ______ '.
24 I should have listened to my colleagues. They warned ______ .

If you are working in class, choose some sentences to read aloud. Ask and answer questions.

20 Verb + *-ing* or infinitive 2

A Verb + *-ing* or infinitive: change in meaning

Some verbs can be followed by *-ing* or *to* + infinitive and the meaning of the verb changes.

REMEMBER AND FORGET. We use *remember/forget doing* for memories. The remembering happens after the action.

I ***remember seeing*** *him before somewhere.*
I'll never ***forget making*** *my first million euros.*

We use *remember/forget to do* for actions someone is supposed to do. The remembering happens before the action.

I must ***remember to call*** *her this afternoon.*
Sorry, I ***forgot to make*** *a back-up file.*

REGRET. We use *regret doing* when we are sorry about something that happened in the past.

I ***regret saying*** *no to the job in Paris.*

We use *regret to do* when we are sorry for something we are going to do, such as giving bad news.

I ***regret to inform*** *you that we are unable to …*

TRY. We use *try doing* when we make an experiment.

I'll ***try talking*** *to him. He might change his mind.*
(the 'talking' will happen, and I'll see the result)

We use *try to do* when we make an effort.

I'll ***try to talk*** *to him today, but I know he's very busy.*
(perhaps the 'talking' won't happen)

STOP. We use *stop doing* when we end an action.

We ***stopped buying*** *from that supplier.*

We use *stop to do* when we give the reason for stopping.

I ***stopped to buy*** *something for my daughter.*

MEAN. We use *mean doing* when one thing results in or involves another.

Globalization ***means being*** *active in every major market.*

We use *mean to do* to express an intention.

I ***meant to*** *let you know, but I got side-tracked.*

GO ON. We use *go on doing* when we continue doing something.

They ***went on trading****, even though they were technically insolvent.*

We use *go on to do* when we change and do something else.

After leaving IBM he ***went on to start*** *his own company.*

B Verbs of perception

Verbs of perception include: *feel, hear, listen to, notice, see, watch*. These verbs can be followed either by an object + *-ing* or a bare infinitive (without *to*).

If we see or hear only part of the action, we use the *-ing* form.

I ***saw*** *her* ***giving*** *her presentation.*
(I saw part of the presentation)

I ***heard*** *the machine* ***making*** *a strange noise.*
(I heard the noise and it continued afterwards)

If we see or hear the whole action from beginning to end, we use the bare infinitive without *to*.

I ***saw*** *her* ***give*** *her presentation.*
(I saw the whole presentation)

I ***heard*** *the machine* ***make*** *a strange noise.*
(I heard the noise and it stopped)

C Verb + *-ing* or infinitive: little change in meaning

Some verbs can be followed by *-ing* or *to* + infinitive and there is little change in meaning. These include: *begin, continue, intend, start.*

What do you ***intend doing/to do*** *about it?*

However, with these verbs we do not usually have two *-ing* forms together.

It was ***starting to get dark****.*
(NOT ~~starting getting~~)

The verbs *like, love, prefer, hate* can be followed by either form. *To* + infinitive suggests something is a good/bad idea. The *-ing* form shows your feelings.

I ***like to do*** *my tax returns early, but I* ***don't like doing*** *them.*

D Passive forms

Unit 19 gave lists of verbs that are followed by *-ing* or *to* + infinitive. Only the active forms were given.

The passive form of 'verb + *-ing*' is 'verb + *being* + past participle'.

If the share price falls any more, we ***risk being taken over*** *by a larger company.*
It's not worth being sued *over this issue.*

The passive form of 'verb + *to* + infinitive' is 'verb + *to be* + past participle'.

I think I ***deserve to be given*** *a pay rise.*
I don't ***want to be seen*** *as a time-waster.*

Exercises

Section A

20.1 Underline the correct words.

1 I stopped in Paris for a few days *to meet/meeting* Henri.
2 We've stopped *to meet/meeting* so often. It was a waste of time.
3 Learning a language means *to be/being* interested in the culture as well.
4 I meant *to make/making* some more copies of the report, but I didn't have time.
5 Please remember *to speak/speaking* to Josie when you see her.
6 I don't remember *to say/saying* anything like that.
7 I tried *to open/opening* the window, but it was too high to reach.
8 I tried *to open/opening* the window, but it was still too hot in the room.
9 I'll never forget *to give/giving* my first presentation to the Board.
10 Don't forget *to look at/looking at* the audience when you speak.
11 We regret *to announce/announcing* the death of our founder, Mr Obuchi.
12 I really regret *to quit/quitting* my MBA course.
13 We should go on *to sell/selling* this model for at least another six months.
14 First I'll give you an overview of the company, then I'll go on *to describe/describing* our new range of products.

Section B

20.2 Match each sentence 1–6 to the situations a–f below.

1 Sorry to interrupt, but I heard you talking about e-books. [a]
2 I heard you talk about e-books at the seminar. [ ]
3 I saw Barbara showing the visitors round the factory. [ ]
4 I saw Barbara show the visitors our new machine. [ ]
5 I felt the spider walking down my neck. [ ]
6 I felt the spider walk down my neck. [ ]

a) I heard part of your conversation.
b) I heard the whole presentation.
c) I saw Barbara's complete demonstration.
d) I saw Barbara and the visitors briefly as I walked through the factory.
e) In the story, the listener imagines that the spider is still walking.
f) In the story, the listener wonders what happened after the spider finished walking.

Section D, unit 19

20.3 Complete the sentences with *being* or *to be*. This exercise includes some revision of unit 19.

1 I enjoy *being* taken out for expensive meals.
2 The Minister denied ________ given a bribe.
3 The Minister refused ________ questioned about the bribe.
4 I expect ________ asked some tough questions at the interview.
5 All our staff are going to be busy. Do you mind ________ picked up by taxi?
6 How awful! Imagine ________ asked to give a presentation at such short notice!

Exercises

Sections A, C, unit 19

20.4 Complete this mini-dialogue between two colleagues with the correct form of the verb, either *-ing* or *to* + infinitive. This exercise includes some revision of unit 19.

THOMAS: Hi, Carla, I've been meaning [1] *to speak* (speak) to you all day. We're trying [2]__________ (book) a table at that new Chinese restaurant tonight. Would you like to come too?

CARLA: Thanks, I'd really like to, but I was intending [3]__________ (start) work on my monthly sales report tonight.

THOMAS: You're a real workaholic!

CARLA: Of course I want [4]__________ (go) out with you all tonight, but I really have to get this report done. I'm sorry it means [5]__________ (miss) dinner with you guys.

THOMAS: Well, perhaps next time then.

CARLA: Yes, and please don't forget [6]__________ (give) me as much notice as possible beforehand so I can keep the evening free.

THOMAS: OK! But the trouble with you, Carla, is that you never stop [7]__________ (work). You should remember [8]__________ (have) some fun sometimes. If you go on [9]__________ (work) like you do at the moment, you'll start [10]__________ (get) really stressed. You'll become ill, and you'll look back and regret [11]__________ (miss out) on your social life. It happened to a friend of mine – at first it was just stress at work but then in the end he went on [12]__________ (have) a nervous breakdown.

CARLA: Oh, come on. Stop [13]__________ (be) so dramatic. I don't enjoy [14]__________ (take) work home like tonight, it's just that I like [15]__________ (finish) my reports on time.

Sections A, C, unit 19

20.5 Complete this email with the correct form of the verb, either *-ing* or *to* + infinitive. This exercise includes some revision of unit 19.

Send

To... customerservice@gamesworld

Subject: your policy re old video games

I am writing to complain about your change of policy re old video games. I have been buying games from you for many years, and I really liked the fact that you allowed customers [1] *to trade in* (trade in) their old games for credit towards new ones. However, I have now found out that you have stopped [2]__________ (do) this. For me, this means [3]__________ (lose) a lot of value – I bought the games from you on the expectation that I could trade them in. When I visited your store last week I had two old games with me, and your salesman refused [4]__________ (accept) them. This was very annoying, as I had even remembered [5]__________ (bring) the receipts with me.

I can't help [6]__________ (think) that you will lose a lot of business if you go on [7]__________ (do) this. As a gamer, I strongly advise you [8]__________ (go back) to the old system of part-exchange – otherwise you will just encourage people [9]__________ (move) to online gaming. In fact, many of my friends who used to buy from your stores are already beginning [10]__________ (do) this.

Frantz Christensen

Tasks

Speaking: listen and repeat

1 20 **You are going to hear eight phrases. Listen and repeat.**

Translate

2 **Translate these short texts taken from the Internet into your own language. Remember not to translate word for word, but rather to make it sound natural.**

'In the second quarter, when the market began to go down, we began selling some of the equity position in our fund. It dropped to around 70% and we held the remainder in cash. That way, I was able to minimize the impact of the downturn.'

Asiaweek website

Bank of America's acquisition of Merrill Lynch stands out as an example of the central problem in many failed mergers. The company cultures of the two firms simply weren't compatible. Many at Merrill resented being acquired because they felt superior to anyone at a commercial bank.

Forbes website

Writing: personalized practice

3 **Complete the sentences with the verb form given in brackets.**

1 (*-ing*) I remember *going for my first job interview after university* .
2 (*to* + inf) I must remember *to water the plant in the office* .
3 (*-ing*) I'll never forget ______ .
4 (*to* + inf) Sorry – I forgot ______ .
5 (*-ing*) Is there a problem? Why don't you try ______ ?
6 (*to* + inf) I know it won't be easy, but you could try ______ .
7 (*-ing*) You're a big boy now. It's time that you stopped ______ .
8 (*to* + inf) I'll catch up with you. I need to stop for a moment ______ .
9 (*-ing*) The situation is impossible. We can't go on ______ .
10 (*to* + inf) After joining the company as a sales consultant, she went on ______ .

Rehearsal for the real world

4 **Look again at section D on page 86. Now complete the sentences with a past participle.**

1 I dislike being *asked to attend meetings at such short notice* .
2 I can't imagine being ______ .
3 Not again! I keep on being ______ .
4 If we continue like this, we risk being ______ .
5 Your results this year have been excellent. You deserve to be ______ .
6 At my performance review meeting I expect to be ______ .
7 I need regular feedback from you. I want to be ______ .
8 The restaurant is very busy. We'll have to wait to be ______ .

If you are working in class, choose some sentences to read aloud. Ask and answer questions.

21 Verbs and objects

A Transitive verbs

Transitive verbs are followed by an object. This information is shown in dictionaries with the letter [T]. The object can take a variety of forms.

noun: *I really appreciate* ***your help***.
pronoun: *It's too expensive – I can't afford* ***it***.
reflexive pronoun: *I enjoyed* ***myself*** *yesterday.*
clause: *I decided (****that****)* ***it was too risky***.

Note that you do not have *it* as an object if you already have a *that* clause.

I doubt it. ✓
I doubt (that) their idea will work. ✓
(But NOT ~~I doubt it their idea will work~~)

B Intransitive verbs

Intransitive verbs do not take an object. This information is shown in dictionaries with the letter [I].

Her flight has arrived. ✓
Her flight arrives at Heathrow. ✓
(But NOT ~~Her flight arrives Heathrow.~~)

Our sales in Turkey fell. ✓
Our sales fell last year. ✓
(But NOT ~~Our company fell its sales last year.~~)

Common intransitive verbs include:

ache, appear, arrive, come, depart, disappear, exist, fall, go, graduate, happen, live, occur, rain, remain, rise, sleep, stay, talk, wait, walk, work

C Verbs with both [T] and [I] forms

Many verbs can have both a transitive and an intransitive form. This information is shown in dictionaries with the letters [I/T].

I opened the door.	*The door opened.*
We began the meeting.	*The meeting began.*
We increased sales.	*Sales increased.*

Sometimes the transitive and intransitive meanings are different.

recover [T] = get back something
We recovered everything that was lost.

recover [I] = return to normal after a difficulty
The housing market is slowly recovering.

pick up [T] = collect in a car
He's gone to pick up Mr Chen from the airport.

pick up [I] = improve
Sales picked up slightly last month.

D Verb + two objects

Some verbs can have two objects: an indirect object (IO) – a person who receives something – and a direct object (DO) – the thing received.

After a lot of negotiation they offered (IO) ***us*** (DO) ***a better deal***.
They paid (IO) ***the consultants*** (DO) ***a lot of money***.
It took (IO) ***me*** (DO) ***a long time to understand***.

Verbs like this include:

award, bring, buy, cause, cost, email, fine, give, hand, leave, lend, make, offer, owe, pass, pay, promise, read, refuse, sell, send, show, take, teach, tell, write

E Verb + two objects: the use of *to*

Notice that in the examples above we do not use *to*.

NOT ~~they offered to us a better deal~~
NOT ~~they paid to the consultants~~

With most of the verbs in the previous list you can put the direct object first, and in this case you do use *to* + indirect object.

They offered (DO) *a better deal* (IO) ***to our competitors***.
They paid (DO) *a lot of money* (IO) ***to the consultants who came here last month***.

This structure is also common when both objects are pronouns.

They offered (DO) ***it*** (IO) ***to us***.

Some verbs must have *to* + indirect object. They cannot have the structure in section D above.

She explained (DO) ***the situation*** (IO) ***to me***.
(NOT ~~explained me the situation~~)

I suggested (DO) ***an alternative*** (IO) ***to them***.
(NOT ~~suggested them an alternative~~)

Verbs like this include:

admit, announce, demonstrate, describe, explain, introduce, mention, propose, prove, recommend, repeat, report, say, suggest

F Verb + two objects using *for*

With some verbs we use *for* to introduce the indirect object, not *to*.

I'll reserve (IO) ***us*** (DO) ***a table***.
I'll reserve (DO) ***a table*** (IO) ***for six people***.

Verbs like this include:

bring, build, buy, change, charge, choose, cook, do, find, get, keep, leave, make, order, prepare, reserve, save

Exercises

Sections A, B

21.1 Tick (✓) the sentences that are correct and cross (✗) the ones that are incorrect.

1 The company needs. ✗
2 My tooth aches. ☐
3 The box contains. ☐
4 It's finally happened. ☐
5 I've really enjoyed. ☐
6 I waited. ☐
7 I waited hours. ☐
8 I waited the bus. ☐
9 There exists a problem. ☐
10 There is a problem. ☐
11 The company is growing. ☐
12 The company is cutting. ☐
13 He reminded. ☐
14 He remembered. ☐
15 I got. ☐
16 What did you get? ☐

Section A

21.2 If the sentence is correct, put a tick (✓). If the sentence has a word that should not be there, cross it out.

1 I believe ~~it~~ that the new version of this software is much better.
2 Our prices can't be beaten – we guarantee it.
3 We guarantee it our prices can't be beaten.
4 I hear that they're building a new shopping centre.
5 I hear it they're building a new shopping centre.
6 Here's the invoice – please check it carefully.
7 Please check it that the figures are correct.
8 Thanks for all your help – I really appreciate it.

Sections A, B, C

21.3 Tick (✓) the sentences that are correct and cross (✗) the ones that are incorrect.

1 Unfortunately we had to increase our prices. ✓
2 Unfortunately we had to raise our prices. ☐
3 Unfortunately we had to rise our prices. ☐
4 Last quarter we fell our advertising budget. ☐
5 Last quarter we cut our advertising budget. ☐
6 I've been studying the company for two years. ☐
7 I've been working the company for two years. ☐
8 I've been working at the company for two years. ☐
9 If the CEO leaves, who will run the company? ☐
10 If the CEO leaves, what will happen the company? ☐
11 If the CEO leaves, what will happen to the company? ☐
12 I've always lived Paris. ☐
13 I've always liked Paris. ☐
14 The airport shuttle leaves the hotel every half hour. ☐
15 The airport shuttle arrives the hotel every half hour. ☐
16 They told that the order was being shipped this week. ☐

"Somewhere out there, Patrick, is the key to increased sales. I want you to find that key, Patrick, and bring it to me."

Exercises

Sections A, B, C, D, E

21.4 Underline the correct words.

1 He *lent me/lent to me* the article about Turkey from The Economist.
2 I'm going to *suggest them/suggest to them* that we postpone the meeting.
3 They *promised me/promised to me* a full refund if I wasn't satisfied.
4 At tomorrow's press conference she's going to *announce the journalists the news/announce the news to the journalists*.
5 I *explained them/explained to them* that I was just following company policy.
6 This delay is *causing us problems/causing problems to us*.
7 Maria ate here last week and recommended *me the fish/the fish to me*.
8 I described *them the whole situation/the whole situation to them*.
9 Changing suppliers will *cost us/cost to us* a lot of time and money.
10 I reported *to the technician the fault/the fault to the technician*.

Sections D, E

21.5 Put the words and phrases into the correct order to make a sentence.

1 I/to Louisa from marketing/lent/my Macmillan dictionary.
I *lent my Macmillan dictionary to Louisa from marketing* .
2 I/Louisa from marketing/lent/my Macmillan dictionary.
I ______ .
3 I/an email/them/sent/yesterday.
I ______ .
4 I/an email/to their customer services/sent/yesterday.
I ______ .
5 I/reported/to the technician/the fault.
I ______ .
6 I/reported/to him/the fault.
I ______ .
7 I/him/the display model that's been in the showroom/sold.
I ______ .
8 I/to a man who came in this morning/the display model/sold.
I ______ .

Sections D, E, F

21.6 Complete the sentences with *to* or *for*.

1 I've sent the artwork *to* the printers and left a copy *for* you on your desk.
2 Can you give this note ______ Jan and ask him to make some coffee ______ our visitors?
3 I've prepared a report ______ the Board meeting. Here, I'll show it ______ you.
4 Please write a letter ______ our gas supplier and save a copy ______ our files.
5 I want to leave this package ______ him. Perhaps you could take it ______ him?
6 I'll bring some samples ______ the office ______ you.
7 She described ______ me how they chose the location ______ their new factory.
8 Hand the documents ______ my secretary and she'll keep them ______ me.

Tasks

Speaking: listen and repeat

1 21 **You are going to hear eight phrases. Listen and repeat.**

Translate

2 Translate these short texts taken from the Internet into your own language. Remember not to translate word for word, but rather to make it sound natural.

A bigger test of Asian governments' resolve to shift the balance of growth from exports towards domestic spending is whether they will allow their exchange rates to rise. A revaluation would lift consumers' real purchasing power and give firms reason to shift resources towards producing for the domestic market. But, so far, policymakers have been reluctant to let currencies rise too fast.

The Economist website

I want to suggest a new feature to the team at Google who program and design AdSense. Is there a way to contact them or post my idea somewhere? It's really frustrating me that they don't have this feature, so I'd like to bring it to their attention somehow.

Google website

Writing: personalized practice

3 Look again at section B on page 90. Now make sentences using the words in brackets and your own ideas. You may have to change the order of the words.

1 (aches, my back) *My back really aches – I need a massage!*
2 (hurts, my back) *Doing the gardening hurts my back.*
3 (fall, profits) ___
4 (cut, the budget) ___
5 (happen, the accident in the factory) ___
6 (cause, the accident in the factory) ___
7 (rise, my salary) ___
8 (raise, my salary) ___

4 Look again at section D and section E on page 90. Use the words in brackets and your own ideas to write two sentences with the objects in a different order each time.

9 (she, give, me, instruction manual)
a *I couldn't figure out what to do, so she gave me the instruction manual.*
b *I couldn't figure out what to do, so she gave the instruction manual to me.*

10 (bank, lend, €50,000, company)
a ___
b ___

11 (save, delicious-looking cake, me)
a ___
b ___

12 (local agent, find, us, better distribution channel)
a ___
b ___

13 (show, me, factory, on my last visit to Poland)
a ___
b ___

14 (pay, 25%, us, upfront)
a ___
b ___

22 Phrasal verbs 1

A Understanding phrasal verbs

Verbs are often followed by particles like *back, off, through, up,* etc. The word 'particle' means adverb or preposition.

Sometimes both verb and particle have their normal meanings. Other times there is a new meaning when the verb and particle are put together. Compare:

*It took 20 minutes to **go through** passport control.*
(normal meaning)

*Can we **go through** your proposal again?*
(new meaning = 'look at something carefully')

A phrasal verb is where there is a special meaning of verb + particle together. These verbs are common in informal English.

Often one phrasal verb can have several different meanings, and the correct one is only clear from the context.

1 *Don't worry, I'll **deal with** it.*
(= take action)
2 *We **deal** mainly **with** German companies.*
(= do business with)
3 *The report **deals with** our future strategy.*
(= be about)

B Separable phrasal verbs

With some phrasal verbs we can separate the two parts.

If the object is a noun, we can put it before or after the particle.

*Could you **fill** this form **in**, please?*
OR *Could you **fill in** this form, please?*

If the object is a pronoun (*me, you, it,* etc.) it must come before the particle.

*Could you **fill** it **in**, please?*
(NOT ~~fill in it~~)

Here is a list of separable phrasal verbs commonly used in business, and their approximate meanings:

back up (give support to, provide evidence for)
bring in (use the skills of a person or group)
bring out (start to sell a new product)
call off (decide an event will not happen, cancel)
check out (look at something to see if you like it)
draw up (think about and then write)
drop off (take to a place in a car and leave)
figure out (be able to understand; solve)
fill in/out (complete by writing information)
find out (discover a fact)
give up (stop doing, quit)
hand in (give something to a person in authority)
head up (be in charge of a group, team, etc.)
hold up (cause a delay)
keep down (prevent from increasing)
lay off (dismiss, stop employing)
look up (find information in a book or list)
pick up (collect in a car)
point out (tell, indicate something important)
roll out (introduce a new product)
set up (start, establish)
shut down (close, stop operating)
sort out (organize, put right, find a solution)
take on (accept work/responsibility; employ)
take over (take control of)
throw away (get rid of, waste an opportunity)
turn down (refuse, say 'no' to)
turn on/off (start/stop a piece of equipment)

*Will you **back** me **up** in the meeting?*
*Hey! **Check out** this cool new design.*
*Our lawyers will **draw up** a new contract.*
*We **turned down** their offer. It was too low.*

C Inseparable phrasal verbs

With some phrasal verbs we cannot separate the two parts. See the list below. Those marked with an asterisk* do not have objects.

*break down** (stop working)
call on (visit for a short time)
*check in** (register, report your arrival)
come across (find by chance)
*come in** (interrupt a discussion)
do without (manage without)
*end up** (be somewhere after doing something)
enter into (start a formal discussion or activity)
*fall through** (fail to happen)
file for (officially ask a court for something)
get into (start enjoying, start discussing)
go into (start a type of job, talk about in detail)
*hold on** (wait a moment)
look after (take care of)
look into (investigate, examine the facts)
look through (search among a lot of things)
*pay off** (bring some benefit, repay in full)
take up (use an amount of time or space)
*take off** (suddenly become successful)
*turn out** (how something develops or ends)
*turn up** (arrive)

*I couldn't **do without** my secretary.*
*Both sides must **enter into** serious negotiations.*
*They are going to **file for** bankruptcy.*
*I'm sorry to **take up** so much of your time.*

Exercises

Sections B, C

22.1 Choose the best verb from A, B, C or D below.

1 She left the company to _C_ up her own business.
A create B put C set D take
2 Here are some figures that ____ up what I've been saying.
A put B back C support D turn
3 This is a great opportunity. We can't just ____ it all away.
A remove B get C take D throw
4 I might need some help. I've never ____ across a situation like this before.
A come B been C found D looked
5 Their long-term strategy is in crisis. The merger has ____ through.
A gone B fallen C ended D passed
6 We won the contract. Congratulations! All your hard work really ____ off.
A went B brought C took D paid
7 He started as a salesman and ____ up as the CEO of the same company.
A went B got C ended D picked
8 After a relatively slow start in May, sales really ____ off in June.
A took B went C rolled D launched

Sections A, B, C

22.2 Complete the sentences with a phrasal verb that means the same as the words in brackets. The particle has been given to help you.

1 Did you _find_ out why they haven't paid their invoice? (discover)
2 Can you ________ on here until I get back? (wait a moment)
3 There's another way to finance the deal. I'm going to ________ into it. (investigate)
4 You need to ________ out this customs declaration. (complete by writing)
5 Rita is in reception. Can you ________ with it? I'm really busy. (take action)
6 You need determination to succeed. Don't ________ up now! (quit)
7 When he retires his son will ________ over the business. (take control of)
8 I'd like you to ________ up the design team for the new model. (be in charge of)
9 If Bob Pinker arrives, could you ________ after him until I return? (take care of)
10 This job is going to ________ up most of the morning. (use an amount of time)

Sections B, C

22.3 Underline all the possible word orders from the four alternatives. Sometimes two are possible, sometimes three are possible.

1 I'm too busy to *deal with this/deal this with/deal with it/deal it with* right now.
2 I'm going to *look up the information/look the information up/look up it/look it up* on the Internet.
3 In the current economic climate we're trying to *keep down our costs/keep our costs down/keep down them/keep them down* as much as possible.
4 I couldn't *do without my BlackBerry/do my BlackBerry without/do without it/do it without*.

Exercises

Sections A, B, C **22.4 Complete the memo with phrasal verbs from the box that mean the same as the words in brackets. Two verbs need an *-ing* form.**

bring out	call off	call on	check in	draw up	drop off
get into	hold up	look through	~~pick up~~	sort out	turn up

Memo

Simon – I'm leaving for Benelux tonight. There are a few things I need you to do while I'm away:

1 Mr Yamanaka

Mr Yamanaka will be arriving at the airport at 10.55 on Thursday morning. Can you [1] pick him up (collect by car) from there and [2] ______ him ______ (take in a car and leave) at his hotel? He's staying at the Marriott. Perhaps you could also be with him just to make sure there are no problems [3] ______ (registering), etc. After that he can just go to his room and freshen up. I'll probably [4] ______ (arrive) there around 1.00 pm and will call his room from reception.

2 Spain trip

I'm trying to [5] ______ (organize) the itinerary for my trip to Spain next month. Can you [6] ______ (think about then write) a list of all our Spanish customers by [7] ______ (searching) our customer accounts database? I'd like to know exactly who I need to [8] ______ (visit) while I'm there.

3 Product launch

As you know, we were going to [9] ______ (start to sell) our XJ6 model next month – it's the replacement to the XJ5. Unfortunately production issues are going to [10] ______ (delay) the launch by at least six weeks. Unfortunately this means that we will have to [11] ______ (cancel) the launch event. When I'm back in the office we need to [12] ______ (start discussing) details re who to contact about this. Can you give it some thought?

Thanks, Grace

Sections B, C **22.5 Complete this extract from a newspaper article by choosing the correct particle from those in the brackets.**

New crisis at eTravel

Online travel site eTravel announced yesterday that revenues were down 15% on the same period last year. Earlier in the year eTravel laid [1] ______ (off/up/out) a quarter of its staff in a bid to keep costs [2] ______ (off/down/out), but these measures were not enough to make the company profitable. Now they are going to bring [3] ______ (up/through/in) an outside consultancy firm who will take [4] ______ (through/up/on) the task of finding areas for further cost savings while creating a viable long-term strategy.

Tasks

Speaking: listen and repeat

1 22 **You are going to hear eight phrases. Listen and repeat.**

Translate

2 **Translate these short texts taken from the Internet into your own language. Remember not to translate word for word, but rather to make it sound natural.**

Entrepreneurs figured out years ago they could make a profit by taking on some of the tasks that businesses don't like – managing an employer's payroll, keeping up with tax payments, benefits deductions and the like. Today, a new breed of outsourcing specialist is offering to take over the entire financial operation of its clients – essentially everything below the level of the Chief Financial Officer.

CNN Money website

Even in a slow economy, Procter and Gamble ends up doing a lot of air freight. The sluggish economic climate hasn't had a major impact on Procter and Gamble's express shipping strategies. If an object needs to move fast, it goes by express. It might be anything from documents to raw materials (if something is needed at a plant quickly for finished products) to getting an item to market for sale or promotion.

WorldTrade Magazine website

Writing: personalized practice

3 **Complete the sentences with a phrasal verb from section B on page 94.**

1 We don't have that kind of specialized expertise. We'll need to bring *in an external management consultant* .

2 Can you help me to set up this spreadsheet? I can't figure ______ .

3 Can I introduce you to Angela Hoogstad? She heads ______ .

4 Times are hard, and the company is going to have to lay ______ .

5 We have some great new products. In the autumn we're going to roll ______ .

6 He's a real entrepreneur. He set ______ .

7 I'll join you later. First I have to sort ______ .

8 When he retires, his son will probably take ______ .

4 **Continue as before, using a phrasal verb from section C on page 94.**

9 Here's a very interesting article which I came ______ .

10 If we carry on like this, we're going to end ______ .

11 Recently I've really been getting ______ . I never knew about it before.

12 All our hard work will pay ______ .

13 Can I have a quick word? I know you're busy, and I don't want to take ______ .

14 The project was not very well defined initially, but everything turned ______ .

23 Phrasal verbs 2

A Phrasal verb + preposition + object

Many phrasal verbs can be used either alone or followed by a preposition + object.

*Any more comments? OK, shall we **move on**?*

*Shall we **move on to the next item** on the agenda?*

Here is a list of common phrasal verbs of this type, and their approximate meanings:

back out (of) (refuse to do something you agreed to do)
bring something forward (to) (change to an earlier time)
carry on (with) (continue doing)
catch up (with) (reach the same place as)
cut back/down (on) (reduce, do less of)
fit in (with) (be part of a group or plan)
get along/on (with) (be friendly with)
get on (with) (continue after an interruption)
get through (to) (succeed in reaching by phone)
keep up (with) (know the latest things about)
move on (to) (begin doing another thing)
put something back/off (to/until) (change to a later time)
put someone through (to) (connect by phone)
run out (of) (finish a supply of)
sit in (on) (attend a meeting as an observer)
stand in (for) (substitute for)

*Your idea **fits in** nicely **with** our existing plans.*
*I try to **keep up with** developments in my field.*
*Sandra is **standing in for** Mike while he's away.*

B Phrasal verbs with two particles

Some phrasal verbs have two particles, and both must be used. The parts are usually not separable. Here is a list of verbs of this type:

come in for (receive criticism or blame)
come up with (think of an idea or plan)
face up to (deal with a bad situation)
fall back on (do something else after other things have failed)
get back to (speak or phone again later)
get around to (finally do something)
go along with (accept existing decisions)
put up with (accept something unpleasant in a patient way)

In a few phrasal verbs there are two particles which can be separated.

*We can **play** one supplier **off against** another.*
*She **puts** her success **down to** hard work.*
*I've decided to **take** you **up on** your offer.*

C Particle meanings in phrasal verbs

Each particle has a range of meanings, sometimes literal but often metaphorical. The categories below are based on *Macmillan Phrasal Verbs Plus.*

Increasing and decreasing
up: *Can you speak up, please?*
out: *We're branching out into cosmetics.*
down: *We need to cut down on waste.*

Communication
across: *What message do you want to get across?*
through: *I tried to call but I couldn't get through.*

Exploring and revealing information
into: *I won't go into details right now.*
out: *I need to find out the truth.*
up: *I'd like to bring up the issue of costs.*

Checking and reviewing
over: *Can I just go over that again?*
through: *Could you look through these figures?*

Time – past and future
back: *I'd like to go back to what you said before.*
ahead: *Let's think ahead to next year.*
forward: *I look forward to seeing you in Paris.*

Progress
ahead: *They are pressing ahead with the reforms.*
along: *The building work is coming along nicely.*
on: *She just kept on until the job was finished.*
through: *We have a lot of work to get through.*
behind: *I've fallen behind with my work.*

Involvement in an activity
in: *Are you all going for lunch? Can I join in?*
into: *We're trying to break into that market.*
away: *I've been slaving away in the kitchen.*
out: *We've pulled out of that market.*

Preventing problems
around: *We'll work around the problem somehow.*
aside: *We need to put aside our differences.*
off: *Keep off the grass.*

Completeness
up: *The next slide sums up my whole presentation.*

Ending
away: *The snow just melted away.*
off: *They broke off negotiations.*
out: *We've sold out of size 14.*
up: *He's just broken up with his girlfriend.*

Relationships
together: *Let's all get together after work.*
up: *Let's meet up for lunch some time.*

Happiness and unhappiness
up: *Cheer up! Things are looking up!*
down: *The cold weather was getting me down.*

Exercises

Sections A, B **23.1 Complete the sentences with one word from list A and one word from list B.**

A: along back ~~in~~ in out up	B: for on of ~~with~~ with with

1 It's not just a question of choosing a candidate with the right experience. They also have to fit *in* *with* the company culture.
2 Our office is a friendly place. I get ________ ________ just about everyone.
3 We have to make a decision. We're beginning to run ________ ________ time.
4 If it's not successful, we can always fall ________ ________ plan B.
5 The situation is changing so fast I find it hard to keep ________ ________ what's happening.
6 He came ________ ________ a lot of criticism after taking that decision.

A: along back down through up up	B: on to to to with with

7 I'm sorry, I'm going to be away next week. Can we put the meeting ________ ________ the following week?
8 We might have to withdraw this product from the market and face ________ ________ the fact that it hasn't been such a great success.
9 He agreed to go ________ ________ our decision, but now he spends the whole time complaining and criticizing.
10 I'm starting to get a bit overweight. I'm going to have to take more exercise and cut ________ ________ alcohol and fatty food.
11 We will all have to put ________ ________ the noise of the building work until the extension is finished.
12 I've been trying to get ________ ________ Miguel all morning, but it keeps going to his voicemail.

Section C **23.2 Read sentences 1–6 and think carefully about the meaning of the particle 'up' in each one. Remember that the meaning might be metaphorical, not literal. Then match each use of 'up' to meanings a–f below.**

1 The Turkish market is opening up for new investment. [e]
2 We need more ink for the printer. It's nearly used up. [ ]
3 A key goal for the bank is to build up their asset management business. [ ]
4 Many technical issues have come up in the negotiations. [ ]
5 It's going to take them a long time to catch up with their competitors. [ ]
6 This project will tie up all our resources for weeks and weeks. [ ]

a) increase in amount
b) arise/appear
c) do/finish something completely
d) restrict, prevent or fasten
e) start to happen
f) move closer to something

"Coles, we've decided to cut back on people named Coles."

Exercises

Sections A, B, C

23.3 Complete this email extract from a financial advisor to his client with the particles in the box. You will need to guess some answers from the context.

back	behind	~~down~~	in	on	up

Unfortunately, since I last contacted you the value of stocks has come [1] *down* significantly in all global markets. In addition, there are increasing signs of inflation, and Central Banks are starting to put [2] ________ interest rates. Investors are nervous, and it is likely that market volatility will carry [3] ________. Your own portfolio is weighted towards the financial sector, and this sector has fallen even further [4] ________ the general market. In the current climate we recommend that you cut [5] ________ on your exposure to this sector and switch to energy and infrastructure instead. These areas will fit [6] ________ nicely with the rest of your portfolio.

Sections A, B, C

23.4 Complete the telephone call with phrasal verbs in the box that mean the same as the words in brackets. You will need to guess some answers from the context.

breaking up	cut off	get back to	get through	go ahead
go over	hold on	look into	~~put through~~	sort out

RECEPTIONIST: Good morning, Media Solutions, how can I help you?

DEREK: Can you [1] *put* me *through* (connect) to Christine Moreau, please?

RECEPTIONIST: Of course, hold the line. ... I'm sorry, caller, I can't [2] ________ (succeed in reaching her) at the moment, the line's busy.

DEREK: Can I leave a message?

RECEPTIONIST: Of course. Just [3] ________ (wait) a second while I look for a pen. Right, [4] ________ (continue).

DEREK: My name is Derek Richardson, from Weston Security. Ms Moreau wanted me to [5] ________ (investigate) the cost of installing an alarm system for your premises. I said I'd [6] ________ her today (phone again later).

RECEPTIONIST: Hello? Hello? I'm sorry, you're [7] ________ (separating into small parts). Hello?

DEREK: Sorry about that. I'm on a train and we were [8] ________ (disconnected). Yes, as I was saying, I've managed to [9] ________ something ________ (organize). I wanted to talk to her directly, but perhaps I'll email the quotation to her along with some other details about our services.

RECEPTIONIST: Right, can I just [10] ________ (check carefully) that again? Your name is Derek Richardson, from Weston Security, and you're going to email some details about an alarm system.

DEREK: Yes, that's right. Thank you for your help. Goodbye.

Tasks

Speaking: listen and repeat

1 23 **You are going to hear eight phrases. Listen and repeat.**

Translate

2 Translate these short texts taken from the Internet into your own language. Remember not to translate word for word, but rather to make it sound natural.

Retailers are cutting back on variety. For years supermarkets, drugstores, and discount retailers packed their shelves with an ever-expanding range of products in different brands, sizes, colors, flavors, fragrances and prices. Now, though, they believe less is more. They are trying to cater to budget-conscious shoppers who want to simplify shopping trips and stick to familiar products.

Wall Street Journal website

Executives will have to face up to inevitable changes in the corporate governance of their companies. One such measure would enhance shareholders' ability to propose alternative candidates to management's choice of directors. Another would give them a chance to voice their disapproval of executive compensation. And it is likely more companies will move to split the roles of chief executive and chairman, a move that will help advance the independence of boards from company managements.

FT website

Writing: personalized practice

3 Complete the sentences with a phrasal verb from section A on page 98 and your own ideas. You will need to begin with a preposition + object.

1 It's too late. We can't back out *of the deal now. They would never do business with us again* .
2 I'm going to be busy all morning. I need to carry on ____________ .
3 Korean car manufacturers like Hyundai are trying hard to catch up ____________ .
4 In the current economic climate we're going to have to cut back ____________ .
5 He's a genius, but he's not really a team player. I don't think he'll fit in ____________ .
6 I go to the main annual conference in my field. I like to keep up ____________ .
7 That's all I have to say about trends in the market. Now I'd like to move on ____________ .
8 Our Marketing Director is away all this week, but I'm standing in ____________ .

4 Continue as before, using a phrasal verb from section B on page 98 and your own ideas.

9 Their share price has fallen dramatically and the CEO has come in ____________ .
10 He's in a state of denial. Sooner or later he'll have to face up ____________ .
11 If her ideas for becoming self-employed don't work, she can always fall back ____________ .
12 I need to look into this to see what's happening. I'll get back ____________ .
13 It's taken a long time, but this week I've finally got around ____________ .
14 I don't think it's the right decision, but I'm going to go along ____________ .

24 The *-ing* form

A *-ing* form in previous units

The *-ing* form can be used in a variety of verb tenses: units 1–8.

The *-ing* form follows certain verbs: units 19–20.

B *-ing* form as a noun

The *-ing* form can be used as a noun, either as the subject or the object.

***Marketing** requires careful **planning**.*

It can also be part of a noun phrase.

***Giving a successful presentation** is closely related to the enthusiasm of the presenter.*

-ing forms often begin items in a list, for example in job descriptions and CVs:

The job involves:
- ***Leading** a sales team of six people.*
- ***Ensuring** that sales targets are met.*
- ***Liaising** with senior managers.*

C *-ing* form as an adjective

The *-ing* form can be used like an adjective, before a noun.

*We are a small **manufacturing company** with about 50 employees.*

There is a small group of adjectives which can have either an *-ing* form or an *-ed* form. Examples include: *bored / boring, excited / exciting, interested / interesting, tired / tiring.*

*The meeting was very **interesting**. I was **interested** in your comments about Cisco.*

Adjectives ending *-ing* describe something we are reacting to (outside us).

Adjectives ending *-ed* describe our feelings (inside us).

D *-ing* form after prepositions

We use the *-ing* form after prepositions.

*Walmart became successful **by** sell**ing** high volumes at low prices.*
*We never launch a new product **without** do**ing** extensive market research first.*
***After** wash**ing** the fruit, we sort it according to size and put it into boxes.*

Prepositions are often associated with particular verbs, adjectives and nouns (units 47–49).

*Success in this business **depends on** hav**ing** the right contacts.*
*I'd be very **interested in** hear**ing** your suggestions.*
*I need some **advice on** do**ing** business in the Balkans.*

Be careful with the word *to*. Very often *to* is followed by an infinitive. However, when *to* is a preposition it is followed by the *-ing* form in the normal way.

*Outdoor posters are an alternative **to** us**ing** expensive TV advertisements.*

A few verbs have *to* used as a preposition. Examples include: *look forward to, object to, be used to, respond to.*

*I **look forward to** see**ing** you next week.*
(NOT ~~to see~~)

*He **responds** well **to** work**ing** under pressure.*
(NOT ~~to work~~)

E *-ing* form used to begin a clause

An *-ing* clause can give more information about a noun. This is like a defining relative clause (unit 29D).

*A lot of the small mining companies **operating in Canada** are likely to be taken over.*
(= companies which are operating)

An *-ing* clause can give the reason for an action in the past.

*I went over to him, **thinking he was a sales assistant**.*
(= because I thought he was a sales assistant)

An *-ing* clause can describe a background situation for another action.

***Coming into work on the metro**, I met Celia who used to work in Accounts.*
(= while I was coming into work)

An *-ing* clause can give more information about a verb. This is like an adverb.

*She left the meeting, **smiling at the size of her bonus payment**.*
(answers the question: 'how did she leave?')

F *-ing* form: negative, perfect and passive

There is a negative form with *not*.

*I started the job **not knowing** what to expect.*

There is a perfect form with *having* + past participle. This is used to refer to the past.

***Having done** business with them myself, I know exactly what you mean.*

There is a passive form with *being* + past participle.

*I think your boss likes **being listened to**.*

Exercises

Sections B, C

24.1 Match the beginnings of sentences 1–6 with their endings a–f.

1 Manufacturing in the UK has been [c]
2 In the UK, the service sector is much more important than the [ ]
3 Our manufacturing process [ ]
4 Car manufacturing in Poland is [ ]
5 Developing and promoting Poland's manufacturing base will [ ]
6 Developing manufacturing in Poland is a central part [ ]

a) manufacturing sector.
b) is now almost completely automated.
c) in decline for many years.
d) of the government's economic strategy.
e) concentrated in the Katowice area.
f) need a lot of investment.

Sections B, C

24.2 For each sentence in exercise 24.1 above, decide if the word 'manufacturing' is a noun or an adjective.

Noun: *1c* ______ ______ Adjective: *2a* ______ ______

Section C

24.3 Complete the sentences with adjectives formed from the *-ing* form of the verbs in the box.

confuse	cut	last	meet	sell	~~tire~~	wear	welcome

1 I'm going to take a long bath – it's been a very *tiring* day.
2 There's a ______ point in front of the ticket office. I'll see you there at six.
3 Her presentation was a little ______ at times.
4 This carpet is very hard-______ , and so it will be very long-______ .
5 The new reception area should be ______ , not cold and formal like before.
6 One of the strongest ______ points of this machine is its ______-edge technology. We have a patent on it and you won't find it anywhere else.

Section D

24.4 Underline the correct words.

1 Thanks for calling, and I hope to *meeting/meet* you next week.
2 Thanks for calling, and I look forward to *meeting/meet* you next week.
3 I'm expecting to *taking/take* the train to work when I move to my new house.
4 I don't object to *taking/take* the train, but I prefer coming to work by car.
5 In my summer holidays I used to *working/work* at a café on the beach.
6 I can help you with your spreadsheet – I'm used to *working/work* with Excel.

Exercises

Section D

24.5 Complete the sentences by choosing a preposition from list A followed by an *-ing* form from list B.

A: ~~after~~ before by instead of of without

B: being going ~~leaving~~ raising using taking over

1 *After leaving* university I worked in IT recruitment for a while.
2 I was aware ________ ________ very nervous at the start of my talk.
3 Vodafone grew ________ ________ local operators.
4 ________ ________ on, I'd like you to look at one more thing on this slide.
5 We could switch to open source software ________ ________ Microsoft Office.
6 It's almost impossible to reduce inflation ________ ________ interest rates.

Section E

24.6 Cross out either <u>two</u> or <u>three</u> unnecessary words in each sentence.

1 A lot of the firms ~~which are~~ developing tidal energy are based in Scotland.
2 ~~While I was~~ listening to his presentation, I started to think about the lunch menu.
3 The woman who is replacing Kay Walker used to work at Omnicom.
4 The thing that is worrying me most is the fluctuation in raw materials prices.
5 As I was passing his office just now, I noticed a huge potted plant in the corner.
6 The visitors who are coming this afternoon are a Chinese Trade Delegation.

Sections D, E, F

24.7 Rewrite the underlined part of each sentence using an *-ing* form. Note that in some examples there may be a negative form or a perfect form.

1 I got to the airport at ten <u>because I expected</u> the flight to arrive on time.
I got to the airport at ten, *expecting* the flight to arrive on time.
2 <u>I wasn't used to</u> the company culture so I found it hard to fit in.
Not being used to the company culture, I found it hard to fit in.
3 I invested $8,000 in a China fund <u>because I hoped</u> the market would go up.
I invested $8,000 in a China fund, ________ the market would go up.
4 <u>As I wasn't</u> an experienced negotiator, I think I made too many concessions.
________ an experienced negotiator, I think I made too many concessions.
5 <u>I assumed</u> she wouldn't mind, so I asked her about her salary.
________ she wouldn't mind, I asked her about her salary.
6 I said yes <u>because I didn't know</u> it would create so many problems.
I said yes, ________ it would create so many problems.
7 After <u>we had reviewed</u> the budget we decided to cut one of the projects.
After ________ the budget we decided to cut one of the projects.
8 <u>He lost</u> all his money on the stock market, so he got a job serving fries.
________ all his money on the stock market, he got a job serving fries.
9 Before <u>I started</u> here, I used to work at UBS.
Before ________ here, I used to work at UBS.
10 <u>Now that I've heard</u> what went wrong, I can see what needs to change.
________ what went wrong, I can see what needs to change.

Tasks

Speaking: listen and repeat

1 24 **You are going to hear eight phrases. Listen and repeat.**

Translate

2 Translate these short texts taken from the Internet into your own language. Remember not to translate word for word, but rather to make it sound natural.

'In the military, I saw that you need someone at the top who is capable of running a strong organization: establishing a chain of command, maintaining a list of priorities, and making sure that everyone is working toward the same goals. I used that experience in business.'

BNET website

The reality now is thousands of emails, fax messages, telephone calls and internet orders coming into a company every day. Integrating that information intelligently so that the customer gets what it needs is a very complex task demanding a very complex solution.

Eurobusiness website

Writing: personalized practice

3 Look again at page 102, and then complete the following sentences, beginning with an *-ing* form used in the way shown in brackets.

1 (*-ing* form as a noun or part of a noun phrase)
Advertising on billboards and public transport seems to work well in my business.

2 (*-ing* form as a noun or part of a noun phrase)
______________________________ is a very important part of my job.

3 (*-ing* form as a noun or part of a noun phrase)
______________________________ is a very difficult part of my job.

4 (*-ing* form like an adjective, before a noun)
I went on a training course to improve my ______________________ skills.

5 (*-ing* form after a preposition)
We became successful by ______________________________ .

6 (*-ing* form after a preposition)
All my life I have been interested in ______________________________ .

7 (*-ing* form after a preposition)
My new job is different to my old one, and I'm still not used to ______________________ .

8 (*-ing* clause giving information about a noun, like a defining relative clause)
A lot of the small firms ______________________________ will probably merge or be taken over in the next few years.

9 (*-ing* clause giving information about a noun, like a defining relative clause)
Many of the people ______________________ are on temporary contracts.

10 (*-ing* clause giving the reason for an action)
I put on my smartest clothes, ______________________________ .

11 (*-ing* clause giving the reason for an action)
Not ______________________________ before, I was a bit nervous.

12 (*-ing* clause describing a background situation for another action)
______________________________ I noticed how quiet it was.

13 (*-ing* clause giving more information about a verb, like an adverb)
I walked along the street, ______________________________ .

14 (*-ing* clause giving more information about a verb, like an adverb)
I went into the room, not ______________________________ .

If you are working in class, choose some sentences to read aloud. Ask and answer questions.

25 make & do, have, get

A *make & do*

There are many common expressions using *make* and *do*. A very approximate guideline is that *make* is used for a result and *do* for an activity.

You can *make* …

> *an appointment with sb, an arrangement with sb, sb angry/sad/etc., an attempt to do sth, sth better/lighter* (comparative adjectives), *a bid for sth, a call to sb, sth clear, a complaint against sb, contact, a decision, a difference to sth, an exception, an effort, inquiries, an excuse, a good/poor impression on sb, an investment, a loss, a mess, a mistake, money, a noise, a note of sth, an offer, a plan, sth possible, a profit, a promise, progress, sense of sth, a start, a suggestion, sure, yourself understood*

Note: *sth* = something; *sb* = somebody

You can *do* …

> *the accounts, your best, business with sb, the cleaning/shopping/etc., a course in sth, damage to sth, economics at university, everything you can to help, sb a favor, a job for sb, nothing, overtime, research, something about it, a test on sth, well/badly at sth, without sth, work for sb*

We use *make* to mean 'produce' or 'manufacture'. Products are *made in* a country, *made by* a company and *made of* a material like plastic/steel, etc.

We use *do* to mean 'perform an action' when we are speaking generally.

*Can I **do** anything to help you?*
*What did you **do** at the weekend?*

B *have*

We use the verb *have* either like 'possess' or as an action (= do something).

*I **have** a flat in the city centre.*	(possess)
*We **have** a meeting every morning.*	(action)

When *have* is used like 'possess', it is a state verb and so does not form continuous tenses. See unit 2D for state verbs.

*Sorry, I **don't have** any change for the meter.*
(NOT ~~I'm not having~~)

We can use *have got* in place of *have* when it means 'possess'. This is very common in British English.

*He**'s got** an MBA from INSEAD.*
***I've got** a new job.*

Using *have* like 'possess', you can *have* …

> *a new car/job, a brother, brown hair, glasses, an appointment, a chance (to do sth), a day off, a holiday/vacation, good/bad luck, time (to do sth), second thoughts, a good sense of humour, a lot of energy, an idea, an/no alternative, a/no doubt, a cold, a headache, a bad back*

Using *have* as an action verb, you can *have* …

> *a coffee, a glass of wine, a meal, lunch/dinner, the steak, a discussion, a meeting, a drink, a look, a break, a wash, a rest, a guess, an accident, difficulty (+ -ing), trouble (+ -ing), a word (with sb)*
> Imperatives: *Have fun! Have a good time! Have a nice day! Have a go! Have a try!*

C *get*

Get has many different meanings. The following are all common, and are given in approximate order of frequency.

1. obtain/receive/be given
   *Her husband **got** a new job.*
   *I **got** an email from Frank yesterday.*
   *You'll **get** the chance to travel abroad.*
2. buy sth
   *I **got** this shirt from Harrods.*
3. become
   *It's **getting** late – I have to go.*
4. bring sth (fetch)
   *Will you **get** me a glass of water?*
5. get sth done/fixed/finished, etc.
   *I can **get** the report finished today.*
   *Joran managed to **get** my email working again.*
6. make sb do sth/persuade
   *I'll **get** Estera to give you a call.*
   *We tried to **get** them to agree, but they refused.*
7. move
   *I saw him **get** out of the taxi.*
   *I **got** into marketing many years ago.*
8. arrive at a place
   *I **get** to work at nine.*
9. make progress
   *I'm not **getting** anywhere with this report.*
10. fit/put sth in a place
    *You can **get** a lot of things into this bag.*
11. understand
    *I'm sorry, I didn't **get** that.*
12. travel by/catch
    *I **got** a taxi from the airport.*

Exercises

Section A **25.1 Complete the sentences with *make* or *do*. You may have to use a past simple or present continuous form.**

1 I'm sorry, Mr Kreiner is busy. You'll have to *make* an appointment.
2 The insider dealing scandal ________ a lot of damage to his reputation.
3 Manchester United are going to ________ a bid for Real Madrid's striker.
4 Could you ________ me a favour? Could you ________ some coffee for us all?
5 I think we should use another contractor to ________ the office cleaning.
6 Don't worry, just ________ your best. We all ________ mistakes.
7 OK, are we all here? Shall we ________ a start?
8 The builders ________ so much noise that it was difficult to ________ any work.
9 At my previous company, we ________ business in the Ukraine for three years before we ________ a profit.
10 We ________ some quality tests last week and I think we're ________ progress.
11 We have to ________ a decision. We can't just ________ nothing.
12 I hope they can send a technician to ________ the job this afternoon.

Section B **25.2 Look at the form of the word *have* in the sentences below. Put a tick (✓) if the sentence is possible. Put a cross (✗) if it is not possible.**

1 It's OK, I don't need any help, I'm just having a look. ☐
2 I'm having one brother and one sister. ☐
3 She's a good team member – she's having a lot of energy. ☐
4 Why not join us later? We'll be having a drink in the bar. ☐

Section C **25.3 Study the uses of *get* in sentences 1–12, then match them with meanings a–l below.**

1 Where did you *get* that jacket? It really suits you. *b*
2 Can I *get* you a drink while you're waiting? ☐
3 The factory is very busy. We *got* a large order from Qatar last week. ☐
4 I couldn't *get* her to sign the contract. She needs more time to decide. ☐
5 We have a new CEO. Things are going to *get* interesting. ☐
6 I need to *get* my hair cut. ☐
7 What time do you usually *get* to the office? ☐
8 I'm sorry, I didn't quite *get* the last point. Could you explain it again? ☐
9 I flew to Schiphol and then *got* a train to Amsterdam Central Station. ☐
10 How far did you *get* with the PowerPoint slides? Are they ready yet? ☐
11 The graphic designer couldn't *get* all the text onto one page. ☐
12 It's going to be difficult to *get* the conference table down the corridor. ☐

a) obtain/receive
b) buy
c) become
d) bring sth (fetch)
e) have sth done
f) make sb do sth
g) move
h) arrive at
i) make progress
j) fit sth in a place
k) understand
l) travel by/catch

"Mr. Herman, you made me laugh and you made me cry, but you didn't make me money."

Exercises

Section B **25.4 Complete the sentences with a word or phrase from the box.**

appointment	chance	break	day off	difficulty	discussion			
doubt	fever	the fish	go	holiday	look	~~meeting~~	time	word

1 I'm having a *meeting* with my bank manager this afternoon.
2 Did you have a good ______ ? You went to Greece, didn't you?
3 If you have a ______ , could you have a ______ at these figures?
4 I was really busy yesterday, and I didn't have any ______ to do it.
5 We've had a very full ______ of this issue. Let's have a short ______ now and reconvene in about 15 minutes.
6 (reception desk) I have an ______ with Benedicte Bouchet at ten o'clock.
7 Let me see. I think I'll have ______ . It's normally very good here.
8 I have no ______ at all that he's telling the truth. He's very honest.
9 I had a lot of ______ understanding the technical details in his talk.
10 I've got a bit of a ______ – I'm going to take an aspirin. If I still feel like this in the morning I think I'll have the ______ .
11 I'd like to have a quick ______ with you about the seminar tomorrow.
12 Have a ______ ! I'm sure you can do it!

Section A, C **25.5 Complete the dialogue with a correct form of *make, do* or *get*.**

IAN: Eva, you've been [1] *doing* a lot of overtime recently! Are you hoping to [2] ______ promoted?

EVA: No, it's just that I haven't been [3] ______ this job very long and I really want to [4] ______ a good impression. In the last place I worked they laid off a lot of people, including me.

IAN: Really, why was that?

EVA: Well, the company just wasn't [5] ______ very well. Basically they [6] ______ into difficulties by expanding too quickly. They [7] ______ a big investment in Latin America but they hadn't [8] ______ their market research properly beforehand. They just couldn't [9] ______ money. So they had to cut back.

IAN: So what did you [10] ______ after you lost your job?

EVA: The first thing I [11] ______ was put my CV on the web. I [12] ______ quite a few replies. I contacted the companies who were interested, and that's how I [13] ______ an interview here. They [14] ______ me an offer the next day and I accepted it straightaway.

IAN: Being able to do a job search and things like that online [15] ______ a big difference. You don't even have to leave the house! I'm using the Internet for everything now. I couldn't [16] ______ without it. I even use it to [17] ______ my main weekly shopping.

EVA: I know what you mean. A friend of mine [18] ______ married last week and I was so busy at work that I didn't have time to go to the shops. So I looked on the Internet and [19] ______ her a really nice bag. It's [20] ______ by Prada.

Tasks

Speaking: listen and repeat

1 25 You are going to hear eight phrases. Listen and repeat.

Translate

2 Translate these short texts taken from the Internet into your own language. Remember not to translate word for word, but rather to make it sound natural.

'The stock market is what it is. You live with that,' says the CEO of Nokia Corp, 'You just do the best you can on a daily basis, try to get the right balance of short-term and long-term actions. That's the only attitude to have to avoid losing sleep unnecessarily.'

IndustryWeek website

Could Apple make a bid for one of the world's biggest game developers and publishers? There is chatter that Apple is eyeing Electronic Arts as a takeover target, and the notion of a deal between the two companies may not be so far-fetched. Apple has been promoting its iPod touch as a gaming device, and a major gaming-related acquisition could make sense.

The Tech Report website

Writing: personalized practice

3 Look again at section C on page 106 and exercise 25.3. Write a sentence using *get* with the meaning in brackets.

1 (obtain/receive) *I get so much spam in my inbox. Does anyone really reply to this junk?*
2 (buy) ______
3 (become) ______
4 (bring/fetch) ______
5 (get sth done) ______
6 (make sb do sth) ______
7 (move) ______
8 (arrive at) ______
9 (make progress) ______
10 (fit sth in a place) ______
11 (understand) ______
12 (travel by) ______

Rehearsal for the real world

4 Look again at the list of expressions using *make* and *do* in section A on page 106. Now use the expressions to write three or four true sentences about yourself. Here are some examples:

As a sales consultant I have to make a good impression on clients, so personal appearance is important.
I'm trying to save money for my holidays, so I'm doing a lot of overtime at the moment – they pay me one and a half times the usual rate.

Look again at the list of expressions using *have* in section B on page 106. Now use the expressions to write another three or four true sentences about yourself. Here are some examples:

I have no doubt that we'll all be working beyond the present retirement age of 65.
My English is quite good, but I have trouble understanding native speakers with a strong regional accent.

If you are working in class, choose some sentences to read aloud. Ask and answer questions.

26 Reported speech 1

A Reported speech

We often tell people what other people said. This is called reported or indirect speech. We very rarely try to report the exact words. Usually we give the general meaning with a summary.

(actual words): *'**I'll** get the third quarter sales numbers and bring them to the meeting.'*
→ (report): *He said **he'd** bring the figures to the meeting.*

Note the change of tense and person in the example above: *I will* to *he would.*

This unit uses *said* as the reporting verb. Other verbs are given in unit 27.

In writing we can repeat the exact words using speech marks (' … '). This is called 'quoting' the words.

The company press officer said yesterday, 'The situation is completely under control.'

B Tense changes

When the verb tense changes, it 'moves back' in time.

*'I **work** for IBM.'*
→ *She said she **worked** for IBM.*

*'**I'm working** for IBM.'*
→ *She said she **was working** for IBM.*

*'**I've worked** for IBM.'*
→ *She said she **had worked** for IBM.*

*'**I've been working** for IBM.'*
→ *She said she **had been working** for IBM.*

*'I **worked** for IBM.'*
→ *She said she **had worked** for IBM.*
→ OR *She said she **used to work** for IBM.*
→ OR *She said she **worked** for IBM.*

*'I **had worked** for IBM.'*
→ *She said she **had worked** for IBM.*

*'**I'm going to work** for IBM.'*
→ *She said she **was going to work** for IBM.*

*'I **can/will/may** work for IBM.'*
→ *She said she **could/would/might** work for IBM.*

There is no change for *must, might, could, should, would.*

Note that if the actual words were in the past simple (*worked*), the reported speech can take a variety of forms, including no change.

Note that there is no change for the past perfect (*had worked*).

C No tense change

It is not always necessary to change tenses. If the information is still true, we can keep the same tense as the original.

(actual words): *'What a great advertising campaign – one of our most successful ever.'*

→ (report – the campaign is finished): *She **said** the campaign **was** a great success.*

→ (report – the campaign is still happening): *She **says/said** the campaign **is/was** a great success.*

We do not change tense if we report something which is always true.

(actual words): *'There **is** always a period of uncertainty after a merger.'*
→ (report): *He **says/said** there **is** always some uncertainty when a merger happens.*

D People, places, times and things

In reported speech the terms used to refer to people, places, times and things often change, because the point of view changes.

*'**I'll** see **you here tomorrow**.'*

*Sue said **she'd** see **me there the next day**.*

*'**I've** read **your** report about **this** project.'*

*He said **he'd** read **my** report about **the** project.*

Here is a list of typical changes:

PEOPLE	
I	he/she
you	me
my	his/her
your	my
PLACE	
here	there, at the office
TIMES	
now	then, at that time
today	that day, last Monday
this afternoon	that afternoon
yesterday	the day before, the previous day
last week	the week before, the previous week
tomorrow	the next day, the following day
next week	the week after, the following week
a few days ago	a few days before, a few days earlier
THINGS	
this project	the project

Exercises

Section B **26.1 Write the actual words that each person says. Use contractions where possible.**

1 Anna said she had already finished the three tasks.
(Anna's actual words) '*I've already finished the three tasks*.'

2 Claudia said she would be back after lunch.
(Claudia's actual words) ' ______________________________________ .'

3 He said Paula was going to contact the printers.
(His actual words) ' ______________________________________ .'

4 Bill said he wanted to call Head Office.
(Bill's actual words) ' ______________________________________ .'

5 She said she was meeting the bank manager at 11 am.
(Her actual words) ' ______________________________________ .'

6 Pierre said he had found out about the problem a long time ago.
(Pierre's actual words) ' ______________________________________ .'

7 David said he had to be back in the office by 3.30.
(David's actual words) ' ______________________________________ .'

Section D **26.2 Look at the actual words spoken. Underline the correct words in the reported version.**

1 (Helen's words) 'I won't do it until tomorrow.'
Helen said *I/she* wouldn't do it until the *previous/following* day.

2 (Peter's words) 'It's very busy in here. I'll call you later.'
Peter said it was very busy *here/there*, and he'd call *me/him* later.

3 (The sales manager's words) 'We received your order last week.'
He said *they'd/we'd* received *our/their* order the week *after/before*.

4 (Melanie's words) 'I'm sorry about the delay. I'll deal with this right now.'
She said *she/I* was sorry about the delay, and she'd deal with it *right then/later*.

Sections B, D **26.3 Rewrite each sentence in reported speech. Use contractions where possible.**

1 'I won't put it in the January Sales, because it's selling very well,' he said.
He said *he wouldn't put it in the January Sales, because it was selling very well*.

2 'I've read the report but I don't understand section four,' she said.
She said ______________________________________ .

3 'When I finish my presentation, I'm going to have a drink,' he said.
He said that when ______________________________________ .

4 'I'm preparing the figures but I won't be long,' she said.
She said __________________________
__________________________ .

5 'I like tennis, but I don't play very often,' he said.
He said __________________________
__________________________ .

6 'I'm going to visit our Polish subsidiary, but I'm not sure when,' she said.
She said __________________________
__________________________ .

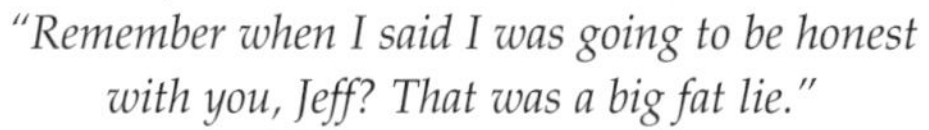

"Remember when I said I was going to be honest with you, Jeff? That was a big fat lie."

Exercises

Sections B, C **26.4 Read the words spoken in a conference presentation about the role of the Chief Executive Officer (CEO).**

> I'm going to talk to you today about CEOs. Did you know that over the last five years, two-thirds of all major companies worldwide have replaced their CEO? What's the reason for this? The reason is that expectations of CEO performance are far too high. Boards of companies look at their CEO as a kind of superhero who can solve all the company's problems. This mythology comes from high-profile CEOs of the recent past like Bill Gates and Steve Jobs – people who managed to produce constantly rising share prices while they were in charge. But the situation is very different now.

Now look at ways to report these words to a colleague who missed the presentation. If the sentence is grammatically correct, put a tick (✓). If it is incorrect, put a cross (✗). Remember it is not necessary to change tenses if the information is still true.

The speaker said that ...

1 Boards look at their CEOs as superheroes. ☑
2 Boards looked at their CEOs as superheroes. ☐
3 Boards had looked at their CEOs as superheroes. ☐
4 Bill Gates produced a constantly rising share price. ☐
5 Bill Gates had produced a constantly rising share price. ☐
6 Bill Gates had been produced a constantly rising share price. ☐
7 the situation is different now. ☐
8 the situation was different now. ☐

Sections B, D **26.5 A few days ago you went to your advertising agency to have a meeting. The person you met there spoke the words on the left. This morning you tell a colleague about the discussion. Underline the correct words on the right.**

The advertising person's words:

'Did you get my email I sent yesterday about this campaign we've been working on? I hope so. I'm sorry to ask you to come here at such short notice, but it's quite urgent. The situation is this: we use an outside printing company for all the brochures and leaflets, and a few days ago the workers there went on strike. I have no idea what it's all about, but I'm having a meeting with the production manager this afternoon. Anyway, I thought I should talk to you first.'

What you say to your colleague:

'He said he [1] *hopes/hoped* I'd got [2] *his/my* email that [3] *he'd send/he'd sent* [4] *yesterday/the day before* about [5] *the/this* advertising campaign. And he apologized for asking [6] *me/you* to go [7] *here/there* at such short notice – he said it [8] *is/was* urgent. Well, apparently a few days [9] *ago/before*, the printers they use [10] *have gone/had gone* on strike. He said he [11] *is meeting/was meeting* the production manager [12] *this/that* afternoon, but he wanted to talk to me about it first.'

Tasks

Speaking: listen and repeat

1 26 **You are going to hear eight phrases. Listen and repeat.**

Translate

2 Translate these short texts taken from the Internet into your own language. Remember not to translate word for word, but rather to make it sound natural.

Earlier in the week, a labor union report said that 751 deaths had occurred 'on the job' in Italy during the first six months of this year, up from 621 for the same period last year.

International Herald Tribune website

The European Union will ask Lufthansa for more concessions to approve the carrier's purchase of Austrian Airlines, Austrian government sources said on Monday. The sources said it was looking as if the EU Commision would examine the deal more closely, rather than rubber-stamping it when a deadline expires this Wednesday. Lufthansa has said from the outset that it would walk away from the deal if EU conditions were too severe. Chief Executive Wolfgang Mayrhuber last week reiterated he was not interested in buying what he called a 'little Austrian Airlines'.

Reuters website

Writing: personalized practice

3 You went to an internal company presentation yesterday where the CEO spoke to all the employees. One of your colleagues missed the presentation. Answer your colleague's questions using reported speech and your own ideas.

1 'What did he say about the performance of the company last year?'
He said *we had missed most of our sales targets* .
2 'Did he give a reason?'
He said we ______ .
3 'So what changes does he want?'
He told us he ______ .
4 'They must have a plan for that. How are they going to implement the changes?'
He said ______ .
5 'What about in our department specifically?'
He said we ______ .
6 'Are they going to monitor the process to see how the changes are working?'
He said they ______ .
7 'And do they have any plans for developing the business? New products? New markets?'
He told us ______ .
8 'So how did he finish? Was he optimistic or pessimistic?'
He said ______ .

Rehearsal for the real world

4 Think of a real meeting that you recently had. It could be a large, formal meeting; a smaller meeting with colleagues; or a one-to-one meeting with a customer, supplier or business partner. Now write an email to your boss, where you report on what was said.

If you are working in class, put all the emails on the desks or on the walls. Go round the room and read the emails. Return to your seats and say which email you liked best, and why.

27 Reported speech 2

A *Say* or *tell*?

We *say* something and we *tell* somebody.

*Simon **said** the project was going well.*
*Simon **told me** the project was going well.*

We never use *to* between *tell* and the object.

*He **told me** what happened in the meeting.*
(NOT ~~told to me~~)

We can use *to* after *say*.

*What did he **say to** you?*
*The boss wanted to **say** something **to** Susan.*

B Other reporting verbs

Unit 26 used *say* as the reporting verb, but there are many verbs to report what people say. Each verb has one or more possible patterns. Common reporting verbs include:

Verb + *-ing* form (unit 19)
admit, deny, mention, propose, suggest
*I **suggested changing** the supplier.*

Verb + *to* + infinitive (unit 19)
agree, ask, demand, decide, offer, promise, refuse, threaten
*They **refused to lower** their price.*

Verb + object + *to* + infinitive (unit 19)
advise, ask, convince, encourage, invite, order, persuade, remind, tell, warn
*They **advised us to wait** until next year.*

Verb + *that* clause
admit, agree, announce, answer, claim, complain, confirm, deny, explain, mention, promise, propose, reply, reveal, say, suggest
*She **promised that** she'd call me today.*

Verb + object + *that* clause
advise, assure, convince, inform, notify, persuade, promise, reassure, remind, tell
*I **reminded them that** there was a 25% deposit.*

We use the same tense change rules as in unit 26.

(actual words): *'**I'll** definitely call you.'*
➜ (report): *She **promised** she**'d** call me.*

We can also report what people think or know. Verbs include: *know, notice, think, realize, have no idea*, etc.

*Sorry, I **didn't realize** you **were** busy. I **thought** you **had** finished.*

C *It was agreed that*

We use *It* + passive of a reporting verb + *that* to report what people in general feel or believe.

***It was agreed** at the meeting **that** expansion plans would be put on hold until next year.*
***It was announced** yesterday **that** Private Equity Partners would take a 50% stake in BioTech.*

This is a formal use, found, for example, in newspaper stories, scientific reports or written summaries of meetings. Verbs that are often used in this way are:

be agreed, be announced, be claimed, be confirmed, be decided, be estimated, be expected, be feared, be felt, be found, be pointed out, be proposed, be reported, be rumoured, be said, be shown, be suggested, be thought

D Reporting questions

In reported questions we use the same tense change rules as in unit 26. The word order is like a normal statement.

(actual words) *'When **will** the goods arrive?'*
➜ *They **asked** me when the goods **would** arrive.*
(NOT ~~when would the goods arrive~~)

(actual words) *'Where **do you work**?'*
➜ *He **asked** me where **I worked**.*
(NOT ~~where I did work~~)

When we report *yes/no* questions, we use *if* or *whether*.

(actual words) *'**Have you spent** all your budget?'*
➜ *She **asked** me **if** we**'d spent** all the budget.*

(actual words) *'**Are you going to** pay in cash?'*
➜ *He **asked** me **whether I was going to** pay in cash.*

Notice in the examples above that reported questions have no question mark in writing.

E Reporting commands and requests

Commands are reported with *tell* and the infinitive.

(actual words) *'Take us to the airport.'*
➜ *She **told** the driver **to take** us to the airport.*

(actual words) *'Don't worry. I'll deal with it.'*
➜ *He **told** me **not to worry**.*

Requests are reported with *ask* and the infinitive.

(actual words) *'Would you mind waiting for a moment?'*
➜ *He **asked** me **to wait**.*

Exercises

Section A

27.1 Underline the correct words.

1 Sally *told me/told* that she'd lost the memory stick with the presentation.
2 Chris *said me/said* he must leave the meeting early.
3 This is confidential. Please don't *say/tell* anything about it.
4 This is confidential. Please don't *say/tell* anyone about it.
5 I *said/told* them about the party on the boat, and they *said/told* they would come.
6 'Look,' I *told to/said to* her, 'please *tell me/say me* what really happened.'

Section B

27.2 Match the actual words 1–12 with the reported statements a–l.

1 'Well done! You've done it!'	a) She advised me to do it.
2 'Who, me? No, I never did it.'	b) He apologized for not doing it.
3 'I'm sorry. I just completely forgot to do it.'	c) She reminded me to do it.
4 'If I were you, I'd do it.'	d) He denied doing it.
5 'Would you like to do it?'	e) She invited me to do it.
6 'Don't forget to do it!'	f) He congratulated me on doing it.
7 'Oh, I see that you've done it.'	g) She refused to do it.
8 'Oh, by the way, I've done it.'	h) He didn't realize I'd done it.
9 'Oh! I thought you hadn't done it!'	i) She promised she'd do it.
10 'Don't do it! It could be a disaster.'	j) He noticed I'd done it.
11 'I'll do it, you can count on me.'	k) She mentioned she'd done it.
12 'No, I won't do it. It's out of the question.	l) He warned me not to do it.

Section D, unit 26

27.3 Rewrite each sentence in reported speech. Write *if/whether* for yes/no questions. This exercise includes revision of unit 26.

1 'Are you on vacation for the whole of August?' she asked me.
She asked me *if/whether I was on vacation for the whole of August* .
2 'What do the letters 'URL' mean?' I asked him.
I asked him ______________________________ .
3 'Have you prepared the figures?' my boss asked me.
My boss asked me ______________________________ .
4 'When is your talk?' I asked Francesca.
I asked Francesca ______________________________ .
5 'Did you remember to back up the file?' she asked him.
She asked him ______________________________ .
6 'Why have you turned off the air conditioning?' Dana asked me.
Dana asked me ______________________________ .
7 'Do you speak German?' they asked me at the interview.
They asked me at the interview ______________________________ .
8 'How much did you pay for your car?' I asked Jitka.
I asked Jitka ______________________________ .

Exercises

Section C **27.4 Read the following extract from a meeting, chaired by Tessa. Then underline the most appropriate reporting verbs in the written summary below.**

TESSA: I'd like to hear your views on the talks we're having with BCP about the possible merger. Do you think we should go ahead with the talks?

NIGEL: No, I don't think so. Our company cultures are totally different, and I can't see many opportunities to cut costs in a combined operation. I'm against it.

TONY: But Nigel, can't you see that we're too small to stand alone in the global economy? There's going to be consolidation in our market and now is the right time to act.

TESSA: How long do you think it would take to integrate the two companies?

TONY: Probably about six months, maybe more.

NIGEL: That's six months of chaos and falling investor confidence. It's just too risky.

TESSA: I don't think we have enough information at the moment. Perhaps we could set up a task force to look into the whole issue in more detail? Tony – would you be willing to chair it?

TONY: OK, I'll chair a task force, but I'll need representatives from every department. And it'll involve a lot of management time.

TESSA: When do you think you'll be able to get the report done?

TONY: Four weeks, max, if we work hard.

TESSA: Right, that's settled. We'll meet again after the report is ready and we've all had a chance to study it. Let's say July 28th, same time same place.

1 It was **decided/estimated/announced** that it would take about six months to integrate the two companies in the event of a merger.

2 It was **shown/rumoured/suggested** that we could set up a task force to produce a report on the implications of the merger.

3 It was **agreed/claimed/shown** that the task force would be chaired by Tony, with representatives from all departments. Report to be ready in four weeks.

4 It was **felt/feared/decided** that the next meeting would be on July 28th at 9 am in the main conference room.

Sections A, B, D **27.5 Nigel (from exercise 27.4 above) is talking to a colleague about the same meeting later in the week. Underline the correct words.**

“Tessa asked 1 *that we give/us to give* our opinions about the merger talks. I 2 *told them/told to them* that I thought the whole thing was a bad idea, but they refused 3 *to listen/listening*. Of course Tony disagreed, as usual. He 4 *told/said* we were too small for the global market. Then Tessa asked how long 5 *would it/it would* take to integrate the two companies, and Tony claimed it would take six months. I 6 *reminded them that/reminded that* it would be six months of chaos. Well, Tessa suggested 7 *setting up/to set up* a task force to look into the whole thing. I decided 8 *not saying/not to say* anything. Guess what? Tony offered 9 *to chair/that he would chair* the task force. No surprises there. Anyway, we decided 10 *to meet/meeting* again at the end of July.”

Tasks

Speaking: listen and repeat

1 27 **You are going to hear eight phrases. Listen and repeat.**

Translate

2 Translate these short texts taken from the Internet into your own language. Remember not to translate word for word, but rather to make it sound natural.

13% of finance professionals admitted that they would be phoning in to work to pick up voice mail messages between Christmas and the New Year.

AccountancyAge website

A recent report revealed that nearly half of the employers it surveyed were not planning to recruit school leavers or graduates this summer. For many young adults hit by the downturn, who are relying on the generosity of parents or claiming state benefits, the normal process of growing up has been delayed: 35 is the new 25.

The Observer website

Writing: personalized practice

3 Look again at section B on page 114. Complete the sentences with the verbs in brackets.

1 There was a job vacancy at a competitor's company and I …
(encourage) *encouraged her to apply for it* .
2 The discussion in the meeting was going round and round in circles, so I …
(suggest) __________ .
3 Our Communications Director called a press conference to …
(announce) __________ .
4 I was worried about the forthcoming departmental reorganization but he …
(reassure) __________ .
5 I've just spoken to our suppliers on the phone and they've …
(promise) __________ .
6 Our lawyers have now looked at the contract in detail and they've …
(advise) __________ .
7 They said that the warranty was no longer valid and they …
(refuse) __________ .
8 I went out for a drink with Melanie after work yesterday and she …
(tell) __________ .

Rehearsal for the real world

4 Respond with surprise to the following comments.

1 'The project is behind schedule and over budget.'
Really? I thought *it was going well* .
2 'We'll have to wait two to three months for delivery.'
Really? I had no idea __________ .
3 'They're a huge company – they operate all over the world.'
Really? I didn't realize __________ .
4 'Linda is at the airport – she just called me.'
Really? I thought __________ .
5 'Here's my new business card.'
Oh. I didn't realize __________ .
6 'Here's a photograph of my wife and two children.'
Oh. I didn't know __________ .

28 Relative clauses 1

A Relative clauses

Relative clauses are short phrases beginning with words like *who, that* and *which* that define or describe people and things. There are two types.

DEFINING RELATIVE CLAUSES
We use these to identify exactly which person or thing we mean.

The candidate ***who we interviewed on Friday*** *is better than this one.*

The information in the clause is necessary for the sentence to make sense.

NON-DEFINING RELATIVE CLAUSES
We use these to add extra information about a person or thing.

Anna Hoefer, ***who we interviewed last Friday****, is the best candidate in my opinion.*

The information is not necessary for the sentence to make sense. To show this, we use commas in writing or pause briefly where the commas are in speech.

Non-defining clauses are much more common in writing. In speech we usually just use two short sentences. Compare the examples below:

in an email: *I'd like to thank you for your help,* ***which was much appreciated****.*
speech: *Thanks for all your help. I really appreciate it.*

B Relative pronouns

The words *who, which, that* and *whose* can begin a relative clause. They are called relative pronouns.

For people, both *who* and *that* are used, but *who* is more common.

The sales assistant ***who I spoke to on the phone*** *said you had this model in stock.*

For things or ideas, both *which* and *that* are used, but *that* is more common, especially in speech.

I have your order on my screen. The items ***that you wanted*** *were shipped yesterday.*

The relative pronoun *whose* shows that something belongs to someone or something.

I've invited to the meeting everyone ***whose work is relevant to the project****.*
The European Union is an organization ***whose policies change quite slowly****.*

The relative pronoun *whom* is formal and rare in modern English. It can be used where *who* is the object of the sentence.

The candidate ***who/whom*** *we chose has an MBA in management accounting.*

C Leaving out the relative pronoun

We can leave out *who, which, that* (but not *whose*) in a defining relative clause if they are followed immediately by a noun or pronoun. This is usual in spoken English.

*The sales assistant (****who****)* ***I spoke to on the phone*** *said you had this model in stock.*
*I have your order on my screen. The items (****that****)* ***you wanted*** *were shipped yesterday.*

We must keep the relative pronoun if it is followed immediately by a verb.

The technician ***who spoke to Tony*** *said the network was working fine.*
The sauce ***that came with the fish*** *was superb.*

D Non-defining relative clauses

We must keep the relative pronoun in non-defining relative clauses. We cannot leave it out.

The technician, ***who spent over an hour here****, said the network was working fine.*
The sauce, ***which was creamy with lemon and herbs****, was superb.*

The word *that* is never used in a non-defining relative clause.

I have your order on my screen. The items, ***which were shipped yesterday****, are all in stock, with the exception of part number KL453.*

E Relative pronouns and prepositions

Normally we put prepositions at the end of the relative clause.

*Unilever is a company (****that****)* ***we know quite a lot about****.*
*The person (****who****)* ***I spoke to*** *was called Pam.*

In formal English we can put the preposition in front of *which* and *whose*, but not *that*.

Unilever is a company ***about which we know quite a lot****.*
(But NOT ~~about that~~)

After a preposition we change *who* to *whom*. This is rare and very formal.

The person ***to whom*** *I spoke was called Pam.*
(Normally: *The person who I spoke to was called Pam.*)

We do not put another pronoun after the preposition.

(NOT Unilever is a company that we know quite a lot about ~~it~~.)

Exercises

Section A

28.1 Read sentences a–d, and then answer the questions below. In speech there would be a pause at the commas.

a) The projector, *which has a new bulb*, is over there.
b) The projector *which has a new bulb* is over there.
c) The train *which leaves at 8 am* is direct.
d) The train, *which leaves at 8 am*, is direct.

1 In which sentence is there more than one projector, and the speaker needs to make it clear which projector they mean? ☐
2 In which sentence is the information about the bulb interesting but not essential? ☐
3 In which sentence is '8 am' essential to the meaning? There are several trains and the listener needs to know which train is being referred to. ☐
4 In which sentence is '8 am' not essential to the meaning? At this point the speaker is only talking about one train and so doesn't need to identify it. ☐

Section B

28.2 Complete the sentences with *who*, *whose*, *which* or *that*. If more than one answer is possible, choose the word that is most common in speech.

1 The customer *whose* company I visited has placed an order.
2 The manual ________ they sent explains everything.
3 The manual, ________ is translated into about twenty languages, can be downloaded as a pdf file from the Internet.
4 The business leader ________ I most admire is Jeff Bezos, the founder of Amazon.
5 The candidates ________ CVs I looked at this morning were all very good.
6 Your colleague, ________ I met this morning, had a different opinion.
7 The contract ________ you showed me before was different to this one.
8 Toyota is a manufacturer ________ reputation is excellent all over the world.

Sections C, D

28.3 Put a bracket around the relative pronoun if you can leave it out. Put a tick (✓) at the end if you must keep the relative pronoun.

1 The book (that) you lent me about influencing skills is really interesting.
2 The company that is our main competitor is Apollo. ✓
3 The name which they chose for the new model is Prima.
4 The meeting room, which wasn't very large, became hot and stuffy.
5 In the end, the sales campaign was the best that we'd ever had.
6 These are the people whose names appear on the database.
7 The people who attended the presentation found it very useful.
8 The supplier who we visited last week had better quality than this one.
9 Richard Branson, who started with almost nothing, is a typical entrepreneur.
10 Newsweek is the English-language magazine that I read most often.

"Miss Dugan, will you send someone in here who can distinguish right from wrong?"

Exercises

Sections C, E

28.4 Rewrite each formal sentence as a sentence from everyday speech. Remember that in spoken English we usually leave out the relative pronoun if it is possible to do so.

1 These are the colleagues with whom I went to the conference.
These are the colleagues *I went to the conference with* .

2 Here is the latest edition of the catalogue from which we order.
Here's the latest edition of the catalogue ______________________________ .

3 I will give you an overview of the area for which I am responsible.
I'll give you an overview of the area ______________________________ .

4 This is the breakthrough for which we've been waiting.
This is the breakthrough ______________________________ .

5 That is the hotel at which I stayed.
That's the hotel ______________________________ .

6 When I call the accountants, Richard is the person with whom I usually deal.
When I call the accountants, Richard is the person ______________________________ .

Section E

28.5 Put the preposition in brackets into the correct position in the sentence.

1 (from) This is the customer we received the complaint *from*.
2 (on) This is the product we're depending to recover our market position.
3 (about) It's a question I've been thinking since our last conversation.
4 (to) The presentation I most enjoyed listening was the one about nanotechnology.
5 (for) We got the contract! It's the news we've been hoping all year.
6 (on) The areas we need to focus in the meeting are highlighted in yellow.
7 (in) The training course I'm interested starts next month.
8 (from) The sales force needs to push the product lines we get the most profits.

Sections A, B, C, D

28.6 Read this newspaper extract about interest rates, which includes four relative clauses a–d. Then decide whether each statement below is True or False by circling T or F below about each relative clause.

Which Way Now For The Dollar?

YESTERDAY the Federal Reserve made the rise in interest rates [a]*which the markets had been expecting*. The Fed Chairman, [b]*who was back at his desk yesterday after a short trip to Japan*, made the announcement after trading on Wall Street had closed. The reaction [c]*which will follow on the currency markets* is difficult to predict, as the dollar has probably already discounted this move, [d]*which was widely expected by traders*.

	a	b	c	d
1 The relative clause identifies a person, event or thing.	T/F	T/F	T/F	T/F
2 The relative pronoun can be replaced with 'that'.	T/F	T/F	T/F	T/F
3 You can leave out the relative pronoun.	T/F	T/F	T/F	T/F

Tasks

Speaking: listen and repeat

1 28 You are going to hear eight phrases. Listen and repeat.

Translate

2 Translate these short texts taken from the Internet into your own language. Remember not to translate word for word, but rather to make it sound natural.

Investors are constantly searching for stocks that are fundamentally sound. But which criteria are a good indicator of the health of a company? Three of the most important performance measures are sales, profit margins, and return on equity. Sales figures are a start, but they are only one piece of the puzzle. Net profit margin – after-tax profits as a percentage of sales – is also needed as a measure of profitability. And finally return on equity, which is profits divided by the total owners' equity, is an indication of how efficiently stockholders' capital is being employed.

BusinessWeek website

Clearly the recession – which has cost the American economy more than five million jobs, including an estimated 1.5 million in the white-collar sector – has placed a new premium on the art of social networking among workers who see their jobs threatened.

Knowledge@Wharton website

Writing: personalized practice

3 Complete the sentences with a defining relative clause.

1 I work for a company *that makes parts for the automobile industry* .
2 I have a boss ________ .
3 I have a colleague called '____' ________ .
4 I am working on a project ________ .
5 Our company operates in a market ________ .
6 In my job I deal with a lot of people ________ .
7 I have a nightmare customer ________ .
8 I have a salary ________ .
9 There are many things about my job ________ .
10 In an ideal world, I would like a job ________ .

4 Complete the sentences with a non-defining relative clause between the commas. See the first example.

11 *Basketball* (name of sport), *which is more popular in the US than Europe* , is my favourite sport.
12 ________ (name of film), ________ , is my favourite film.
13 ________ (name of actor), ________ , is my favourite actor.
14 ________ (name of singer/musician), ________ , is my favourite singer/musician.
15 ________ (name of company), ________ , is the market leader in my field.

Rehearsal for the real world

4 Write a paragraph or two from your company's (or university's) Annual Report using relative clauses. See the example.

Our company, which has been in the market for over twenty years, had an outstanding year. The figures that show this most clearly are turnover and market share – the former rising by 8% year-on-year and the latter by 3%.

If you are working in class, choose some examples to read aloud. Ask and answer questions.

29 Relative clauses 2

A Combining sentences

Look at this example of two short separate sentences:

I'm taking a flight. It goes via Frankfurt.

We can combine the sentences using a relative clause. There are two ways, but the meanings are the same.

a) *I'm taking a flight* ***that goes via Frankfurt****.*
OR
b) *The flight (****that****)* ***I'm taking*** *goes via Frankfurt.*

Note that articles often change when sentences are combined. Example a) above has ***a*** *flight*, like the original short sentence, because the flight is mentioned for the first time and there are several of them. Example b) above has ***the*** *flight*, because there is only one in the speaker's mind. These are the normal, regular uses of articles (unit 34).

Remember that we often leave out the relative pronoun *(that)* in spoken English if it is possible to do so (unit 28C).

When we combine sentences, we do not add another pronoun.

Example a) above:
NOT I'm taking a flight that ~~it~~ goes via Frankfurt.

Example b) above:
NOT The flight that I'm taking ~~it~~ goes via Frankfurt.

B Use of *what*

We can use the relative pronoun *what* to mean *the thing(s) that*.

I didn't understand ***what*** *she said.*
(= the things that she said)

What *we need is a better marketing strategy.*
(= The thing that we need is)

C Use of *where, when* and *why*

We can use the relative adverbs *where, when* and *why* with their normal meanings to identify which thing we are talking about.

This is the site ***where the new shopping centre will be built****.*
I'll email you as soon as I know the time ***when we're meeting****.*
It is difficult to understand the reason ***why they're reducing their dividend payments****.*

In the examples above we can leave out *when* or *why*, or use *that*.

*I'll email you as soon as I know the time (****that****) we're meeting.*
*It is difficult to understand the reason (****that****) they're reducing their dividend payments.*

But we must keep *where*.

NOT ~~This is the site the new shopping centre will be built.~~

Where is not used if there is a preposition at the end of the clause.

The hotel ***I stayed in*** *was quite cheap.* ✓
The hotel ***that I stayed in*** *was quite cheap.* ✓
The hotel ***where I stayed*** *was quite cheap.* ✓
(NOT The hotel ~~where I stayed in~~ was quite cheap)

D Relative clauses with a participle (*-ing, -ed*)

The relative clause can have a continuous verb form (with an *-ing* ending) or a passive verb form (with an *-ed* ending).

The people ***who are making the real decisions*** *are all at Head Office.*
The products ***that were attracting the most interest*** *were the smaller, lighter models.*
Passengers ***who are seated in rows J to P*** *can now board the aircraft.*
Food ***which is sold in supermarkets*** *needs a clearly defined shelf life.*

In these cases we can simplify the sentence by leaving out both the relative pronoun and the verb *be*.

The people ***making the real decisions*** *are all at Head Office.*
The products ***attracting the most interest*** *were the smaller, lighter models.*
Passengers ***seated in rows J to P*** *can now board the aircraft.*
Food ***sold in supermarkets*** *needs a clearly labelled shelf-life.*

The above examples are with defining relative clauses. With a non-defining clause we can only leave out the relative pronoun + *be* where there is a passive verb form.

*The products, (****which are****)* ***manufactured using the latest German-designed machine tools****, offer superb quality at a reasonable price.*
*The company, (****which was****)* ***founded in 1981****, is a leading player in the adventure travel market.*

Exercises

Section A

29.1 Combine each pair of sentences by including the word given in brackets.

1 Last year we introduced a new line. It is aimed at the youth market. (that)
The new line *that we introduced last year* is aimed at the youth market.

2 I'd like you to meet a colleague. He could be a useful contact for you. (who)
I'd like you to meet a colleague ______ .

3 A candidate's CV is on your desk. She deserves an interview. (whose)
The candidate ______ deserves an interview.

4 A visitor is coming next week. She's from our Paris office. (who)
The visitor ______ is from our Paris office.

5 Tom took me to a restaurant. It was called 'Noodle Heaven'. (that)
The restaurant ______ was called 'Noodle Heaven'.

6 I heard a man's presentation. He was a private equity investor. (whose)
The man ______ was a private equity investor.

7 Over there is a site. They're going to build a new factory. (where)
The site ______ is over there.

8 Here is a mobile phone. I was telling you about it. (that)
Here is ______ .

Section A

29.2 If the sentence is correct, put a tick (✓) at the end. If the sentence has a word which should not be there, cross it out.

1 The woman who I asked didn't know the way. ✓
2 The firm whose ~~their~~ stand was at the back of the hall had very few visitors.
3 That was the longest meeting I've ever been in.
4 The train which it goes to Brussels leaves from here.
5 The products which sell best they are those with nice packaging.
6 This model, which it was launched last year, is selling very well.
7 Everyone that I spoke to advised me to try again.
8 The company where I used to work it was called Interlink.

Sections C, D, unit 28

29.3 Underline the correct words. This exercise includes some revision of unit 28.

1 Everyone *who/which* was at the meeting will receive a copy of the minutes.
2 She's from the company *which/whose* products we distribute.
3 Notice. To *whom/who* it may concern: Please do not leave dirty coffee cups here.
4 There were some interesting ideas at the meeting *that/what* I went to.
5 *That/What* I like best about my job is the contact with people.
6 Has anybody seen the folder *what/that* I left on this desk?
7 The room *where/that* I work has very little natural light.
8 The room *where/that* I work in has very little natural light.

Exercises

Sections B, C **29.4 Complete the sentences with *what, which* or *who*, or tick (✓) the space if the sentence is already correct.**

1 There's a lot of noise from the builders ✓ working next door.
2 Mike doesn't really know *what* he wants in his career.
3 I was talking to a man ______ going to the same conference as us.
4 I was talking to a man ______ is going to the same conference as us.
5 I asked her ______ she was thinking.
6 This is a new drug ______ was developed at our Cambridge laboratories.
7 This is a new drug ______ developed at our Cambridge laboratories.
8 This drug, ______ was developed at our Swiss laboratories, is a breakthrough.
9 This drug, ______ developed at our Swiss laboratories, is a breakthrough.
10 ______ we need now is better brand recognition.
11 The 'assets' include everything ______ owned by the company.
12 I didn't really understand ______ he was talking about.

Section A **29.5 Complete the article by writing relative clauses based on the notes below. Begin each time with either *who* or *which*.**

The Battle for GUCCI

In 1999 there was a major battle in the luxury goods sector [1] *which has become a standard case study in business schools all over the world*. Bernard Arnault's LVMH fought a battle to take over Gucci, [2] ______________________. Arnault had been acquiring shares in arch-rival Gucci, and he said that he should be allowed to name a director to its board. This would give him access to inside information regarding stores, publicity and designers. De Sole decided to fight: this was going to be the battle [3] ______________________. He used the two classic tactics to fight a hostile takeover: a poison pill and a white knight. The poison pill was to offer stock options to his employees. These gave voting rights to the staff, who were all against the takeover. The white knight [4] ______________________ arrived in the form of Francois Pinault, [5] ______________________. Pinault wanted a chance to build a global group, and Gucci provided that opportunity. He bought the shares in Gucci [6] ______________________, paying a premium price. This gave him a majority stake and representatives on a new strategic committee. However, he had previously agreed to leave control of the company with De Sole and the senior Gucci team. The battle was over – De Sole had won, but Arnault pocketed a nice profit on his shares.

1 There was a battle in the luxury goods sector. It has become a standard case study in business schools across the world.
2 LVMH fought with Gucci. Gucci was run by Domenico De Sole.
3 This was going to be a battle. It would decide the future of the industry.
4 A white knight arrived. Gucci had been looking for one.
5 Pinault was the white knight. He was the head of a retail group called PPR.
6 Pinault bought shares in Gucci. LVMH owned them.

Tasks

Speaking: listen and repeat

1 29 **You are going to hear eight phrases. Listen and repeat.**

Translate

2 Translate these short texts taken from the Internet into your own language. Remember not to translate word for word, but rather to make it sound natural.

What is the reason why customers are so indecisive? It's a factor called the Whole Story. We need to know anything and everything that helps us decide in favour of something, not just price or terms or warranties. Telling the Whole Story eliminates a big hurdle called risk. To use a metaphor, when you add the spices to your marketing curry, your customer will be captivated by the aroma.

BNET website

Chrysler, now owned by Fiat in a swift exit from bankruptcy, is ready to become a viable, competitive company. The first redesigned vehicle will be a new Jeep Grand Cherokee that will be a bit smaller and more fuel efficient than its predecessor. Fiat's technology will be one of the biggest benefits it will bring to Chrysler, which is known for large vehicles.

About website

Writing: personalized practice

3 Complete the sentences with your own ideas.

1 The job I'm doing is *essential for the smooth running of the company* .
2 I'm doing a job ______ .
3 The colleague I'm sharing an office with is ______ .
4 I'm sharing an office with ______ .
5 What we need in our department is ______ .
6 This is the place ______ .
7 I still don't know the exact date ______ .
8 I can't understand the reason ______ .
9 The people making the real decisions ______ .
10 The products attracting most interest ______ .

Rehearsal for the real world

4 Complete the sentences with *where*, *when*, *why* or *whose* (in the first space) and your own ideas in the second, longer space.

1 Someone ______ opinions I respect is ______ .
2 One place ______ I'll never return is ______ .
3 One of the reasons ______ I like my city/town is ______ .
4 The time ______ I think I was at my happiest was ______ .

If you are working in class, choose some sentences to read aloud. Ask and answer questions.

30 Countable and uncountable nouns

A Countable nouns

A countable noun has a singular and a plural form.

*The new model **is** a big improvement.*
*The new model**s are** a big improvement.*

We can use numbers: *one bank, four banks, one person, ten people.*

B Uncountable nouns

An uncountable noun only has one form, and the verb is always singular.

*The new **equipment is** a big improvement.*
(NOT ~~The new equipments are~~)

We cannot use numbers.

Here are some examples:

substances, materials
water, rice, air, oil, money, steel, food, fire

abstract ideas
life, fun, freedom, progress, health, time, trouble, supply, demand, experience, power, influence, ownership, productivity

activities
work, travel, sleep, football, help, music, research, training, production

human qualities/feelings
honesty, patience, hope, respect, courage, love

Be careful! The following nouns are uncountable in English:

accommodation, advice, baggage, behaviour, cash, equipment, expenditure, furniture, health, homework, information, knowledge, luggage, machinery, money, permission, scenery, traffic, travel, wealth, work

A few uncountable nouns end in -s: *athletics, diabetes, economics, gymnastics, news, politics.*

Uncountable nouns cannot be counted directly. However, we can count them using phrases like: *a piece of, a bit of, an item of, a glass of, a bottle of, a kilo of,* etc.

*two **pieces of** information*   *two **items of** news*

C Singular or plural verb?

Some nouns can be followed by either a singular or a plural verb.

*The company **is**/**are** doing very well.*

Examples are:

army, audience, board, committee, company, data, family, government, group, management, media, press, public, staff, team, union

Some nouns only have one form and only take a plural verb. Examples are:

clothes, contents, earnings, expenses, feelings, goods, headquarters, means (of transport), police, premises, refreshments, remains, surroundings, trousers

D *a / an, a lot of, many / much, few / little*

Study the table and the examples to see how different words are used before countable and uncountable nouns.

a/an – singular countable nouns only
*We have **a** new **customer**.*

a lot of/lots of – plural nouns and uncountable nouns
*They have **a lot of** new **customers**.*
*I have **lots of** free **time**.*

many/few/a few – plural nouns only
*They don't have **many** new **customers**.*
***A few customers** replied to our online questionnaire.* (positive: I'm pleased)
***Few/Not many customers** replied to our online questionnaire.* (negative: I'm disappointed)

much/little/a little – uncountable nouns only
*I don't have **much** free **time**.*
***A little time** is still left.* (positive: luckily)
***Little/Not much time** is left.* (negative: unfortunately)

(NOT '~~an~~ information' – instead say 'some information')
(NOT ~~much~~/~~little~~/~~a little~~ customers/people, etc.)
(NOT ~~many~~/~~few~~/~~a few~~ time/information, etc.)

Note that the negative uses of *few* and *little* are rather formal. It is more common to say *not many/not much.*

E Specific and general meanings

Some nouns can be either countable (with a specific meaning) or uncountable (with a general meaning).

*The machine is making **a** strange **noise**.*
***Noise** inside factories can be a problem.*
*This is **a** new **business**.*
***Business** is going well at the moment.*
*There aren't **many spaces** in the car park.*
*There isn't **much space** in my office.*

a coffee (a cup of coffee)   *coffee* (the substance)
a glass (for drinking)   *glass* (the material)
a paper (at a conference)   *paper* (the material)

Exercises

Sections A, B, C, D

30.1 Underline the correct words.

1 *Is/Are* there *many/much* traffic in Jeddah?
2 *Is/Are* there *many/much* traffic problems in Jeddah?
3 *How much/How many* information have we got about this company?
4 He gave me *an advice/some advice* which *was/were* really useful.
5 We bought some new *equipment/equipments* last month.
6 We bought some new *machine/machines* last month.
7 This is *an equipment/a piece of equipment* that controls the heating process.
8 They're a start-up company and they don't have *much/many* sales yet.
9 We don't have *much/many* time before we get serious cashflow problems.
10 We're making *a little/a few* progress, but not *many/much*.
11 We're making *a little/a few* sales, but not *many/much*.
12 We have *a lot of demand/many demands* for our services.

Sections A, D

30.2 Complete the sentences with *a*, *an*, *some*, *much* or *many*.

1 That's a good idea.
2 Well, that's ______ progress, I suppose.
3 We do some business in Turkey, but not ______ .
4 We have a few customers in Turkey, but not ______ .
5 I'd like to make ______ inquiry about train times to Paris.
6 Can I have ______ information about trains to Paris?
7 I'll see you in an hour. I don't have ______ more emails to write.
8 I'll see you in an hour. I don't have ______ more work to do.
9 Do you have ______ trouble with the quality of your raw materials?
10 Do you have ______ difficulties with the quality of your raw materials?
11 I'm not going to claim ______ expenses for my trip, just a few.
12 We didn't study ______ macroeconomics at university, just a little.

Section E

30.3 Look at the underlined noun in each sentence. Write S if it has a specific, countable meaning, or G if it has a general, uncountable meaning.

1 a) Do you see this material? This is unbreakable glass. ☐
b) What a beautiful wine glass! Where did you get it? ☐
2 a) In this job, experience is more important than qualifications. ☐
b) This is going to be an experience I'll remember for a long time. ☐
3 a) Claire runs a business designing websites. ☐
b) It's not good for business when interest rates are too high. ☐
4 a) You should meet Mark – he's had a very interesting life. ☐
b) Life is complicated sometimes. ☐

"We have lots of information technology. We just don't have any information."

Exercises

Section B

30.4 Match each phrase 1–12 with the best continuation a–l.

1 A cup of	j	5 A pint of		9 A barrel of	
2 A glass of		6 A litre of		10 A packet of	
3 A bottle of		7 A sheet of		11 A tin of	
4 A kilo of		8 A tonne of		12 A slice of	

a) weight is quite easy to lose if you go on a diet.
b) wine is acceptable at a business lunch, but no more.
c) beer is the traditional drink in an English pub.
d) petrol will take a small car about 15 to 20 kilometres.
e) dried fruit is good to take on a walk in the countryside.
f) concrete is the same as 1000 kilograms of concrete.
g) whisky costs less at the airport.
h) wholemeal bread goes well with tomato soup.
i) oil cost as little as US$35 in 2009.
j) coffee is a good way to start the day.
k) paper can sometimes get stuck in the photocopier.
l) paint should be stored with the lid put on tightly.

Note that phrases 1–12 give a way to count the uncountable nouns in a–l.

Sections A, B, C, D

30.5 Underline the correct words in this dialogue.

ANGELA: Jack, there [1]*is/are* [2]*an/some* important work that we need to do.

JACK: Really?

ANGELA: Yes. [3]*Some piece of/A piece of* empty land has come onto the market on the other side of town. And, as you know, we don't have [4]*many/much* space at our present site.

JACK: That's true.

ANGELA: Well, we think it's an ideal opportunity to expand. We're thinking about building completely new offices over there. We'd like you to do [5]*a/some* research on the whole thing and then write [6]*a/some* report on whether to go ahead or not. Are you interested?

JACK: Well, I don't have [7]*many/much* [8]*experience/experiences* of this kind of thing. And I have very [9]*little/few* spare time at the moment – I'm doing [10]*a/some* training and I have to read a lot of background material for it.

ANGELA: I know you're busy, but you're one of the few people we have with some [11]*knowledge/knowledges* of costing and evaluating large projects. We need to make [12]*a progress/progress* on this as quickly as possible.

JACK: OK, but there [13]*is/are* [14]*many/a lot of* [15]*information/informations* to collect. Will I get any help?

ANGELA: There are some people who we can reassign from other projects to help you for [16]*a little/a few* hours each week. It's not [17]*much/many* help, but it's something. Oh, I forgot to say – we'd also pay you more to take account of the extra [18]*work/works*.

JACK: Really? Well, yes, it does sound like an interesting challenge. I'll do it.

Tasks

Speaking: listen and repeat

1 30 **You are going to hear eight phrases. Listen and repeat.**

Translate

2 Translate these short texts taken from the Internet into your own language. Remember not to translate word for word, but rather to make it sound natural.

Toulouse is the home of French aerospace research and has been considered a center of innovation for many years. Recently, thanks to explosive growth in the biotech and computer industries, it has become one of Europe's most fashionable hubs for young tech workers.

The Industry Standard website

Broadcasters with online content are increasingly looking for ways to boost falling revenues, and many have begun exploring the introduction of payment models. Any methods to increase revenue streams will be welcomed by the industry, because the ad-funded model can only stretch so far.

newmediaage website

Writing: personalized practice

3 Complete the sentences with *a/an* or *some* (in the first space) and your own ideas in the second, longer space.

1 I have *a* bag *that hasn't come round on the belt yet* .
2 I have *some* luggage *in the room next to the reception desk* .
3 I've ordered ______ furniture ______ .
4 I've ordered ______ office chair ______ .
5 There's ______ job that needs doing in my ______ .
6 There's ______ work that needs doing in my ______ .
7 In the factory there's ______ machinery which ______ .
8 In the factory there's ______ machine which ______ .
9 I'm having ______ trouble with ______ .
10 I'm having ______ problem with ______ .
11 I discovered ______ very interesting fact ______ .
12 I discovered ______ very interesting information ______ .
13 Can I give you ______ suggestion about ______ ?
14 Can I give you ______ advice about ______ ?
15 I need ______ time to decide ______ .
16 I need ______ week to decide ______ .

Rehearsal for the real world

4 You are an expert on the meaning of life. Write something philosophical on the following topics.

1 Music *is the food of love* .
2 Money ______ .
3 Freedom ______ .
4 Courage ______ .
5 Life ______ .
6 Travel ______ .
7 Sleep ______ .
8 Time ______ .
9 Football ______ .
10 Business ______ .

If you are working in class, choose some sentences to read aloud. Discuss them.

31 Pronouns

A Indefinite pronouns: *anything*, etc.

The words in the list below are called indefinite pronouns.

People:	*someone / somebody, anyone / anybody, everyone / everybody, no one / nobody*
Things:	*something, anything, everything, nothing*
Places:	*somewhere, anywhere, everywhere, nowhere*
Time:	*sometime, anytime*

There is no difference between the *-one* forms and the *-body* forms with people.

Indefinite pronouns are followed by a singular verb, but we refer back to them in a sentence with *they / them / their*.

***Someone is** waiting for you in reception. I told **them** you wouldn't be long.*

B *some- / any-*

AFFIRMATIVE SENTENCES
Some- is used in affirmative sentences.

*There's **something** you should know.*

Any- is also used, particularly when we want to show that there is no limit to the possibilities.

*You can fly **anywhere** you want from here.*

Compare *some-* and *any-*:

*I can bring it to you **sometime** tomorrow.*
(I don't know when yet, but I'll tell you)
*I can bring it to you **anytime** tomorrow.*
(there's no limit – you decide)

Any- is common in sentences with *if*.

*If there's **anything** you want to know, just ask.*

QUESTIONS
Any- is used in questions.

*Does **anyone** understand this new software?*

Some- is used with offers and requests.

*Can I give you a lift **somewhere / anywhere**?*

Compare *some-* and *any-*. *Any-* emphasizes that there is no limit to the possibilities.

*Is there **something** I can do to help?*
(a normal offer)
*Is there **anything** I can do to help?*
(I'll do whatever I can)

NEGATIVE SENTENCES
Any- is used in negatives. *Not … any-* means the same as *no-*.

*There is**n't anybody** here with that name.*
*= There is **nobody** here with that name.*

C *every- / no-*

Everyone (one word) means all the people in a group.

*I'd like to say a big 'thank you' to **everyone**.*

Every one (two words) means 'each single one' and gives emphasis. In pronunciation, both words have equal stress.

***Every one** of our clients is important, even the smallest companies.*

Be careful with *no-*, because double negatives are not used.

There is nothing we can do. ✓
There isn't anything we can do. ✓
(But NOT ~~There isn't nothing we can do~~.)

D Reflexive pronouns

The reflexive pronouns are: *myself, yourself, himself, herself, itself, ourselves, yourselves, themselves*. Note that there is a plural 'you' form.

We use a reflexive pronoun if the object of the verb is the same as the subject. Compare:

***I**'m enjoying **the trip**.*
***I**'m enjoying **myself**.*

Some verbs may be reflexive in your language, but are usually not in English. Examples include: *change (clothes), complain, decide, dress, feel, hurry, meet, relax, remember, rest, sit down, stand up, wake up, wash, wonder, worry.*

Note that actions that we do to ourselves do not have a reflexive pronoun in English.

*When I got back to the hotel, I **washed** and **changed** before going out to the restaurant.*

We can use a reflexive pronoun for emphasis. In pronunciation, we stress *self* or *selves*.

*I **myself** haven't seen the new design, but I believe it's very good.*

If the meaning is 'without help' or 'alone', we can use *by* + reflexive pronoun.

*Are you doing all the work (**by**) **yourselves?***
(without help)

*I travelled to the conference **by myself**.*
(alone / on my own)

Be careful with *themselves*.

*Steve and Melinda emailed **themselves**.*
(a strange meaning: Steve sent an email to himself, and Melinda sent an email to herself)

In this case the correct version is probably:

*Steve and Melinda emailed **each other / one another**.*

Exercises

Sections A, B, C **31.1 Complete the sentences with the words in the box.**

anyone	anything	anything	everyone	everything
no one	nothing	someone	~~something~~	something

1 It's just not right – *something* is worrying me about this.
2 The office is empty. There's ______ here except me.
3 I'm sorry, I don't think there's ______ I can do to help you.
4 We need someone to go to Head Office tomorrow. Is ______ free?
5 We handle ______ for you, from design to delivery.
6 There's ______ to see you. Shall I ask them to wait?
7 I see that ______ has a copy of the agenda, so let's begin.
8 Is there ______ else we need to discuss?
9 I think there's ______ wrong with the printer. It's not working.
10 Sorry, I've decided, and ______ you could say would make me change my mind.

Sections A, B, C **31.2 Underline the correct or most likely words.**

1 There's *anything/nothing* in the mail for you this morning.
2 There isn't *anything/nothing* in the mail for you this morning.
3 We can't blame *anyone/no one* but ourselves for this mess.
4 *Anyone/Someone* called you earlier, but I don't know who.
5 Isn't there *anywhere/nowhere* to go that's open at this time of night?
6 Can I ask you *anything/something*?
7 There's *anyone/someone* on the phone to speak to you.
8 You can do *anything/something* you want; it won't make any difference.
9 Sorry, I don't know *anything/nothing* about it.

Section D **31.3 Complete the sentences with a word from the box in an appropriate form + a reflexive pronoun.**

~~ask~~	blame	enjoy	hurt	introduce	make	prepare	teach

1 I keep *asking* *myself* what I would do in his situation.
2 It wasn't your fault. Don't ______ ______ !
3 Last year James ______ ______ Spanish using an online course.
4 Be careful! It's very heavy! Don't ______ ______ !
5 It was a great holiday. We really ______ ______ .
6 Mary, ______ ______ for a shock. I'm going to resign.
7 Let me ______ ______ . My name is Susan Conway.
8 Sara and Nick! What wonderful flowers! And little Anna – look how you've grown! Great to see you all. Come in and ______ ______ at home.

Exercises

Sections A, B, C, D

31.4 Circle the correct or most likely words.

1 Pizza Express! We deliver your pizza *sometime, somewhere / anytime, anywhere*.
2 I *felt myself/felt* quite nervous at the start of the presentation, but after a few minutes I *relaxed myself/relaxed*.
3 The figures in this spreadsheet don't correspond to the ones on the invoices. We're going to have to check *everyone/every one*.
4 Everyone *has/have* to meet in the lobby at nine o'clock to collect *his/their* conference registration forms.
5 Rome isn't *somewhere/anywhere* near Milan.
6 Rome isn't *somewhere/anywhere* I'd like to go in August. It's too hot.
7 Your two colleagues introduced *themselves/each other* to me yesterday. First I met Peter, then after lunch I met Susan.
8 I met Peter and Susan and they introduced *themselves/each other* to me. Peter told me a little about what Susan does, and Susan told me about Peter.

Sections B, C

31.5 Complete the dialogue with the words in the box.

anyone	anything	anywhere	everyone	everything
~~everywhere~~	someone	something	somewhere	

DAVID: I can't find my BlackBerry. I've looked 1 *everywhere* . I must have put it down 2 ________, but I just can't remember where. Oh, how annoying! It could be 3 ________ .
RITA: Perhaps 4 ________ has picked it up by mistake? 5 ________ in the company has the same type of phone. 6 ________ could have picked it up.
DAVID: This is driving me crazy.
RITA: Don't worry. There must be 7 ________ we can do to find it.
DAVID: But what? I've tried 8 ________ . I've looked. I've asked people. I can't think of 9 ________ else I can do.

Section D

31.6 Vicky and her husband Charles are staying in a hotel. Complete what Vicky says by using the verbs in brackets with or without a reflexive pronoun.

"Charles, come on, try to 1 *enjoy yourself* (enjoy). 2 *Remember* (remember) you're on holiday. Look, why don't you 3 ________ (help) to another drink, go on. Oh, look – there's Daniel Westlake over there. What on earth is he doing in Marrakech? Have you two 4 ________ (met) before? You know you'd have a lot in common with Daniel. Why don't you go over there and 5 ________ (introduce) to him? While you do that I'll go back to the room and 6 ________ (change) in time for dinner. I don't know. Sometimes I 7 ________ (ask) whether you can ever 8 ________ (relax) when you're away from the office."

Tasks

Speaking: listen and repeat

1 31 **You are going to hear eight phrases. Listen and repeat.**

Translate

2 Translate these short texts taken from the Internet into your own language. Remember not to translate word for word, but rather to make it sound natural.

Airlines such as British Airways lease aircraft complete with crew, have their accounts and computer operations organised by somebody else, and sub-contract booking to online agents. There is practically nothing that cannot be outsourced. These days everything is being shifted to an outside contractor except the core activities.

Telegraph website

Derivatives are contractual arrangements between two parties – at least one of which is likely to be a giant financial institution – that transfer risk. Warren Buffett tagged derivatives with the name that follows them everywhere, 'financial weapons of mass destruction.'

Fortune website

Writing: personalized practice

3 Answer the following questions using the words in brackets and your own ideas.

1 Do we need to go to the supermarket?
(anything) *Yes, we do – we don't have anything in the fridge.*
2 Have they moved their head office?
(somewhere) ______
3 What do you think about UFOs and flying saucers?
(nobody) ______
4 Are you going to go to London for the Christmas sales?
(everything) ______
5 Are these seats reserved?
(anywhere) ______
6 I can see you're having problems. Can I help?
(nothing) ______
7 Is the phone call for me?
(someone) ______
8 Can I invite my partner to the office party?
(anyone) ______

Rehearsal for the real world

4 Look again at exercise 31.3. Now write your own sentences using the word in brackets in an appropriate form + a reflexive pronoun.

1 (ask) *Ask yourself this simple question: why are we losing so many customers?*
2 (blame) ______
3 (enjoy) ______
4 (hurt) ______
5 (introduce) ______
6 (make) ______
7 (prepare) ______
8 (teach) ______

If you are working in class, choose some sentences to read aloud. Ask and answer questions.

32 Determiners

A Determiners

A determiner is a word used in front of a noun to show which thing you mean, or to show the quantity of something. Determiners include: *a/the, my/your, this/that, all/most, some/any, no/none, much/many, a little/a few, each/every, both/either/neither.*

Some determiners are covered in units 30, 34 and 35.

Note that we do not use a determiner if we are talking generally (units 30E and 35E).

***These/Many/Both** mobile devices have GPS.*
(particular mobile devices)
***Mobile devices** are becoming more powerful.*
(mobile devices in general)

B *all / many / much / a few / a little,* etc.

Note the structures for plural nouns:

All/most/many/some/a few ***workers***
All/most/many/some/a few ***of the workers***
All/most/many/some/a few ***of our workers***
All ***the workers*** (But NOT ~~Most the workers,~~ etc.)

With uncountable nouns we use *much* in place of *many* and *a little* in place of *a few*. See unit 30D.

With singular nouns we do not use the words above, except for a few special expressions: *all day, all night.*

C *all* meaning 'everything' or 'the only thing'

We can use *all* + subject + verb to mean 'everything' or 'the only thing'.

*I've told you **all** I know.* (all = everything)
***All** we need is a signature.* (all = the only thing)

All is rarely used as a single-word subject or object. Instead we use *everything.*

***Everything is/All the preparations are** going well.*
(NOT ~~All is~~ going well.)

*I want to hear **everything/all your news**.*
(NOT I want to ~~hear all~~.)

A few fixed expressions do have *all* on its own.

That's all!
All's well that ends well.

D *no, none*

We can use *no* with all types of noun.

***No employee** has more than 20 days holiday.*
***No** new **ideas** were put forward at the meeting.*
*There was **no** useful **information** in the report.*

We do not use *no* if there is a second negative in the sentence. In this case we use *any*.

*Our food does**n't** contain **any** additives.*
(NOT ~~doesn't contain no additives~~)

We do not use *no of*. Instead, we use *none of* or *none* on its own as a pronoun.

***None of** the machines are faulty.*
***None** are faulty.*

To emphasize the idea of *none* we can use *None at all, Not one* or *Not a*.

A: *How many people came to the talk?*
B: ***None at all**!/**Not one**!/**Not a** single person!*

E *each, every*

The meaning of *each* and *every* is similar, and often either word is possible. They are both followed by a singular noun.

We use *each* when we think of the members of a group as individuals, one by one. It is more usual with smaller groups and can mean only two.

*Make sure that **each parcel** has a label.*

We use *every* when we think of all the members together, and it is usual with a larger number.

*Sales have increased **every year** for the last five years.*
*I believe **every word** he says.*

We can use *each of*, but we cannot use *every of*.

***Each of the parcels** needs a label.*

Each can also be used after the subject or at the end of a sentence.

***The parcels each** need a label.*
*The parcels need a label **each**.*

F *both, either, neither*

We use *both, either* and *neither* to refer to two things.

Both means 'the one and the other'. Note the structures:

***Both emails/both the emails/both of the emails** are important.*
*The emails are **both** important.*
*I've read them **both**.*

Either means 'the one or the other'. *Neither* means 'not the one or the other'.

*Monday or Tuesday? Yes, **either day/either of the days** is fine.*
*Monday or Tuesday? I'm sorry, but **neither day/neither of the days** is convenient.*

We say *either ... or* and *neither ... nor.*

*I can meet you **either** Monday **or** Tuesday.*
(NOT ~~or~~ Monday or Tuesday)

Exercises

Sections A, B

32.1 Put the phrases in the box into order from 0% (#1) to 100% (#6). Two have been done for you.

~~none of them~~	most of them	a few of them
many of them	some of them	~~all of them~~

1 *none of them* ______
2 ______
3 ______
4 ______
5 ______
6 *all of them* ______

Sections B, C, D, E, F

32.2 <u>Underline</u> the correct words.

1 There were *none/no* messages on my voicemail.
2 *Not one/Not any* question has been answered.
3 *Some of/Some* restaurants here have service included in the price.
4 Check your webcams. I can't see *either/neither* of you on my screen.
5 *Each our clients/Our clients each* have a separate file on the database.
6 I can't come at the weekend. I'm busy *both days/every day*.
7 *All of/Every of* the files are corrupted by the virus.
8 I can't see *no/any* solution to the problem.
9 The flight and hotel are booked. *All/Everything* is organized.
10 We gave the sales reps *each a mobile phone/a mobile phone each*.
11 *Every option has been/Every options have been* explored.
12 OK, I think that covers *all/everything*. Shall we move on?

Sections B, C, D, E, F

32.3 Complete the sentences with a word or phrase from the box.

all (x2)	any	no	~~not one~~	none	
each (x2)	every (x2)	both	either (x2)	neither	

1 We sent letters to sixty customers, but *not one* replied!
2 I can't go. There are only two flights, and there are ______ seats left on ______ of them.
3 I can't go. There are only two flights, and ______ of them has any seats left.
4 ______ I want is a bit of peace and quiet to finish writing this report.
5 I called ______ store in the Yellow Pages and they were ______ out of stock.
6 We have three models, and ______ one has its own special features.
7 I was nervous at the start of my talk, but after that I enjoyed ______ minute.
8 I got three letters, but there were ______ for you, I'm afraid.
9 I got three letters, but there weren't ______ for you, I'm afraid.
10 The Trade Fair is important. We need ______ Sue and Mike on the stand.
11 Both roads lead to the city centre. You can take ______ one.
12 We forecast cashflow of at least €50m in ______ of the next three years.

"We are neither hunters nor gatherers. We are accountants."

Exercises

Sections B, C, D, E, F

32.4 Rewrite each sentence so it has a similar meaning and contains the word in brackets.

1 This idea won't work, and the other one also won't work. (neither)
Neither idea will work.

2 We only have a week left. (all)
______ a week.

3 All the participants will be sent an agenda. (every)
______ will be sent an agenda.

4 At the end of my talk nobody at all asked a question. (single person)
At the end of my talk ______ asked a question.

5 Not all the audience understood her talk. (some)
______ understand her talk.

6 Not one of my colleagues speaks German. (none)
______ German.

7 All we want is clarity in government policy. (The only)
______ clarity in government policy.

8 No documents were inside this package. (any)
There ______ inside this package.

9 The hotels were both unsuitable. (neither)
______ suitable.

10 I'm sorry, we have absolutely none. (all)
I'm sorry, we have none ______ .

Sections B, C, D, E, F

32.5 Complete this article by choosing the correct alternative A, B or C below.

The Cola Wars

One of the most famous battles in the business world is that between Coke and Pepsi. [1]*B* a core product that is little more than sugary, brown, fizzy water – with Pepsi perhaps being a little sweeter. Surprisingly, [2]____ has diversified very much: Coke still gets [3]____ from cola and drinks, although Pepsi does have a snack food business as well. [4]____ for being very big spenders on advertising – [5]____ on the planet must surely be familiar with Coke and Pepsi through TV, sponsorship, billboards and drinks machines. They [6]____ have a slightly different marketing strategy. Pepsi decided long ago to focus on the youth market, leaving Coke to be the drink of everyone. For this reason Coke is considered to be a more valuable brand: it is more deeply rooted in the collective psyche and is closer to the 'essence' of cola. However, there isn't [7]____ to stop Pepsi from challenging strongly in particular local markets.

	A	B	C
1	A Both them have	B Both of them have	C Both of them has
2	A either of them	B neither of the company	C neither company
3	A all its revenue	B most its revenue	C much its revenue
4	A Each are famous	B Every one is famous	C Both are famous
5	A all person	B all peoples	C every person
6	A each	B each one	C both of them
7	A nothing	B something	C anything

Tasks

Speaking: listen and repeat

1 32 **You are going to hear eight phrases. Listen and repeat.**

Translate

2 Translate these short texts taken from the Internet into your own language. Remember not to translate word for word, but rather to make it sound natural.

Nutritionists talk about proteins, carbohydrates, fats, and fibre. Instead of having a few helpings from each group every day, they recommend having something from each of the four groups every time you sit down to eat. Research suggests that meals with more protein and fats are associated with better-sustained attention, focus, and concentration, while meals that have a higher carbohydrate content seem to be more calming and have fairly consistent positive effects with memory.

Money Watch website

Until recently it wasn't unusual for manufacturers to keep a mere day or two of stock on hand. After all, many of their lead times were measured in hours. Most of their transportation providers were known quantities. And the routes and infrastructure they used were highly familiar and time-tested. Today, that kind of lean inventory is a luxury most companies can't afford, because deliveries from global sources depend upon a far wider variety of factors, which a manufacturer can't always predict or control.

World Trade Magazine website

Writing: personalized practice

3 Complete the sentences with your own ideas.

1 Most of our employees *say that they agree in principle with moving to a system of performance-related pay* .
However, not one of them *has made any concrete suggestions for how individual productivity could be measured* .

2 None of our competitors ______ .
However, a few of them ______ .

3 The majority of our customers ______ .
However, not one single customer ______ – none at all!

4 Both my parents ______ .
However, neither of them ______ .

5 Every product we sell has ______ .
And each time we sell a product we make sure ______ .

6 All I need now is ______ .

Rehearsal for the real world

4 Look again at exercise 32.5. Now write a short text where you compare two similar companies working in the same market.

If you are working in class, read some texts aloud and discuss them.

33 Possessives and compound nouns

A Possessive adjectives and pronouns: *my / mine*, etc.

My / your / her / his / its / our / their are adjectives and come before a noun.

*This was **your** suggestion.*

Mine / yours / hers / his / ours / theirs are pronouns, and we use them on their own.

*This suggestion was **yours**.*

There is no 'its' form as a pronoun.

We can add *own* to a possessive adjective for emphasis.

***My own** view is that the project is too ambitious.*

There is no apostrophe (*'s*) in possessive adjectives or pronouns.

We worked for one year on its design.
(NOT We worked for one year on ~~it's~~ design.)

B *'s* (apostrophe *s*)

We use *'s* to show that something belongs to a person or organization. Many other languages use 'of' in these cases. We add *'s* even if the name ends in *s*.

*The CEO**'s** office   Charles**'s** email address*

With plural nouns we add the apostrophe only.

*The auditor**s'** investigations are continuing.*

We can use the *'s* form without a following noun if the meaning is clear.

*The project was a team effort, but the original idea was **Helen's**.*
(= Helen's idea)

A special use of *'s* is to refer to someone's home or a workplace.

*I'll be at **Jack's** this evening.*
(Jack's house)
*I must go to the **acountant's**.*
(the accountant's office)

If there is no possession, we do not use an apostrophe.

Special offer on Epson printers!
(NOT Epson ~~printer's~~)

Note that apostrophes can also be a short form of *is* or *has*.

***It's** a lovely day.* (= It is)
***It's** been a pleasure meeting you.* (= It has)

C using *of*

We use *of* to show that one thing belongs to another thing.

*The end **of the street**.*
(NOT ~~the street's end~~)
*The time **of the meeting**.*
(NOT ~~the meeting's time~~)

Here are some common phrases with *of*, and examples of nouns that follow:

choice of (flights)   *piece of (advice)*
error of (judgment)   *range of (colours)*
flood of (complaints)   *strength of (the euro)*
lack of (funds)   *stroke of (luck)*
level of (commitment)   *success of (the project)*
method of (payment)   *time of (arrival)*
number of (factors)   *waste of (time)*

We can use *a ... of* + possessive form to show a connection between people.

*She's **a** colleague **of mine**.*
(= She's my colleague.)

We can use *of* or apostrophe for places and organizations.

*the historic centre **of Prague***
OR ***Prague's** historic centre*
*the future **of the company***
OR *the **company's** future*

D Compound nouns

A compound noun is two nouns together. Compound nouns are common in English, especially in business language:

sales report   ***management decision***
research results   ***manufacturing productivity***
exchange rate   ***insurance document***
stock market   ***customer service***

When we use two nouns together, the first noun is like an adjective and describes the second noun.

The first noun is usually singular.

*reductions in **costs** ➜ **cost** reductions*
*the law relating to **companies** ➜ **company** law*

We can use more than two nouns. To understand the meaning, start at the end.

*an **executive search company***
(a company that searches for executives)
*a **stock market launch***
(a launch in the market for stocks)

In certain fixed phrases we cannot use a compound noun. We have to use *of*.

*lack **of** confidence*   *freedom **of** choice*
*the price **of** success*   *the cost **of** progress*

Sometimes we can use *of* or a compound noun.

time of arrival   *arrival time*
rate of inflation   *inflation rate*

Over time there is a tendency for some compound nouns to be written as one word.

database   *timescale*   *businessman*
network   *workshop*   *motorcycle*

Exercises

Section A

33.1 Underline the correct words.

1 *My/mine* office is at the end of the corridor.
2 It's not really *her/hers* decision.
3 The committee had *its/it's* final meeting yesterday.
4 Excuse me, is this *your/yours* seat?
5 Excuse me, is this seat *your/yours*?
6 We do all *ourselves/our own* design and printing.
7 We do all the design and printing *ourselves/our own*.
8 Is this pen *yours/your's* or mine?

Section C

33.2 Complete the sentences with the phrases in the box.

error of	flood of	lack of	level of	method of
piece of	range of	stroke of	success of	~~waste of~~

1 I went there, but they were closed. It was a complete *waste of* time.
2 The product launch is a disaster. There's a complete ________ interest.
3 You shouldn't have told them about that. It was an ________ judgment.
4 Our hotel offers a wide ________ facilities for the business traveler.
5 We have a relatively low ________ unemployment in our country.
6 I heard a very interesting ________ information the other day.
7 We arrived just at the right time. What a ________ luck!
8 The ad has been very successful. There's a ________ inquiries.
9 The results must be correct. We use a very reliable ________ analysis.
10 I'd like to congratulate everyone on the ________ the project.

Section D

33.3 Make two compound nouns from the nouns in each group.

1 profits course training company *company profits* *training course*
2 staff forecast meeting sales ________ ________
3 card store credit department ________ ________
4 Internet sale summer access ________ ________
5 figures price inflation range ________ ________
6 survey market hour rush ________ ________
7 technology keys car information ________ ________
8 assistant shop failure power ________ ________
9 shopfloor working worker lunch ________ ________
10 insurance loan contract bank ________ ________
11 features costs production product ________ ________
12 market marketing budget leader ________ ________
13 margin capital profit expenditure ________ ________
14 control sheet balance quality ________ ________

Exercises

Sections A, B

33.4 Rewrite the sentences using apostrophes where necessary.

1 Ingrid knows that its Marys area of work, not hers.
Ingrid knows that it's Mary's area of work, not hers.

2 When its Christmas, all our competitors sales go up more than ours.

____

3 Alices friends called Bill. Hes one of Morgan Stanleys top analysts.

____

4 My bosss PA reads all the customers emails.

____

5 I went to my doctors and hes computerized all the patients records.

____

6 Look at those two Mercedes. Ones our directors and the others a visitors.

____

Sections A, B, C, D

33.5 Write the second sentence so it has a similar meaning to the first sentence.

1 I'll see you in the room we use for meetings in ten minutes.
I'll see you *in the meeting* room in ten minutes.

2 This pen doesn't belong to me.
This isn't _______________ .

3 This pen doesn't belong to me.
This pen isn't _______________ .

4 These documents belong to James.
These are _______________ .

5 Fatima met one of her colleagues at the conference.
Fatima met a _______________ at the conference.

6 What is your boss called?
What _______________ name?

7 You should consult an expert in law about companies.
You should consult an _______________ law.

8 This graph shows the figures for sales for last year.
This graph _______________ figures for last year.

9 I just sent an email to one of our customers.
I just sent an email to a _______________ .

10 I'm going on a course to train managers.
I'm going on _______________ course.

Section D

33.6 Cross out the one word in each group that does not make a common compound noun with the first word in bold.

1 **sales** *forecast/figures/~~trade~~/target*
2 **market** *forces/sector/check/share*
3 **price** *offer/list/range/rise*
4 **brand** *image/leader/loyalty/process*
5 **tax** *relief/benefits/output/allowance*
6 **product** *manager/range/features/share*
7 **advertising** *slogan/line/campaign/agency*
8 **production** *market/line/capacity/target*
9 **company** *car/policy/accounts/trade*
10 **stock** *option/decision/market/exchange*

Tasks

Speaking: listen and repeat

1 33 **You are going to hear eight phrases. Listen and repeat.**

Translate

2 Translate these short texts taken from the Internet into your own language. Remember not to translate word for word, but rather to make it sound natural.

"There are four main elements to our business model – product, distribution, communication and price," explains an executive at LVMH, the world's largest luxury-goods group. "Our aim is to do such a fantastic job on the first three that people forget all about the fourth." At Louis Vuitton, LVMH's star company, the model's pricing power has produced consistent profit margins of around 40–45%, the highest of any luxury-goods brand.

The Economist website

From a business perspective, Australia is not one market; it is nine. There is a set of regulations for each state. Whether it is business taxation, occupational health and safety rules, workers' compensation, product standards, trade practices legislation, food laws and regulation, shop trading hours, road transport regulation, or many other areas, businesses face countless different demands. There is extra paperwork and record keeping; multiple licence, inspection and audit fees; and other extra costs.

Sydney Morning Herald website

Writing: personalized practice

3 Look again at section C on page 138 and exercise 33.2. The phrases that you see are common fixed expressions (e.g. *error of judgment*). Write a sentence of your own using the words in brackets in a fixed expression.

1 (error of) *We shouldn't have outsourced our recruitment process. It was an error of judgement.*

2 (flood of) ______

3 (lack of) ______

4 (level of) ______

5 (method of) ______

6 (piece of) ______

7 (range of) ______

8 (stroke of) ______

9 (waste of) ______

Rehearsal for the real world

4 Look again at exercise 33.6. Choose one compound noun from each group 1–10 and use it to write a sentence of your own. Add another sentence (or two) for interest. See the example:

Our sales targets are very ambitious, and I'll be very surprised if we can achieve them. If we don't manage to get enough sales, I probably won't get my annual bonus – and that means no skiing in Austria this year.

If you are working in class, choose some sentences to read aloud. Ask and answer questions.

34 Articles 1

A Articles

A/an is called the indefinite article, and we use it to introduce new information.

The is called the definite article, and we use it when the listener knows which person or thing we are talking about.

'No article' is the noun by itself, without an article. We use no article when we want to speak generally.

Compare:

I read ***an*** *interesting* ***report*** *last week.*
('report' is mentioned for the first time)
I read ***the report*** *you gave me.*
(the listener knows which report)
Reports *are sent out four times a year.*
(speaking generally)

B *a/an*

We use *a/an* to introduce new information. The listener does not know which person or thing we are talking about.

We use *a/an* to refer to something for the first time.

I have ***an idea*** *I'd like to discuss.*

We use *a/an* to refer to one of a group of things.

Can you pass me ***a paper clip*** *from that box?*

We use *a/an* to describe someone's job.

Fiona is ***a financial consultant****.*

We use *a/an* with an adjective to describe something.

Cairo is ***an enormous city****.*

We use *a/an* in expressions of measurement. *Per* can also be used.

twice ***a/per*** *month   300 units* ***an/per*** *hour*

A/an mean 'one', so we cannot use *a/an* with plurals or uncountable nouns.

Can you give me ***some information****?*
(NOT ~~an information~~)

C *a* or *an*?

We use *a* in front of a consonant sound and *an* in front of a vowel sound.

consonant sounds
a manager, a job, a university, a one-way street, a European law

vowel sounds
an idea, an employer, an hour, an MBA

D *the*

We use *the* for old information. It is clear which person or thing we are talking about.

We often know which one because we mentioned it before, using *a/an*.

We must have ***a meeting*** *next week.* ***The meeting*** *should focus on the auditors' report.*

Sometimes we know which one because it is clear from the context, or it is shared knowledge from the lives of the speaker and listener.

Where's ***the newspaper****?*
(we know which one from the context)

The talk *will begin at 10.00.*
(both the speaker and listener know which talk)

Note that in cases like these we can use *the* to refer to something for the first time.

We use *the* when there is only one of something, and so it is clear which one.

I'll speak to ***the boss*** *when he gets back.*

We use *the* with nationalities and other groups.

I admire ***the Italians*** *for their sense of design.*
This is how ***the rich*** *live.*

We use *the* with superlatives (unit 37B).

This is ***the fastest*** *machine in our range.*

There are special rules for place names (unit 35).

E No article

No article is used when we are talking generally.

Study this example for a plural noun:

I got ***the emails*** *you sent.*
(we know which emails)
We try to reply to ***emails*** *within 24 hours.*
(emails in general)

Study this example for an uncountable noun:

The information *in this report gives us* ***the power*** *to target our advertising.*
(we know which information and power)

Information *is* ***power****.*
(information and power in general)

A common mistake is to use *the* with plural nouns and uncountable nouns used in a general way.

Jobs *are hard to find these days.*
(NOT ~~The jobs~~ are hard to find)

Time *is* ***money****.*
(NOT ~~The time~~ is ~~the money~~)

For me, ***football*** *is like* ***life****.*
(NOT For me, ~~the football~~ is like ~~the life~~)

We use no article for most companies.

I work for ***HSBC*** *in Hong Kong.*

Exercises

Sections A, B, D

34.1 Underline the correct words.

1 Where's *a/the* package we received this morning? I can't find it.
2 I have *an/the* appointment at *a/the* bank.
3 I had *a/the* very good holiday. *A/The* weather was marvellous.
4 I've been working so hard that I need *a/the* break.
5 They are *a/the* largest manufacturer of wind turbines in *a/the* world.
6 *A/The* presentation was *a/the* great success.
7 We need to reach *a/the* decision as soon as possible.
8 There must be *an/the* answer to *a/the* problem.
9 Mike is *an/the* office worker. He works on *another/the other* side of town.
10 His office is *a/the* biggest one in *a/the* building.
11 Where have you saved *a/the* document we were looking at?
12 *Portuguese/The Portuguese* are very good negotiators.

Sections A, B, C, E

34.2 Put either *a/an* or a dash (~) to show no article.

1 ~ money makes the world go round.
2 It's all ____ question of ____ supply and ____ demand.
3 Rita works in ____ insurance company in ____ Cologne.
4 I think that ____ good health is the most important thing in ____ life.
5 This is ____ good time for ____ sales of new cars.
6 This is the number to call for ____ information.
7 I've got ____ colleague who is ____ systems analyst.
8 ____ product knowledge is very important for ____ sales consultant.
9 He's ____ engineer. He studied ____ engineering at University.
10 We produce ____ income statement four times ____ year.

Sections A, B, C, D, E

34.3 Put either *a/an*, *the* or a dash (~) to show no article.

1 *The* Spanish have given us *a* lot of ~ business.
2 ____ most people thought that it was ____ very good product.
3 I like to drink ____ glass of ____ wine in ____ evening.
4 I wish I could speak ____ English like ____ English.
5 As soon as ____ Hanna gets off ____ plane, ask her to give me ____ call.
6 ____ smoking is not permitted in this building.
7 There's ____ visitor at ____ reception desk.
8 When I arrived at ____ airport, I had ____ drink and waited for ____ flight.
9 I want ____ action, not ____ words.
10 ____ person with ____ MBA usually gets ____ good job.
11 ____ retailing is still in recession, but ____ B2B sector is doing OK.
12 Marie-Flore comes from ____ France.

"We reward top executives at the agency with a unique incentive program. Money."

Exercises

Sections A, B, C, D, E

34.4 Complete this interview between a journalist and the CEO of Biotek, a biotechnology company. Use either *a/an*, *the* or a dash (~) to show no article.

JOURNALIST: Can you begin by telling me 1 _a_ little about 2 _the_ recent changes at 3 _~_ Biotek?

CEO: Well, a few years ago we made 4 ___ important decision. This was to move our operations to 5 ___ Cambridge, because it's very important for 6 ___ biotechnology companies to recruit 7 ___ scientists from 8 ___ best universities. It's 9 ___ very competitive job market in Cambridge, and we attract and motivate employees by offering them 10 ___ good salaries and 11 ___ excellent working conditions. We've built up 12 ___ exceptional team here, and we're focusing more and more on our cutting-edge research in 13 ___ field of 14 ___ gene therapy.

JOURNALIST: Many people say that 15 ___ biotechnology promises more than it delivers. Is that true at Biotek?

CEO: That may be true in general, but 16 ___ biotechnology that we do is already producing 17 ___ results. Last year we made 18 ___ small profit for 19 ___ first time, and 20 ___ revenue is increasing steadily. Also, we've recently made 21 ___ distribution deal with 22 ___ large pharmaceutical company. They have the marketing skills that we lack, and 23 ___ partnership is working well for both sides. Our aim going forward is to enter 24 ___ American market, and we're confident of 25 ___ success.

Sections A, B, C, D, E

34.5 Complete this article with *a/an*, *the* or a dash (~) to show no article.

How Clean Is Their Money?

'Money laundering' is 1 _the_ name given to one of 2 ___ world's biggest financial problems: moving money that has been obtained illegally into 3 ___ foreign bank accounts so that 4 ___ people do not know where it has come from. Putting 5 ___ value on money laundering is of course very difficult, but the International Monetary Fund estimate that it is huge – perhaps \$1 trillion 6 ___ year, equivalent to about 4% of global economic output.

7 ___ international payment systems allow money to be moved in seconds between banks in different parts of 8 ___ world who know very little about each other. This payment system is crucial to 9 ___ stability of the world's financial markets, but it also provides 10 ___ opportunity for criminals to hide their money.

Private banking is 11 ___ best-known laundering channel. Clients of these banks are wealthy people who want their affairs handled with discretion, especially because they want to minimize 12 ___ amount of 13 ___ tax they pay. In these banks there is 14 ___ culture of 'don't ask, don't tell'. And within 15 ___ private banking 16 ___ biggest problem of all is offshore banks. There are around 5,000 offshore banks controlling about \$5 trillion in assets, and some have no physical presence in any location.

Tasks

Speaking: listen and repeat

1 34 **You are going to hear eight phrases. Listen and repeat.**

Translate

2 Translate these short texts taken from the Internet into your own language. Remember not to translate word for word, but rather to make it sound natural.

Once people have a website, they start to realize the importance of search engine optimization. Why? Because without it, you just have a website, and what good is a website if you don't get lots of targeted traffic looking for the products and services which you provide. The base of all SEO is content. Content is the text you see on the page. The search engine's job is to provide the most relevant content available on the Internet, and this is why Google is so successful – because they do it better than anyone else.

Advisor website

The scenario goes something like this: the ongoing depletion of the world's oil resources, coupled with soaring demand from emerging economies like India and China, will send the price of oil through the roof. This will seriously escalate transportation costs, which in turn will cripple international trade, reverse commercial interdependence and disable the global economy. The resulting age will be one in which nations are isolated, technological progress is sluggish and travel is infrequent.

Newsweek website

Writing: personalized practice

3 Complete the sentences with your own ideas. Add another sentence or two for interest if you want to.

1 I have an idea *I'd like to discuss in the meeting tomorrow. How can I put it on the agenda?*

2 I like the idea *you put forward in the meeting yesterday. Perhaps we could talk about it over lunch one day this week?*

3 We're developing a product ______________________________________ .

4 Have I shown you the product ______________________________________ ?

5 I work as a/an ______________________________________ .

6 I speak to someone from head office several times a ______________________________________ .

7 I have a boss ______________________________________ .

8 I'll speak to the boss ______________________________________ .

9 Among all the cultures I know, I think the best negotiators are the ______________________________________ .

10 If you want quality and are prepared to pay for it, this is the ______________________________________ in our range.

11 The information ______________________________________ .

12 Information ______________________________________ .

If you are working in class, choose some sentences to read aloud. Ask and answer questions.

35 Articles 2

Unit 34 gives some basic rules for articles. This unit gives additional points.

A Place names and no article

In general, no article is used for continents, countries, states, islands, mountains, lakes, cities, parks, roads and streets, squares, palaces, castles, cathedrals, stations and airports.

Europe	*China*	*California*
Malta	*Mount Everest*	*Lake Lucerne*
Budapest	*Hyde Park*	*Church Street*
Times Square	*Elysée Palace*	*Windsor Castle*
Köln Cathedral	*Milan Station*	*Orly Airport*

B Place names and *the*

Note that all the following use *the*:

Plurals: *the Alps, the Bahamas, the Netherlands*

'Adjective + place': *the Black Sea, the Middle East, the West End* (but NOT where 'place' is a country or continent: *Northern Italy*)

Phrases with 'of': *the Houses of Parliament, the South of France*

Political constitutions: *the Irish Republic, the United Kingdom (the UK), the United States (the US)*

Rivers and canals: *the Danube, the Suez Canal*

Oceans and seas: *the Atlantic, the Mediterranean*

Roads with numbers: *the A8*

Theatres and art galleries: *the Scala, the Louvre*

Hotels: *the Marriott (Hotel)*

Famous buildings: *the Eiffel Tower, the Taj Mahal, the White House*

C Special uses of *the*

We use *the* with:

International institutions: *The EU, The United Nations, The IMF, The WTO*

Adjectives that refer to nationalities and groups: *The Spanish, The unemployed*

Some time phrases: *in the past, at the moment, in the future* (but 'at present'), *the 1960s (decades), the 21st century (centuries)*

Points of the compass: *(in) the south-west*

Playing instruments: *I play the guitar*

Job titles and official titles: *the Marketing Director, the Prime Minister*

Magazines and newspapers: *The Economist, The Wall Street Journal*

D Special uses of no article

We use no article with:

Company names: *I work for Accenture.*

Years, months, days: *in 2001, on Thursday*

Special times of the year: *at Christmas / Easter*

Some parts of the day: *at night, at midnight*
(BUT 'in the morning', 'in the afternoon')

Languages: *English* (spoken by 'the English')

Means of transport (in general): *by car / taxi / train / bus / coach / plane, on foot*
(BUT 'the train to Barcelona')

Meals (in general): *breakfast / lunch / dinner*
(BUT 'the dinner we had last night')

Note the use of 'preposition + no article' with certain places, when the purpose of the place is more important than the actual place itself.

in / to *hospital / prison / bed / class / court*
I spent two days ***in hospital****.*
I went ***to hospital*** *for a check-up.*

at / to *work / school / university*
I was ***at work*** *yesterday until 8 pm.*
Usually I go ***to work*** *by bus.*

Note how we use 'home':

I was ***at home*** *yesterday evening* (NOT ~~at the home~~)
What time did you ***go home****?* (NOT ~~go to the home~~)

E General and specific meanings

When we use a plural noun or an uncountable noun with no article, it has a general meaning. When we put *the* in front, it has a specific meaning.

Cars *are a big problem in city centres.*
The cars *our salesforce use are all VWs.*
I can't set up complicated ***spreadsheets****.*
The spreadsheets *for May and June are here.*
People *can be difficult sometimes.*
The people *in my office are all very friendly.*
I prefer ***fish*** *to meat.*
The fish *I had for lunch was superb.*
Money *makes the world go round.*
The money *we've invested is close to €1m.*
How's ***business****?*
The clothing business *is very competitive.*
Negotiating *with suppliers is my responsibility.*
The negotiating *was much easier last time.*

Exercises

Sections A, B, C, D

35.1 Underline the correct words.

1 I went to *Pisa/the Pisa* by *car/the car* and saw *Leaning Tower/the Leaning Tower*.
2 They wouldn't pay, so we took them *to court/to the court*.
3 *Crete/The Crete* is very beautiful at this time of year.
4 Helmut Kohl was *Chancellor/the Chancellor* who helped to reunite *Germany/the Germany*.
5 My son is *in hospital/in the hospital* and can't go to *school/the school*.
6 We flew over *Alps/the Alps* and saw *Mont Blanc/the Mont Blanc*.
7 On our trip to *UK/the UK* we visited *Canterbury Cathedral/the Canterbury Cathedral*.
8 In *past/the past* people telephoned from cabins in the street. Can you believe it!?!
9 I'm tired! Thank goodness it's time to *go home/go to home*.
10 I used to work for *Deutsche Bank/the Deutsche Bank*.
11 My daughter wants to go to *university/the university* after her exams.
12 I bought this suit from *Fifth Avenue/the Fifth Avenue* when I was in *States/the States*.
13 Do you know *Lake Windermere/the Lake Windermere*? It's in *Lake District/the Lake District*, in *north-west/the north-west* of *England/the England*.
14 The government wants *the rich/the rich people* to pay more tax.
15 When I am *at work/at the work,* I usually have *lunch/the lunch* at about one.
16 *Danube/The Danube* is the main river in *Central Europe/the Central Europe*.

Section E

35.2 In each pair of sentences, fill in one space with *the* and the other space with a dash (~) to show no article.

1 a) ~ sales are increasing across every division of the company.
b) *The* sales we made last month were up 6% year-on-year.
2 a) ______ information in your report will be very useful to us.
b) ______ information about the Kazakh market is hard to find.
3 a) ______ visitors should sign their name at the reception desk.
b) ______ visitors from Algeria will be arriving at eleven.
4 a) This magazine article gives ______ advice about which stocks to buy.
b) Thank you for ______ advice you gave me last week.
5 a) ______ bonds I have are all long-term investments.
b) ______ bonds are a good investment when interest rates are falling.
6 a) ______ fashion right now is to look like an American gang member.
b) ______ fashion in music changes all the time.
7 a) ______ French exports to the rest of Europe are up 4% this year.
b) ______ French are world leaders in the luxury goods market.
8 a) ______ time is money.
b) ______ time it takes to do the job properly is well worth it.

Exercises

Sections C, D

35.3 Complete the second sentence so it has a similar meaning to the first sentence.

1 I was a student until last year.
I was *at* university until last year.

2 Please don't call me too early – I'll be sleeping.
Please don't call me too early – I'll be ______ bed.

3 I had a quiet weekend in my house.
I had a quiet weekend ______ home.

4 We walked to the station.
We went to the ______ foot.

5 David is still in his office.
David is ______ work.

6 We employ 250 people right now.
We employ 250 people ______ present.

7 I drink coffee at 10 am but never at 10 pm
I drink coffee in ______ morning but never ______ night.

8 I catch the bus in the morning.
I go ______ work ______ bus.

Sections A, B, C, D, E

35.4 Complete this text with *the* or a dash (~) to show no article.

Poland and the Poles

1 *~* Poland is a large territory at the heart of 2 ____ Europe. It is bordered by 3 ____ Germany to 4 ____ west; 5 ____ Czech Republic and Slovakia to the south; Ukraine, Belarus and Lithuania to the east; and 6 ____ Baltic Sea and Kaliningrad to the north. Much of the country is a flat, fertile plain, although in the south there are 7 ____ Tatra mountains. Poland has one of 8 ____ highest numbers of lakes in 9 ____ world (over ten thousand), the largest being 10 ____ Lake Sniardwy. Poland's rivers include 11 ____ Vistula and 12 ____ Odra, both of which frequently flood, causing major problems for 13 ____ authorities in towns such as 14 ____ Wroclaw.

Poland joined 15 ____ EU in 2004, and in the next few years an interesting social phenomenon took place. At that time 16 ____ unemployment rate in Poland was high, and 17 ____ Polish currency was weak. But there was work in 18 ____ UK and 19 ____ Ireland, and more than one million young Poles went looking for it. They found jobs in 20 ____ restaurants, hotels, agriculture and construction. On the streets,

21 ____ Polish could be heard everywhere – from 22 ____ biggest cities to 23 ____ most remote areas of Scotland and Wales. Then, just as suddenly, they all went back. 24 ____ pound was weakening against 25 ____ złoty, and 26 ____ opportunities in the UK and Ireland in general were becoming fewer and fewer as 27 ____ economy slowed.

No one knows what will happen in 28 ____ future, but Poland does have a tradition of 29 ____ migration and an adaptable and skilled workforce. If there is a strong economy somewhere in Europe, and 30 ____ jobs that need doing, Poles are likely to be there.

Tasks

Speaking: listen and repeat

1 35 **You are going to hear eight phrases. Listen and repeat.**

Translate

2 **Translate these short texts taken from the Internet into your own language. Remember not to translate word for word, but rather to make it sound natural.**

What will be the impact of global warming? Rising sea levels will threaten to flood islands like the Maldives in the Indian Ocean. The risk of tidal waves could rise in Florida and other coastal states. Diseases common in the tropics would move north. Diseases carried by mosquitoes, for example, have become more common in Central America and Mexico.

Fortune website

Taxis in Singapore are abundant and reasonably priced, but hard to find during rush hours, when it rains, and between 11 pm and midnight. The taxis from the airport to the central business district cost around $16.

Asia-Inc website

Writing: personalized practice

3 **Look again at sections A–D on page 146. Write a sentence on the topic in brackets using your own ideas.**

1 (a continent) *In the 21st century Asia is likely to become the most important region in terms of growth and global development.*

2 (an island or a lake) ______

3 (a palace or a castle) ______

4 (a river or canal) ______

5 (a theatre or an art gallery) ______

6 (a famous building) ______

7 (a part of the day without 'the') ______

8 (a meal, talking generally) ______

9 (a place, where the purpose is more important than the actual place itself) ______

4 **Complete the sentences with your own ideas.**

10 People ______ .

11 The people ______ .

12 Life ______ .

13 The life ______ .

If you are working in class, choose some sentences to read aloud. Ask and answer questions.

36 Adjectives and adverbs

A Adjectives and adverbs

An adjective describes a noun.

*We need a **significant increase** in sales.*

An adverb describes a verb and says how (*quickly*), when (*tomorrow*) or where (*over there*) something happens.

Adverbs can come in different positions. 'How' adverbs usually come after the verb.

*We **planned** everything very **carefully**.*

Frequency adverbs (unit 1) come after *be* and auxiliaries, but before other verbs.

*She **is never** late. She **never goes** there.*

Other 'when' adverbs can come before or after the verb.

***Last year** profits **rose**.* *Profits **rose last year**.*

If we have several adverbs together, the usual word order is:

HOW – WHERE – WHEN

*Our profits **rose slightly in Benelux last year**.*
(NOT ~~last year in Benelux~~)

As well as describing verbs, adverbs can also describe adjectives and other adverbs.

*It's **relatively expensive**.* (adverb + adjective)
*I did it **very easily**.* (adverb + adverb)

Adverbs are covered in other units in this book: 1, 3, 5, 7, 39, 40, 43, 44 and 49.

B Form of adverbs

Many 'how' adverbs are formed by adding *-ly* to an adjective. A few add *-y*, *-ally*, or *-ily*, depending on the spelling of the original adjective.

*slow – slow**ly*** *full – full**y***
*dramatic – dramatic**ally*** *steady – stead**ily***

Some adverbs and adjectives have the same form. Examples include: *fast, hard, early, late, high, low, right, wrong, daily / weekly / monthly / quarterly.*

*This is a **fast machine**.* *(adj.)*
*This machine **goes** very **fast**.* *(adv.)*
*It's a **hard decision**.* *(adj.)*
*He's **working** very **hard**.* *(adv.)*

Note that the adverb *hardly* is not related to the meaning of *hard*.

*It's so noisy I can **hardly** think.*
('hardly' = almost not)

Note that *good* is an adjective and *well* is an adverb.

*She's **a good negotiator**.*
*She **negotiates well**.*

C Gradable and non-gradable adjectives

Look at these sequences:

boiling ← hot, warm, cool, cold → freezing
excellent / fantastic ← good, bad → terrible / awful
enormous ← large / big, small → tiny / minute

Adjectives in the middle of the sequence are 'gradable'. We can make them stronger or weaker with words like: *a bit, quite, reasonably, relatively, very, extremely.*

*The weather was **quite** hot / cold.*
(NOT ~~quite boiling / freezing~~)
*The sales figures were **very** good / bad.*
(NOT ~~very excellent / awful~~)

Adjectives at the end are 'non-gradable'. With these adjectives we use *absolutely*.

*The talk was **absolutely** excellent / awful.*
(NOT ~~absolutely good / bad~~)

D Order of adjectives

When we have more than one adjective, we use this order:

Opinion: *wonderful, lovely, nice, difficult, important, well-made*
Size: *large, small, long, short*
Other qualities: *cheap, clean, quiet, fast*
Age: *new, old, second-hand*
Shape / pattern: *circular, rectangular, short-sleeved, striped*
Colour: *white, red and blue*
Origin / nationality: *German, French*
Material: *metal, plastic, steel, cotton*
Type (what kind?): *company (policy), mobile (device), cash (payment)*

Words in the final two categories can be nouns used as adjectives.

Here are some examples:

*a **10-page American legal** contract*
(size, nationality, type)
*an **efficient worldwide distribution** network*
(opinion, size, type)
*a **cheap clean energy** source*
(quality, quality, type)

E *interesting / interested*

Adjectives ending *-ing* describe what we are reacting to (outside us).

Adjectives ending *-ed* describe our feelings (inside us).

*I found her comments quite **surprising**.*
*I was **surprised by** her comments.*

Other pairs like this are: *bored / boring, confused / confusing, excited / exciting, interested / interesting, tired / tiring.*

Exercises

Sections A, B

36.1 Complete the second sentence so it has a similar meaning to the first sentence.

1 There was a slight fall in profits in April.
In April profits *fell slightly* .

2 We saw a dramatic improvement in our share price last month.
Last month our share price ______ .

3 There has been a significant drop in demand for oil over the last few months.
Demand for oil has ______ over the last few months.

4 There was a slow recovery in consumer confidence last year.
Consumer confidence ______ last year.

5 There has been a gradual rise in unemployment.
Unemployment ______ .

6 There was steady growth in Korean GDP for many years.
For many years Korean GDP ______ .

Sections C, E

36.2 Underline the correct adjectives.

1 I couldn't do any more work last night. I was just so *tired/tiring*.
2 I don't think the audience liked the talk. They looked *bored/boring*.
3 I don't think the audience liked the talk. It was a bit *bored/boring*.
4 Your new e-learning project sounds really *excited/exciting*.
5 They made very *big/enormous* profits last year.
6 They made absolutely *big/enormous* profits last year.
7 The sales figures last month were extremely *bad/terrible*.
8 Warsaw is absolutely *cold/freezing* at this time of year.

Section A

36.3 Complete the sentences with one word from list A and one from list B. Read the whole line first.

A: badly completely easily extremely heavily quite unexpectedly ~~well~~

B: delayed designed helpful illegal late ~~made~~ promoted recognizable

1 This suitcase is very *well made* . It will last for years and years.
2 The new product is being ______ . You see the posters everywhere.
3 This website is very ______ . I can't find the information I need.
4 You've been ______ . I really appreciate it.
5 Our offices are ______ . Look out for the large flags at the front.
6 I'm sorry, my flight has been ______ . I'll call you when I arrive.
7 Taking bribes is ______ . You'll lose your job if they find out.
8 I arrived at the presentation ______ and missed the first part.

Exercises

Section D **36.4 Put each group of words into the best order.**

1 new package an amazing software — *an amazing new software package*
2 old-fashioned a large machine cutting ______
3 wooden square two cartons ______
4 period a transition three-month difficult ______
5 chips computer Taiwanese high-quality ______
6 a strategy well-planned investment ______
7 a new revolutionary device handheld ______
8 awful plastic cheap souvenirs ______

Section A, B **36.5 Complete the sentences with the words in the box. At the end of each sentence write *adj.* (adjective) or *adv.* (adverb) to show how the word in the gap is being used.**

good	well	fast	fast	hard	hard	hardly	late	late	~~monthly~~

1 We're going to introduce a *monthly* newsletter for all employees. *adj.*
2 I'm sorry, your goods are going to arrive about a week ______ . ___
3 That departure time is too ______ . Don't you have anything earlier? ___
4 Everything's fine. The negotiations are going very ______ . ___
5 The hotel was ______ , but we didn't like the food in the restaurant. ___
6 I was so tired that I could ______ keep my eyes open. ___
7 It's a ______ choice, but I think Carla is the better candidate. ___
8 I had to work very ______ to get everything finished on time. ___
(*late* is possible for #8 but is not the answer)
9 I'm sorry, I don't understand. You're talking too ______ . ___
10 We'll have to make a ______ exit if things start going wrong. ___

Section A, B **36.6 Read this article about home networks. Underline the correct adjective or adverb each time.**

All Your Home Content Under One Roof

In the Dark Ages, many years ago (long before you were born), homes just had one computer. People shared it. This may seem [1]*strange/strangely* to you, but it's true. Nowadays, of course, a home might have a [2]*large/largely* variety of computers, plus a games console and a set-top TV box. Music, video and photos all need to be managed and shared. Everything needs to be integrated [3]*proper/properly*, connected to the Internet, and, of course, connected to the printer/s in different rooms and to the flat screen/s hanging around the house. Oh, yes – it would be [4]*good/well* if it was all wireless as well. Finally, all the files need to be backed up [5]*regular/regularly* and [6]*invisible/invisibly* to the user.

Don't worry – it's [7]*easy/easily*! What you need is a home network with a server at its heart, and in fact developments in consumer electronics are moving very [8]*quick/quickly* in this field. The companies that get everything [9]*right/rightly* are going to do very [10]*good/well*.

Tasks

Speaking: listen and repeat

1 36 **You are going to hear eight phrases. Listen and repeat.**

Translate

2 **Translate these short texts taken from the Internet into your own language. Remember not to translate word for word, but rather to make it sound natural.**

LG was previously known as Lucky Goldstar before its name change in 1995. It has since developed a more sophisticated image, created a catchy tagline of 'Life's Good', and is a rapidly growing name in consumer electronics with an especially strong presence in white goods and mobile phones.

Asia-Inc website

Q: What is the importance of non-verbal communication in a negotiation?
A: Non-verbal communication is absolutely critical. The areas where you have to be especially careful are those that show internal calm. The most positive non-verbal language is displayed when we lean our bodies forward and smile; when we move firmly and slowly, without any nervous ticks; and when we nod to show that we are listening to the other person – to show that we hear and we understand.

Knowledge@Wharton website

Writing: personalized practice

3 **Write sentences using the words in brackets and your own ideas.**

1 (slightly/last year) *Our turnover fell slightly last year, especially in the North American market.*
2 (significantly/in our domestic market) ______
3 (late, *adj.*) ______
4 (late, *adv.*) ______
5 (right, *adj.*) ______
6 (right, *adv.*) ______
7 (relatively successful) ______
8 (reasonably good) ______
9 (absolutely awful) ______
10 (well-made, reliable, German) ______
11 (beautifully-designed, expensive, French) ______
12 (horrible, cheap, plastic) ______

Rehearsal for the real world

4 **Write a paragraph describing each of the following. Give details using a good variety of adjectives.**

1 (your house or flat) *I live in a …*
2 (your clothing) *I'm wearing a …*
3 (an electronic device that you own) *It's a …*

If you are working in class, choose some paragraphs to read aloud. Ask and answer questions.

37 Comparing 1

A Comparatives and superlatives

We use the comparative form of an adjective to compare two separate things, situations, people, etc.

Model C40 is ***more powerful than*** *model C30.*
Model C20 is ***less powerful than*** *model C30.*

We use the superlative form to say that one thing in a group has more or less of a quality than all the others.

The most powerful *model we make is the C60.*
The least powerful *model we make is the C20.*

B Form

The form depends on the number of syllables in the word and the spelling.

Adjective	Comparative	Superlative
One syllable		
cheap	*cheap**er***	***the** cheap**est***
nice	*nice**r***	***the** nice**st***
One syllable ending in a vowel + consonant		
big	*big**ger***	***the** big**gest***
hot	*hot**ter***	***the** hot**test***
One or two syllables ending in -*y*		
risky	*risk**ier***	***the** risk**iest***
easy	*eas**ier***	***the** eas**iest***
Two or more syllables		
modern	***more** modern*	***the most** modern*
	***less** modern*	***the least** modern*
expensive	***more** expensive*	***the most** expensive*
	***less** expensive*	***the least** expensive*

Note in the table above that one-syllable adjectives ending in 'vowel + consonant' double the final consonant, and that -*y* becomes *i*.

Some two-syllable adjectives can form in either way. Examples include: *clever, common, narrow, polite, quiet, simple, tired.*

common	*common**er***	***the** common**est***
OR		
common	***more** common*	***the most** common*

Note that long adjectives have a *less/least* form that short adjectives do not have. To make this meaning with short adjectives we just use another word.

This piece of metal is ***shorter/smaller****.*
(NOT ~~less long/less big~~)

Note the following irregular forms:

good	*better*	*the best*
bad	*worse*	*the worst*
far	*farther/further*	*the farthest/furthest*

Of all the hotel breakfasts I have had in my life, this one is ***the worst****.* (NOT ~~the worse~~)

C Other points (use of *than, the, ever,* etc.)

We use *than* after a comparative form.

This year's profits will be a little ***higher than*** *last year's.*
It's a lot ***more difficult than*** *I thought at first.*

We use *the* before a superlative form. We can also use a possessive.

This is ***the/our/Digicom's*** *most powerful model.*

Comparative and superlative adjectives can be used without a noun if the meaning is clear from the context.

Their level of customer service is good, but ours is ***better****.*
Digicom produces a range of models, but this one is ***the most powerful****.*

The present perfect with *ever* is often used with superlatives.

This is the ***most fuel-efficient car*** *we* ***have ever produced****.*
This is one of ***the worst years*** *we* ***have ever had****.*

D *as ... as ...*

We can compare two equal things with *(just) as ... as.*

The C60i is ***(just) as powerful as*** *the C60.*

We say that two things are not equal with *not as ... as.*

The C40 is ***not as powerful as*** *the C60.*

E Comparing actions

When we compare actions we can use an auxiliary at the end of the sentence.

The C60 runs faster than the C40.
OR *The C60 runs faster than the C40* ***does****.*
You've done more work than me.
OR *You've done more work than I* ***have****.*

Exercises

Sections
A, B, C, D

37.1 Underline the correct words.

1 Hopefully the new line will be *so profitable as/as profitable as* the old one.
2 This handset is *the most profitable/the more profitable* we've ever made.
3 This version of the software is *the most recent/the most recenter.*
4 The guarantee is a year longer *than/that* with our older models.
5 Nothing is *worse/worst* than missing a flight because of traffic.
6 This printer is one of *the best/the better* on the market.
7 The situation is *not as bad as/not as bad* it looks.
8 The situation is *more bad/worse* today than it was yesterday.
9 I'm sorry, the journey here took *longer than/the longest* we expected.
10 We'll be there soon. It's not much *farer/further.*

Sections
A, B, C, D

37.2 Complete the sentences with a comparative or superlative form of the adjective in brackets. Include any other necessary words like *the, more, less, as* or *than*.

1 Intel is *the biggest* (big) manufacturer of microchips in the world.
2 This keyboard is quite difficult to use. It's ________ (small) the one I'm used to.
3 The conference was a little disappointing. It was ________ (interesting) I expected.
4 Yesterday was one of ________ (hot) days of the year.
5 I think this suggestion is ________ (good) the other one.
6 It's impossible to choose between these two products. One is just ________ (good) the other.
7 The first round of negotiations was easy. The next will be ________ (difficult).
8 We're only a small company. We're not ________ (large) some of the other players in our sector.
9 Unfortunately our sales figure are ________ (bad) last year.
10 This is ________ (bad) case of corruption I've ever seen.

Sections
A, B, C, D, E

37.3 Put one suitable word in each space.

1 We are a bigger company *than* GNC, but Satco are *the* biggest.
2 We can meet up either day. One day is ______ good ______ the other.
3 Nobody knows more about marketing ______ Tina ______ .
4 Of course I'll send you a sample. It's the ______ I can do after all your help.
5 It's not perfect but it's the ______ I can do in the time.
6 He is one of the ______ difficult customers I have ever dealt with.
7 Everyone else had worked a lot longer on the project ______ I ______ .
8 This market is not ______ risky ______ it used to be.
9 Both hotels are very upscale. One is ______ as expensive ______ the other.
10 This restaurant attracts more students than the other one. It's ______ as expensive.

BASICALLY IT MAKES THE SAME MISTAKES THAT WE'VE ALWAYS MADE — BUT IT MAKES THEM SO MUCH FASTER!
MARKETS
Smith

Exercises

Sections A, B, C, D

37.4 Complete the second sentence so it has a similar meaning to the first sentence.

1 Liam is a better analyst than Chris.
Chris is not *as good an analyst as* Liam.

2 I haven't read as many sections of the report as you.
You've read ______________________________ .

3 I expected the meeting to last longer.
The meeting didn't last ______________________________ expected.

4 Our department's training budget isn't as big as yours.
Your department's training budget is ______________________________ .

5 No presentation I've given is more important than this one.
This is the ______________________________ .

6 This speaker is more interesting than the last one.
The last speaker was not ______________________________ this one.

7 No one in the team has better communication skills than Jane.
Jane has ______________________________ in the team.

8 I have rarely met a more interesting person.
He is one of ______________________________ .

Sections A, B

37.5 Complete the magazine article about investment options with the comparative or superlative forms of the adjectives in brackets.

Investment choices: risk and reward

In this article we're going to look at the three main types of investments: cash, bonds and stocks.

The [1] *safest* (safe) place for your money is cash in the bank, and because this has a very low level of risk it also has a [2] __________ (low) return than the other options. However, in a falling market cash is the [3] __________ (good) place to be – you can buy stocks later at a [4] __________ (cheap) price. If it's a normal market and you want a [5] __________ (good) return on your money, you should consider bonds. A bond is like a long-term loan you give to a government or company, and in return you receive a fixed rate of interest. Bonds are often a [6] __________ (attractive) option than cash, particularly when interest rates at the bank are falling.

The [7] __________ (risky) form of investment is stocks. They offer the chance of much [8] __________ (great) profits over the long term, but you might make a loss if the company does badly. The [9] __________ (bad) case scenario is that the company goes bankrupt and you lose everything. You can reduce the risk by investing in a fund rather than individual stocks.

So what should you do? In fact, most financial advisors recommend a balance. In the middle of your career you can afford to have a [10] __________ (large) part of your investments as stocks, with some bonds for stability. As you get [11] __________ (near) retirement, the [12] __________ (sensible) thing to do is to switch your money into bonds, and also have some cash available for emergencies.

Tasks

Speaking: listen and repeat

1 37 **You are going to hear eight phrases. Listen and repeat.**

Translate

2 Translate these short texts taken from the Internet into your own language. Remember not to translate word for word, but rather to make it sound natural.

As the tallest, longest, largest and most expensive cruise ship ever built, Queen Mary 2 provides her guests with unprecedented amenities and accommodation at every turn. And no matter which itinerary you choose, you may well find that the most enchanting island of all is the one you're sailing on.

GoDirectCruises website

It's still good to be king of your corporation – just not as good as it used to be. In fact, falling markets and a slowing economy actually seem to be putting the brakes on executive compensation packages.

BusinessWeek website

Writing: personalized practice

3 Write a paragraph comparing the things in brackets. See the example.

1 (pasta, pizza, risotto) *A ready-made pizza is the easiest to cook, but a better option is perhaps to buy a pizza base and add your own topping. Pasta is just as easy to cook if you buy a sauce in a jar, but, again, making your own sauce is healthier and nicer. Risotto is the most difficult to prepare – you have to add the water bit by bit and get the timing right. It can also be more expensive if you use ingredients like asparagus or porcini mushrooms.*

2 (Johnny Depp, Brad Pitt, George Clooney) ______________________________

3 (Kia, VW, Ferrari) ______________________________

4 (Sales jobs, Marketing jobs, Finance jobs) ______________________________

Rehearsal for the real world

4 Write a few paragraphs comparing your own company with two other named companies operating in the same market. If you are a student, do the same for two other educational institutions.

If you are working in class, choose some examples to read aloud. Ask and answer questions.

38 Comparing 2

A Small and large differences

We can use adverbs before a comparative structure to talk about small and large differences. Compare product A with product B:

more … than …
*A is **a bit/a little/slightly** more expensive than B.*
*A is **considerably/much/a lot/far** more expensive than B.*
as … as …
*A is **not nearly as** expensive **as** B.*
*A is **almost/nearly/not quite as** expensive **as** B.*
*A is **twice as** expensive **as** B.*
*A is **more than twice as** expensive **as** B.*

We can use *even* to emphasize a comparison.

*A is **even** more expensive than B.*

B Other structures with comparatives

We can say that something is increasing or decreasing by repeating a comparative word with *and*.

*The personal pensions market is growing **bigger and bigger**.*
*Investors are becoming **more and more** sophisticated.*

We can say that one situation depends on another by using *the* + one comparative followed in the next phrase by *the* + another comparative.

***The bigger** the company and **the larger** its costs, **the greater** is the opportunity for savings and efficiencies.*

The phrases below are also useful for comparing things.

exactly/just/almost/nearly/virtually/more or less/roughly ***the same … as …***
exactly/just/very/more/less/quite/a bit/a little ***like***
completely/quite/slightly ***different from (to)***
very ***similar to***
compared to/in comparison with
comparatively/relatively

*Customers expect **exactly the same** service online **as** they get in traditional retailing.*
*The new BMW is **more like** an Audi.*
*The new BMW is **slightly different from** its predecessor.*
***Compared to** Finnish, English is easy.*
*It's **relatively** cheap, given the quality.*

C Phrases with superlatives

The phrases below are common with superlatives.

One of the	*largest retailer**s** in the US …*
By far the/Easily the	*largest retailer in the US …*
The second/third/fourth	*largest retailer in the US …*

D Comparing adverbs

Adverbs follow the same rules as adjectives.

One syllable
*hard, hard**er**, **the** hard**est***

Two syllables ending *-y*
*early, earl**ier**, **the** earl**iest***

Two or more syllables
*effectively, **more** effectively, **the most** effectively*

The adverbs *well* and *badly* are irregular.

well, better, the best
badly, worse, the worst

We can use many of the same structures as adjectives (see sections A and B opposite).

*Their share price rose **almost as** rapidly **as** it fell.*
*Employees have to work **harder and harder** to get promotion.*
***The quicker** we can sign the deal, **the sooner** we can start production.*

We often need comparative and superlative adverbs when the verb has the form of a present participle (*doing*) or a past participle (*done*).

*Vietnam is **developing more rapidly** than its neighbours.*
*Vietnam is one of **the most rapidly developing** countries in the world.*
*This product is **more attractively designed** and **more solidly built**.*
*Her CV was **the most carefully writtten**.*

E Comparing nouns

We compare nouns using the words below.

Countable nouns (products, people, banks)
more, the most, fewer, the fewest, (not) as many … as

*We have **fewer people** working for us now **than** two years ago.*
*There are**n't as many products** on the market now **as** there used to be.*

Uncountable nouns (time, money, information)
more, the most, less, the least, (not) as much … as

*I'm working as a freelancer now and I earn considerably **less money**.*
*I do**n't** have **nearly as much time** for reading **as** I would like.*

Exercises

Sections A, B, C, D, E

38.1 Underline the correct words.

1 The new design is *considerable/considerably* lighter than the old one.
2 There are nearly twice as many people working here *as/than* last year.
3 The sooner they decide, *it's better/the better* for us all.
4 There's *each time more/more and more* investment in Turkey.
5 We have *the nearly largest/the second largest* market share in Brazil.
6 This model might be better for you. It's *slightly less/quite less* expensive.
7 This is by far our *faster/fastest* selling product.
8 We need to check the figures *more careful/more carefully* next time.
9 We need to be *more careful/more carefully* with the figures next time.
10 It's a little more expensive, but the quality is *much better/more better*.
11 Our sales this year are virtually *the same as/the equal of* last year.
12 This is one of *the best-/the well-* organized conferences I've ever been to.

Sections A, B

38.2 Match a word or phrase from list A with one from list B that has the same meaning. Then write the pairs in the correct spaces below.

A: a bit comparatively exactly much ~~roughly~~ virtually

B: far just a little ~~more or less~~ nearly relatively

1 They're similar in many ways. They're *roughly/more or less* the same.
2 They're very similar. They're ________________ the same.
3 They're identical. They're ________________ the same.
4 X costs $580 and Y costs $600. X is ________________ cheaper.
5 X costs $400 and Y costs $600. X is ________________ cheaper.
6 X costs less than other similar products. X is ________________ cheap.

Section D

38.3 Rewrite each sentence using a superlative with a present participle (*doing*) or a past participle (*done*).

1 Few credit cards are accepted as widely as Visa.
Visa is probably *the most widely accepted* credit card.
2 No market is growing as fast as China.
China is ________________ market.
3 Few watches on the market are designed as cleverly as the new Seiko.
The new Seiko is one of ________________ watches on the market.
4 Few of our products are selling as well as this.
This is one of our ________________ products.
5 Few facts about Amazon are less known than this.
This is one of ________________ facts about Amazon.
6 No area of business is changing as rapidly as biotechnology.
By far ________________ area of business is biotechnology.

Exercises

Sections A, B, C, E

38.4 A company wants to move the location of its offices and there are several options. Read the details in the table and then complete the sentences below with the phrases in the box.

Location	size (m^2)	rent (per m^2)	running costs per year	distance to city centre (km)
Docklands (converted warehouse)	290	€500	€120,000	3
City View Tower	300	€350	€125,000	5
Greenfield Business Zone	320	€200	€105,000	15

~~slightly~~	not nearly	more than twice	roughly the same
slightly less	considerably less	as much	as many

1 The locations all have a similar size, but Greenfield is *slightly* larger.
2 There's almost ______ square metres at Docklands as at City View.
3 There's almost ______ space at Docklands as at City View.
4 The rent at Greenfield is ______ than at the other two places.
5 The rent at Docklands is ______ the rent at Greenfield.
6 The running costs at Docklands and City View are ______ .
7 The running costs at Greenfield are ______ than at the other two locations.
8 To get to the centre, Greenfield is ______ as convenient as City View.

Sections A, B, C, D, E

38.5 Study the table, which shows financial information for three large oil companies in millions of US dollars.

Company	Total Revenues	% change y-o-y	Operating Profit	% change y-o-y
Exxon Mobil	477,000	32	82,000	34
BP	361,000	29	32,000	30
Total	205,000	17	30,000	16

Make phrases by matching an item from column A with an item from column B. Then use the phrases to complete the report extract.

A	B
by	comparison with
in	more
considerably	much as
the fastest	far the largest
roughly	growing
half as	the same

The table shows that all three companies did well [1] *in comparison with* the previous year. However, there are significant differences. Exxon is [2] ______ company, with [3] ______ revenues than the other two companies. It is also [4] ______ company: last year revenues and profit were both up by more than 30% compared to the previous year. BP also had a successful year, with year-on-year growth [5] ______ as Exxon. The results at Total were mixed: revenues are increasing steadily, but profit growth is only [6] ______ its two competitors.

Tasks

Speaking: listen and repeat

1 38 **You are going to hear eight phrases. Listen and repeat.**

Translate

2 **Translate these short texts taken from the Internet into your own language. Remember not to translate word for word, but rather to make it sound natural.**

The foreign exchange (FX) markets are far more volatile and unpredictable than commodities markets. Trader sentiment can change abruptly, by the minute, fuelled by speculation and rumours. Traditionally, exchange rate movements are determined by relative economic growth, inflation and interest rates expectations, as well as a country's external trade balance.

AllBusiness website

America's top CEOs have ranked California 'the worst place in which to do business' for the fourth straight year. They won't bring their businesses there because of the oppressive tax and regulatory climate. California has the highest corporate income tax in the US, by far the highest sales tax, the fourth-highest capital gains tax, and the lowest bond rating of any state.

Advisor website

Writing: personalized practice

3 **Look again at this unit and notice how the language used for comparing is more varied than the simple comparisons of unit 37.**

Now turn to exercise 38.4 and cover everything except for the information table at the top. Write two or three sentences of your own comparing the three locations, using the topics below. You can also refer to your present location (imaginary).

1 (size) *Docklands has the least space, but, to be honest, the size at all three locations is virtually the same . All the locations offer considerably more space than we have now, which is good as the company is growing bigger and bigger every year.*

2 (rent) ______________________________

3 (running costs) ______________________________

4 (distance to the city centre) ______________________________

Rehearsal for the real world

4 **Write a few paragraphs comparing the different products that your company sells. If you are a student, do the same for different courses/classes. You might find it useful to organize your ideas into tables, charts or diagrams before you start writing.**

If you are working in class, choose some examples to read aloud. Ask and answer questions.

39 Adverbs of degree

A Intensifying adverbs

Intensifying adverbs (also called 'modifiers') make the meaning of the following word stronger or weaker.

Strong: *absolutely, completely, considerably, extremely, highly, incredibly, quite, really, terribly, totally, very*
Moderate: *fairly, moderately, pretty, quite, rather, reasonably, relatively, significantly, somewhat*
Weak: *a bit, a little, marginally, slightly*

Look at these examples with adjectives, adverbs, verbs and comparatives:

*The whole thing was **highly professional**.*
*Their rates are **a little expensive**.*
*The job was done **very professionally**.*
*They replied **quite quickly**.*
*I'm sorry but I **really disagree** with that.*
*I **marginally prefer** option B.*
*It's **slightly more expensive**.*
*It's **relatively expensive**.*

Not all adverbs can be used in every case. Some combinations do not make sense together.

They replied ~~slightly quickly~~. ✗
His presentation was ~~marginally good~~. ✗

See unit 36C for the rules with gradable and non-gradable adjectives.

B *too, enough, not enough*

Here are the meanings:

Too: 'more than is necessary or good'
Not enough: 'less than is necessary or good'
Enough: 'as much as is necessary'/'sufficient'

Look at these examples with adjectives, adverbs and nouns:

*His salary is **too low**.*
*His salary is/is**n't high enough**.*

*The negotiation is going **too slowly**.*
*The negotiation is/is**n't** going **fast enough**.*

*I have **too many jobs** to do.*
*I have **too much work** to do.*
*I have/do**n't** have **enough time**.*

Note the positions: *too* comes before adjectives, adverbs and nouns; *enough* comes after adjectives and adverbs, but before nouns.

We use *too many/few* + plural nouns and *too much/little* + uncountable nouns.

*We spent **too many euros** on the consultants.*
*We spent **too much money** on the consultants.*

C Other structures with *too* and *enough*

After *too* and *enough* we can use a phrase with *for*.

*Sales are **too** low **for an annual bonus**.*
*Have we got **enough** chairs **for everyone**?*

After *too* and *enough* we can use a *to* infinitive.

*Sales are **too** low **to justify** an annual bonus.*
*We don't have **enough** time **to do** everything.*

D *so, such a, such*

We use *so* and *such* for emphasis.

***So* with adjectives and adverbs**
*The meeting finished **so quickly**.*

***Such a* with adjective + singular noun**
*It was **such a** quick **meeting**.*

***Such/So many/So few* with plural nouns**
*You have **such** friendly **colleagues**.*
*There were **so many people** in town today.*

***Such/So much/So little* with uncountable nouns**
*It was **such** good **advice**.*
*I have **so much work** to do.*

So and *too* are different. *So* expresses an opinion which can be either positive or negative. *Too* is always negative and suggests a problem or bad situation.

*There are **so many people** working on this project.*
(it's just a comment and could be a good thing)

*There are **too many people** working on this project.*
(and therefore we need to reduce the number)

So can be used with *that* to express a result. *Too* cannot be used with *that*.

*We finished **so** quickly **that** I was home by 5.30.*

E *fairly, quite, rather* and *pretty*

Fairly suggests a moderate degree.

*I speak French **fairly well** – around intermediate level.*

Quite (mainly British English) suggests a higher degree than *fairly*. It often suggests surprise in a positive way.

*The film was **quite good** – I enjoyed it.*

Rather is stronger than *quite*. It often suggests surprise in a negative way.

*It's **rather late** to do anything about it now.*

Pretty is similar to *rather* but is more informal.

*It's **pretty strange** – don't you think?*

Note that the exact meaning of these words can depend on the intonation used.

Exercises

Sections A, B, E **39.1 Match each phrase 1–8 with the phrase a–h with the closest meaning. Be careful – some are very similar.**

1 It's slightly slow. [b] a) It's moderately slow.
2 It's quite slow. [ ] b) It's a little slow.
3 It's rather slow. [ ] c) It's comparatively slow.
4 It's relatively slow. [ ] d) I'm surprised it's slow and I don't like it.

5 It's so fast. [ ] e) I want it to be even faster.
6 It's too fast. [ ] f) I want it to be slower.
7 It's fast enough. [ ] g) It's very fast.
8 It's not fast enough. [ ] h) OK. That's as fast as it needs to be.

Sections B, C, D **39.2 Underline the correct words.**

1 There were *so few/so little* customers that I went home early.
2 We can't back out now. There's *too much/too many* money involved.
3 It was *such a/so* boring meeting that I nearly fell asleep.
4 The meeting was *such a/so* boring that I nearly fell asleep.
5 The price they wanted was *so high/too high* for my budget, so I said no.
6 We had *so much/so many* new business that we needed extra staff.
7 I had *so much/so many* reports to write that I completely missed lunch.
8 We have *so few/so little* information that we can't make a decision.
9 The salary they are suggesting sounds *so good/too good* to be true!
10 The meeting was *so short/too short*. We couldn't cover everything.
11 Can you help me? I'm not *enough tall/tall enough* to reach the top shelf.
12 There isn't *enough money/money enough* in the budget.

Sections B, C, D **39.3 Complete the sentences with *too, enough, so, such, much, many, little* or *few*. Some words are used more than once.**

1 Is your coffee *too* hot? Would you like a little cold water?
2 I had ________ ________ trouble finding somewhere to park that I arrived late.
3 I had ________ ________ problems finding somewhere to park that I arrived late.
4 I had ________ ________ cash on me that I couldn't even buy a sandwich.
5 There were ________ ________ restaurants open that we had to eat in the hotel.
6 The price of their shares is ________ high to buy any more right now.
7 We're making ________ good progress that we should finish a week early.
8 We're expecting a lot of people. This room won't be large ________ .
9 I couldn't do any work on the train. I was ________ tired that I fell asleep.
10 She speaks ________ quickly for me to understand.
11 They pay ________ late that we won't receive the money until June.
12 That's ________ a great idea. It'll save us thousands of dollars.

"My fees are quite high, and yet you say you have little money. I think I'm seeing a conflict of interest here."

Exercises

Section D **39.4 Look at the table. Sentences a) and b) can be combined with the sentence on the right using either *so ... that* or *such ... that*. Write the two possible combined sentences below.**

1 a) There was a big drop in their share price. b) The drop in their share price was very big.	+ Investors became very nervous.

a) There was *such a big drop in their share price that* investors became very nervous.
b) The drop in their share price was *so big that* investors became very nervous.

2 a) That company has very large debts. b) That company's debts are very large.	+ There's a risk it will have to close down.

a) That company has ______ there's a risk it will have to close down.
b) That company's debts are ______ there's a risk it will have to close down.

3 a) Our order fulfilment system works very well. b) We have a very good order fulfilment system.	+ Most goods are shipped within 48 hours.

a) Our order fulfilment system works ______ most goods are dispatched within 48 hours.
b) We have ______ most goods are dispatched within 48 hours.

4 a) The advertising campaign was very successful. b) The advertising campaign was a success.	+ Sales increased by 25% per month.

a) The advertising campaign was ______ sales increased by 25% per month.
b) The advertising campaign was ______ sales increased by 25% per month.

Sections B, D **39.5 Complete the second sentence so it has a similar meaning to the first sentence and contains the word in brackets.**

1 I didn't buy that laptop because the screen was too small. (enough)
I didn't buy that laptop because *the screen wasn't large enough* .
2 The problem was so difficult that I referred it to my line manager. (such)
It ______ that I referred it to my line manager.
3 There weren't enough copies of the agenda. (few)
There ______ of the agenda.
4 There's not enough space on this spreadsheet for all the results. (little)
There's ______ on this spreadsheet for all the results.
5 It was such a good presentation that we easily won the contract. (so)
The ______ that we easily won the contract.
6 I sold too few units last month to get a bonus. (enough)
I ______ last month to get a bonus.
7 We've sent out lots of brochures and we'll need to print some more. (many)
We've sent out ______ we'll need to print some more.
8 I haven't got enough time to prepare for the meeting. (too)
I've got ______ to prepare for the meeting.

Tasks

Speaking: listen and repeat

1 39 **You are going to hear eight phrases. Listen and repeat.**

Translate

2 Translate these short texts taken from the Internet into your own language. Remember not to translate word for word, but rather to make it sound natural.

The Greens and Socialists oppose Mr Barroso's re-election on the grounds that he is too oriented toward free trade and free markets. If only. Our complaint with Mr. Barroso's leadership is that he hasn't been bold enough in working toward liberalizing Europe's economy.

Wall Street Journal website

Most retailers build their marketing and display plans around the assumption that shoppers are overwhelmingly female, but that's not such a safe bet anymore. A Nielsen Co. report demonstrates that male shoppers are becoming increasingly important and need to be recognized. Today, according to the report, 31.5 percent of men act as primary household shopper, up from 14.3 percent in 1985.

BNET website

Writing: personalized practice

3 Complete the sentences with your own ideas.

1 Right now I am extremely *interested in intensifying adverbs, but please don't my tell friends* .

2 Taking everything into consideration, I am reasonably ______ .

3 The builders who worked on our house did the job pretty ______ .

4 I'm sorry but I really ______ .

5 Compared to other similar companies, my own is relatively ______ .

6 The situation in our market has changed somewhat ______ .

7 On the whole, I think I marginally prefer ______ .

8 In my life I have too much ______ and not enough ______ .

9 I think we have enough money in the budget for ______ but not enough to ______ .

10 In my job I have so much ______ and so little ______ .

11 In my business, there are too many ______ .

12 I really like '______' – s/he's so ______ and s/he's such a ______ .

Rehearsal for the real world

4 Write a short text to explain what you like or dislike about one of the topics below.

- an actor/singer/sports personality you like
- a film/book you disliked
- a place you like
- a previous job you disliked

If you are working in class, choose some texts to read aloud. Ask and answer questions.

40 Time adverbs

A *in, on, at,* no preposition

in	*the morning / June / the summer / the third quarter / 2012 / the nineties / the twentieth century*
on	*Friday / Friday morning / the 2nd of April / the second / Christmas Day*
at	*three fifteen / the weekend / the end of the week / night / Easter, Christmas / breakfast, lunch, dinner*
no preposition	*this morning / yesterday afternoon / tonight / last night / the day before yesterday / a few days ago / last week / tomorrow morning / the day after tomorrow / next week*

The word *night* has some special forms.

*I woke up three times **in the night**.*
(= during the night)

*It happened **on Friday night**.*
(= one particular night)

*The hotel is quite noisy **at night**.*
(= in general when it is night)

We can use *in* for the time it takes to complete something.

*The line can assemble 80 vehicles **in** a day.*

We can also use *in* to talk about 'future time from now'. In this case we sometimes add the word 'time' at the end.

*The new offices will be ready **in** two months (**time**).*

(NOT ~~after~~ two months)

B *on time* or *in time*?

On time means 'at the right time'. *In time* means 'with enough time in advance'.

*The plane took off exactly **on time**.*
(not late and not early)
*We arrived at the airport **in time** to have a meal.*
(early enough to do something before the flight)

C *for, since, during, ago*

We use *for* and *since* with the present perfect to talk about something continuing up to now. We use *for* to talk about the period of time and *since* to say when it started (unit 5C).

*I've worked here **for two years**.*
(period of time)

*I've worked here **since January**.*
(point in time when it started)

We can also use *for* with other tenses, and sometimes we can leave it out.

*I'm staying in the UK **for a year**.*
*The training period lasted (**for**) three months.*

We can use *during* to talk about periods of time. *During* answers the question 'When?'. *For* answers the question 'How long?'.

*I didn't feel nervous **during my presentation**.*
(when didn't you feel nervous?)

*She talked **for about thirty minutes**.*
(how long did she talk for?)

Ago means 'before the present'. It is used with the past simple.

*I came here **four years ago**.*
(NOT ~~since four years~~)

To refer to a time before another time we use *before (that)* or *previously*.

*I came here four years ago. **Before that/Previously**, I lived in Budapest.*

D *during* or *while*?

During is a preposition and comes before a noun phrase. *While* is a linking word and comes before a clause (subject + verb).

*I moved into marketing **during my time at Bacardi**.*
*I moved into marketing **while I was working at Bacardi**.*

E *by* or *until*?

By means 'on or before'. *Until* means 'up to'.

*I need your report **by Friday**.*
(on or before Friday – perhaps Thursday)
*He'll be away **until Friday**.*
(all the time up to Friday)

F *then, after, afterwards*

Then is used like 'next' in a sequence.

*First we discussed sales, and **then** new markets.*

After is usually followed by an object.

***After the meeting** I need to speak with you.*

Afterwards means 'at a later time' and can come at the end of a sentence.

*It was a long meeting and (**afterwards**) we went for a drink (**afterwards**).*

G Calendar references

In the UK people say *the tenth of June* or *June the tenth* and write Day/Month/Year: *10/6/09*.

In the USA people say *June ten* and write Month/Day/Year: *6/10/09*.

Exercises

Section A

40.1 Put *in*, *on* or *at*.

1 *in* + parts of day (*the evening*)
2 ______ + longer religious holidays (*Easter, Ramadan*)
3 ______ + meal times (*dinner*)
4 ______ + special days (*my birthday*)
5 ______ + long periods (*the nineteenth century*)
6 ______ + clock times (*four thirty*)
7 ______ + day + part of day (*Monday morning*)
8 ______ + seasons (*the winter*)
9 ______ + years (*2008*)
10 ______ + days (*Monday*)
11 ______ + dates (*5 May*)
12 ______ + months (*August*)
13 ______ *the weekend*
14 ______ *the moment*
15 ______ *that day*
16 ______ *the end of the year*

Section A

40.2 It is now Wednesday afternoon. Put these phrases into order, with 1 as the most distant in the past, and 14 as the most distant in the future.

1 *g* 2 ___ 3 ___ 4 ___ 5 ___ 6 ___ **NOW** 7 ___ 8 ___ 9 ___ 10 ___ 11 ___ 12 ___ 13 ___ 14 ___

a) a few days ago
b) tonight
c) in a few weeks' time
d) in a fortnight
e) in an hour
f) last night
g) last week
h) this time next week
i) this evening
j) this morning
k) the day before yesterday
l) tomorrow evening
m) yesterday morning
n) the day after tomorrow

Sections A, B, C, D, E, F

40.3 Underline the correct words.

1 Sorry, I was out of the office *this morning/in this morning*.
2 Bye. I'll see you *the day after tomorrow/the next day*.
3 We have a security guard to look after the premises *at the night/at night*.
4 It's very important to arrive at meetings *on time/in time* in this country.
5 If you arrive *on time/in time,* we can talk a little before the meeting starts.
6 The joint venture has been operating successfully *for/during* three years.
7 We had a few problems *for/during* the summer, but things are OK now.
8 I started working here *since two years/two years ago*.
9 The market crashed, but I had sold my shares a few months *ago/before*.
10 *During/While* the meeting I made a lot of notes.
11 *During/While* she was talking I made a lot of notes.
12 It happened *during/while* house prices were crashing in 2009.
13 It happened *during/while* the crash in house prices in 2009.
14 We have to finish this project *by/until* the end of the month.
15 I have to work late. I'll be here *until/by* eight this evening.
16 We reviewed the training plans, and *after/then* talked about the cost.
17 We had lunch, and *afterwards/after* I showed them round the factory.
18 *Afterwards lunch/After lunch* I showed them round the factory.

Exercises

Section C

40.4 Make questions using *How long* and the present perfect. Make answers using *for* or *since*.

1 Q: (How long/you/work here?) *How long have you worked here?*
A: (about six months) *For about six months.*

2 Q: (How long/you/have a subsidiary in Poland?) ______
A: (2009) ______

3 Q: (How long/Peter Middelhoff/be CEO?) ______
A: (the start of last year) ______

4 Q: (How long/your company/have the same logo?) ______
A: (about twenty years) ______

5 Q: (How long/you/know Lei Huang?) ______
A: (a long time) ______

6 Q: (How long/you/have this particular job?) ______
A: (the company was restructured) ______

7 Q: (How long/you/be interested in antiques?) ______
A: (ages and ages) ______

8 Q: (How long/you/live in this town?) ______
A: (I was born) ______

Sections C, D, F

40.5 Complete this extract from a job interview by with *for, since, during, while, ago, before, after* or *afterwards*.

INTERVIEWER: Perhaps you could begin by telling us a little bit about your career history? 1 *Afterwards* we'll move on to your current job.

ALESSANDRO: Yes, of course. I graduated from Bocconi University in Milan five years 2 ______ . I was at Bocconi 3 ______ about six years, and 4 ______ that period I worked part-time as an analyst in my uncle's consultancy firm.

INTERVIEWER: Did you manage to find a job easily 5 ______ you left university?

ALESSANDRO: Well, eventually I was offered a job in an Italian bank, but 6 ______ that I had been looking for work 7 ______ quite a long time.

INTERVIEWER: So how long did you work at the Italian bank?

ALESSANDRO: I worked there 8 ______ about two years.

INTERVIEWER: And why did you leave that job?

ALESSANDRO: Well, I enjoyed my time there a lot, and 9 ______ I was there I learned a lot of techniques for financial analysis. But I wanted the chance to do something more challenging in an international environment. It had been my dream to work in an international company 10 ______ leaving school.

INTERVIEWER: So what did you do?

ALESSANDRO: I decided to take a risk and move to London – that was about two years 11 ______ . I just left Italy, with no job to go to. I thought that it would be easier to find a job 12 ______ I was actually living in London. It was only 13 ______ that I realized how much competition there was! Anyway, eventually, 14 ______ some months, I did find a job at an investment bank in the City. That's where I'm working now.

Tasks

Speaking: listen and repeat

1 40 **You are going to hear eight phrases. Listen and repeat.**

Translate

2 Translate these short texts taken from the Internet into your own language. Remember not to translate word for word, but rather to make it sound natural.

Why should you pay your invoices on time? As well as being unethical, the practice of deliberately paying later than the agreed terms is wrong for sound economic reasons: it weakens your organisation because it harms your reputation; it damages your relations with suppliers; it weakens the economy as a whole because it constricts growth; it indicates that the buyer is in difficulties, and this may mean the terms worsen next time.

PayOnTime website

Korean automaker Hyundai is offering to guarantee low fuel prices for a year for American consumers who buy its vehicles during the next two months. Hyundai says it is targeting the large number of potential car buyers in the US who are holding back because they are unsure about the direction of fuel prices.

BusinessWeek website

Writing: personalized practice

3 Complete the sentences with your own ideas.

1 In summer, at the weekends, I often *take my family to the beach and we have a barbeque* .
2 In winter, in the mornings, I often ________ .
3 On Friday evening, at the end of the week, I often ________ ________ .
4 On Christmas Eve, at night, we usually ________ ________ .
5 When you have a small baby you ________ ________ in the night.
6 The day before yesterday I ________ and the day after tomorrow I'll probably ________ .
7 I arrived at the airport on time and ________ .
8 I arrived at the airport in time to ________ .
9 I've been in my current job since ________ .
10 I've been in my current job for ________ .
11 How long? She was talking for ________ .
12 When was she talking? You'll never believe it, but she was talking during ________ ________ .
13 When was she talking? You'll never believe it, but she was talking while ________ ________ .
14 He's out of the office but he should be back by ________ .
15 He's away on holiday until ________ .
16 The meeting should end around 5 pm, and afterwards ________ ________ .
17 In the UK, people would say my birthday (day and month) either as '________ ________' or as '________', while in the USA they would say '________'.

If you are working in class, choose some sentences to read aloud. Ask and answer questions.

41 Linking words 1

A Linking words

We use some linking words to join parts of sentences. Examples include *and, but, because, so*. This unit and unit 42 deal with these words.

We use other linking words and phrases to make a link across sentences and between paragraphs. Examples include *Firstly, Actually, In general*. Units 43 and 44 deal with these words.

B Addition: *and, also, as well*, etc.

To emphasize the fact that there are two things we can use *both ... and ...* .

*I need to call **both** Andy **and** Patricia.*

We use *too, as well, as well as* and *also* to add another fact. Note the positions.

*I need to call Andy, Patricia **and** Giselle **too/as well**.*
*I need to call Andy **and** Patricia **as well as** Giselle.*
*I need to call Andy, Patricia **and also** Giselle.*

C Contrast / Surprise: *but, although, though*, etc.

But makes a simple contrast. It expresses a conflict between two ideas/facts/feelings.

*In theory it's a good idea, **but** I don't think it'll work in practice.*

We can use *yet* in place of *but*. It is slightly formal.

Although introduces information that is less important, or makes something in the sentence seem surprising.

*It's a great idea, **although** it'll need careful costing.*
*We chose option B, **although** it was a little more expensive.*

The clause with *although* can come at the beginning.

***Although** I disagreed, I didn't say anything.*

We can emphasize *but* and *although* with *still* and *anyway*.

*I wasn't feeling well, **but** I **still** went to work.*
*I wasn't feeling well, **but** I went to work **anyway**.*
*I **still** went to work, **although** I wasn't feeling well.*
***Although** I wasn't feeling well, I went to work **anyway**.*

We can use *though* in informal speech like *although*. We often use two separate sentences and put *though* at the end.

*I really disagreed with him. I didn't say anything, **though**.*

(= Although I disagreed with him, I didn't say anything.)

We can use *even though* like *although* to give a stronger contrast.

***Even though** I wasn't feeling well, I **still** went to work.*

D Contrast / Surprise: *despite / in spite of*

Despite and *in spite of* are like *although* (they suggest surprise), but they are followed by a noun or noun phrase.

***Although I was ill**, I went to work.*
= ***In spite of my illness**, I went to work.*
***Although sales increased**, operating profit fell.*
= ***Despite the increase in sales**, operating profit fell.*

Remember that a gerund (verb with *-ing*) can act as a noun.

***Despite** feel**ing** ill, I went to work.*
(NOT ~~Despite I felt ill~~)

E Compare and contrast: *whereas*

We can use *whereas* to compare two facts and emphasize the difference between them. The clause with *whereas* can come at the beginning or end.

*Indonesia has a lot of natural resources, **whereas** Singapore has none.*
***Whereas** Indonesia has a lot of natural resources, Singapore has none.*

Whereas is typical of careful speech and writing.

F *although* or *whereas* or *while*?

Although in a sentence suggests surprise. Sometimes the clause with *although* seems surprising, sometimes the other clause does.

*We had a reasonable year in Asia, **although** sales fell a little in Japan.*
(Japan sales figures seem surprising)

***Although** sales fell a little in Japan, we had a reasonable year in the rest of Asia.*
(Asia sales figures seem surprising)

Whereas simply compares two facts. It makes a strong contrast, but there is less suggestion of surprise.

*We had a reasonable year in Asia, **whereas** sales in Europe were quite disappointing.*

We can use *while* like *although* or *whereas*.

***While** there are still some issues to resolve, I think we should go ahead.*
(like 'although')

*Inflation rose by 2% last year, **while** house prices went up 4%.*
(like 'whereas')

Exercises

Sections C, D, E, F

41.1 **<u>Underline</u> the correct words.**

1 *Although/Even* I like this company, I probably won't work here long.
2 Kate gave a good presentation, *although/despite* having very little time to prepare.
3 *In spite of/Although* their shares are rising, their future is still uncertain.
4 This year our earnings are close to $8m, *while/despite* last year they were just $6m.
5 *Whereas/In spite of* these three candidates have an MBA, these other ones don't.
6 I saw that movie you were talking about. I didn't enjoy it, *although/though*.
7 I didn't have much time, *but/whereas* I managed to visit the whole factory.
8 I drive a Peugeot, *but/whereas* my wife drives a VW.
9 The product launch was way over budget, but we did it *still/anyway*.
10 *Although/In spite of* the delay, we still arrived on time.
11 I didn't manage to close the deal, *although/whereas* I really tried.
12 *Although/Whereas* their share price is falling at the moment, the company is still a good long-term investment.

Section B

41.2 **Rewrite each sentence using the word/s in brackets so that it emphasizes the fact that there are two things.**

1 We can handle the transport arrangements and the insurance.
a) (also) *We can handle the transport arrangements and also the insurance.*
b) (both) ____________
c) (too) ____________

2 I want the sales figures for October and November.
a) (as well) ____________
b) (as well as) ____________
c) (also) ____________

Sections C, D, E, F

41.3 **Complete the sentences with *although, anyway, but, in spite of, still, though* or *whereas*.**

1 Carol didn't recognize Mark Larner, *although* she had met him before.
2 I don't like karaoke bars, ____________ I went with my Japanese clients anyway.
3 I offered my best price, but they ____________ didn't seem interested.
4 I think we'll have to change our suppliers. It's a pity, ____________ .
5 ____________ the early problems, the project has been a great success.
6 Korea is a mature market, ____________ Vietnam is still an emerging economy.
7 We don't have all the facts, but it's worth discussing the basic ideas ____________ .

"And as your department representative, let me just say that I am both proud and honoured to be taking credit for your accomplishments."

Exercises

Sections C, D, E, F

41.4 Join each pair of sentences using the words given. There are two ways each time.

1 It was snowing. The flight left on time.
   a) Although *it was snowing, the flight left on time* .
   b) Despite *the snow, the flight left on time* .

2 I had a headache. I still went to the meeting.
   a) In spite of ______ .
   b) ______ , but ______ .

3 Some analysts think that stocks will fall in value. Others disagree.
   a) ______ , whereas ______ .
   b) Although ______ .

4 There were difficulties in the negotiations. We won the contract.
   a) Despite ______ .
   b) Even though ______ .

5 Oil prices rose slightly last year. This year they have gone down.
   a) Whereas ______ .
   b) ______ , although ______ .

6 They've never been successful. They keep on trying.
   a) ______ , yet ______ .
   b) Despite ______ .

Sections B, C, D, E, F

41.5 Complete this article about the use of phones to track peoples' movements with the words in the box.

~~as well~~	as well as	both	despite	even though	whereas	yet

Geo-Tracking:
We Know Where You Are

Imagine that your company had a complete and exact record of your customers' movements – commuting to work, going to the supermarket, and walking the dog [1] *as well* . What about if you knew that information in real time every minute of the day? How could you use that knowledge? What sort of goods and services could you sell them? [2] ______ this might seem like science fiction, it isn't. If you carry a mobile phone, there are now various ways to track your movements across the planet. You leave a digital trail via cell phone base stations and satellites [3] ______ numerous Wi-Fi access points inside buildings.

This 'geo-tracking' has a synergy with another trend: how people access the Net. [4] ______ ten years ago most people used laptops or PCs to surf the Web, these days mobile platforms are equally important.

However, [5] ______ progress with the technology, there are serious privacy issues at stake. Do people really want you to know where they are [6] ______ night and day? (Especially night!). Will they accept location-specific marketing on their phones? These are certainly problem issues, [7] ______ consumers are becoming less resistant to having location-based advertising 'pushed' at them. The key seems to be to make it relevant, timely, and to give people the ability to opt in or out.

Tasks

Speaking: listen and repeat

1 41 **You are going to hear eight phrases. Listen and repeat.**

Translate

2 Translate these short texts taken from the Internet into your own language. Remember not to translate word for word, but rather to make it sound natural.

Although the Scandinavian states and the Asian tigers were culturally, politically, economically, geographically and historically as far apart as possible, they both adopted development models that went against the neo-liberal orthodoxy and were very successful.

African Business website

In its annual report the OECD found that private pensions plans lost 23 per cent of their value last year, while higher unemployment "leaves little room for more generous public pensions". The OECD secretary general said, "Reforming pension systems now to make them both affordable and strong enough to provide protection against market swings will save governments a lot of financial and political pain in the future".

FT website

Writing: personalized practice

3 Complete the sentences with your own ideas.

1 I agree with you in principle, although *I have one or two technical questions that I would like to ask* .
2 Although she doesn't have much experience of the marketing area, ______ .
3 ______ . I didn't say anything, though.
4 Even though the product is still at the developmental stage, it still ______ .
5 Russia and Brazil are rich in energy resources, whereas China and India ______ .
6 Whereas our turnover is up 8% this year, ______ .
7 While there are still some issues to resolve, I think ______ .
8 Shares of IBM rose 2% yesterday, while shares of ______ .
9 In spite of ______ , sales growth has been disappointing.
10 Despite not having ______ , she got to the top of her profession.

Rehearsal for the real world

4 Write a sentence or two saying something surprising about each of the following, using a variety of grammatical constructions:

your career path so far — your company — your national culture

5 Write a sentence or two contrasting each of the pairs of items below.

you and a close family member
sales this year (so far) and last year
the Chinese and Indian economies

If you are working in class, choose some sentences to read aloud. Ask and answer questions.

42 Linking words 2

A Reason: *because, as, because of, due to*

We use *because, as* and *since* when we want to explain the reason for something. *As* and *since* are a little more formal.

I'm calling to complain ***because*** *the goods are damaged.*
I am returning the goods inside this package, ***as/since*** *they were damaged on arrival.*

As and *since* can come at the beginning of the sentence. *Because* is not common in this position.

As/since *the goods were damaged on arrival, I am returning them inside this package.*

We use *because of, due to, owing to* and *as a result of* before a noun or noun phrase.

I'm calling to complain ***because of*** *the damaged goods.*

B Result: *so*

We use *so* to express a result. Note the relation between *because* and *so*:

I'm calling to complain ***because*** *the goods are damaged.* (reason)
The goods are damaged, ***so*** *I'm calling to complain.* (result)

C Purpose: *to* and *for*

We use the *to* infinitive to express purpose (to say why we do things).

He went to the airport ***to meet*** *Mr Li.*
(NOT ~~for to meet~~) (NOT ~~for meet~~)
I'm calling ***to talk*** *about the sales conference.*
(NOT ~~for to talk~~) (NOT ~~for talk~~)

We can use *in order to* or *so as to* in place of *to*. They are more formal.

He called a press conference ***in order to*** *explain the background to the merger.*

We use the negative *in order not to* or *so as not to*. We cannot use *not to* on its own.

I'll call a taxi ***so as not to*** *miss my flight.*
(NOT ~~I'll call a taxi not to miss my flight~~)

We can use *for* followed by a noun to say why we do something.

I'm here ***for a meeting*** *with Elena Kopytina.*
(= to have a meeting)
Shall we go out ***for some lunch****?*
(= to have some lunch)

D Purpose: *so that*

We can use *so (that)* to express purpose. After *so (that)* we use subject + verb.

We have to be more flexible ***so (that) we can*** *respond to changing customer expectations.*

For a present purpose we use the present simple, *will* or *can*. For a past purpose we use the past simple, *would* or *could*.

I'll send it by DHL Express today ***so (that)*** *it* ***gets****/it* ***'ll get*** *to them on time.*
I sent it by DHL Express yesterday ***so (that)*** *it* ***got****/it* ***'d get*** *to them on time.*

If the subject of the first part of the sentence and the subject of the purpose clause are the same, we use *to*. If not, we use *so (that)*.

I'm *calling* ***to talk*** *about the sales conference.*
('calling' and 'talk' both have 'I' as the subject)
I'm *calling* ***so (that) we can talk*** *about the sales conference.*
('calling' and 'talk' have different subjects)

E Manner: *like, as, as if*

We can use *like* or *as* to mean 'in the way that'. *Like* is more common, and *as* is more formal.

He runs the company ***like/as*** *his father used to.*
We'll have four people working on the stand, ***like/as*** *we did last year.*

Before a noun or noun phrase we must use *like* if we mean 'in the way that'.

He runs the company ***like*** *his father.*
(NOT ~~as his father~~)

We use *like* to give examples.

Only a few companies, ***like*** *Areva and GE, can provide the technology for a nuclear power plant.*
(NOT ~~as Areva and GE~~)

We use *as* to say what job/function/role a person or thing has.

She works ***as*** *a financial controller.*
We're using the Croatian market ***as*** *a test for the whole Balkans region.*
We use this room ***as*** *a storage area.*

Like would be wrong in the last three examples because it means 'something is similar to something' not 'something is something'.

We can use *as if* or *like* before a clause to say how someone or something feels, looks, sounds or behaves.

I have a temperature. I feel ***as if/like*** *I should go home.*
(NOT ~~I feel as I should go home~~)
It looks ***as if/like*** *we're going to break even by the end of the year.*
(NOT ~~It looks as we're going to break even~~)

Exercises

Sections A, B

42.1 Complete the second sentence so it has a similar meaning to the first and contains the word in brackets.

1 I sent Karen a copy of the minutes because she missed the meeting. (so)
Karen missed the meeting, *so I sent her a copy of the minutes* .

2 She doesn't know, so I'll ask someone else. (since)
Since ______ .

3 I'll call you back. I have to go now because I have a meeting. (so)
I'll call you back. I have a meeting, ______ .

4 I had a lot of paperwork to do, so I finished work late. (because)
I finished work late ______ .

5 I had to do all the paperwork, so I finished work late. (because of)
I finished work late ______ I had to do.

Sections C, D

42.2 Underline the correct words.

1 We're not in this business just *to make/for to make* short-term profit.
2 I'll explain in more detail *so/in order to* our objectives are clear.
3 I wrote the date in my diary *so that/so to* I wouldn't forget.
4 He resigned *in order to/for* spend more time with his family.
5 Alesha came to me *in order to/for* advice.
6 We'll agree to your offer so that we *can/could* close the deal.
7 We agreed to their offer so that we *can/could* close the deal.
8 She rechecked the figures so that the auditors *won't/wouldn't* find any errors.
9 I'll recheck the figures so that the auditors *won't/wouldn't* find any errors.
10 Many visitors come here *to see/for to see* our automated production line.

Sections C, D

42.3 Match the beginning of each sentence 1–12 with an ending a) or b).

1	I went to Barcelona to	*b*	a) the trade fair.
2	I went to Barcelona for		b) attend the trade fair.
3	I'm here for		a) a meeting with Manuel Lopez.
4	I'm here to		b) meet Manuel Lopez.
5	I kept his business card so that I		a) 'd remember his name.
6	I'll keep his business cards so that I		b) remember his name.
7	I think it's time to		a) a short coffee break.
8	I think it's time for		b) have a short coffee break.
9	I'll deal with it personally so I		a) could check everything was OK.
10	I dealt with it personally so I		b) can check everything is OK.
11	It's worth shopping around for		a) a better price.
12	It's worth shopping around to		b) get a better price.

Exercises

Sections C, D **42.4 Write ✓ if the sentence is possible. Write ✗ if it is grammatically incorrect.**

1 I'll speak louder so that everyone can hear. ✓
2 I'll speak louder in order to everyone can hear. ☐
3 Sorry, I'll explain my proposal again to avoid any confusion. ☐
4 Sorry, I'll explain my proposal again so avoid any confusion. ☐
5 Sorry, I'll explain my proposal again so we avoid any confusion. ☐
6 We send a monthly newsletter not to lose contact with our clients. ☐
7 We send a monthly newsletter so as not to lose contact with our clients. ☐
8 I'll take an umbrella so I won't get wet. ☐
9 I'll take an umbrella so I wouldn't get wet. ☐
10 I'll take an umbrella so I don't get wet. ☐

Section E **42.5 Complete the sentences with *as* or *like*, or put *as/like* if both are possible.**

1 While I was at university, I sometimes worked __as__ a waiter to earn some extra money.
2 In a situation like this, you should do exactly ________ it says in the book.
3 I'll take my annual leave in August, ________ last year.
4 It sounds ________ the negotiations are not going very well.
5 We sent the order in two consignments, ________ we agreed in the meeting.
6 Some countries, ________ Sweden, have strong environmental policies.
7 I'm lucky. I have a small room at home that I use ________ my study.
8 This crisis is not ________ the last one. It's worse!

Sections A, B C, D, E **42.6 Underline the correct words in this dialogue between two managers.**

PAMELA: I've just seen the last set of sales figures, and it looks [1] *as if/as* we'll make a loss this quarter. Things are getting serious, and the CEO is talking about laying people off, [2] *like/as* our competitors. We need to look for some imaginative solutions [3] *so/for* we can avoid that.

JACK: You're right. We have a great team here, and we don't want to lose anyone. It would be good to reassure people that their jobs are safe, [4] *not to/so as not to* worry them unnecessarily.

PAMELA: That's right, and [5] *since/so that* I work [6] *like/as* the Director of Human Resources it's my responsibility to come up with some ideas.

JACK: So what are you thinking of?

PAMELA: Obviously we'll begin by having a freeze on hiring new people, [7] *like/as if* we did last year. Beyond that, I'm thinking of unpaid vacations and reducing employees' work hours.

JACK: Well, [8] *since that/as* the situation is serious I think people might be prepared to accept that.

PAMELA: They'll have to accept it. It's a crisis, [9] *so/because* crisis measures are necessary. And people will have to do a greater variety of jobs as well. We'll train staff [10] *that/so* they can move from one department to another with ease.

JACK: Even people [11] *as/like* me?

PAMELA: Yes, even you. I'm calling a meeting next week [12] *to/for* explain my ideas.

Tasks

Speaking: listen and repeat

1 42 **You are going to hear eight phrases. Listen and repeat.**

Translate

2 Translate these short texts taken from the Internet into your own language. Remember not to translate word for word, but rather to make it sound natural.

Nations are constructing futuristic science parks, with nearby housing and city amenities, to gain a competitive edge in the next generation of knowledge industries.

BusinessWeek website

A chemical maker reduced the time to market of its top R&D project by more than 12 months. How? It killed three zombie projects, redeployed the resources to accelerate its most promising new product, and improved early-stage R&D collaboration between engineers and marketers so that executives could make better decisions.

BNET website

Writing: personalized practice

3 Complete the sentences with your own ideas.

1 I'm going to call head office to *check a few details about the new pricing policy* .
2 I'm going to call head office so as not to ______________________________ .
3 Hello? Is that customer services? Yes, I'm calling to complain because of ______________________________ and because you ______________________________ .
4 I'm here in Paris for ______________________________ .
5 I'm here in Paris so that ______________________________ .
6 These days we don't do business like ______________________________ .
7 A plastic ice-cube tray can also be used as ______________________________ .
8 When I fell in love for the first time I felt as if ______________________________ .

Rehearsal for the real world

4 Answer these questions using a 'reason/purpose' word or phrase from page 174 and ideas of your own. Write a complete paragraph each time.

1 Why do some people climb mountains?
2 Why do people yawn/sneeze/shiver?
3 Why do people get married?
4 Why are you doing this exercise?

Answer these questions using a 'manner' word or phrase from page 174 and ideas of your own. Write a complete paragraph each time.

5 How does your boss treat you? How do you treat your boss?
6 How do you treat your boss's boss?
7 How do you use the largest room in your workplace? How could you use it?
8 How did you feel when your first child/nephew/niece was born?

If you are working in class, choose some paragraphs to read aloud. Ask and answer questions.

43 Developing an argument 1

A Linking across sentences

Units 41 and 42 gave short, everyday words to join parts of a sentence. We can use longer, more formal words and phrases to link across sentences and within more complex sentences. Look at the examples below for *and, but* and *so*:

and: *In addition, Besides, Moreover, Furthermore*
but: *However, Nevertheless, On the other hand*
so: *Therefore, Consequently, As a result*

These words are typical of careful speech (e.g. presentations) and writing. They usually come at the start of a sentence and have a comma afterwards, but can come after a comma in the middle of a sentence.

Supplier A is cheaper and has good delivery times. ***However****, supplier B has better quality and is more flexible with volume.*

This new process produces less waste, and ***as a result*** *it's much better for the environment.*

B Numbering points and concluding: *firstly, in addition, finally, overall, in conclusion*

We can use *First/Firstly/First of all* to begin a list of points. For other points we say *Second/Secondly/Third/Thirdly*, etc.

To add a point without numbering we can say *In addition, As well as this* or *Besides this.*

To finish the points we can say *Finally.*

Why choose the Czech Republic? Well, ***first of all****, it has a trained, flexible and relatively inexpensive workforce.* ***As well as this****, it has a good location in Central Europe near to key markets.* ***Finally****, it has good infrastructure.*

To conclude one particular discussion point we can say *Overall* or *Taking everything into consideration.*

So, ***overall****, things are improving.*

To finish and conclude more formally we can say *In conclusion.*

In conclusion*, I'd like to thank you all very much for coming here today.*

C Examples: *for example, for instance, such as*

We can use *for example* or *for instance.*

Our costs have gone up. ***For instance****, the cost of steel has nearly doubled.*
Our costs have gone up. The cost of steel, ***for example****, has nearly doubled.*

We use *such as* in the middle of a sentence to give examples. It is the same as 'like'. *Such as* is followed by a noun phrase, not a whole clause.

Some delays are beyond our control, ***such as*** *strikes or bad weather.*

D True but surprising: *in fact, actually*

We use *In fact, Actually* or *As a matter of fact* to say what is really true, when this is surprising or different to what people think.

We have plenty in stock. ***In fact****, we could deliver tomorrow.* (surprising)
I thought we had some in stock, but ***actually*** *we don't.* (different)

E Alternatives: *either ... or, instead of*

We use *either* to begin a list of possibilities. We do not begin with *or*.

Either *we could cancel the launch,* ***or*** *we could simply postpone it.* (NOT ~~Or we could ..., or we could ...~~)

We use *instead (of)* to mean 'in the place of something else'. At the end of a sentence, *instead* is used without *of.*

Can we meet on Friday ***instead of*** *Thursday?*
Instead of *Thursday, can we meet on Friday?*
Can we meet on Friday ***instead****?*

F Exceptions: *except for, apart from*

We use *except, except for, with the exception of* or *apart from* to mean 'not including'.

I contacted everyone ***except (for)*** *Irina.*

G Generalizing: *in general, on the whole*

To talk generally we can say: *In general, On the whole, As a rule, Typically, Broadly speaking.*

In general*, large public companies have five key relationships: customers, business partners, suppliers, employees and shareholders.*

If we want to make a balanced argument, we often use one of these phrases followed by a word like *but* + a contrasting idea.

On the whole*, I think you're right,* ***although*** *I disagree with you about the level of risk.*
As a rule*, we usually ask for an upfront payment on a first-time order.* ***However****, I think we can be flexible on that.*

H Summarizing: *so, basically, to sum up*

To summarize quickly we can use *So, Basically, In short* and *To put it simply.* To summarize more formally we can use *To sum up* and *In summary.*

Basically*, the whole idea is ridiculous.*
So, to sum up*, I've looked at three main issues in my presentation. First, ...*

Exercises

Sections A, C, D, E, F, G

43.1 **Underline the correct words.**

1 If you don't want the Canon, what about this Panasonic *instead/instead of*?
2 The fall in share prices has made investors nervous. On the other *side/hand*, it could be an excellent buying opportunity.
3 *As a rule/As a whole,* I don't normally have a big lunch, but I'll come with you to the restaurant today.
4 All commodity prices rose last week, *apart/except* soybeans and wheat.
5 We can *either/or* wait for a train, or go by taxi.
6 I know Madrid very well. *As a matter of fact/On the whole*, I worked there for a short time many years ago.
7 *For instance/On the whole* I am a supporter of the green movement. However, I think that they are wrong to oppose nuclear energy.
8 I like to drive to work because I can go door-to-door. *On the other hand/Besides*, the train would probably be quicker.
9 I like to drive to work because I can go door-to-door. *On the other hand/Besides*, the company pays for my petrol.
10 Investment in areas *for example/such as* biotechnology can be risky.
11 Investment in some areas, *for example/such as* biotechnology, can be risky.
12 The résumés are all very strong, *except for/instead of* these two here.

Sections A, C, D, E, F, G

43.2 **Complete the sentences with the words or phrases in the box.**

~~actually~~	moreover	either	except	in general
instead	nevertheless	so	such as	therefore

1 People think it's expensive, but *actually* over the long term it isn't.
2 The restaurant is open every day ________ Monday.
3 She is out of the country and ________ unable to attend the meeting.
4 I was going on Tuesday, but now I'm going on Monday ________ .
5 ________ , I think the meeting went very well, although we didn't manage to agree on a budget for next year.
6 Some areas, ________ recruitment, are outsourced to other companies.
7 I'm sorry, I've had enough. ________ he goes, or I go.
8 It's reliable, safe and easy to use. ________ , it's excellent value for money.
9 It's reliable, safe and easy to use. ________ , the maintenance costs can be quite high.
10 ________ , in short, we offer a full range of insurance products to both corporate and private clients.

"On the one hand, eliminating the middleman would result in lower costs, increased sales, and greater consumer satisfaction; on the other hand, we're the middleman."

Sections A, C, G

43.3 **Put four commas in this short paragraph.**

In general taking an MBA is a good idea for an ambitious young professional. However you do have to make some sacrifices. You miss out on two years' valuable work experience for example and it can be very expensive.

Exercises

Sections A, B, C, D, E, F, G, H

43.4 Read this article about traffic in city centres. Complete the article by choosing the best alternative from A, B, C or D below.

Want to enter the city? Sorry, you'll have to pay.

Traffic congestion in city centres is a big problem for both businesses and residents. Policy makers are being forced to think of solutions based on public transport, road pricing and restricted use of various kinds. What are the reasons for this? [1] *B* , cars cause noise and pollution in areas where people walk, shop or go sightseeing. [2]_____ this, they require parking areas, and space in city centres is limited. And [3]_____ , cars cause traffic jams and [4]_____ many hours of work time are lost.

[5]_____ , people do like the freedom and convenience of using their own car, and alternatives are often unavailable or of poor quality. What can be done? Public transport has to become more reliable and more comfortable. [6]_____ , bicycle use should be encouraged – [7]_____ , by having more cycle lanes. Some large cities, [8]_____ Cologne and Amsterdam, are already organized in this way. But the most radical measure is road pricing. Asking motorists to pay to enter city centres is controversial, but is an increasingly common solution. So, [9]_____ , we can see that imaginative and sometimes unpopular measures will be needed to make the city centre a more pleasant place to work and live.

	A	B	C	D
1	A As well	B First of all	C In fact	D As a result
2	A Besides	B Also	C For example	D Except
3	A for example	B however	C instead	D finally
4	A either	B both	C as a result	D instead of
5	A However	B Therefore	C So	D In conclusion
6	A To sum up	B In addition	C Actually	D For example
7	A on the whole	B in addition	C actually	D for example
8	A such as	B as well as	C instead of	D except
9	A thirdly	B in conclusion	C instead	D also

Sections A, B, D, E, G

43.5 Complete this speech made by the leader of a Korean trade delegation in Slovakia with the words and phrases in the box.

as a rule	~~first of all~~	however	in addition
in conclusion	in fact	instead of	therefore

"Could I just say a few words? Thank you. Well, [1] *first of all* I'd like to thank everyone here at the Bratislava Chamber of Commerce for organizing our short tour of Slovakia. We have enjoyed looking round all the factories and meeting the employees. [2]__________ , I would like to thank the Korean Ministry of Foreign Affairs and Trade, who made the whole trip possible. As you know, we see the European market as very important for our company. [3]__________ , it is central to our future plans. [4]__________ I look forward to a close cooperation between our two countries in the future. [5]__________ I think it's better to keep the ceremonies short on occasions like this. [6]__________ , I would just like to take this opportunity to leave you with something to remember our visit. I have great pleasure in presenting this book with photographs of Korea to Mr Telensky, who took such good care of us. [7]__________ , I hope that we may have the pleasure of welcoming some of you to our country in the near future. Perhaps the next time we meet it will be in Seoul [8]__________ Bratislava! Once again, thank you all very much."

Tasks

Speaking: listen and repeat

1 43 **You are going to hear eight phrases. Listen and repeat.**

Translate

2 **Translate these short texts taken from the Internet into your own language. Remember not to translate word for word, but rather to make it sound natural.**

As a result of the reforms in the area of banking, trade, and investment, the economy grew significantly and achieved high annual growth rates. In fact, last year the economy grew by 8%.

Asia Econ website

Researchers found that while underweight and extremely obese people die earlier than people of a normal weight, people who are slightly overweight actually live longer than those of a normal weight.

Reuters website

Writing: personalized practice

3 **Complete the sentences with your own ideas.**

1 I've divided my presentation into three parts. First of all I'm going to give you an overview of *the company and its product range* .
Secondly, I'm going to ______ .
And finally I'll ______ .
If you have any questions, please feel free to interrupt.

2 As you can see, our products offer excellent value for money. As well as this, ______ .

3 Our costs have gone up significantly this year. For instance, ______ .

4 Some delays are beyond our control, such as ______ .

5 We have a lot of experience in this market. In fact, ______ .

6 I thought that working in a cross-cultural team would present some challenges, but actually ______ .

7 At the rate we're working we're not going to meet the project deadline. The way I see it we have two options. Either we ______ ,
or we ______ .

8 Why don't we outsource our recruitment process instead of ______ ?

9 The planning for the conference is all complete, except for ______ .

10 In general I think that ______ ,
although ______ .

11 Yes, I listened to everything she said. Basically, ______ .

12 So, to sum up, the main message that I want you to take away from this presentation is ______ .

44 Developing an argument 2

A Other linking words and phrases

Study this list of common linking words and phrases. It extends the list given in unit 43.

Emphasizing something important
Especially, Particularly, In particular, Above all, Specifically

Explaining in another way
In other words, To put it another way, That is (to say), To put it simply

Correcting yourself
I mean, Or rather

Changing the topic (informal)
By the way, Talking about, On the subject of

Announcing a change of topic (more formal)
In relation to, With regard to, As far as … is concerned

Preparing to finish
Anyway

We need to keep our costs down, ***especially*** *in the current economic climate.*
We need to keep our costs down, ***especially as/because*** *the company is not doing so well.*
By the way*, how is Claudia? I haven't seen her for ages.*
And that's the situation in Europe. ***As far as*** *Latin America* ***is concerned****, we only have a presence in Brazil at the moment.*
Anyway*, I really must be going now. It was very nice to meet you.*

B Personal comment

There are many words and short phrases that come at the beginning of a sentence and help us to make a personal comment.

Giving your own ideas (often to disagree)
I think, From my point of view, In my opinion, In my view, Personally, I am convinced that

You heard something but are not sure
Apparently, It seems that, It appears that

Something is already known or not surprising
Clearly, Of course, Obviously

Good/bad luck
Fortunately, Luckily, Unfortunately, Sadly

You are being honest
To be honest, Frankly, Actually, To tell you the truth

Apparently*, she resigned because they refused to give her a promotion.*
Of course*, we'll have to do some market research before we take a final decision.*
Frankly*, I don't really care what he thinks.*

Other words used to make a personal comment include:

admittedly, coincidentally, curiously, incredibly, interestingly, ironically, naturally, paradoxically, predictably, significantly, surprisingly, unbelievably, understandably, unexpectedly

Admittedly*, option B is a little more expensive. I still think it's better, though.*
Ironically*, the talk about mass communication was cancelled because no one knew it was on the programme.*
Predictably*, Production complained about Sales promising unrealistic delivery times – again.*
Understandably*, she was upset by the news.*

C *at the end, in the end, at last*

The phrases *at the end*, *in the end* and *at last* do not have the same meaning.

At the end refers to a point in time
There were a lot of questions ***at the end*** *of my talk.*

In the end means 'after a lot of time'/'eventually'
I waited until ten, and ***in the end*** *I left.*
(used with a past tense)

At last means we are pleased because a long wait has ended
At last *I've finished this report!*
(used with a present tense, e.g. present perfect)

D *if, unless, otherwise*

Conditionals with *if* (units 17 and 18) are important for developing an argument.

The linking words *unless* and *otherwise* have the meaning 'if not'. Look at the next three examples, which all have the same meaning:

If *we* ***don't pay*** *the invoice now, they'll cut our credit line.*
Unless *we* ***pay*** *the invoice now, they'll cut our credit line.*
We should pay the invoice now, ***otherwise*** *they'll cut our credit line.*

E Abbreviations in written English

Note the following abbreviations, which are common in written English. The first two can also be spoken (simply as letters).

i.e. = 'that is to say' (from the Latin 'id est')
e.g. = 'for example' (from the Latin 'exempli gratia')
NB = 'note' (from the Latin 'nota bene')

Exercises

Sections A, B, C, D, E

44.1 Underline the correct words.

1 I like all the marketing ideas, but *in particular/in particularly* the free samples.
2 And that's the situation in France and Germany. *In relation to/In relationship with* the UK market, things are a little different.
3 *It seems that/Apparently that* the Board is looking for a new CEO.
4 *Fortunately/With good fortune,* our department is not affected by the restructuring.
5 *Actually/Truly*, I've never really trusted him.
6 *With regard to/With regard* the question of finance, we'll need to raise about $2m.
7 I tried arguing with them, but *at the end/in the end* I just gave up.
8 Frankie's managed to get a job *at last/in the end*!
9 *Unless/Otherwise* we decide within the next few weeks, it'll be too late.
10 We must decide within the next few weeks, *unless/otherwise* it'll be too late.
11 We're expanding into some of the smaller European markets, *i.e./e.g.* Slovenia and the Baltic States.
12 We need a sales network in each of Europe's three biggest economies, *i.e./e.g.* Germany, France and the UK.

Sections A, B

44.2 Complete the replies to the comments in speech marks by following the instructions in brackets and using the words and phrases in the box.

above all	anyway	apparently	by the way	
frankly	of course	or rather	~~personally~~	unfortunately

1 'We should have the prototype ready by June.'
→ (give your own ideas) *Personally* , I think August is more realistic.
2 'The insurance premium doesn't look too expensive.'
→ (something is already known) ______ , it will need to be renewed annually.
3 'I've got two spare tickets for the opera tonight. Are you interested?'
→ (you would like to go but can't) ______ , I've got a previous commitment.
4 'So, I had lunch with Magda and Viktor, and then I had a meeting with the auditors.'
→ (change the topic) ______ , what did Magda say about Paris?
5 'The joint venture with Optika is running into all sorts of problems.'
→ (be honest) ______ , we should never have entered into it in the first place.
6 'Why didn't Robert get the new sales job?'
→ (you heard something) ______ , his interview was a complete disaster.
7 'Yes, the conference should be very interesting. And there's a choice of hotels.'
→ (prepare to finish) ______ , we can sort out the hotels nearer the time.
8 'Carmen really deserves to be the team leader on this project.'
→ (emphasize one important point) ______ , because of her experience in this area.
9 'I think we should target our next line of clothes at a younger market.'
→ (correct yourself) It's a good idea. ______ , it could be a good idea if we don't lose our existing customers by doing so.

Exercises

Sections A, B, C, unit 43

44.3 <u>Underline</u> the correct words in this presentation about robotics. This exercise includes some revision of unit 43.

> Today I'm going to be talking about robotics, and [1]*anyway/in particular* the commercial exploitation of robots. [2]*Especially/Clearly* there's a huge interest in the subject, as can be seen by the number of people in the audience today. And this is not surprising, as we predict that over the next decade robotics is going to be one of the world's fastest growing industries. Tens of millions of dollars are being invested in the development of personal robots, and [3]*instead/as a result* progress has been rapid. Scientists now understand the technology necessary for complex actions like walking on two feet without falling over. [4]*On the other hand/At the end*, it's clear that the development of 'robo sapiens' – with something that approximates human intelligence – will take longer, [5]*especially/or rather* a lot longer.
>
> Let's take one example where robotics is making a big impact now: health care. Robots are doing a whole range of tasks: reminding patients to take medicines, interacting with patients who show cognitive decline, collecting data and monitoring patients, and assisting people with limited mobility. [6]*Specifically/In fact*, they'll soon be doing almost everything [7]*except for/instead of* peeling the grapes!
>
> Who is taking the lead in developing robotics worldwide? [8]*Nevertheless/In general* it's the Japanese, [9]*although/apart from* the Americans are trying hard to catch up. But the market is big enough for everyone. Small companies across Europe are developing and selling robots in areas [10]*such as/for example* automated manufacturing, materials handling in dangerous or dirty environments, and security and military applications.
>
> However, [11]*as far as start-up companies are concerned/concerning start-up companies*, home entertainment is perhaps a safer area to launch the robot revolution. Compared to the other areas, singing and dancing robots don't do anything essential, and so it's OK if they make a mistake sometimes. [12]*Especially/Furthermore*, home entertainment is likely to be the biggest market [13]*in the end/at last*, with some households having two or three robots, just like they have computers today.
>
> So, [14]*in fact/to sum up*, I've tried to show you how I believe we're entering a new age, the age of the robot, and it's an age that's full of business opportunities.

Sections A, B, C

44.4 Check the answers to exercise 44.3 before you do this exercise. Then find words and phrases from the answers to 44.3 that are similar to the expressions below.

1	on the whole	*in general*	8	however	______
2	apart from	______	9	in short	______
3	because of this	______	10	eventually	______
4	as a matter of fact	______	11	above all	______
5	with regard to	______	12	I mean	______
6	despite the fact that	______	13	like	______
7	in addition	______	14	obviously	______

Tasks

Speaking: listen and repeat

1 44 **You are going to hear eight phrases. Listen and repeat.**

Translate

2 Translate these short texts taken from the Internet into your own language. Remember not to translate word for word, but rather to make it sound natural.

'Yahoo is not immune to the ongoing economic downturn,' said chief executive Carol Bartz, who was appointed at the beginning of the year with a mandate to transform Yahoo's fortunes. In response to a drop in revenue, Yahoo intends to trim its workforce of 13,500 by a further 5% as it adapts to the increasingly difficult environment. David Garrity, an industry analyst, said cuts to Yahoo's extensive operation were bearing fruit: 'We're actually seeing some benefit as far as the bottom line is concerned.'

Guardian website

Bear markets are a natural part of stocks, in the same way that fires are a natural force in the forests. Even though it's tough to watch, the market is usually healthier in the end.

Wall Street Journal website

Writing: personalized practice

3 Complete the sentences with your own ideas.

1 I thought there were some very strong candidates for the new job. In particular, *the first two people we saw should be called back for another interview* .
2 They're going to downsize the company. In other words, ______ .
3 Yes, very interesting idea about the product launch. By the way, ______ .
4 So that's the story in our banking division. As far as the insurance side of the business is concerned, ______ .
5 I was speaking to Gina from Accounts yesterday. Apparently, ______ .
6 The TD600 has more functionality than the TD400. Of course, ______ .
7 Kate was in favour of the idea but Angelo was against it. Frankly, ______ .
8 In the end I found that ______ .
9 At last ______ . Now I can go home.
10 Admittedly ______ , but at least it works.
11 Senior managers, i.e. ______ , each have an executive office on the top floor.
12 Some departments, e.g. ______ , have had their budgets cut this year.

Rehearsal for the real world

4 Look again at the longer texts in units 43 and 44 that use several linking words and phrases (exercises 43.4, 43.5 and 44.3). Now write a few paragraphs on one of the following topics:

- The script for a guided tour of my factory/offices/campus
- The script for a guided tour of my city/town
- Marketing successes and failures in my business
- The impact of new technology on my business
- Money-making ideas from my favourite hobby

If you are working in class, choose some texts to read aloud. Ask and answer questions.

45 Developing an argument 3

A Emphasizing: preparatory *it*

We can emphasize information by using *It* plus a form of *be* at the beginning of the sentence. Compare a) and b) each time:

a) *Magda really does all the work in that team.*
b) ***It's Magda who** really does all the work in that team.* (not anybody else)

a) *I spoke to you on the phone last week.*
b) ***It was me who** spoke to you on the phone last week.* (not somebody else)

a) *They were discussing my suggestion.*
b) ***It was my suggestion that** they were discussing.* (not anybody else's)

a) *We should move our production to Morocco.*
b) ***It's Morocco that** we should move our production to.* (not somewhere else)

B Emphasizing: *The thing is*

We can emphasize a whole sentence with the phrase *The thing is.*

***The thing is (that)** the idea is just too risky.*
***The thing is**, how much money will all this cost?*

Other nouns used with this structure include:

The answer is	*The fact is*	*The idea is*
The point is	*The problem is*	*The question is*
The solution is	*The trouble is*	*The truth is*

***The fact is**, we should just use a different supplier.*
***The question is**, what are we going to do about it?*
***The trouble is (that)** it's going to be very expensive.*

C Emphasizing: *What we need is*

We can emphasize a whole sentence with a clause that begins with *What* and has a form of *be*.

***What we need is** a bigger budget.*
***What we can't do is** just walk away.*
***What I'm going to do is** call them right now and explain the whole situation.*
***What worries me is (that)** the costs for this project keep escalating.*
***What happened was (that)** the road was closed and I had to come by a different route.*

Note. Sections A–C above are all examples of 'cleft sentences' ('cleft' is a grammar word meaning 'divided'). There are two parts to a cleft sentence, one with the verb *be* and the other with the main verb.

D Emphasizing: negative frequency + inversion

We can emphasize a negative frequency expression such as *never (before)* by putting it at the beginning of the sentence. This is then followed by auxiliary + subject (so an inversion of the order of a normal statement).

***Never (before) have I received** such good customer service. Their sales staff were outstanding.*
(normally: I have never (before) received such good ...)

Other phrases that are followed by an inversion are shown below. These structures are mostly quite formal.

***Under no circumstances** can we agree to their proposal.*
***On no account** must we repeat the mistake we made last year.*
***At no time** was our Marketing Director aware that the advertising agency was working for a competitor at the same time.*
***Not only** did we lose our money, but we seriously damaged our reputation as well.*
***Only then** did I realize that I was speaking to their CEO, not just a regular middle manager.*

E Emphasizing: position of adverbs

Unit 36 mentioned that the usual order of adverbs is manner-place-time ('How–Where–When').

*Our sales rose **slightly in Benelux last year**.*

Place or time can be moved to the front for emphasis. This can be done over several sentences to organize a paragraph around a time frame or a series of locations.

***In Benelux** our sales rose slightly last year. **In Germany and France** sales were unchanged, while **in Spain** they actually fell a little.*

F Emphasizing: *do / did* with affirmatives

Do / Did can be used to emphasize an affirmative verb.

*Yes, we **do** have that in stock. So you can order as many as you want.*
(normally: Yes, we have that in stock)
*I **did** make a back-up copy, just like you suggested. It's on my USB stick.*
(normally: I made a back-up copy)

G Emphasizing: field of relevance

If we want to emphasize one particular aspect of an issue, we can use a phrase like:

From a technical / financial / commercial / economic / administrative point of view, ...

We can also say:

Technically / financially / commercially / economically / administratively (speaking), ...

Exercises

Section A

45.1 Rewrite each sentence using *It* + a form of *be* so that you emphasize the underlined word.

1 We get paid in <u>dollars</u>, not in euros.
It's dollars that we get paid in, not euros.

2 <u>Brand image</u> really differentiates products.

3 <u>Nouriel Roubini</u> gave the best analysis of the recession in 2008.

4 They implemented <u>my</u> ideas.

5 We should invest in <u>emerging markets</u>, not our domestic market.

6 <u>I</u> negotiated that deal.

Sections B, C

45.2 Complete the sentences with the phrases in the box. Several answers are possible but only one solution uses each phrase in the most appropriate way.

The answer is	~~The idea is~~	The question is	The trouble is	The truth is

1 Leyla told us about Head Office's plans for next year. *The idea is* to launch a new line of bathtime products for babies – body washes, shampoos, towels made from organic cotton, that sort of thing.

2 Sales are falling and several of our best managers have left. What, then, should we do? ______ we need to replace our CEO with one who has the commitment and vision to turn the company around.

3 We've trained him, coached him and given him every chance. But it doesn't seem to make much difference. ______ , the job is just too big for him.

4 Our products are not differentiated in the market. They appeal to everyone and no one. ______ , who exactly do we want to target?

5 Customers like our products, but they complain they can't find them in the shops. ______ our distributors carry products from many different companies, and we don't get the focus we need.

Continue as before.

What I'm going to do is	What we can't do is
What we need is	What happened was
What worries me is	

6 ______ that no one is giving me straight answers to my questions.

7 ______ just wait and hope that the problem goes away.

8 ______ that Sandra forgot to tell me the meeting time had changed.

9 ______ a better and faster management information system.

10 ______ talk to my boss and see what she says about it.

"I was going to say, 'Well, I don't make the rules.' But, of course, I <u>do</u> make the rules."

Exercises

Section D **45.3 The first few words in the sentences below are in the wrong order. Write the sentences again with a capital letter and the correct word order.**

1 before never I have seen such incompetence.
Never before have I seen such incompetence.

2 under circumstances he will no sell his shares in the company.

____

3 account no on you must talk to the press about this.

____

4 at time I no did authorize this payment.

____

5 only not they did offer me a promotion, they're also upgrading my car to a Lexus.

____

Section E **45.4 Move three time expressions to a new position in this paragraph about the early history of SAP. The new version should emphasize the time frame. The first has been done for you.**

> Five former IBM employees launched a company (in 1972) to develop some software for processing real-time business information. The first component was complete one year later: a financial accounting package. 50 of the 100 largest German companies were SAP customers by the middle of the 1980s, and revenues had reached around $50 million.

Section F **45.5 Rewrite these sentences using *do/did* to emphasize the underlined verb.**

1 Yes, I <u>understand</u> what you're saying, but I still disagree.
Yes, I do understand what you're saying, but I still disagree.

2 I <u>ordered</u> the spare parts, but they haven't arrived yet.
______________________________, but they haven't arrived yet.

3 <u>Have</u> a seat. Would you like anything to drink?
______________________________. Would you like anything to drink?

4 Believe me, I <u>did</u> everything I could, but it just wasn't enough.
Believe me, ______________________________.

Section G **45.6 Complete the sentences with *commercial, commercially, financial, financially, technical* or *technically*.**

1 From a *technical* point of view, the new turbine is an engineering masterwork.
2 ____________, the new turbine is an engineering masterwork.
3 ____________ speaking, the new turbine was very expensive to develop.
4 From a ____________ point of view, the new turbine was very expensive to develop.
5 ____________ speaking, the new turbine will have a limited market.
6 From a ____________ point of view, the new turbine will have a limited market.

Tasks

Speaking: listen and repeat

1 45 **You are going to hear eight phrases. Listen and repeat.**

Translate

2 Translate these short texts taken from the Internet into your own language. Remember not to translate word for word, but rather to make it sound natural.

There is no doubt that changes are happening in the accountancy sector. The question is, which of the Big Four firms will be the strongest? Based on revenues and current strategy, PwC, KPMG and Deloitte are likely to survive, and Ernst & Young are not.

AccountancyAge website

Never before have leaders experienced the scale and complexity of change that they face now. Consider, for example, the competition that businesses face in a flatter world; the impact of global issues like pirating and climate change; social forces shaping the work environment; and the influence of technological advancements.

BusinessWeek website

Writing: personalized practice

3 Complete the sentences with your own ideas.

1 It's Manuela who *organized the whole event. I think she did a great job* .
2 It was me who ______ .
3 It's now that ______
______ , not next week or next month.
4 Yes, yes, I understand that these changes aren't going to be easy. The point is,
______ .
5 I think we all know what the problems are. The question is, ______
______ ?
6 They're one of our biggest customers. What we can't do is ______
______ .
7 I apologize once again for what has happened. What I'm going to do is ______
______ .
8 If everything goes as planned, the new service should attract a lot of new clients. What worries me is ______ .
9 Never before have I seen ______
______ .
10 Under no circumstances can we ______
______ .
11 Not only did we ______ ,
but we also ______ .
12 That's not really true. In fact we do have ______
______ .
13 From a financial point of view, ______
______ .
14 Technically speaking, ______
______ .

Rehearsal for the real world

4 Think of a problem or difficult issue you are facing in your business, professional or personal life. Choose an issue where there are several possible solutions/outcomes. Write a short presentation where you explain the situation and what might happen.

If you are working in class, choose some presentations to read aloud. Ask and answer questions.

46 Prepositions of place

A *at* or *in*?

We use *at* to talk about the position of something, or about the place where something happens. *At* shows a general location.

*There's someone **at the door**.*
(position)
*I'll see you **at the meeting**.*
(where something happens)

We use *in* with the name of a container, place or area to show that someone or something is inside it.

*There's plenty of paper **in the photocopier**.*
*She's **in the third room** on the left.*
*Our head office is **in Paris**/**in the north**.*

Study these examples for public buildings:

*I'll see you **at** the airport.*
(the place in general)
*I'll see you **in** the airport terminal.*
(inside the building)
*I had a hard day **at** the office.*
(perhaps I spent some time out of the building)
*I'll be back **in** the office at three.*
(inside the building)

B Expressions with *at, in* and *on*

Note these fixed expressions with *at*:

***at** the front/back*	***at** the station/airport*
***at** the top/bottom*	***at** home/work/school*
***at** the beginning/end*	***at** the seaside*

Note these fixed expressions with *in*:

***in** the middle*	***in** a book/magazine*
***in** the corner*	***in** the photo/picture*
***in** my hand*	***in** the country*
***in** a queue (BrE)*	***in** hospital/prison*
***in** line (AmE)*	***in** a row/column*
***in** the chair* (= in charge of the meeting)	

Note these fixed expressions with *on*:

***on** the left/right*	***on** television/the radio*
***on** the screen*	***on** the page/map*
***on** the phone*	***on** the platform*
***on** the computer*	***on** the pavement*
***on** the first floor*	***on** the Rhine (rivers)*
***on** the M6 (motorways and roads)*	
***on** the plane/bus/train* (but **in** a car/taxi, because you are contained in a smaller space where you can't stand up)	

With addresses, we use *in* or *on* for the street name and *at* when we say the street number as well.

*I went shopping **in** Oxford Street.* (common in UK)
*I went shopping **on** Fifth Avenue.* (common in US)
*Our offices are **at** 14 High Street.*

C *above/below, over/under*

Above/below mean 'higher/lower than'. They can be used with or without an object.

*The floor **above/below** us is occupied by an insurance company.*
*From the mountain I could see the lake **below**.*

Over/under mean 'directly above/below'. They both need an object.

*We flew right **over** Windsor Castle on our way into Heathrow.*
*There's still a lot of oil **under** the sea.*

Over can also be used for movement. In this case it is like 'across'.

*We have to go **over/across** to the other side of the street.*

Over can also mean 'covering'.

*He put his jacket **over** the back of his chair.*
*They put a plastic sheet **over** the hole in the roof.*

All four words can be used for positions in a management hierarchy.

***Above me** is the Regional Sales Manager. **Under me** there are eight sales consultants.*

D *opposite, next to/beside, near/by*

Opposite means 'exactly on the other side of' a space.

*We sat **opposite** each other in the meeting.*

Next to and *beside* mean 'exactly at the side of'. *Beside* can be more formal.

*Miguel should sit **next to/beside** Irene in the restaurant tonight.*

Near (to) means 'close to'. *By* means 'at the side of'.

*The metro station is very **near** (**to**) our offices.*
*Can we have a table **by** the window?*
*We stayed in a hotel **near** the sea.*
(close to the sea – a few kilometers away)
*We had a holiday **by** the sea.*
(we were on the beach a lot of the time)

E Other prepositions of place

Study these opposites:

into/out of	*inside/outside*
towards/away from	*backwards/forwards*
in front of/behind	*on top of/underneath*

The preposition *past* meaning 'passing' is often used when giving directions.

Go down this road, past the church, and take the first left.

Exercises

Sections A, B, C, D, E

46.1 <u>Underline</u> the correct words.

1 Look in the Appendix *at/by* the end of the report.
2 When I got *in/on* the train, I found out there was a Wi-Fi connection.
3 What a fantastic view! The sky *above/over* and the sea *below/under*.
4 Next week I'll be *at/in* Hungary for a few days.
5 Turn into Western Avenue and you'll see our offices *on/at* your left.
6 I bought this tie *on/at* Madison Avenue in New York.
7 She'll be here in a few minutes – she's just *at/on* the phone.
8 The power socket is over there, *by/at* the door.
9 This graph isn't labeled. You need to write the units *by/next to* the X axis.
10 Put a sheet *above/over* the machine to stop it getting dusty.
11 Siena is *near/by* Florence.
12 I'll see you tomorrow at ten thirty, *at/by* the office.
13 It's a large block. Our offices are *at/on* the fifteenth floor.
14 The customs officer asked me to take everything *out/out of* my suitcase.
15 The waiter took us to a table *by/near* the window. (close to the window)
16 The waiter took us to a table *by/near* the window. (next to the window)
17 I'll meet you *at/in* the front of the building in ten minutes.
18 I'll meet you *at/in* front of the building in ten minutes.

Sections A, B

46.2 Complete the sentences with *at*, *in* or *on*.

1 I live *at* number 295 Manor Road.
2 You shouldn't really park ______ the pavement.
3 I had a lovely meal ______ the plane.
4 I'd like to live ______ the country when I retire.
5 Go to the end of the road, and you'll see the bank ______ the right.
6 I'll be arriving ______ your offices ______ Barcelona at three.
7 I often work ______ home in the evening.
8 I went to visit my son ______ hospital yesterday.
9 I wonder what's ______ television this evening.
10 The size of the text ______ the screen is very small. Can't it be bigger?
11 Is that your daughter I can see ______ the photo?
12 ______ the beginning of my career I worked in telesales.
13 It was a very well-run meeting. Erika was ______ the chair.
14 Wroclaw is ______ the south-west of Poland, ______ the river Odra.
15 She works ______ Seville, ______ the University.
16 The sales figures? Yes, I have them right here ______ my hand.
17 The taxi rank is ______ the back of the station.
18 I must have been standing ______ line for about half an hour.
19 I'm on sick leave right now, but I should be back ______ work next week.
20 The last Finance Minister is still ______ prison.

Exercises

Sections A, B, C, D, E

46.3 Complete this email, which gives directions to someone's office, with the words in the box.

across	at (x2)	backwards	in front of	~~near~~
next to	on (x2)	past	towards	underneath

Hi Jan. As promised, here are the directions for how to get to our offices by car.

The place where you're staying the previous night is actually quite [1] *near* to us – about 40 km away. Leave the city [2] ____________ the A3 motorway heading east [3] ____________ Metroville. Come off the motorway [4] ____________ exit 19 and just carry on for a few minutes. You'll go [5] ____________ a large car showroom [6] ____________ your left, and just after that you'll come to some traffic lights. Go [7] ____________ this first set of lights, and then [8] ____________ the next lights turn right. You're now in Victoria Road. Follow the road to the end and you'll see our offices right [9] ____________ you. You can't miss them.

The car park is actually down a ramp, [10] ____________ the building. There's a little cabin [11] ____________ the ramp where the security guard sits – you'll see it. When you get down into the parking area, there's not much room to manoeuvre, so you might have to go [12] ____________ and forwards a few times before you can fit in the space! We're all used to it.

Just go to reception when you arrive and ask for me – I'll be right down.

Looking forward to seeing you next week

Hendrik

Sections A, B, C, D

46.4 Complete this email about magazine artwork by putting one suitable word in each space.

Sue

Thanks for sending me the artwork for the magazine advert. I have a few comments about the layout [1] *on* the page. The photograph [2] ____________ the top looks good, but instead of being [3] ____________ the middle I think it should be [4] ____________ the left, [5] ____________ to the main block of text. Also, I think we should have the company logo [6] ____________ the bottom right corner.

Did you know there's going to be an article about our company [7] ____________ the same magazine? I hope it will be on the page directly [8] ____________ our advert, but of course that isn't [9] ____________ my hands.

Can you also send the artwork to Steve for his comments? He should be back [10] ____________ work on Monday.

Thanks

Tony

Tasks

Speaking: listen and repeat

1 46 **You are going to hear eight phrases. Listen and repeat.**

Translate

2 Translate these short texts taken from the Internet into your own language. Remember not to translate word for word, but rather to make it sound natural.

He was laid off from his accounting job at a small firm in Michigan right in the middle of the busy tax season. Instead of looking for other accounting positions in the region, which has been particularly hard hit by the recession, he decided he would look anywhere in the US

CNNMoney website

The US Department of Energy estimates that roughly $1 trillion of the $7 trillion economy is subject to weather risk. A surprisingly wide range of companies are captive to the effect on earnings caused by cooler-than-expected summers, mild winters, and above- or below-average rainfall or snowfall.

CFO website

Writing: personalized practice

3 Complete the sentences with your own ideas.

1 At the back of my house *there's a garden with a lawn and some shrubs* .
2 At the beginning of this book, inside the front cover, ______ .
3 At work I often feel ______ , while at home I usually feel ______ .
4 In the middle of my office, ______ .
5 In the corner of this page, ______ .
6 In my country, in the country, ______ .
7 Waiting in line is ______ in my country.
8 At the last meeting I went to, ______ was in the chair.
9 In the spreadsheet I use most often, I have ______ in the rows down the left hand side, and ______ in the columns across the top.
10 I have set up my Internet browser to have ______ on the screen.
11 If I'm talking on the phone, I often ______ .
12 On the first floor of this building there is ______ .
13 On the motorways in my country you can't ______ .
14 I suddenly realized I was on the wrong platform, so I ______ .
15 From the plane I looked down at the ______ below.
16 Under my desk ______ .
17 As we were landing we flew right over ______ .
18 I put a plastic sheet over ______ .
19 Above my boss in the management structure there is ______ .
20 I saw with horror that there was only one chair available for me to sit down. It was next to ______ and directly opposite ______ .
21 A palindrome is a word or a line that can be read the same forwards and backwards. Some examples are: *level*, *radar* and ______ .
22 As the ship sailed away from ______ and towards ______ , I knew that my life would never be the same again.
23 From the outside, it probably looks as though my company is ______ , but from the inside it's ______ .
24 Just before you get to our offices you go past ______ .

If you are working in class, choose some sentences to read aloud. Ask and answer questions.

47 Verb + preposition

A Verb + preposition

Here is a list of verbs and the prepositions normally used with them:

account for	*consist of*	*object to*
allow for	*cooperate with*	*pay for*
apply for	*coordinate with*	*plan on*
approve of	*count on*	*prepare for*
base on	*decide on*	*qualify for*
believe in	*depend on*	*recover from*
belong to	*focus on*	*refer to*
benefit from	*graduate from*	*rely on*
budget for	*hope for*	*specialize in*
cater for	*insist on*	*suffer from*
comment on	*know about*	*take care of*
compete with	*lead to*	*welcome to*
comply with	*liaise with*	*worry about*
concentrate on	*listen to*	*wait for*

*I've **applied for** a job at Siemens.*
*We **cater for** all tastes and budgets.*
*Does your machinery **comply with** safety regulations?*
*Do I **qualify for** a discount?*

Some of the verbs above can be used alone, without a preposition + object.

I hope/insist. It depends. I've decided. I'm listening/waiting.

Others must have a preposition + object.

*It **belongs to** me.*
*The process **consists of** four main stages.*
*This will **lead to** a lot of problems.*
*I'm **relying on** you for your support.*

In questions the preposition goes after the verb, at the end of the sentence or the main phrase. See unit 16B.

*Who does this **belong to**?*
*What did you **decide on** (in the meeting)?*
*What did you **pay** all that money **for**?*

B Verb + object + preposition

With some verbs the object comes before the preposition. In the list below, *sth* means 'something' and *sb* means 'somebody'.

*We can **insure** you **against** fire and theft.*
*We've **spent** €2m **on** advertising this year.*
*I can **split** your order **into** two shipments.*

add sth to sth	*congratulate sb on sth*
ask sb about/for sth	*divide sth into sth*
blame sb for sth	*exchange sth for sth*
borrow sth from sb	*explain sth to sb*
charge sb for sth	*inform sb about/of sth*
compare sth with/to sth	*insure sth against sth*
involve sb in sth	*split sth into sth*
invite sb to sth	*substitute sth for sth*
prevent sb from sth	*supply sb with sth*
protect sb against sth	*tell sb about sth*
share sth with sb	*thank sb for sth*
spend sth on sth	*translate sth into sth*
invest sth in sth	*waste sth on sth*

*We've **spent** €2m **on** advertising this year.*
*I can **split** your order **into** two shipments.*

With *remind* there is a difference between *about* and *of.*

*Dana **reminded** me **about** the appointment.*
(= she told me not to forget)
*Dana **reminds** me **of** my sister.*
(= she is like my sister)

C Verb + different prepositions

Some verbs can go with several different prepositions.

agree with *sb*; agree to/about/on/with *sth*

*I agree **with** you **about** that.*
*They agreed **to** our demands.*
*We agreed **on** a compromise.*

apologize to *sb* for *sth*

*I must **apologize to** Susan **for** my awful behavior last night.*

ask for/about *sth*

*That was a nice lunch. Shall we **ask for** the bill?*
***Ask** the waiter **about** the dish of the day.*

complain (talk, write, etc) to *sb* about *sth*

*I'm going to **complain to** the manager **about** the service in here.*

hear about *sth* from *sb*; hear of *sth*

*I **heard about** your news **from** a colleague. Congratulations!*
*I've never **heard of** that company in my life.*

look at/for *sth*

***Look at** these new designs – they're amazing!*
*We're **looking for** a way out of this contract.*

result from/in *sth*

*This situation **results from** bad planning, and it will **result in** total chaos if we're not careful.*

think of/about *sth*

What did you ***think of*** the meeting?
You look worried – what are you ***thinking about***?

work at/for/on

*I'm working **at** UBS.*
*I've worked **for** this company since university.*
*They worked **on** this proposal for many weeks.*

Exercises

Section A **47.1 Complete the sentences with a word from list A and a word from list B.**

A: approve ~~believe~~ comply depend know lead suffer wait

B: about for from ~~in~~ of on to with

1 If you want to succeed, you really have to *believe in* yourself.
2 Finish what you're doing – I'll ______ you outside.
3 What you're saying can only ______ one possible conclusion.
4 Of course the size of our order will ______ the price.
5 Your CV is strong, but what do you ______ marketing to teenagers?
6 Our export industries always ______ the effects of a strong euro.
7 I have to look smart at work – my boss doesn't ______ informal clothes.
8 Does our customer database ______ data protection legislation?

Section B **47.2 Underline the correct word.**

1 I think we should ask them *for/about/with* more information.
2 Can you supply us *for/about/with* enough parts to upgrade 50 machines?
3 You remind me *about/of/for* someone I used to work with in Toulouse.
4 If I forget, remind me *about/of/for* it again tomorrow.
5 They blamed the union *against/from/for* going on strike unnecessarily.
6 We might have to split the order *for/in/into* two separate consignments.
7 I'd like to congratulate Patricia *on/with/about* winning Employee of the Month.
8 This safety feature prevents the operator *against/from/with* being hurt or injured.
9 This year we'll be investing more than €4m *on/in/to* plant and equipment.
10 This year we'll be spending more than €4m *on/in/to* plant and equipment.

Section C **47.3 Complete the sentences with prepositions. Choose from: *about, at, for, from, in, to, of, with.***

1 I'm writing *to* all our customers *about* some exciting offers this month on selected models in our range.
2 Have you heard anything ______ Head Office? They said they'd decide this week.
3 Who's Giuseppe Saponi? I've never heard ______ him.
4 Do you agree ______ me ______ this?
5 The improved productivity results ______ all the investment that we made last year.
6 The investment that we're making now should result ______ improved productivity next year.
7 I must apologize ______ not contacting you earlier, but I've been very busy.
8 I complained ______ the manager ______ the food and he gave us a free drink.
9 Make sure you look ______ the small print before you sign anything.
10 Unless their quality improves, we'll have to look ______ a new supplier.

Exercises

Sections A, B, C **47.4 Complete the sentences with a word from list A and a word from list B.**

A: agreed	apologized	apply	insist	involve	listen	~~pay~~	rely	remind	wasted

B: about	~~for~~	for	for	in	on	on	on	to	with

1 You can *pay for* the goods in twelve monthly instalments.
2 I've already __________ an hour this morning __________ this report.
3 The first thing is to __________ __________ the client to find out their needs.
4 Everybody __________ __________ the decision. It was unanimous.
(*on* and *to* are possible but are not the answer)
5 The Chief Operating Officer is leaving next month. I wonder if Chris is going to __________ __________ his job.
6 We need to __________ our business partners __________ this discussion.
7 Vanda is very good at working under pressure. You can always __________ __________ her if there's an emergency.
8 They __________ __________ the delay and said that the items are in the mail.
9 I'm certain to forget. Please __________ me __________ it nearer the time.
10 No, no, I __________ __________ paying. You're my guest.

Sections A, B, C **47.5 Complete the sequence of emails with the correct prepositions. The number in brackets after the space shows the number of letters in the word.**

I've just been looking [1] *at* (2) your website and comparing your online banking facilities [2] ______ (4) your competitors. I have a few questions.

a) If I want to borrow money [3] ______ (4) you, how much will you charge me [4] ______ (3) the loan? I assume that as an Internet bank your cheaper operating costs will result [5] ______ (2) a lower interest rate than a normal bank.

b) I see that if I open an account this month I qualify [6] ______ (3) a credit card with special repayment terms. Do you offer insurance [7] ______ (7) online fraud with this card? I read a lot of stories about hackers and cybercrime.

Thank you.

Thank you [8] ______ (3) your recent email. Here is the information you requested.

a) You can rely [9] ______ (2) the fact that our interest rates are very competitive, but I cannot give exact figures, as it depends [10] ______ (2) the amount you want to borrow and changes in line with base rates. I invite you [11] ______ (2) check the table on our website for the current rates. You can click on the link below.

b) Yes, as soon as you inform us [12] ______ (2) any possible fraud associated with your card we take care [13] ______ (2) everything. We investigate the issue and refund any money that you have lost. We have invested heavily [14] ______ (2) IT security over recent years and we do everything necessary to prevent hackers [15] ______ (4) entering the system.

I hope this answers your questions. Please do not hesitate to contact us again if you think [16] ______ (2) anything else.

Tasks

Speaking: listen and repeat

1 47 **You are going to hear eight phrases. Listen and repeat.**

Translate

2 Translate these short texts taken from the Internet into your own language. Remember not to translate word for word, but rather to make it sound natural.

With over ten billion euros invested in various sectors of the Romanian economy, the Austrian business community is determined to consolidate its position in the local market. Investors are staying focused on opportunities in areas such as infrastructure and agriculture.

Bucharest Business Week website

China and Brazil are working on a currency arrangement to allow exporters and importers to settle deals in their local currencies, bypassing the US dollar, the countries' central banks said on Sunday. Other central bankers have also questioned the dollar's future role as the world's dominant reserve currency.

CNBC website

Writing: personalized practice

3 Complete the sentences with your own ideas. The first word you will need is a preposition (look back at page 194 if you can't remember).

1 When we work out the budget we need to allow *for travel expenses* .
2 I've been at this company too long and I'm thinking of applying ________ .
3 I disagree with his whole argument – it's based ________ .
4 Before we take this product to market, I think it would benefit ________ .
5 It's difficult to be profitable in this field – we compete ________ .
6 Are you sure that the waste disposal process complies ________ .
7 Marketing is a big area, and in this talk I'm going to focus ________ .
8 I graduated ________ (+ *place*) with a degree in ________ .
9 He said to me, 'I'm in charge here and I insist ________ .'
10 Our product design team liaises closely ________ .
11 It took the company three years to recover ________ .
12 The financial services area is very wide, but we specialize ________ .
13 While I'm away, Henri will take care ________ .
14 Good morning everyone and welcome ________ .

4 Complete the sentences with your own ideas. The preposition you need is provided.

15 Do you know what? I blame ________ for ________ .
16 To set up my own business I'd need to borrow ________ from ________ .
17 At the hotel they charged me ________ for ________ .
18 Over the next two years we're going to invest ________ in ________ .
19 Wearing this safety clothing will protect ________ against ________ .
20 Things are going crazy. Last month we spent ________ on ________ .
21 We carry a full range of office furniture and can supply ________ with ________ .
22 This is ridiculous! I've already wasted ________ on ________ .
23 Luckily, Max reminded ________ about ________ .
24 Max reminds ________ of ________ .
25 This whole mess results from ________ .
26 This whole mess will result in ________ .

If you are working in class, choose some sentences to read aloud. Ask and answer questions.

48 Adjective + preposition

A Adjective + preposition

Some adjectives can have a preposition after them. The preposition may be followed by a noun or noun phrase.

*We're all **disappointed with** the results.*
*It's **compatible with** your existing IT system.*

When followed by a verb, the *-ing* form must be used.

*I'm **responsible for** authoriz**ing** new loans.*
*Are you **interested in** look**ing** around the plant?*

An adjective can also be followed by a *to* infinitive. If we need to mention a person, we use *for* between the adjective and the infinitive.

*It's **important to follow** the safety procedures.*
*It's **important for us to move** quickly in these negotiations.*

B Feelings

Many examples of adjective + preposition are connected with feelings.

afraid of	*fed up with*	*proud of*
amazed at / by	*fond of*	*satisfied with*
bored with	*interested in*	*serious about*
disappointed with	*keen on*	*shocked at / by*
doubtful about	*nervous of*	*surprised at / by*
enthusiastic about	*optimistic about*	*suspicious of*
excited about	*pessimistic about*	*tired of*
fascinated by	*pleased with*	*worried about*

*I'm just **amazed by** property prices in London.*
*I'm really **excited about** starting my new job.*
*I'm not very **keen on** fried food, to be honest.*

For behaviour towards another person we use adjective + *to*. Examples include *kind to, nice to, polite to, rude to.*

*I thought he was rather **rude to** the waitress.*

Note this meaning of *sympathetic*:

*He wasn't very **sympathetic to / towards** my suggestion.*
(= he didn't support it)

C Other adjectives

Here are some other common examples of adjective + preposition.

accustomed to	*full of*	*related to*
answerable to	*guilty of*	*relevant to*
attached to	*important for*	*rich in*
aware of	*involved in*	*right about*
based on	*lacking in*	*safe from*
capable of	*late for*	*similar to*
certain about	*limited to*	*suitable for*
compatible with	*married to*	*sure of*
covered in	*opposed to*	*typical of*
dependent on	*popular with*	*used to*
experienced in	*prepared for*	*useful for*
famous for	*ready for*	*wrong about*

*Our company is **famous** all over the world **for** the quality of its engineering.*
*She was **full of** enthusiasm when I explained our idea.*
*We're **used to*** (= accustomed to) *delays on the metro. They happen all the time.*

D Adjective + choice of preposition

Some adjectives can be followed by different prepositions. In the list below *sth* means 'something' and *sb* means 'somebody'.

angry / annoyed about sth; angry / annoyed with sb

*I'm very **angry about** the delay.*
*I'm very **angry with** them for causing this delay.*
*He was **annoyed about** what the journalist wrote.*
*He was **annoyed with** the journalist.*

---

good / bad at sth (ability)

*I've never been very **good at** dealing with conflict.*

good / bad for sth / sb

*A new person at the top would be **good for** the company.*
*I think a vacation would be **good for** you.*

good / bad with sth / sb

*She's very **good with** figures.*
*She's very **good with** difficult customers.*

---

happy about / with sth

*Are you **happy with** my suggestion?*

happy for sb

*Congratulations! I'm very **happy for** you both.*

---

responsible for sth

*I'm **responsible for** all the transport and logistics.*

responsible to sb

*The Finance Director is directly **responsible to** the CEO.*

---

sorry about sth

*I'm **sorry about** all the trouble I've caused.*

sorry for (+ *-ing* sth)

*I'm **sorry for** caus**ing** so much trouble.*

(feel) sorry for sb

*I **felt sorry for** George when he didn't get the promotion.*

Exercises

Sections B, C, D

48.1 Match the beginning of each sentence 1–10 with an ending a–j.

1	Are you interested	*g*	a) at motivating people in her team.
2	It's the same hotel		b) with us for sending the wrong items.
3	Are you aware		c) for another drink?
4	They were really annoyed		d) of the difficulties you are creating?
5	He's become very keen		e) about this, but I don't think it's going to work.
6	Jane is really good		f) by the overcrowding problems at Heathrow.
7	I'm so tired. I'm not used		g) in any other items from the catalogue?
8	Are you ready		h) as last time.
9	I was quite surprised		i) to the time difference yet.
10	I could be wrong		j) on golf since his promotion.

Sections B, C

48.2 Complete the sentences with a word from list A and a word from list B.

A: attached tired dependent ~~popular~~ involved safe suitable serious

B: about for from in of on to ~~with~~

1 This fund is very *popular with* investors looking for long-term growth.
2 Our security infrastructure makes your IT network ______ ______ malware.
3 For further details, see the copy of the contract ______ ______ this letter.
4 The starting salary is ______ ______ previous experience.
5 Some time ago he mentioned the possibility of a permanent contract, but I don't think he's ______ ______ it.
6 We're ______ ______ every stage of the process, from design right through to production.
7 I need a change. I'm ______ ______ doing the same thing every day.
8 Hedge funds are very risky. They're not ______ ______ most investors.

Section D

48.3 Underline the correct word.

1 I'm annoyed *about/with* all this confusion with the wrong invoices.
2 I'm annoyed *about/with* them for sending the wrong invoices.
3 I've spoken to Mahmut and I'm happy *with/for* all the arrangements.
4 Maggie deserved to get promoted – I'm really happy *with/for* her.
5 I'm sorry *about/for* arriving so late – I got delayed in traffic.
6 Low inflation is good *at/for/with* every sector of the economy.
7 She'd be excellent in Human Resources – she's really good *at/for/with* people.
8 Richard, can you help us with this translation? You're good *at/for/with* French.
9 If you need to refer the decision upwards, who are you responsible *for/to*?
10 As Sales Director, how many staff are you responsible *for/to*?

"No, Thursday's out. How about never – is never good for you?"

Exercises

Sections B, C, D **48.4 Complete the second sentence so it has a similar meaning to the first.**

1 Consumers find the old models a bit boring.
Consumers are a bit bored *with the old models* .

2 Julia is Adrian's wife.
Julia is married ______________________ .

3 Driving on the left is still strange to me.
I'm not used ______________________ .

4 Do you find archaeology interesting?
Are you ______________________ ?

5 Mathematics was always my best subject.
I was always very good ______________________ .

6 The advertising campaign was a disaster. You said it would be.
You were right ______________________ . It was a disaster.

7 There were lots of people in the conference hall.
The conference hall was full ______________________ .

8 I don't really like her idea.
I'm not really very keen ______________________ .

Sections B, C, D **48.5 Complete the sequence of emails with the words in the box.**

~~aware~~ attached capable compatible covered dependent
involved lacking late opposed prepared right similar useful

David – are you [1] *aware* of the article about Customer Relationship Management (CRM) in the latest Marketing Monthly? I've scanned it and [2] ______ it to this email.

Basically, it says that in the future B2B companies like ours shouldn't be too [3] ______ on their brand name, and that we have to be [4] ______ for a situation where customers show less and less brand loyalty. To retain customers, it says we're going to need CRM software that is [5] ______ of managing all our customer information. Basically, CRM software integrates data from the sales force, the call center and the website. That information also becomes [6] ______ for marketing – things like understanding buying behaviour and so on.

I remember you saying something [7] ______ to this in a meeting last year, and as you are [8] ______ in IT purchasing decisions I thought you should see the article.

Madeleine

Thanks for the email and the article. You're absolutely [9] ______ about the importance of CRM, and if you remember I proposed at that meeting that we invest in new CRM software. Most people were [10] ______ to the idea, partly because of the difficulty in finding software [11] ______ with our other IT systems. I thought at the time they were [12] ______ in vision, but it's not too [13] ______ for us to start. I'll put together a short report based on the ideas [14] ______ in the article and circulate it.

Thanks again for sending it and thinking about this issue.

David

Tasks

Speaking: listen and repeat

1 48 **You are going to hear eight phrases. Listen and repeat.**

Translate

2 Translate these short texts taken from the Internet into your own language. Remember not to translate word for word, but rather to make it sound natural.

Information technology is not important enough on its own to generate a sustained recovery. Rather, sustained growth will be dependent on a recovery in private consumption.

FT website

Although Denmark is lacking in natural resources, it makes up for this with a strong workforce. Denmark has a free market economy coupled with a large welfare state and has one of the world's highest levels of income equality. It is ranked as the second most peaceful country in the world, as well as being the world's least corrupt.

Global edge website

Writing: personalized practice

3 Complete the sentences with your own ideas. The first word you will need is a preposition (look back at page 198 if you can't remember).

1 I think the new product is overpriced. I'm doubtful *about its sales potential* .
2 I have a 90-minute commute twice a day – I'm really fed up ______ .
3 I'd prefer not to go to an Indian restaurant. I'm not very keen ______ .
4 Spring is in the air and I'm feeling quite optimistic ______ .
5 Looking back over my life's work, I'm proud ______ .
6 I went to the office party last week and I was shocked ______ .
7 Antonio is always so negative and I'm getting tired ______ .
8 What? You want to try paragliding? Are you aware ______ ?
9 These customer satisfaction figures are based ______ .
10 Make sure that the software is compatible ______ .
11 In business it's dangerous to be too dependent ______ .
12 Our company is famous ______ .
13 Trade union representatives were fully involved ______ .
14 He's good at his job, but a little shy and lacking ______ .
15 The new rules do not apply to all employees – they are limited ______ .
16 The green movement in my country is opposed ______ .
17 This job doesn't offer me any more challenges – I'm ready ______ .
18 It's an interesting point, but I'm not sure it's relevant ______ .
19 Brazil is a country that is rich ______ .
20 Do you know what? I think you're right ______ .
21 I don't think the film is suitable ______ .
22 My relocation to Hong Kong is going well, but I'm still not used ______ .
23 I apologize – I was completely wrong ______ .
24 The drop in interest rates will be good ______ .
25 Alexander is the office administrator – he's very good ______ .
26 How's your new job? Are you happy ______ ?
27 Congratulations! I'm really happy ______ .
28 In my job I'm responsible ______ .
29 In the management structure, my line manager is directly responsible ______ ______ .
30 I've never been very good ______ .

If you are working in class, choose some sentences to read aloud. Ask and answer questions.

49 Noun + preposition

A Noun + preposition

Here is a list of nouns and the prepositions normally used with them:

ability in	*example of*	*price of*
advantage of	*experience of/in*	*reason for*
advice on	*hope of*	*reply to*
alternative to	*knowledge of*	*solution to*
benefit of/from	*lack of*	*substitute for*
cause of	*matter with*	*success at/in*
cost of	*method of*	*tax on*
difficulty with	*opinion of*	*trouble with*

Words referring to increases and decreases (*rise*, *fall*, etc.) can be followed by *in* or *of*.

In refers to the thing that has increased or decreased. *Of* refers to an amount.

There has been a ***rise in*** *operating profit* ***of*** *3%.*

Words that can be used like this include:

increase, rise, reduction, fall

Nouns meaning 'need' or 'request' have *for* after them. Examples include:

application for, demand for, need for, order for, preference for, request for

Study how we use *with* and *between*:

There is a relationship ***with*** *what happened last year.*
There is a relationship ***between*** *this year* ***and*** *what happened last year.*

Words that can be used like this include:

connection, contrast, difference, link, relationship

B Noun + preposition (from unit 47)

Many of the verbs in unit 47 have related nouns with the same preposition. Here are some examples:

agreement with	*decision about*	*invitation to*
agreement about	*decision on*	*objection to*
approval of	*division into*	*payment for*
belief in	*focus on*	*preparation for*
budget for	*information about*	*protection against*
comparison with	*insistence on*	*reference to*
complaint about	*insurance against*	*responsibility for*
compliance with	*investment in*	*spending on*

C Noun + preposition (from unit 48)

Many of the adjectives in unit 48 have related nouns with the same preposition. Here are some examples:

awareness of	*interest in*	*preparation for*
certainty about	*involvement in*	*satisfaction with*
doubt about	*opposition to*	*similarity to*
excitement about	*optimism about*	*suitability for*
fear of	*pessimism about*	*worry about*

D Preposition + noun

Here is a list of common prepositional phrases (preposition + noun):

at *our expense,* ***at*** *short notice,* ***at*** *cost price,* ***at*** *a good price,* ***at*** *a profit/loss,* ***at*** *first sight*

beyond *our control*

by *accident,* ***by*** *car/taxi,* ***by*** *chance,* ***by*** *(credit) card,* ***by*** *hand,* ***by*** *monthly instalments,* ***by*** *law,* ***by*** *mistake,* ***by*** *courier,* ***by*** *return (of mail)*

for *a change,* ***for*** *lunch,* ***for*** *pleasure,* ***for*** *sale*

in *advance,* ***in*** *bulk,* ***in*** *cash,* ***in*** *charge of,* ***in*** *good condition,* ***in*** *connection with,* ***in*** *debt,* ***in*** *demand,* ***in*** *the end,* ***in*** *favour of,* ***in*** *full,* ***in*** *general,* ***in*** *a hurry,* ***in*** *the market* (companies), ***in*** *my opinion,* ***in*** *stock,* ***in*** *financial terms,* ***in*** *the pipeline,* ***in*** *touch,* ***in*** *transit,* ***in*** *trouble,* ***in*** *other words,* ***in*** *writing*

on *approval,* ***on*** *arrival,* ***on*** *avearge,* ***on*** *a regular basis,* ***on*** *the basis of,* ***on*** *business,* ***on*** *display,* ***on*** *foot,* ***on*** *hold,* ***on*** *holiday,* ***on*** *closer inspection,* ***on*** *the Internet,* ***on*** *the other line,* ***on*** *loan,* ***on*** *the market* (products), ***on*** *order,* ***on*** *the phone,* ***on*** *purpose,* ***on*** *sale,* ***on*** *schedule,* ***on*** *strike,* ***on*** *television,* ***on*** *track,* ***on*** *trial,* ***on*** *the whole*

out of *business,* ***out of*** *date,* ***out of*** *order,* ***out of*** *the question,* ***out of*** *stock,* ***out of*** *work*

under *pressure*

up to *date,* ***up to*** *you*

I apologise for calling this meeting ***at*** *such short notice.*
The concert is cancelled due to circumstances ***beyond*** *our control.*
We met in the street ***by*** *chance.*
We need 25% of the total price ***in*** *advance.*
We don't have that colour ***in*** *stock, but we do have more* ***on*** *order.*
The economy is ***on*** *track for recovery.*
Your software is quite ***out of*** *date.*
You should always keep your antivirus software ***up to*** *date.*
It's ***up to you*** *– I don't mind which restaurant we go to.*

Note: *for sale* and *on sale* both mean 'available for people to buy'. But *on sale* has a second meaning of 'available to buy at less than the usual price'. You only know which meaning from the context.

Exercises

Section A

49.1 Complete the sentences with the prepositions in the box.

between between for for in in of of ~~to~~ to with with

1 Have you received a reply *to* the letter you sent to the lawyers?
2 The demand ________ microchips is very cyclical.
3 There is a strong contrast ________ the workforce here and the one in Germany.
4 There is a strong contrast ________ the workforce in Germany.
5 What's the matter ________ your PC? Try rebooting it.
6 Last year there was a fall ________ unemployment ________ 1.5%.
7 Is there any difference ________ these two designs? They both look the same.
8 At the moment I can't think of any solution ________ the problem.
9 The increase ________ profits was disappointing. There was a rise ________ only 2%.
10 I'd like to place an order ________ forty cases of single malt whisky.

Sections A, B, C

49.2 Complete the sentences with a word from box A and a word from box B.

A: advantage division involvement objection payment price suitability ~~trouble~~

B: of of for for in into to ~~with~~

1 We should change suppliers. We have so much *trouble* *with* them.
2 The ____________ ______ oil has gone up by $20 a barrel since this time last year.
3 The ____________ ______ using a small company is that they're usually cheaper.
4 The restructuring plan proposes a ____________ of the company ______ five business units.
5 We haven't received their ____________ ______ our last invoice.
6 Does anyone have any ____________ ______ that proposal? OK, it's agreed.
7 There are rumours of their ____________ ______ suspicious arms deals.
8 It's a violent film. I'm not sure about its ____________ ______ a young audience.

Section D

49.3 Underline the correct words.

1 *At/In* first sight it looks like a good deal, but we need more details *at/in* a hurry.
2 A: Shall we go to a Thai restaurant *by/for* a change?
B: It's *up to/over to* you.
3 Are you paying *by/in* cash or *by/in* card?
4 The house next door is *for/at* sale. It's been *on/in* the market for ages.
5 Very few Board members are *at/in* favour of the acquisition.
6 We need to keep *in/on* touch with the situation as it develops.
7 Are you here *on/for* business or *on/for* pleasure?
8 A: Did you do it *by/on* purpose?
B: No, of course not, I did it *by/on* mistake.
9 *By/In* financial terms they're not doing well. They're $10m *in/with* debt.
10 A: It's Niels Jensen from Tyco *at/on* the phone.
B: Can you put him *at/on* hold while I look for his file? OK, I've found it – I'll take it *at/on* the other line.

Exercises

Section D **49.4 You can often guess the meaning of a prepositional phrase from the context. Match each phrase a–j with its meaning 1–10 below.**

a) I'm sorry, I think we were talking at cross purposes. Let me make myself clear.
b) For the time being I think we should wait. We can make a decision later.
c) It's to our advantage to work together on this. We're all in the same boat.
d) It was fantastic news. And it came completely out of the blue.
e) There are two new products in the pipeline. They'll be launched later this year.
f) You have to be really on the ball in this job. The situation changes all the time.
g) I'm speaking off the record of course, but the company is in serious difficulties.
h) In a nutshell, we're behind schedule and over budget. It's a disaster.
i) I'm afraid the new CEO is out of his depth with this latest crisis.
j) In the long run stocks are generally a better investment than bonds.

1 about different things without realizing	a	6 unexpectedly	
2 quick-thinking and quick-acting		7 saying it briefly and clearly	
3 being planned and happening soon		8 over a long time period	
4 in the same unpleasant situation		9 for a short period of time	
5 in a situation that is too difficult for him		10 unofficially	

Sections A, B, D **49.5 Complete the sequence of emails with the correct prepositions. The number in brackets after the space shows the number of letters in the word.**

Erika

The interviews for the post of IT manager are happening next week, and HR have just sent me information 1 *about* (5) all the candidates. I thought we should get together to discuss the CVs before the interviews.

Here are my thoughts. 2 ______ (2) my opinion there is a need 3 ______ (3) someone with a good knowledge 4 ______ (2) integrating different applications. The problem 5 ______ (4) our current IT system is that all the parts work separately – our website, the back-office, our supply chain, etc. We need someone who has shown success 6 ______ (2) dealing with all these areas – although HR have warned me that there's a lack 7 ______ (2) really strong candidates.

Also, a lot of our IT infrastructure is quite 8 ______ (3) of date and we'll have to make a big investment 9 ______ (2) new hardware soon. We need someone who's 10 ______ (2) touch with what's available 11 ______ (2) the market and can take responsibility 12 ______ (3) the whole purchasing process.

What do you think?

Pete

Pete

Yes, we should have a meeting. It will be good to discuss these things 13 ______ (2) advance 14 ______ (3) a change. Usually the job interviews are arranged 15 ______ (2) very short notice and we don't get a chance to really look at the CVs in detail.

Are you free on Friday morning to do this? I could make any time betwen 9 and 11. And can I have a quick look 16 ______ (2) the CVs beforehand?

Erika

Tasks

Speaking: listen and repeat

1 49 **You are going to hear eight phrases. Listen and repeat.**

Translate

2 Translate these short texts taken from the Internet into your own language. Remember not to translate word for word, but rather to make it sound natural.

Annual Report: New Opportunities
We increased our sales and marketing investments almost 20 percent from Q2 to Q4 in order to aggressively launch and promote our new products, and we are excited about our success. With a significant increase in the number of R&D engineers over the last two years, we have many more exciting new products in the pipeline for next year and beyond.

National Instruments website

With the housing market still plunging, long-term mortgage rates have risen in response to rising bond yields on the financial markets. The Federal Reserve will meet this week to discuss monetary policy, and Ben Bernanke, its chairman, is under pressure to take action to bring mortgage rates back down. Few options are available, but Bernanke is thought to be considering making a public commitment to keep rates low for a long time.

Guardian website

Writing: personalized practice

3 Complete the sentences with your own ideas.

1 The equipment has the additional advantage of *needing very little maintenance*.
2 Our baby is two weeks old and I'm suffering from lack of ________.
3 In this recipe you can use chicken as a substitute for ________.
4 If the government could, they'd even put a tax on ________.
5 Last quarter we saw a rise in ________ of ________.
6 This summer has been very hot and there's been a high demand for ________.
7 There's a strong contrast between ________ and ________.
8 Her management style makes a strong contrast with ________.

Continue as before. In the shorter space '____' you need a preposition.

9 Amazing! I was walking down the street and ____ chance ________.
10 This new machine is ____ trial while we ________.
11 Can I put you ____ hold while I ________?
12 I'm sorry, I'm ____ a hurry, can you just ________?
13 This menu looks interesting. I think I'll try ________ ____ a change.
14 I need ________ from you ____ writing.
15 Those politicians receive ________ ____ our expense.
16 Is your ________ ____ ____ date?
17 Please write ________ ____ full.
18 The only way to sell this ____ a profit is if we ________.
19 They went ____ ____ business because of ________.
20 I hope we can ________ ____ a regular basis.
21 This ________ isn't mine – it's ____ loan.
22 We have ________ ____ the pipeline.
23 I didn't do it ____ purpose – I was just ________.
24 ____ first sight ________,
but ____ closer inspection ________.
25 We are very sorry but due to circumstances ____ our control ________.
26 We're ____ schedule to ________.

If you are working in class, choose some sentences to read aloud. Ask and answer questions.

50 Trends, graphs and figures

A Verbs describing trends

The box below shows verbs that describe different business *trends* (= tendencies).

Upward movement
go up, increase, rise, climb

Rapid upward movement
take off, jump, rocket, double

Downward movement
go down, decrease, fall, drop, decline

Rapid downward movement
collapse, crash, slump, plummet, halve

Highs and lows
peak, reach a peak, fall back, bottom out, hit a low, pick up

Change in size
grow, expand, shrink, contract

Stability and volatility
stay the same, be flat, be unchanged, be (relatively) stable, fluctuate, vary, move within a range, level off

Good and bad
improve, get better, strengthen, recover, deteriorate, get worse, weaken

Individual points
stand at, be at, be above, be below

States
be up/down, stay high/low, remain high/low

Note these irregular verb forms:

go – went – gone *grow – grew – grown*
rise – rose – risen *fall – fell – fallen*

Note these nouns:

a rise, growth, an improvement, a fall, a drop, a peak, a recovery, a halving, a doubling

Note the following prepositions:

*Sales increased **from** $5.4m **to** $5.8m.*
*There was an increase **in** sales **of** $0.4m.*
*Sales increased (**by**) $0.4m.*
(*by* is usually missed out in AmE)

B Trend verbs with objects

Verbs are used in different ways. Some verbs are always followed by an object.

*We'll **raise/lower/cut** the budget.*
(NOT ~~The budget will raise/lower/cut~~)

Other verbs are never followed by an object.

*Inflation will **rise/fall/go up**.*
(NOT ~~These measures will rise/fall/go up inflation~~)

Some verbs can be used with or without an object.

*We'll **increase/improve** our market share.*
AND *Our market share will **increase/improve**.*

C Speed and amount of change

We can use adverbs to talk about the speed and amount of change.

Speed

*Sales grew ... **quickly**, **rapidly**, **gradually**, **steadily**, **slowly***

Amount

*Sales grew ... **significantly**, **considerably**, **moderately**, **to some extent**, **slightly**, **marginally***

Note the relationship between 'verb + adverb' and 'adjective + noun':

*Sales **grew steadily**.*
*There was **steady growth** in sales.*

D Graphs and charts

The language in section A is often shown visually in a presentation or report by means of *(line) graphs, (bar) charts, (pie) charts* and *tables.*

A graph/chart may have: a *horizontal* and a *vertical* axis; a *solid/dotted/dashed line*; a *segment*; a *shaded area*; *bars*.

A table has *rows* and *columns* with *headings*.

E Figures (decimal point, comma, etc.)

A decimal point is written as a 'dot', not as a comma like in some languages. It is spoken as *point*.

6.5 six point five
0.25 zero point two five
(NOT ~~point twenty five~~)

A comma can be used to separate thousands from hundreds.

6,200 six thousand two hundred (AmE and BrE)
6,280 six thousand two hundred eighty (AmE)
*6,280 six thousand two hundred **and** eighty* (BrE)

Note also:

2m two million (NOT ~~millions~~)
2.5m two point five/two and a half million

F Linking words and phrases

Linking words are used for analyzing trends. They can join parts of a sentence or link across sentences. See units 41–44. Here are just a few examples:

although, and, basically, because, clearly, firstly, however, in addition, in fact, in general, in my opinion, in particular, in relation to, in spite of, so, therefore, whereas

Exercises

Sections A, B, C

50.1 Underline the correct words.

1 There was a *slightly/slight* rise in profits last month.
2 We *rose/increased* our profits slightly last month.
3 There was a sharp fall *in/of* our sales last quarter.
4 Our sales fell *by/of* 6% last quarter. (*or no preposition*)
5 We *fell/improved* our market share last year.
6 Their share price *hit/beat* a *low/down* last month, but it has *recuperated/recovered* since then and now stands *at/in* €3.78.
7 Their share price *met a top/peaked* in May, but it's fallen back since then.
8 Inflation is increasing *slow/slowly* at the moment, *in/by* about 1% a year.
9 There is a *slow/slowly* increase in the rate of inflation *of/by* about 1% a year.
10 Operating profits went from $2.5m *to/until* $3.1m.
11 This year, dividends paid to shareholders *raised/rose* by 6% year-on-year. Last year, in comparison, they *fell/cut* slightly.
12 This year we *raised/rose* dividends to shareholders by 6% year-on-year. Last year, in comparison, we *fell/cut* them.

Section E

50.2 Write in words how you would say the numbers in brackets, using British English. Look at section C and the additional example below to help you.

1 (1,230) *one thousand two hundred and thirty*
2 (12,300) ____________
3 (12,030) ____________
4 (120,300) ____________
5 (123,000) ____________
6 (123,330) ____________
7 (1,230,000) ____________

Section F

50.3 Complete the sentences with the words or phrases in the box. Look carefully at the punctuation to see if the words join parts of sentences or link across sentences.

because	because of	so	although	in spite of	~~in addition~~	however	therefore

1 Sales are up 5%. *In addition*, market share is up 2%.
2 Sales are up 5%. ____________, market share is down 2%.
3 Sales are up 5%, ____________ market share is down 2%.
4 Sales are up 5%, ____________ a drop in market share of 2%.
5 Sales are up 5%. ____________, we should get a bonus at the end of the year.
6 Sales are up 5%, ____________ we'll all get a bonus at the end of the year.
7 Sales are up 5% ____________ the new advertising campaign.
8 Sales are up 5% ____________ the new advertising campaign has started.

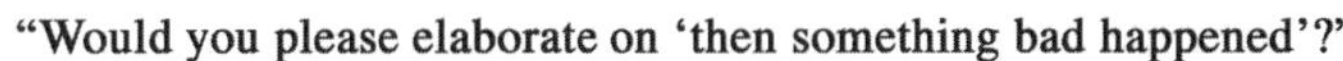

"Would you please elaborate on 'then something bad happened'?"

Exercises

Section E

50.4 Match the rules for numbers in formal writing 1–6 with the examples a–f.

1 Use figures for large amounts	c	a) We'll need twenty four-person teams.
2 Use words for numbers below ten		b) Twelve people took part in the meeting.
3 Use words for two numbers together		c) We employ 24,000 people worldwide.
4 Use words at the beginning of a sentence		d) This is our third annual report.
5 Use words for estimates		e) We have about two hundred employees.
6 Use words for ordinals (*first, second*)		f) There are three main recommendations.

Section E

50.5 In many situations we do not give an exact figure, just an approximate one. Write the phrases in the box on the appropriate lines below.

considerably more than	around	a little over	exactly	almost
a little under	~~much less than~~	about	precisely	slightly more than

40%	1 *much less than* 50%	
48%	2 ______ 50% /	______ 50%
48–52%	3 ______ 50% /	______ 50%
50%	4 ______ 50% /	______ 50%
52%	5 ______ 50% /	______ 50%
60%	6 ______ 50%	

Sections A, B, C, D, E, F

50.6 Complete the conversation between a bank manager, Andrew Cutting (AC), and a business owner, Chris Wood (CW), by underlining the correct words.

AC: Before we decide on the conditions for the loan, we need to have a careful look at your business. I've got the sales [1]*graph/graphic* for last year right here. Can you just go through the [2]*values/figures* for me?

CW: Of course. As you can see, sales at the start of the year were quite [3]*flat/level*, [4]*so/although* that's not surprising [5]*because/due to* we always have a quiet period after Christmas.

AC: OK, but there wasn't much of a [6]*recover/recovery* over the spring period. From your graph I see that in June you were only [7]*increased/up* [8]*by/with* two [9]*million/millions* [10]*euros/of euros* compared to January. What happened?

CW: Well it was a difficult trading period for us – our main competitor [11]*cut/fell* their prices aggressively. [12]*However/In spite of*, in the second [13]*half/halve* of the year things started to improve. We launched a series of new products onto the market, and you'll see that sales [14]*rised/rose* [15]*significant/significantly* over the autumn period. In fact the figure went [16]*to/until* a little [17]*under/over* fifteen million by the end of the year. We were very happy with those results. And we expect the increase [18]*of/in* sales to continue this year. Our sales forecasts are looking very good.

AC: Yes, that looks very promising. I think we can …

Tasks

Speaking: listen and repeat

1 50 **You are going to hear eight phrases. Listen and repeat.**

Translate

2 Translate these short texts taken from the Internet into your own language. Remember not to translate word for word, but rather to make it sound natural.

According to a Business Roundtable survey, US chief executive officers now expect that GDP will decline 2.1% this year, worse than the 1.9% projection made three months ago. But sentiment in other areas is slowly improving: 34% of CEOs expect their sales to increase in the next six months (compared with 24% in the first quarter), 20% see no change, while 46% still expect a drop in sales.

Wall Street Journal website

Productivity in Singapore fell sharply last year. The National Wages Council cautioned the public not to get carried away by the recent stockmarket rebound, as corporate performance has yet to recover. The NWC chairman contradicted suggestions that the Singapore economy had bottomed out, telling a news conference yesterday that the country was 'nowhere near an upturn'.

The Business Times website

Writing: personalized practice

3 Complete the sentences with your own ideas.

1 Last year, *sales of our cholesterol-lowering foods* rose steadily.
2 Last year, ______ fell significantly.
3 Last month, ______ went up marginally.
4 In recent years, ______ reached a peak and then fell back.
5 In recent years, ______ hit a low but then picked up a little.
6 In my country, ______ is/are growing rapidly.
7 In my country, ______ is/are slowly contracting.
8 In my country, ______ has/have levelled off and is/are now relatively stable.
9 In my life, ______ is/are getting worse – dramatically.
10 In my life, ______ is/are improving – gradually.
11 Since I was a child I've noticed a halving in the numbers of ______ and a doubling in the numbers of ______ .
12 It's really important that we raise ______ and lower ______ .

Rehearsal for the real world

4 Choose <u>two</u> related trends from your area of work or from your personal life where you can draw graphs covering several months/quarters/years on the horizontal axis. Write a short presentation describing the trends (this unit) and analyzing them (language from units 41–44). See the example topics below.

- total sales and sales of your most popular product over two years
- production volumes for two different products over six months
- seasonal patterns of spending for two different budget areas
- time spent doing gardening and time spent doing sports over the last year
- your motivation during a language course and your motivation while on a diet

If you are working in class, choose some presentations to read aloud. Draw the graphs on the board before you start. Ask and answer questions.

Test 1 Verb tenses: present (units 1–2)

Test 1.1 **Complete the sentences by putting each verb into the present simple or present continuous. Use contractions (*I'm* instead of *I am*, *don't* instead of *do not*, etc.) where possible.**

1 A: What *do you do* (you/do)?
 B: I'm an engineer.
2 A: What *are you doing* (you/do)?
 B: I'm looking for the document I saved.
3 Can you help me? I ________ (not understand) Spanish.
4 Can I call you back? I ________ (talk) with a client.
5 This product ________ (not sell) – we'll have to put it on special offer.
6 I'll get in touch with you as soon as I ________ (know) the results.
7 We ________ (stay) at the Marriott Hotel. We'll be there until Friday.
8 You'll have to be quick if you want to talk to Darina. She ________ (just/leave).
9 Our company ________ (make) parts for the automobile industry.
10 When ________ (you/usually/get) to work in the morning?
11 When ________ (the auditors/come)? This week or next week?
12 Klaus ________ (come) from Munich, in the south of Germany.

Test 1.2 **Decide if uses a–h are usually associated with the present simple (PS) or present continuous (PC).**

a) facts and permanent situations [*PS*]
b) actions and events in progress now [ ]
c) arrangements for the future [ ]
d) verbs of thinking and feeling [ ]
e) habits and routines [ ]
f) temporary situations [ ]
g) fixed timetables [ ]
h) current trends and changes [ ]

Match each sentence 1–8 with uses a–h.

1 She*'s talking* on another line. Can I ask her to call you back? [*b*]
2 *I'm working* in our Istanbul office for a few months. [ ]
3 We *offer* an IT solution that is customized, reliable and secure. [ ]
4 We *release* figures for sales and earnings every quarter. [ ]
5 Internet fraud and cybercrime *are increasing* all over the world. [ ]
6 OK, I *understand* what the problem is now. [ ]
7 I*'m arriving* in Lyon at 10.30. [ ]
8 The plane *arrives* in Lyon at 10.30. [ ]

Test 1.3 **Put the time expressions in the box into two categories: those most often used with the present simple, and those most often used with the present continuous. Write the expression in the correct column below.**

~~after~~ always as soon as ~~at the moment~~ before currently every day hardly ever most of the time never next time normally nowadays occasionally often right now sometimes these days twice a year until usually when

Present simple	**Present continuous**
after	*at the moment*

Test 1.4 **Put the words into the correct order. The first word is given each time.**

1 I at about 1 o'clock have usually lunch. I *usually have lunch at about 1 o'clock* .
2 Lunch just a sandwich often is. Lunch ______ .
3 I from time to time visit in Paris Head Office. I ______ .
4 I ever hardly am late in the morning. I ______ .
5 I ever hardly take the train to work. I ______ .
6 I prepare once a month a sales report. I ______ .
7 I miss a Board meeting never. I ______ .
8 I am late for a Board meeting never. I ______ .

Test 1.5 **Some of the following sentences are right and some are wrong. Put a tick (✓) next to the right ones, and correct the wrong ones.**

1 I'm invoicing you for your last order. *✓*
2 ~~I'm agreeing~~ with you completely. *I agree*
3 Our chocolates are containing only the finest ingredients. ______
4 Our chocolates are winning prizes all over the world. ______
5 We're setting up subsidiaries in Laos and Cambodia. ______
6 We're owning subsidiaries in Laos and Cambodia. ______
7 I'm knowing they will make a decision this week. ______
8 I'm guessing they will make a decision this week. ______
9 At first sight, it's seeming to be a sensible suggestion. ______
10 At first sight, he's making a sensible suggestion. ______
11 We're having a lot of trouble with our suppliers. ______
12 Unfortunately, we're having no alternative. ______

Test 1.6 **Complete the sentences by putting each verb into a form of the present simple or present continuous. Use contractions where possible. The verbs in each sentence may or may not have different tenses.**

1 Every time inflation *goes up* (go up), people *demand* (demand) higher salaries.
2 Inflation ______ (fall) quite quickly right now, which ______ (mean) that central banks all over the world can keep interest rates low.
3 ______ (you/wait) for Victoria Wilkinson? I ______ (not/think) she'll be long.
4 What exactly ______ (our customers/want)? Nobody around here ______ (seem) to know.
5 Carlo doesn't have much experience of this situation. I ______ (hope) he ______ (know) what he ______ (do).
6 What exactly ______ (you/mean)? I ______ (not/understand).
7 What exactly ______ (you/say)? ______ (you/want) us to renegotiate the whole contract?
8 ______ (your chicken/taste) OK? The food here is usually very good, but of course it all ______ (depend) on which particular chef ______ (work) in the kitchen on that day.
9 Our suppliers ______ (not/be) very flexible at the moment – I ______ (imagine) that they ______ (have) a lot of orders and they ______ (have) problems with the production capacity of their plant.
10 I ______ (agree) – we ______ (waste) our time discussing this. Let's move on.

Test 2 Verb tenses: past (units 3–4)

Test 2.1 **Write the past simple form of these irregular verbs.**

1 become *became*	6 choose ______	11 grow ______	16 rise ______
2 begin ______	7 eat ______	12 keep ______	17 send ______
3 break ______	8 fall ______	13 lead ______	18 shut ______
4 bring ______	9 find ______	14 lend ______	19 spend ______
5 buy ______	10 forget ______	15 meet ______	20 understand ______

Test 2.2 **Underline the correct words.**

1 When I *got/was getting* to the office, I *heard/was hearing* your voicemail.
2 When I worked at Telekom, I *used to claim/was claiming* all my travel expenses.
3 The network suddenly *went down/was going down* just as I *printed out/was printing out* last month's figures.
4 When I *was/used to be* a little boy, I *used to dream/was dreaming* of being an astronaut.
5 While the plane *descended/was descending*, my ears *started/were starting* to ache really badly.
6 We *wanted/were wanting* a reliable firm, so we *chose/were choosing* Philips.
7 We *used to have/were having* offices in Latvia and Estonia, but then we *combined/were combining* all our Baltic operations at our Vilnius office in Lithuania.
8 When I *arrived/was arriving* at the office, Jaroslav *waited/was waiting* for me.
9 The door was open so I *knocked/was knocking* and *went/was going* in.
10 Stavros *lost/was losing* his temper with Dimitri while they *discussed/were discussing* the quality problems in the plant.
11 When I *was/used to be* in Paris last October, I *visited/was visiting* the museums every day.
12 I *was feeling/used to feel* assertive so I *was deciding/decided* to speak to the HR Director about the way I had been treated.

Test 2.3 **Complete the second sentence so it has a similar meaning to the first sentence and contains the word in brackets. This exercise practises the past perfect and *used to*.**

1 Michael made some notes and started writing. (had)
After *Michael had made* some notes, he started writing.
2 This Internet connection is slower than before. (didn't)
This Internet connection ______________ be so slow.
3 I was sure I had my passport with me. (forgotten)
I was sure I ______________ my passport.
4 In the past, the factory produced 4,000 units a month. (used)
The factory ______________ 4,000 units a month.
5 I thought the article seemed familiar. (had)
I thought ______________ the article before.
6 Aisha left before I arrived. (already)
By the time I arrived, Aisha ______________ .
7 When I was younger I went skiing a lot. (used)
I ______________ a lot when I was younger.
8 I left the window open, but I only remembered at the airport. (had)
When I got to the airport, I remembered that ______________ open.

Test 2.4 Complete the sentences with the time expressions in the box.

at	on	in	when	while/when

1 The computer gave an error message *while/when* I was loading up the new software.
2 ____________ did you first notice the fault?
3 We sent you the invoice ____________ the end of last month.
4 Central Europe was changing very rapidly ____________ the nineties.
5 We sent the goods ____________ the fifteenth. Haven't you received them yet?
6 ____________ the ECB raised interest rates last month, the euro rose against the dollar.
7 ____________ she was checking the invoices, she noticed a small mistake.
8 We were acquired by Novartis ____________ 2006.
9 We met ____________ eight for a business breakfast.
10 What were you doing ____________ I called you this morning?
11 We changed our advertising campaign ____________ the beginning of the year.
12 I'll check my files and call you ____________ the morning.
13 This issue came to light ____________ we were assessing the viability of our operations in North America.
14 This issue came to light ____________ I spoke to our North American office.

Test 2.5 Complete the sentences by putting one verb in the past simple and one in the past perfect.

1 When the DVD started, I *realized* (realize) I *had seen* (see) the film before.
2 By the time I ____________ (get) to the phone it ____________ (stop) ringing.
3 How ____________ (you/find out) that you ____________ (got) the job?
4 Before I ____________ (join) ABN Amro I ____________ (work) as an investment analyst at ING.
5 I ____________ (send) her an email just to see how things were going. Meanwhile, my boss ____________ (already/spoke) to her boss.
6 I ____________ (always/suspect) that the contract ____________ (not/be) strictly legal.
7 By the time I ____________ (leave) university I ____________ (gain) a lot of valuable experience working as an intern at Intel.
8 The project ____________ (be) totally underfunded. If only we ____________ (know) right at the start!

Test 2.6 Complete the sentences by putting the verb in brackets into either the past perfect or past perfect continuous.

1 By last Christmas I *had decided* (decide) it was time to change my job.
2 I *had been thinking* (think) about changing my job for some time before I finally decided.
3 I ____________ (wait) for over an hour by the time he arrived.
4 Actually, I ____________ (already hear) the news before she told me.
5 Their share price ____________ (rise) steadily on rumours that they were a takeover target.
6 I couldn't give him a lift because I ____________ (not finish) work.
7 You would think they'd known each other for ages, but in fact they ____________ (never meet) until this year.
8 My eyes were hurting because I ____________ (look) at the screen all day.
9 After I ____________ (see) the new design I realized it was going to be a great success.
10 They closed down the factory because it ____________ (lose) money for years.

Test 3 Verb tenses: connecting past and present (units 5–6)

Test 3.1 **Underline the correct or most likely answers.**

1 *I'm waiting/I've been waiting* here for ages.
2 I'll join you in the restaurant. *I'm waiting/I've been waiting* for my colleagues.
3 The markets *have had/had* a sharp fall last week.
4 The markets *have had/had* a sharp fall this week.
5 If you need the instruction manual, *I've left/I left* it on your desk.
6 *I've left/I left* the instruction manual on your desk yesterday.
7 A: How long *are you working/have you been working* here?
B: About two years. I joined the company when they opened this branch.
8 A: How long *are you working/have you been working* here?
B: About two weeks. Then it's on to Chicago. Head Office send me all over the world.
9 We can't supply the goods because they *haven't paid/didn't pay* the deposit.
10 We couldn't supply the goods because they *haven't paid/didn't pay* the deposit.
11 I'm waiting for Sue. When *have you last seen/did you last see* her?
12 I'm waiting for Sue. *Have you seen/Did you see* her?

Test 3.2 **Cross out the mistake in each sentence and write the correction at the end.**

1 She ~~is~~ sending emails all week but hasn't placed an order yet. *has been*
2 We have started this course three weeks ago. ______
3 A: 'What have you been doing all morning?' B: 'I've been written letters.' ______
4 When have you arrived? ______
5 You have ever been to India? ______
6 Paula has been organized the press conference for Friday at nine. ______
7 Sales have been rising since three months. ______
8 I live in this city since I was born. ______
9 I wait here a long time. Where have you been? ______
10 I didn't give a presentation before, so I'm a bit nervous. ______
11 At last! I'm waiting for this phone call all morning. ______
12 How long do you work here? ______

Test 3.3 **Complete the sentences with the time expressions in the box. Several answers may be possible but one solution uses each expression in the most appropriate way.**

yet	for	~~since~~	often	ever	never	already	so far	just	always

1 I've lived in my city-centre flat *since* 2009. I love it there.
2 Thanks for the present! I've ______ wanted a gold Rolex!
3 We've ______ interviewed four candidates this morning, and none of them is really suitable for the job.
4 Have you ______ worked abroad?
5 I've ______ heard that we've won the contract! Congratulations everybody!
6 Hurry up! Haven't you finished______ ?
7 Nina has worked in this company ______ over five years now.
8 I've ______ been to a karaoke bar before. It's certainly an interesting experience!
9 I've ______ passed this building, but this is the first time I've been inside.
10 We've been very busy on the stand this morning. ______ we've given away over 200 brochures.

Test 3.4 **Complete the second sentence so it has a similar meaning to the first sentence. You may need a new verb, or a time expression like those in Test 3.3. Use contractions where possible.**

1 Jan doesn't work at this company now.
Jan *has left* this company.
2 This is the first time I've been to the United States.
I ________________ to the United States before.
3 That's strange! My copy of *Business Grammar Builder* isn't here!
That's strange! My copy ________________ disappeared.
4 I saw a friend of yours a few moments ago.
I ________________ a friend of yours.
5 I'm still writing this report.
I ________________ this report yet.
6 We started working here three years ago.
We've been ________________ three years.
7 Is this your first visit to Serbia?
Have you ________________ before?
8 It's a long time since I spoke to Goran.
I ________________ to Goran for a long time.
9 Is Anna still out of the office?
Has ________________ back yet?
10 I'm sorry, but Rachel Dawson isn't here.
I'm sorry, but Rachel Dawson has ________________ out.
11 I last saw David in 2008.
I ________________ since 2008.
12 I came to live here three months ago.
I've been ________________ three months.
13 How stupid of me! My laptop is still in the car. I hope it's still there!
How stupid of me! I ________________ my laptop in the car. I hope it's still there!
14 I'm still reading this report.
I ________________ reading this report yet.
15 Ronan left the building a moment ago.
Ronan has ________________ the building.
16 Have you been to Scandinavia at any time?
Have you ________________ to Scandinavia?
17 I've had English lessons at my company since January.
I've been ________________ English at my company since January.
18 It's ages since we last had an order from CWP.
We ________________ an order from CWP for ages.
19 This is the first time I've eaten reindeer steak.
I've ________________ reindeer steak before.
20 I started playing tennis about six months ago.
I've been ________________ about six months.
21 I don't remember Helen's phone number.
I've ________________ Helen's phone number.
22 The last time I saw Marguerite was Monday.
I haven't ________________ Monday.

Test 4 Verb tenses: future (units 7–8)

Test 4.1 **<u>Underline</u> the correct or most likely answers.**

1 Wait for me. *I'll be/I've been* ready in a moment.
2 We need to move forward – we can't just wait until the economy *recovers/will recover*.
3 That looks very heavy. *Will I/Shall I* help you?
4 Notice. This elevator *is going to be/will be* out of service until further notice.
5 Look out! *It's going to fall/It'll fall*!
6 A: 'Do you want me to call them?'
B: 'No, it's all right, *I'll do/I'm doing* it.'
7 Please don't leave until I *come back/will come back*.
8 Julie won't be here next week. *She'll work/She'll be working* at our other office.
9 The flight attendant is calling us. I think *we will/we're going to* board the plane.
10 *They'll probably/They probably will* cut back the training budget next year.

Test 4.2 **Correct these sentences by either crossing out or adding words. Write the correction at the end.**

1 ~~I go to get~~ an accurate valuation of all our properties. *I'm going to get*
2 The visitors from Japan will here at 9.30. ______
3 Justine will probably to get the sales job. ______
4 Sue is going lend me her copy of the report. ______
5 Bye for now. I see you later this evening. ______
6 I not be in the office tomorrow. I'm working from home. ______
7 What exactly you going to discuss at the next meeting? ______
8 It's snowing – the flight probably will be delayed. ______

Test 4.3 **Decide if uses a–h are most often associated with *will*, *be going to*, the present continuous (*I'm doing*), the future continuous (*I'll be doing*) or the future perfect (*I'll have done*).**

a) future facts *will*
b) fixed future arrangements ______
c) instant decisions ______
d) future plans and intentions ______
e) predictions with present evidence ______
f) general opinions about the future ______
g) looking back from the future ______
h) activities in progress in the future ______

Now match the underlined forms 1–8 below with uses a–h.

1 We<u>'re going to launch</u> the new model at the Frankfurt Motor Show. [d]
2 Sorry about this confusion. I<u>'ll look into it</u> right away and I<u>'ll call</u> you back. [ ]
3 I think we<u>'ll</u> probably <u>make</u> a small loss this year. [ ]
4 Judging by these figures, we<u>'re going to make</u> a small loss this year. [ ]
5 I<u>'m meeting</u> my bank manager on Thursday. We<u>'re having</u> lunch together. [ ]
6 During my presentation I<u>'ll be describing</u> the key benefits of our new service. [ ]
7 Next year <u>will be</u> the tenth anniversary of our company. [ ]
8 It's not a difficult job. We<u>'ll have finished</u> by lunchtime. [ ]

Test 4.4 **Complete the second sentence so it has a similar meaning to the first sentence. The answers include these forms: *'ll, won't, shall*, present simple (*I do*), present continuous (*I'm doing*) and future continuous (*I'll be doing*).**

1 I promise to call you when I get back.
When I get back, *I'll call* you.
2 Would you like me to close the window?
__________ close the window?
3 After the conference we can travel back together.
When the __________ we can travel back together.
4 What job will you have after the company reorganization?
What __________ doing after the company reorganization?
5 They refuse to lower their price.
They __________ lower their price.
6 Are you free tomorrow evening?
Are __________ anything tomorrow evening?
7 I'll wait here until it stops raining.
When it stops raining __________ leave.
8 I need to find a new job soon if sales don't improve.
I __________ looking for a new job soon if sales don't improve.
9 How about having a round of golf after work?
__________ we have a round of golf after work?
10 The product launch is at the Berlin Expo in April.
We __________ the product at the Berlin Expo in April.

Test 4.5 **Rewrite each sentence choosing from *'ll/won't, shall* or *going to*. Use the main verb underlined.**

1 Sarah doesn't plan to get married yet.
Sarah isn't going to get married yet.
2 How about having a game of tennis at the weekend?
__________ a game of tennis at the weekend?
3 I've decided to study Arabic in Qatar.
__________ Arabic in Qatar.
4 I promise to be back before midday.
__________ before midday.
5 I have an appointment to see the doctor, so I can't come.
__________ the doctor, so I can't come.
6 I promise not to forget.
__________ .
7 I plan to do my MBA at Insead in France.
__________ my MBA in France.
8 Would you like me to help you with those bags?
__________ with those bags?
9 We're willing to come back later if you like.
__________ back later if you like.
10 I intend to ask my boss about opportunities for promotion.
__________ my boss about opportunities for promotion.
11 I want to have the salmon.
__________ the salmon, please.
12 I've decided to have the salmon. What about you?
__________ the salmon. What about you?

Test 5 Passives (units 9–10)

Test 5.1 **Cross out the mistake in each sentence and write the correction at the end.**

1 Lucas ~~has been offer~~ a new job in Brazil. *has been offered*
2 Your parcel was been posted yesterday. ______
3 A new industrial site is be developed outside the town. ______
4 All the food at the reception was ate. ______
5 Gold is produce in large quantities in South Africa. ______
6 Nothing will being decided before next week. ______
7 The presentation is giving at the Hotel Intercontinental. ______
8 I've just heard that Carla is been promoted to Marketing Director. ______
9 The introduction to the report was writing by the CEO. ______
10 Many customers are losing through poor after-sales service. ______

Test 5.2 **Rewrite each sentence with a passive verb, without mentioning who did the action.**

1 The authorities have closed the casino.
The casino has been closed.
2 Someone broke into our house last week.
______
3 Nowadays people everywhere speak English.
______
4 The local authorities have finally opened the new motorway.
______
5 Someone left this bag in reception.
______
6 The city council will ban all traffic from the city center.
______
7 We leave the liquid for 24 hours after adding the ingredients.
______
8 The organizers are postponing the meeting.
______

Test 5.3 **Complete the second sentence so it has a similar meaning to the first sentence and contains the word in brackets.**

1 They have just serviced all our machines. (had)
We *have just had all our machines serviced* .
2 They are coming to clean the carpet tomorrow. (having)
We ______ .
3 They printed some business cards with the new logo. (had)
We ______ .
4 Tomorrow they are repairing my car. (getting)
Tomorrow I ______ .
5 They have just refused my request for credit. (had)
I ______ .
6 They just fined me for illegal parking. (got)
I ______ .

Test 5.4 **Underline the correct words in this article.**

A Race Against Time

Governments across Europe are [1]*starting/being started* to worry. Why? Because low birth rates combined with longer life expectancy [2]*mean/are meant* that the Continent will soon have fewer people working and fewer people paying taxes. As a result, a whole range of measures must [3]*take/be taken* to deal with the problems that demographic change [4]*will bring/will be brought*.

This whole issue [5]*addressed/was addressed* recently at the World Economic Forum in Davos. Many speakers [6]*highlighted/were highlighted* that this is a global problem, not just a European one. However, the facts cannot [7]*ignore/be ignored*: the situation in Europe is particularly serious. In Europe, 2.1 children per woman [8]*considers/is considered* to be the population replacement level. No country achieves this, and the worst performers (Germany, Italy, Spain and Greece) all have a national average of less than 1.4 children per woman. Spain's population, for example, [9]*expects/is expected* to fall from 40 million to 35 million by 2050. And as the population gets smaller, it is also getting older. From around now onwards the 'baby boomer' generation [10]*will start/will be started* to retire, and their retirement benefits [11]*will fund/will be funded* by fewer and fewer tax-paying young workers.

So solutions will have [12]*to find/to be found*. Increasing immigration is, in theory, one option – although most agree it is politically unfeasible in the current climate. Another option is to raise the retirement age and make people work until later in life. This is almost certain [13]*to do/to be done*. Finally, tax and social security models must [14]*look at/be looked at* in a completely new way, for example by encouraging people to look after themselves in retirement with private pension plans and so on.

Apart from this, governments will have to tackle the root cause of the problem and try to boost birth rates. Tax and cash incentives can [15]*give/be given* to parents who have babies, maternity leave schemes can be extended, and state-subsidized child care can [16]*provide/be provided*.

Test 5.5 **Complete the second sentence so it has a similar meaning to the first sentence. Do not mention who did the action.**

1 Someone checked these figures for me last week.
I *had these figures checked* last week.

2 They grow much less coffee in Columbia these days.
These days ______________________________ .

3 Someone delivered this package this morning.
This package ______________________________ .

4 The city council is redeveloping the old docklands area.
The old docklands area ______________________________ .

5 They've put up interest rates again.
Interest rates ______________________________ again.

6 We'll discuss your idea in the meeting tomorrow.
Your idea ______________________________ tomorrow.

7 The technician installed some new software on the network yesterday.
Yesterday we ______________________________ on the network.

8 Tokyo is my place of birth.
I ______________________________ in Tokyo.

9 When is your date of birth?
When exactly ______________________________ born?

10 Someone stole Peter's car last week.
Peter ______________________________ stolen last week.

11 Did anyone tell Alex about the meeting?
Was ______________________________ about the meeting?

12 Has anyone made a backup copy of this file?
Has ______________________________ made?

Test 6 Modals (units 11–14)

Test 6.1 **Underline the correct or most appropriate words.**

1 That looks like Carlos over there, but it *can't/mustn't* be. He's in Spain.
2 Marie isn't at her office, so she *can/must* be on her way here.
3 I think you *need to/have necessity to* get some advice from your colleagues.
4 Is your car door damaged? Someone *must/must have* tried to break in.
5 It's getting very late. I think *we'd better/we would* pay the bill and leave.
6 I *might/can* be able to help you, but I'm not sure.
7 Yes, it's a good idea – we *should/must* lease rather than buy.
8 It's absolutely necessary – we *should/must* lease rather than buy.
9 Katja *can't have/must have* heard the bad news. She doesn't look very worried.
10 Sorry, I *must to/have to* go now. I don't want to be late.
11 You *might not/don't need to* come to the meeting if you're busy.
12 This invoice *can't/mustn't* be right. It says €890 to repair the photocopier!

Test 6.2 **Complete the sentences with the words or phrases in the box.**

have to	had to	~~don't have to~~	didn't have to	must
mustn't	must have	might have	should	could

1 We're trying a new dress code. We *don't have to* wear formal clothes on Fridays.
2 You ________ touch that red button! The whole production line will stop!
3 I'm not sure, but I think I ________ made a mistake.
4 Before we agree, we'll ________ study the contract in more detail.
5 Is that the time? I really ________ go now.
6 If you needed the goods urgently, we ________ speed up the order.
7 Sorry I'm late, but I ________ talk to a contractor about some maintenance work.
8 It ________ been embarrassing for you to forget his name.
9 I think we ________ accept their offer. It's the best we'll get.
10 Luckily, we ________ borrow too much money for the mortgage on our house.

Test 6.3 **Match the uses of *would* a–j with sentences 1–10 below.**

a) offering help
b) offering something
c) polite request
d) invitation
e) imaginary future with *if*
f) reporting the spoken word *will* (i.e. reported speech)
g) be willing to do something
h) asking or giving opinions about a possible situation
i) past refusal
j) past habit

1 Would you mind calling back later? [c]
2 What would you do if they refused to negotiate? [ ]
3 Would you like some milk in your coffee? [ ]
4 Would you like to join us for dinner tomorrow evening? [ ]
5 Would you like me to open the window? [ ]

6 They wouldn't drop their price under any circumstances. [ ]
7 He said he would call back later. [ ]
8 When I was a student I would go out every night. [ ]
9 Eileen would lend you the money, I'm sure. [ ]
10 Why would anyone do a thing like that? [ ]

Test 6.4 **Complete the second sentence so it has a similar meaning to the first sentence. Use a word or phrase from the box.**

can't	might	~~should~~	have to	don't have to	ought to
can't be	might be	must be	should be		

1 It would be a good idea to bring in a firm of outside consultants.
We *should* bring in a firm of outside consultants.
2 It's not necessary for you to leave a deposit.
You ________ leave a deposit.
3 I'm sure that isn't John, because he's in Paris.
That ________ John, because he's in Paris.
4 Anne is almost certainly with a customer.
Anne ________ with a customer.
5 I expect the meeting will be finished by ten.
The meeting ________ finished by ten.
6 It's possible that I'll be late.
I ________ late.
7 We are not allowed to dispose of waste in that way.
We ________ dispose of waste in that way.
8 Perhaps our interests will differ on this issue.
Our interests ________ differ on this issue.
9 It's the rule that we need to check all bank references.
We ________ check all bank references.
10 At this point it's better that I disclose a personal interest in the matter.
At this point I ________ disclose a personal interest in the matter.

Test 6.5 **Complete the second sentence so it has a similar meaning to the first sentence. Use a word or phrase from the box.**

~~might have~~	could have	should have (x2)	must have
can't have	shouldn't have	might not have	

1 Perhaps David made a mistake.
David *might have* made a mistake.
2 I'm sure that she worked very hard on this project.
She ________ worked very hard on this project.
3 I'm sure the warranty hasn't expired already.
The warranty ________ expired already.
4 It would have been a good idea for you to tell me.
You ________ told me.
5 Perhaps you didn't see the article about us in *The Economist*.
You ________ seen the article about us in *The Economist*.
6 I was expecting them to call by now.
They ________ called by now.
7 It was a bad idea for us to drop our prices so much.
We ________ dropped our prices so much.
8 It was possible for us to see this problem coming.
We ________ seen this problem coming.

Test 7 Questions (units 15–16)

Test 7.1 **When we make questions in spoken English, we often leave out the auxiliary verb and the subject pronoun. For example, instead of saying, 'Do you like it?' we just say, 'Like it?'. Write full questions using the underlined verb.**

1 Finished yet? We're all waiting! *Have you finished yet?*
2 See you tomorrow? Or are you busy all day? ________
3 You look relaxed. Have a nice holiday? ________
4 Steve's a bit difficult sometimes. Know what I mean? ________
5 Hi, Erik. Coming out for a drink later? ________
6 Sorry I'm so late. Been waiting long? ________
7 Interesting conference, isn't it? Enjoying yourself? ________
8 Heard the latest? Isabel is taking early retirement. ________

Test 7.2 **Rewrite each question, beginning as shown.**

1 What's the time?
Could you tell me *what the time is* ?
2 What does this mean?
I'd like to know ________ ?
3 How much does this cost?
Could I ask ________ ?
4 What time does the bank open?
Do you know ________ ?
5 Am I in the right seat?
Could you tell me if ________ ?
6 Where's the Opera House?
Do you know ________ ?
7 Is this the way to the station?
Could you tell me if ________ ?
8 Who is the speaker at the next session?
I'd like to know ________ ?

Test 7.3 **Match the beginnings of the phrases with their endings.**

1 Do you mind if I …	a) closing the window?
2 Would you mind if I …	b) closed the window?
3 Would you mind …	c) close the window?

Somebody asks *Would you mind if I opened the window?* Write (✓) if the answer is appropriate in normal conversation; write (✗) if it is not.

4 Yes, I would. ☐
5 Yes, please. ☐
6 No, of course not. ☐
7 Go ahead. That's fine. ☐
8 Please do. ☐
9 Why? I think it's cold in here. ☐
10 To be honest, I'm fine. It could be a little chilly with the window open. ☐

Test 7.4 Write short answers for each question, beginning as shown. Use contractions (*don't* instead of *do not*) where possible.

1 Do you like Brazil? Yes, *I do* . No, *I don't* .
2 Does Karen like Brazil? Yes, ______ . No, ______ .
3 Do they like Brazil? Yes, ______ . No, ______ .
4 Have you worked here long? Yes, ______ . No, ______ .
5 Has Karen worked here long? Yes, ______ . No, ______ .
6 Are you coming with us tonight? Yes, ______ . No, ______ .
7 Is Karen coming with us tonight? Yes, ______ . No, ______ .
8 Can you come on Friday? Yes, ______ . No, ______ .
9 Will you be here tomorrow? Yes, ______ . No, ______ .
10 Did you have to pay a lot? Yes, ______ . No, ______ .
11 Is that your coat? Yes, ______ . No, ______ .
12 Is that Maria over there? Yes, ______ . No, ______ .

Test 7.5 Complete each sentence with the verb in brackets where there is one.

1 '*You have got* (have got) the file, haven't you?' → 'Yes, of course.'
2 'They'll be back by 4.00, ______ ?' → 'I expect so.'
3 'You ______ (leave) now, are you?' → 'Sorry, I really have to go.'
4 'They've been here before, ______ ?' → 'Yes, I think so.'
5 'You can meet Ida at the station, ______ ?' → 'Yes, of course, it's in my diary.'
6 'You don't happen to know the time, ______ ?' → 'Sorry, I don't.'
7 'You had the same thing for lunch yesterday, ______ ?' → 'Yes, exactly the same.'
8 'You ______ (forget) the product samples, did you?' → 'No, of course not.'
9 'You ______ (give) me a hand, could you?' → 'Of course, what can I do?'
10 'You ______ (be) here yesterday, were you?' → 'No, I wasn't.'
11 'Let's have a break now, ______ ?' → 'OK, good idea.'
12 'I'm late, ______ ?' → 'Only a little. But don't worry about it.'

Test 7.6 Put the words into the correct order to make questions. Add a capital letter at the beginning.

1 take Visa do you? *Do you take Visa?*
2 please I can see the menu? ______
3 excuse me here anyone is sitting? ______
4 from which country do come you? ______
5 by which route you did come? ______
6 to who you were just now talking? ______
7 what mean do you exactly by that? ______
8 a little more specific you could be? ______
9 what time the next train to Brussels is? ______
10 you can tell me what time is the next train to Brussels? ______
11 do need you any help with your suitcase? ______
12 this BlackBerry to who does belong? ______
13 I could ask something you? ______
14 do think you could I ask you something? ______
15 the station where is? ______
16 you could me tell the station where is? ______

Test 8 Conditionals (units 17–18)

Test 8.1 **Underline the correct words.**

1 If we sent the goods by sea, the transport costs *will be/would be* much lower.
2 If they *promote/promoted* the brand better, they'll gain market share.
3 If you *left/had left* earlier, you might have got there on time.
4 If anyone from Head Office visits, they always *stay/will stay* in a five-star hotel.
5 If I were you, *I'd call/I'll call* their technical support number.
6 If I *have/had* more time, I'd be able to come up with a solution.
7 If it *breaks down/will break down*, it takes days for the service engineer to arrive.
8 If you needed the money urgently, I *could phone/could have phoned* Accounts to try and speed up your payment.
9 If you enter the date in the wrong format, the computer *doesn't recognize/didn't* recognize the information.
10 If *we'd been/we were* more careful, we wouldn't have lost so much money.
11 If I'd bought more shares, *I'd become/I'd've become* rich by now.
12 If your second interview *goes/will go* well, I'm sure they'll offer you the job.
13 If you *would have backed up/backed up* your files more often, you *wouldn't risk/didn't risk* losing all your work.
14 If you *hadn't acted/wouldn't acted* so quickly, *we'd be/we are* in big trouble.
15 They're asking a lot of detailed questions about the contract. I wish I *have/had* it with me.
16 I wish it *is/was* Friday!

Test 8.2 **Complete each sentence with the verb in brackets in one of these forms: *will do, would do, would have done*. Use contractions typical of speech where possible (*'ll do, 'd do, 'd've done*).**

1 If we got a virus on the network, we *'d lose* (lose) all our data.
2 We ______ (be) in Paris by six if the train isn't late.
3 If you'd given a handout for your talk, I think they ______ (ask) more questions.
4 If you tell me what you want, I ______ (get) it for you at the airport.
5 We ______ (get) more inquiries if we advertised more often.
6 If we hadn't left so early, we ______ (miss) the flight.
7 Don't worry – if you haven't got any change on you, I ______ (leave) the tip.
8 We ______ (sort out) the problem much sooner if we'd had the manual.
9 If you were in his situation, what ______ (you/do)?
10 If you'd been in his situation, what ______ (you/do)?
11 If I worked abroad, I ______ (not see) my family so often.
12 We ______ (not get) the contract if we hadn't shown them these testimonials from our clients.

Test 8.3 **Complete the sentences with *if*, *unless* or *otherwise*.**

1 Their offices are very near. We'll walk there, *unless* it's raining.
2 We would probably get the contract ______ we dropped our price a little.
3 Come on! ______ we hurry, we'll miss the plane.
4 If the cost is under €10,000, it's worth doing. ______ it's not a good idea.
5 ______ you have any more questions, please feel free to call.
6 What would you do ______ they only implemented a part of the plan?
7 See if we can do the job with fewer people; ______ we don't have much scope for cutting costs.
8 I don't feel able to take a decision ______ I have all the figures.

Test 8.4 **Complete the *if* sentence that comments on each situation. The *if* sentence imagines the opposite to what really happened.**

1 Situation: Emma didn't leave early, and so she missed her flight.
If Emma *had left early*, she *wouldn't have missed* her flight.

2 Situation: He didn't make more copies, so we didn't have enough handouts for everyone.
If he ________________, we ________________ enough handouts for everyone.

3 Situation: I forgot to bring your map, so I went to the wrong building.
If I ________________, I ________________ to the wrong building.

4 Situation: They didn't invest in new technology, so they didn't survive the recession.
If they ________________, they ________________ the recession.

5 Situation: You didn't wait, so this has happened.
If you ________________, this ________________.

6 Situation: I didn't realize you were so busy when I asked you to help me.
If I ________________, I ________________ to help me.

7 Situation: The Government didn't collapse, so there wasn't a crisis.
If the Government ________________, there ________________ a crisis.

8 Situation: They didn't bring out their new model on time, so they lost market share.
If they ________________, they ________________ market share.

Test 8.5 **Choose the correct continuation for each sentence.**

1 I wasn't taking notes, and now I can't remember what she said. [*b*]
a) I wish I took notes. b) I wish I'd taken notes.

2 This is a very unusual situation. [ ]
a) I wish I'd known what to do. b) I wish I knew what to do.

3 Our offices are in the city center and the rent is very high. [ ]
a) I wish we were outside the center. b) I wish we are outside the center.

4 They gave the job to an external candidate, but now they regret it. [ ]
a) They wish they hadn't done it. b) They wish they didn't do it.

5 I can't enter the system because I don't have the password. [ ]
a) If only I'd have the password. b) If only I had the password.

6 There are too many similar models on the market right now. [ ]
a) If only we launched our version earlier. b) If only we'd launched our version earlier.

7 I'm worried about the meeting next Friday. We need to get agreement. [ ]
a) I wish we succeed. b) I hope we succeed.

8 My presentation is going from bad to worse! People are actually leaving the room! [ ]
a) I wish I could start again. b) I wish I would start again.

Test 8.6 **Complete the sentences with a form of the verb in brackets. Use contractions where possible.**

1 We're not the market leader, but I wish we *were* (be).
2 He made a mess of all my photocopying. I wish I ____________ (do) it myself.
3 I told them all our product development ideas. If only I ____________ (not say) so much.
4 I can't understand anything Marie says. I wish I ____________ (can speak) French.
5 Your dessert looks good. I wish I ____________ (order) that too.
6 I'm hopeless at choosing clothes for my wife. If only I ____________ (have) our daughter here.
7 They're meeting at the moment. I wish I ____________ (can be) a fly on the wall.
8 This information is important. I wish you ____________ (give) it to me before the meeting.

Test 9 Verbs + *-ing* or infinitive (units 19–20)

Test 9.1 **Underline the correct words.**

1 I really can't afford *to eat/eating* in such an expensive restaurant.
2 Do you mind *to come/coming* back in half an hour?
3 Do you want *to come/coming* back in half an hour?
4 Kate denied *to give/giving* the office keys to anyone else.
5 He admitted *to make/making* a serious mistake.
6 *Remind/Remember* me to call Sylvia this afternoon.
7 I really enjoyed *to visit/visiting* your company and meeting all your colleagues.
8 I hope *to be/being* at the next meeting, but I'm not sure if I can make it.
9 I expect *to be/being* at the next meeting. I think I can make it.
10 If she isn't in the office when you call, keep *to try/trying*.
11 We tend *to recruit/recruiting* people who can show some experience of working in a similar environment.
12 I refuse *to believe/believing* that we can't implement the plans.
13 We managed *to get/getting* the outcome we were looking for, but it wasn't easy.
14 I can't stand people *to interrupt/interrupting* all the time. It's so rude.
15 Where do you fancy *to go/going* for lunch today?
16 I've arranged *to meet/meeting* them at their hotel.
17 We guarantee *to deliver/delivering* the goods by the end of June.
18 Imagine *to win/winning* the lottery!
19 The manager refused *to see/seeing* me.
20 I realized I had forgotten *to pack/packing* my phone recharger.
21 If I miss my connection, it means *to arrive/arriving* in Frankfurt after midnight.
22 I tried *to lift/lifting* it, but it was too heavy.
23 I enjoy *to get away/getting away* to the coast at the weekend.
24 I'd love *to get away/getting away* to the coast this weekend.
25 I tried to persuade him, but he refused *to listen/listening* to me.
26 I admit *to be/being* a little careless last time, but I won't do it again.
27 We need to take drastic action, because we risk *to lose/losing* everything.
28 It's not worth *to think/thinking* about using the profits for reinvestment, because we said we'd pay shareholders a higher dividend.
29 They've decided *to order/ordering* 1000 pieces this time.
30 He offered *to meet/meeting* me at the airport.

Test 9.2 **Complete the sentences with the verbs in the box. Choose either the *-ing* form or *to* + infinitive.**

be	cause	come	compromise	get	get through	give	~~make~~	rise	unpack	wait

1 They admitted *making* a mistake on the paperwork.
2 Wages tend ________ faster than inflation.
3 We're all going out for a drink after work. Do you fancy ________ with us?
4 I can't manage ________ when I call them. I keep ________ an engaged tone.
5 Do you mind ________ for a couple of minutes while I finish off what I'm doing here?
6 They agreed ________ us thirty more days to pay the invoice.
7 The logistics firm denies ________ the damage.
8 Their negotiating position was very rigid. They refused ________ .
9 I saw him ________ the goods, and there was no damage visible at the time.
10 I enjoyed ________ self-employed for a while, but my income was quite insecure.

Test 10 Phrasal verbs (units 22–23)

Test 10.1 **Match the beginnings of sentences 1–12 with their endings a–l.**

1 In my job I deal [c]
2 The Government is trying to cut [ ]
3 Here's the application form. Can you fill [ ]
4 I deal with the retail side of the business, and Kate looks [ ]
5 I hope John gets better soon. We can't do [ ]
6 Thanks for your call, and I look [ ]
7 First I'll give you an overview of the company, and then I'll move [ ]
8 Before you switch off the PC, make sure you back [ ]
9 We're going through a period of consolidation, and some smaller companies in the market will probably be taken [ ]
10 We need some new typists chairs. I'll look [ ]
11 These days you need to do a lot of reading to keep [ ]
12 It's important to find a candidate who fits [ ]

a) after the wholesale side.
b) up with developments in the field.
c) with all the paperwork related to customer accounts.
d) without him on the negotiating team.
e) up all your files.
f) in with the company culture and the other people in the department.
g) down on bureaucracy in the public sector.
h) on to outline the services we offer and some plans we have in the pipeline.
i) over in the next few years.
j) forward to meeting you on the tenth.
k) through some online catalogues and see what I can find.
l) in both sides and sign it at the bottom.

Test 10.2 **Rewrite each sentence by replacing the underlined words with a phrasal verb from the box in the correct form.**

come across	deal with	get through	go over	~~look forward to~~
pick up	put back to	run out of	sort out	take up

1 I think I'm going to enjoy the weekend very much.
I'm looking forward to the weekend very much.
2 The machine occupies about four square meters of floor space.
The machine ______ about four square meters of floor space.
3 I think we'll have to delay the meeting until next week.
I think we'll have ______ next week.
4 They are not an easy company to do business with.
They are not an easy company ______ .
5 There's a small problem. We're just trying to put it right now.
There's a small problem. We're just trying ______ now.
6 Can you collect me from the airport in your car?
Can you ______ from the airport?
7 Before we finish, I'd just like to summarize the main points again.
Before we finish, I'd just like ______ the main points again.
8 We have a lot of work to complete.
We have a lot of work to ______ .
9 I've lost my pen. Let me know if you find it by chance.
I've lost my pen. Let me know if ______ .
10 We'll have to continue the meeting tomorrow. We have no more time left.
We'll have to continue the meeting tomorrow. We have ______ .

Test 10.3 Complete the sentences with the words in the box.

away	back	by	down	into	off	~~on~~	over	out	through	up

1 Hold *on* a moment, that's not exactly what I said.
2 Clare will take ________ my job when I'm given my new assignment next month.
3 I hate it when they put you on hold and you can't get ________ .
4 The total bill for four nights works ________ at €460.
5 The factory will close ________ next year. They're moving production to Vietnam.
6 It's going to be difficult to get ________ with such a small budget.
7 Paula grew ________ in a little village outside Venice.
8 I'll drop you ________ at the station on my way home.
9 I'll look ________ the problem and get ________ to you tomorrow.
10 No, I don't have it any more. I threw it ________ .

Test 10.4 Complete the sentences with the phrasal verbs in the box.

catch up with	cut down on	face up to	~~fall back on~~	get back to
get along with	get around to	move on to	run out of	sit in on

1 There have been a number of unexpected developments. It's lucky we have a contingency plan to *fall back on* .
2 He's a very easy-going kind of guy – he can ________ just about anyone.
3 The quality report says we can ________ a lot of waste in the factory by reducing defects and scrap.
4 We've tried everything and, basically, we've completely ________ new ideas.
5 Sorry it's taken so long to ________ answering your email.
6 Are you going to the restaurant now? I have a few things to do here in the office, but I'll ________ you later.
7 Estera has just started working with us and I thought it would be useful if she could ________ the meeting.
8 It's not going to be easy, but you have to ________ your responsibilities.
9 Now I'd like to ________ this next slide, which shows our sales by region.
10 I need some time to look into this. Can I ________ you later?

Test 10.5 Match the beginnings of sentences 1–12 with their endings a–l.

1 My parents were quite strict and brought me [c]
2 When are you arriving? Would you like me to pick [ ]
3 When are you leaving? Would you like me to drop [ ]
4 Peter? Any comments? Would you like to come [ ]
5 Are you working late? Please make sure you turn [ ]
6 I can't make the meeting on Thursday. Can we bring [ ]
7 I can't make the meeting on Thursday. Can we put [ ]
8 I have no idea what it means. Have you tried looking [ ]
9 The cost of our raw materials should come [ ]
10 I'll try and find her. Can you just hold [ ]
11 Sorry about that – I think we were cut [ ]
12 My doctor says I should give [ ]

a) it back to Friday?
b) it forward to Wednesday?
c) up in a very traditional way.
d) off the lights when you leave.
e) up smoking and go on a diet.
f) you off?
g) you up?
h) off when I entered a tunnel.
i) in here?
j) on for a moment?
k) it up in an online dictionary?
l) down as the recession deepens.

Test 11 *make & do, have, get* (unit 25)

Test 11.1 **Complete the sentences with *make, do* or *have*. You may have to change the form.**

1 What are you *doing* at the weekend?
2 I'm ______ serious doubts about the whole thing.
3 OK, shall we ______ a start?
4 Are you going to the post office? Yes? Could you ______ me a favour?
5 Can I ______ a suggestion? Why don't we ______ a meeting to discuss what to ______ .
6 I think we need to ______ more tests before we ______ a final decision.
7 The company ______ a lot of money last year, but this year we're not ______ so well.
8 It ______ me really mad when people can't ______ their jobs properly.
9 I'm ______ great difficulty in ______ plans when everything is so confusing.
10 Go on! ______ a go! It doesn't matter if you ______ a mistake.
11 The help I got from my employer ______ it possible for me to ______ an MBA. I'm going to ______ the course at ESADE in Barcelona.
12 I'm ______ my best but I really can't ______ sense of these figures. I'm ______ a lot of trouble seeing what they all refer to.
13 The new line for the Prague metro has gone out to tender. We ______ a good chance to win some of the work, and I ______ no doubt that we should ______ a bid.
14 I've been ______ a lot of overtime recently. I need to ______ a rest – I'm exhausted.
15 The builders are ______ some work on the floor below and they're ______ a lot of noise. Unfortunately, we can't ______ anything about it.
16 We don't normally offer those terms to first-time customers, but in this case I think we can ______ an exception.
17 I've just been ______ the accounts and it looks like we finally ______ a profit last quarter.
18 The menu looks really good. I'm going to ______ French onion soup as a starter, and then the pasta with seafood. But I think I'll ______ without dessert. I'm ______ a bit of an effort to lose weight.

Test 11.2 **Match the uses of *get* in sentences 1–8 with their dictionary definitions a–h *(sth = something, sb = somebody).***

1 I didn't get home until eight last night. [d]
2 I'm getting a direct flight to Amsterdam. [ ]
3 We're only getting a 4% pay rise this year. [ ]
4 Did you get what she was saying? [ ]
5 It's no good. We'll never get them to agree. [ ]
6 I'm getting tired. Shall we continue tomorrow? [ ]
7 I should get something for my wife at the airport. [ ]
8 I'll get last year's figures. Just wait a moment. [ ]

a) obtain/receive/be given
b) buy
c) become
d) arrive at a place
e) bring sth/fetch
f) understand
g) make sb do sth/persuade
h) travel by/catch

Now match each sentence 9–14 with some of the definitions a–h above.

9 I'm sorry, I didn't quite get that last point. [ ]
10 Don't worry, you'll soon get used to it. [ ]
11 I'm getting eye strain from looking at the screen for too long. [ ]
12 Is that your new car? When did you get it? [ ]
13 Can I get you a drink while you're waiting? [ ]
14 I got here by taxi. [ ]

Test 12 Reported speech (units 26–27)

Test 12.1 **Rewrite each question in reported speech. Use contractions where possible.**

1 'Are you going out for lunch?' Rahul asked me.
Rahul asked me *if (whether) I was going out* for lunch.

2 'What did you do yesterday?' Carol asked me.
Carol asked me ______________________ the day before.

3 Dmitry asked us, 'Do you often go to Germany for meetings?'.
Dmitry asked us ______________________ for meetings.

4 'How many interviews have you done today?' Patricia asked me.
Patricia asked me ______________________ that day.

5 'Are you going to change jobs, Sue?' asked José.
José asked Sue ______________________ .

6 'Who did you talk to at the conference?' Yanmei asked me.
Yanmei asked me ______________________ at the conference.

7 The technician asked me, 'Will you be here tomorrow?'.
The technician asked me ______________________ there the next day.

8 'Where are your new offices?' Mary asked me.
Mary asked me ______________________ .

9 'Have you seen Anton recently?' he asked me.
He asked me ______________________ recently.

10 He asked me 'Will you be seeing Masumi over the next few days?'.
He asked me ______________________ over the next few days.

Test 12.2 **Remember that in reported speech there are other changes as well as the verb change. Rewrite each sentence below in reported speech, changing all the underlined words.**

1 Tony said to me, 'I'll see you here tomorrow'.
He said ______________________ .

2 'We received your email update about this issue last week,' they said.
They said ______________________ .

Test 12.3 **Rewrite each sentence in reported speech, using a verb from the box.**

advised	apologized for	congratulated on	invited	offered	~~promised~~	refused	suggested

1 'I'll meet you at the airport, Ekaterina,' said Jaroslav.
Jaroslav *promised to meet Ekaterina* at the airport.

2 'Would you like to come to the product launch, Jean?' asked Chris.
Chris ______________________ the product launch.

3 I wouldn't sign the contract if I were you, Todd,' said Patsy.
Patsy ______________________ the contract.

4 'How about getting an alternative quote?' said Ronan.
Ronan ______________________ an alternative quote.

5 'I'm sorry for arriving so late,' said Serena.
Serena ______________________ so late.

6 'Shall I give you a lift?' said Leon.
Leon ______________________ me a lift.

7 'Well done, you've won the Employee of the Year award!' he said.
He ____________ her ____________ Employee of the Year award.

8 'No, I can't accept any further delays,' said Pat.
Pat ______________________ any further delays.

Test 13 Relative clauses (units 28–29)

Test 13.1 **Complete the sentences with *who*, *whose*, *which* or *that*. Sometimes two answers are possible.**

1 The stationery *that/which* you ordered has arrived.
2 The speaker ______ presentation I heard before lunch was very good.
3 The speaker, ______ was an academic from an American business school, gave an overview of green business opportunities.
4 Everyone ______ I met in the Warsaw office asked how you were.
5 This product, ______ features are described in the leaflet, sells very well.
6 This product, ______ is our best seller, is available in four colours.
7 The first thing ______ your customers will notice is the price.
8 The information, ______ is strictly confidential, comes from a very good source.
9 The person ______ book this is wants it back.
10 The person, ______ had been seen earlier by the security guard, tried to run off with my handbag.
11 The person ______ lent me this book wants it back.
12 The person ______ I borrowed this book from wants it back.

Test 13.2 **Look back at the previous exercise and decide if you can miss out the relative pronoun (*who*, *whose*, *which*, *that*). If you can, put a bracket around the word/s. If you can't, write a tick (✓) at the end. See the examples:**

1 The stationery *(that/which)* you ordered has arrived.
2 The speaker *whose* presentation I heard before lunch was very good. ✓

Test 13.3 **In Test 13.1, two answers were possible in 1, 4, 7, 11 and 12. Answer these questions:**

1 For people, which relative pronoun is more common in speech: *who or that*?
2 For things, which relative pronoun is more common in speech: *which or that*?

Test 13.4 **Rewrite each pair of sentences as one sentence using the word in brackets.**

1 Rani showed me a magazine article. It was really interesting. (which)
Rani *showed me a magazine article which was* really interesting.
2 We went to a presentation yesterday. It was very interesting. (that)
The presentation ______ very interesting.
3 We went to a presentation yesterday. It was very interesting. (that)
We went to a ______ very interesting.
4 I borrowed a friend's laptop. He wants it back. (whose)
The friend ______ back.
5 Some Japanese visitors came yesterday. They gave me this gift. (who)
The Japanese visitors ______ this gift.
6 This is a gift. The Japanese visitors who came yesterday gave it to me. (that)
This is the gift ______ gave me.
7 An administrator runs our office. She's getting married tomorrow. (who)
The administrator ______ getting married tomorrow.
8 I met a woman. Her sister works for ABN. (whose)
I met ______ ABN.
9 A man is waiting in reception. He wants to see you. (who)
The man ______ see you.

Test 14 Nouns, pronouns and articles (units 30–35)

Test 14.1 **Cross out the mistake in each line and write the correction at the end.**

1 I spent ~~a time~~ talking to Stanislav, and then I went home. *some time*
2 Kate's sister is doctor. ______
3 Is this conference programme your or mine? ______
4 They say that the wine is good for you in small amounts. ______
5 Write down the full product code all the time you sell something. ______
6 Can you give me an advice? ______
7 I'm sorry, we have two elevators but either one is in service. ______
8 I need some informations about accommodation in London. ______
9 We all tried to get the machine working but no one of us could do it. ______
10 Walking will take too long – let's go with the taxi. ______
11 Sorry I'm late, the traffic were very busy. ______
12 Our marketing director is excellent. She has so much good ideas. ______
13 A: 'How many people visited your stand this afternoon?' B: 'No at all.' ______
14 Have you ever met the colleague of Jane? ______
15 There's coffee and there's tea. You can have both. ______
16 There is too few information to make a decision. ______
17 We have two basic models – every one has slightly different features. ______
18 Have you seen the inflation predictions in the Ministrys report? ______
19 We haven't got chairs enough for the meeting. ______
20 There are none spare parts in stock at the moment. ______
21 Turn on the TV – the news are on in a few minutes. ______
22 You'll find all the statistics at the report's end. ______
23 We're a leading player in either the film and music industries. ______
24 There are enough free samples for one every. ______
25 Luisa keeps talking about that idea of her's. ______
26 Could you give me an information, please? ______
27 Can you speak up? I can't hear nothing. ______
28 We looked at two possible sites but either of them were too small. ______
29 At the end of my presentation, there wasn't no single question. ______
30 Please come back tomorrow. There isn't no one to see you today. ______
31 Please put the manual back in it's proper place when you finish. ______
32 He's only got the job because he's the boss son. ______

Test 14.2 **Each pair of words contains one countable noun and one uncountable noun. Write the words in the correct column below and write *a/an* or *some* before the word.**

accommodation/apartment desk/furniture bag/luggage work/job travel/trip trouble/problem chance/luck wine/litre equipment/machine dollar/money email/correspondence fact/information advice/suggestion hour/time training/course law/legislation progress/step forward idea/brainstorming policy/insurance

Countable nouns	**Uncountable nouns**
an apartment	*some accommodation*

Test 14.3 **Complete the second sentence so that it has a similar meaning to the first sentence and contains the word in brackets.**

1 The box isn't empty. (something)
There's something in the box.

2 Let me tell you what I think you should do. (advice)
Let me give you ______________________________.

3 We traveled there on the train. (by)
We traveled there ______________________________.

4 I feel worried. (something)
______________________________ me.

5 Every morning I walk to the office. (foot)
Every morning I go to the office ______________________________.

6 Martin is a friend of my boss. (one)
Martin is ______________________________.

7 Sinead advises people about their tax. (advisor)
Sinead is ______________________________.

8 Manuela knows this business better than anyone. (knows)
______________________________ better than Manuela.

9 I haven't got anything to do. (got)
I've ______________________________ do.

10 We are all tea drinkers here. (everybody)
______________________________ tea.

11 Are we going to be driven there? (driving)
Is ______________________________ us there?

12 People who are unemployed need better training programmes. (the)
______________________________ better training programmes.

13 The prototype needs to be changed a lot. (redesigning)
The prototype needs ______________________________.

14 We can't do anything. (nothing)
There ______________________________ do.

15 What did that piece of machinery cost? (how)
______________________________ that piece of machinery cost?

16 There is little travel in my job. (much)
There ______________________________ travel in my job.

17 Clara does people's accounts for her job. (accountant)
Clara is ______________________________.

18 No one was on time yesterday. (late)
______________________________ yesterday.

19 There was nothing I could do about it. (couldn't)
I ______________________________ about it.

20 Nobody at all was available to see me. (single)
Not ______________________________ was available to see me.

21 There isn't any reason to worry. (no)
______________________________ reason to worry.

22 The report did not contain the information I wanted. (in)
The information I wanted ______________________________ the report.

23 This copy belongs to the customer. (copy)
This is ______________________________.

24 There's nothing in the post this morning. (anything)
______________________________ in the post this morning.

Test 15 Adjectives and adverbs (units 36–40)

Test 15.1 **Cross out the mistake in each line and write the correction at the end.**

1 I'm really ~~interesting~~ in the area of innovation in online retailing. *interested*
2 They say they'll finish the new shopping mall until the end of the year. ______
3 Peter has been working very hardly on the C-Plan project. ______
4 I bought a blue lovely silk tie. ______
5 We had a great time on holiday. The people were too friendly. ______
6 This magazine article is extremely excellent – it's worth reading. ______
7 On the whole I thought the meeting went very good. ______
8 Using my PC for a long time makes my eyes feel tiring. ______
9 Never we give discounts on these products – we just don't need to. ______
10 Are you interesting in extending the warranty? ______
11 There is too much new information that I'm still a little confused. ______
12 It was so a risky project that we decided to cancel it. ______
13 In my opinion their management team is not enough experienced. ______
14 I don't have time enough to do it now – can it wait until next week? ______
15 Their company is larger as ours. ______
16 Their company is just as large than ours. ______
17 It's the better price I can offer. ______
18 I've been working in this company since three months. ______
19 The negotiation was such tense we had to call a short break. ______
20 When I will get back, I'll give you a ring. ______
21 I have to go out to mail this package until the post office closes. ______
22 You work much harder as they do – you deserve the promotion. ______
23 In my opinion our prices are so high in relation to our competitors. ______
24 Last week's meeting was very productive, but this one was little useful. ______
25 Golf isn't as good for fitness and health than swimming. ______
26 I'll wait here by six, then I'll assume you're not coming. ______

Test 15.2 **Complete the sentences with a time adverb or preposition. Choose from: *in, on, at, for, since, during, while, ago, afterwards, after, then*.**

1 Shall we all go out for a meal *on* my birthday?
2 He started working here four years ______ .
3 He's been working here ______ four years.
4 He's been working here ______ leaving university.
5 The flight arrives ______ Tuesday afternoon ______ four thirty ______ the afternoon.
6 I arrived at the meeting ______ time to chat with some of the other participants.
7 Let's try to start the meeting ______ time.
8 My presentation will finish at midday, so we could meet for lunch ______ .
9 I'll give my presentation, ______ I'll need a little time to relax.
10 Don't worry! ______ your presentation you'll be able to relax.
11 I've been waiting ______ more than an hour.
12 We make up our accounts ______ the end of every quarter.
13 We have three shifts in the factory, including one that works ______ night.
14 I haven't heard from them ______ three weeks.
15 I haven't heard from them ______ last week.
16 ______ my presentation the projector suddenly stopped working.
17 ______ I was talking the projector suddenly stopped working.
18 ______ the summer we usually have a sale. (*two answers*)

Test 15.3 **Complete the second sentence so it has a similar meaning to the first sentence and contains the word/s in brackets.**

1 Your speech was really excellent. (spoke)
You *spoke really well* .

2 We started working on the project in January. (working/since)
We ______ .

3 Retail banking isn't as profitable as investment banking. (more)
Investment banking ______ .

4 She's a very careful worker. (works)
She ______ .

5 I've never seen worse service than this. (ever)
This is ______ .

6 Monica left Paris in July (stayed)
Monica ______ July.

7 Do you find opera interesting?
Are ______ ?

8 The meeting had a positive finish. (finished)
The meeting ______ .

9 This last week has been hard work for you. (worked)
You have ______ this last week.

10 Lee is a bad golfer. (plays golf)
Lee ______ .

11 Lee is a good golfer. (plays golf)
Lee ______ .

12 Could you not talk so fast, please? (slowly)
Could you ______ , please?

13 The Chinese market is bigger than the Indian market. (as)
The Indian market ______ .

14 Alain sells the same number of products as Thierry. (just)
Alain sells ______ .

15 The other members of the team are more experienced than Romy. (least)
Romy ______ .

16 While they were interviewing me I noticed a stain on my shirt. (the interview)
______ I noticed a stain on my shirt.

17 I started this job in 2008. (doing/since)
I ______ .

18 Diane is on holiday. She's back next week. (away on holiday)
Diane is ______ next week.

19 The train arrived exactly when it was supposed to. (time)
The train arrived ______ .

20 His intervention was too late to save the negotiations. (time)
He didn't intervene ______ .

21 I need your report on Friday at the latest. (by)
I need ______ Friday.

22 We tried hard but finally we gave up. (end)
We tried hard but ______ .

23 We've been building this prototype for four months. (started/ago)
We ______ .

24 It's twelve and I've been waiting for you since ten. (two)
I've been waiting for you ______ hours.

Test 16 Prepositions (units 46–49)

Test 16.1 **Complete the sentences with a preposition. Choose from: *at, in, on, over, to, under*.**

1 My brother works *at* the airport.
2 Can you call me back? I'm ________ the middle of a meeting.
3 The taxi dropped me off ________ my hotel ________ the city centre.
4 We flew ________ the new sports stadium as we were landing.
5 He had a suitcase ________ one hand, and his golf clubs ________ the other.
6 Go down the corridor and my office is ________ the right.
7 There's a fire escape ________ the back of the building.
8 She wasn't feeling well and the doctor sent her ________ hospital.
9 She's speaking ________ the phone right now – can I ask her to call you back?
10 He had a portrait of himself hanging ________ the wall.
11 The author's name is ________ the bottom of the page.
12 In the old days, before the tunnel was built, you had to drive ________ the Alps.
13 I have six junior managers working ________ me.
14 I'll be working ________ home for most of tomorrow.
15 Hello. This is Ulrike speaking. I'm ________ Paris, ________ the Hotel Versailles.
16 Susanna's just rung. She's ________ the restaurant having a drink.
17 Susanna's just rung. She's ________ the bus stop.
18 Jim gave me a lift ________ the station ________ his car.
19 I met Kati ________ the bus yesterday.
20 Stratford is ________ the river Thames.
21 Who is going to be ________ the chair ________ the next meeting?
22 Our offices are ________ the fourth floor.

Test 16.2 **Decide which preposition from the box goes with each verb.**

about (x2)	against	for (x3)	from (x2)	in (x2)	into	of (x2)	on (x3)	to (x3)	with (x2)

1 I must apologize *for* being late.
2 Welcome ____________ Cologne!
3 I'd just like to add something ____________ what Jawad just said.
4 Is the factory insured ____________ fire damage?
5 The cost? Well, it depends ____________ what you're looking ____________ .
6 The whole package consists ____________ the main unit plus these four accessories.
7 I've divided my presentation ____________ three main parts.
8 We need to diversify to prevent us ____________ becoming too dependent on just one product.
9 Please, let me pay ____________ this.
10 We can supply your outlets ____________ a full range of sizes.
11 We specialize ____________ catering equipment for the restaurant and hotel sectors.
12 Do you know anything ____________ the market in the Gulf states?
13 He congratulated us ____________ getting the contract.
14 Lisbon reminds me a bit ____________ San Francisco: the bridge, the hills, the weather.
15 Please remind me ____________ her birthday nearer the time.
16 I agree ____________ you.
17 Does this bag belong ____________ anyone here?
18 In the next meeting I think we should focus ____________ the planning schedule.
19 I invested all my savings ____________ stocks in 2007, and a few years later I had almost nothing left.
20 We had a temporary cash-flow problem and had to borrow money ____________ the bank.

Test 16.3 Underline the correct word in these adjective + preposition combinations.

1 Are you certain *to/about/from* that?
2 I hope their workers don't go on strike. We're dependent *of/on/by* them for our parts.
3 This line is very popular *for/to/with* customers looking for value for money.
4 Our country is lacking *in/of/for* energy resources – we have to import all our oil and gas.
5 Our country is rich *in/of/for* energy resources – we export a lot of oil and gas.
6 Are you aware *to/by/of* just how serious this problem is?
7 Are you interested *in/for/of* long-term capital growth or regular income?
8 I'm annoyed *with/for/about* them *with/for/about* being so inflexible.
9 What guarantees can you give about your quality? It's important *to/for/by* us.
10 Our network solution will keep you safe *against/for/from* hackers and viruses.
11 My job is very unpredictable – you have to be ready *for/about/to* anything.
12 I felt sorry *for/about/to* Edi when he got the results from the hospital.
13 Let me use a calculator. I'm not very good *at/for/by* maths.
14 It's often good *at/for/by* your career if you work abroad for a few years.
15 I'm responsible *for/to/of* a team of six consultants.
16 If anything goes wrong, I'm directly responsible *for/to/of* the CEO.

Test 16.4 Complete the sentences with a noun from list A and a preposition from list B.

A: advantage advice compliance increase investment lack matter pessimism ~~price~~ reason reply solution substitute trouble

B: about for for in in ~~of~~ of of on to to with with with

1 At the moment the *price of* oil is about $75 a barrel.
2 Can you tell me the __________ the delay? We've been waiting a long time.
3 The main __________ proposal B is that it's much cheaper.
4 The __________ proposal A is that it's very expensive.
5 What's the __________ Jill? She looks rather upset.
6 Have they sent a __________ your last email?
7 There's a __________ experience at senior management level.
8 I'm sure we can find a __________ this problem, but it may take some time.
9 Clever advertising is no __________ good quality at a reasonable price.
10 This year we're making a major __________ new technology.
11 Can you give me some __________ the best way to invest my savings?
12 Everyone's worried about the future. There's a lot of __________ the economy.
13 The tender has to be an open and transparent process, in __________ EU regulations.
14 Last year there was an __________ operating costs of 4%.

Test 16.5 Complete the text with the prepositions in the box.

across at (x3) down inside near next to off on (x3) opposite to

Liz left early to go to her job interview. She got 1 *on* the bus, paid her fare to the driver and went 2 __________ . She sat down 3 __________ a friendly-looking woman and started chatting. They discovered they were both going 4 __________ the same stop. 'I've got an interview 5 __________ a place called Park House,' said Liz. 'Is it 6 __________ the stop where we get off?' 'Yes, it's not far. You walk 7 __________ the park, 8 __________ Forbes Road, and it's 9 __________ the right, 10 __________ the end of the road,' the woman replied. 'In fact, I live 11 __________ the other side of the road, just 12 __________ , so I can show you the way.' When they arrived 13 __________ their stop they got 14 __________ together.

Appendix 1 Regular verbs: all forms

Present simple (unit 1)

Affirmative: I/you/we/they **work**. She/he/it **works**.
Question: **Do** I/you/we/they **work**? **Does** she/he/it **work**?
Negative: I/you/we/they **don't work**. She/he/it **doesn't work**.

Present continuous (unit 1)

Affirmative: I **am helping**. You/we/they **are helping**. She/he/it **is helping**.
Question: **Am** I **helping**? **Are** you/we/they **helping**? **Is** she/he/it **helping**?
Negative: I'm **not helping**. You/we/they **aren't helping**. She/he/it **isn't helping**.

Past simple (unit 3)

Affirmative: I/you/she/he/it/we/they **started**.
Question: **Did** I/you/she/he/it/we/they **start**?
Negative: I/you/she/he/it/we/they **didn't start**.
For irregular past simple forms see Appendix 2.

Past continuous (unit 3)

Affirmative: I/she/he/it **was helping**. You/we/they **were helping**.
Question: **Was** I/she/he/it **helping**? **Were** you/we/they **helping**?
Negative: I/she/he/it **wasn't helping**. You/we/they **weren't helping**.

Past perfect (unit 4)

Affirmative: I/you/she/he/it/we/they **had arrived**.
Question: **Had** I/you/she/he/it/we/they **arrived**?
Negative: I/you/she/he/it/we/they **hadn't arrived**.

***used to* (unit 4)**

Affirmative: I/you/she/he/it/we/they **used to work**.
Question: **Did** I/you/she/he/it/we/they **use to work**?
Negative: I/you/she/he/it/we/they **didn't use to work**.

Present perfect (unit 5)

Affirmative: I/you/we/they **have looked**. She/he/it **has looked**.
Question: **Have** I/you/we/they **looked**? **Has** she/he/it **looked**?
Negative: I/you/we/they **haven't looked**. She/he/it **hasn't looked**.

Present perfect continuous (unit 6)

Affirmative: I/you/we/they **have been waiting**. She/he/it **has been waiting**.
Question: **Have** I/you/we/they **been waiting**? **Has** she/he/it **been waiting**?
Negative: I/you/we/they **haven't been waiting**. She/he/it **hasn't been waiting**.

***will* (unit 7)**

Affirmative: I/you/she/he/it/we/they**'ll** + **understand**.
Question: **Will** I/you/she/he/it/we/they + **understand**?
Negative: I/you/she/he/it/we/they **won't** + **understand**.

be going to (unit 7)

Affirmative:	I**'m**/you**'re**/she**'s**/he**'s**/it**'s**/we**'re**/they**'re going to** + **check**.
Question:	**Am** I/**Are** you/**Is** she/**Is** he/**Is** it/**Are** we/**Are** they **going to** + **check**?
Negative:	I**'m not**/You **aren't**/She **isn't**, etc. **going to** + **check**.

Future perfect (unit 8)

Affirmative:	I/you/she/he/it/we/they **will have finished**.
Question:	**Will** I/you/she/he/it/we/they **have finished**?
Negative:	I/you/she/he/it/we/they **won't have finished**.

Passive (unit 9)

Active	**Passive**
She helps.	She **is helped**.
She is helping.	She **is being helped**.
She helped.	She **was helped**.
She was helping.	She **was being helped**.
She had helped	She **had been helped**.
She has helped.	She **has been helped**.
She will help.	She **will be helped**.
She will have helped.	She **will have been helped**.

Reported speech (unit 26)

Actual words spoken	**Report**
'I work there.'	He said (that) he **worked** there.
'I'm working there.'	He said (that) he **was working** there.
'I took it.'	He said (that) he **took** it/**had taken** it.
'I was reading it.'	He said (that) he **had been reading** it.
'I had left by then.'	He said (that) he **had left** by then.
'I've forgotten it.'	He said (that) he **had forgotten** it.
'I've been reading'	He said (that) he **had been reading**.
'I can help.'	He said (that) he **could** help.
'I will help.'	He said (that) he **would** help.
'I may help.'	He said (that) he **might** help.
'I could/would/might go.'	He said (that) he **could/would/might** go.
'I must/should go.'	He said (that) he **must/should** go.

Infinitives

Present:	**to like**
Present passive:	**to be liked**
Perfect:	**to have liked**
Perfect passive:	**to have been liked**

Appendix 2 Irregular verbs

Verb	Past simple	Past participle
arise	arose	arisen
be	was, were	been
bear	bore	born(e)
beat	beat	beaten
become	became	become
begin	began	begun
bend	bent	bent
bet	bet	bet/betted
bind	bound	bound
bite	bit	bitten/bit
bleed	bled	bled
blow	blew	blown
break	broke	broken
breed	bred	bred
bring	brought	brought
broadcast	broadcast	broadcast
build	built	built
burn	burnt/burned	burnt/burned
burst	burst	burst
buy	bought	bought
catch	caught	caught
choose	chose	chosen
come	came	come
cost	cost	cost
creep	crept	crept
cut	cut	cut
deal	dealt	dealt
dig	dug	dug
do	did	done
draw	drew	drawn
dream	dreamt/dreamed	dreamt/dreamed
drink	drank	drunk
drive	drove	driven
eat	ate	eaten
fall	fell	fallen
feed	fed	fed
feel	felt	felt
fight	fought	fought
find	found	found
flee	fled	fled
fly	flew	flown
forbid	forbade	forbidden
forget	forgot	forgotten
forgive	forgave	forgiven
freeze	froze	frozen
get	got	got/gotten
give	gave	given
go	went	gone
grind	ground	ground
grow	grew	grown
hang	hung	hung
have	had	had
hear	heard	heard
hide	hid	hidden
hit	hit	hit
hold	held	held
hurt	hurt	hurt
keep	kept	kept
kneel	knelt	knelt
know	knew	known
lay	laid	laid
lead	led	led
lean	leant/leaned	leant/leaned
leap	leapt/leaped	leapt/leaped
learn	learnt/learned	learnt/learned
leave	left	left
lend	lent	lent
let	let	let
lie	lay	lain
light	lit/lighted	lit/lighted
lose	lost	lost
make	made	made
mean	meant	meant
meet	met	met
pay	paid	paid
put	put	put
read	read	read
ride	rode	ridden
ring	rang	rung
rise	rose	risen
run	ran	run
say	said	said
see	saw	seen
seek	sought	sought
sell	sold	sold
send	sent	sent
set	set	set
sew	sewed	sewn/sewed
shake	shook	shaken
shine	shone	shone
shoot	shot	shot
show	showed	shown
shrink	shrank	shrunk
shut	shut	shut

Verb	Past simple	Past participle
sing	sang	sung
sit	sat	sat
sleep	slept	slept
slide	slid	slid
smell	smelt/smelled	smelt/smelled
speak	spoke	spoken
speed	sped/speeded	sped/speeded
spell	spelt/spelled	spelt/spelled
spend	spent	spent
spill	spilt/spilled	spilt/spilled
spin	span	spun
spit	spat	spat
split	split	split
spoil	spoilt/spoiled	spoilt/spoiled
spread	spread	spread
spring	sprang	sprung
stand	stood	stood
steal	stole	stolen
stick	stuck	stuck

Verb	Past simple	Past participle
sting	stung	stung
strike	struck	struck
swear	swore	sworn
sweep	swept	swept
swim	swam	swum
swing	swung	swung
take	took	taken
teach	taught	taught
tear	tore	torn
tell	told	told
think	thought	thought
throw	threw	thrown
understand	understood	understood
wake	woke	woken
wear	wore	worn
weep	wept	wept
win	won	won
wind	wound	wound
write	wrote	written

Note: Where two alternative forms are given, the second form is used in American English.

Appendix 3 Diagram of the English verb system

Notes to the diagram

The diagram is a way of showing the whole English tense system in a simplified form. Using the diagram has three benefits:

- You can see the 'big picture' of how all the tenses are related, and this can help you when you study the individual tenses separately.
- You can see that there is a pattern and logic to English verbs.
- You get a visual picture, and some people find this helps them to understand and learn.

Read through these notes and refer to the diagram and the Key at the top:

1 The first row shows the three **simple** tenses. The past simple refers to a completed action/situation. The present simple refers to actions/situations that are usually/always true (facts, habits, etc.) and so do not really have a time reference. The future simple has lost that name and is now more often called the *will* future; it refers to future facts or general beliefs.

2 The second row shows the three **continuous** tenses, which all have the meaning of 'an action in progress'. There is also an associated meaning that the action has a limited duration.

3 The third row shows the three **perfect** tenses, which all have the meaning of 'looking back'. The past perfect looks back from the past, the present perfect looks back from the present, and the future perfect looks back from the future.

Note the two example sentences for the present perfect: the first showing time that goes from the past until now (*I've been in this job for three years*), and the second showing the present result of a past action (*I've finished the report*). In both cases the meaning of 'looking back from the present' is retained.

4 The fourth row shows the three **perfect continuous** tenses, which all have the meaning of 'looking back at an action in progress'. Note from the diagram how this is a combination of the meanings of the previous two lines: 'looking back' + 'action in progress'.

5 The fifth row shows the use of *be going to*, which has a meaning of 'looking forward'. *Was/were going to* looks forward from the past (to an action which didn't happen; if it did, we would just use the past simple). *am/is/are going to* look forward from the present.

Units 1–8 of the book have a much fuller explanation of all these verb tenses.

There are some uses of English verbs that a diagram cannot show. Many of these other uses can be explained by one simple idea: a past form in English can refer to *social distance* and *distant probability* as well as the more obvious meaning of *distance in time*. So:

- knowing that we can use the past to show *social distance* helps to understand why *I was wondering if I could …?* is more formal or polite than *Can I…?*
- knowing that we can use the past to show *distant probability* helps to understand why *if I could, I would* is imaginary, whereas *if I can, I will* is a real possibility.

Diagram of the English verb system

Key

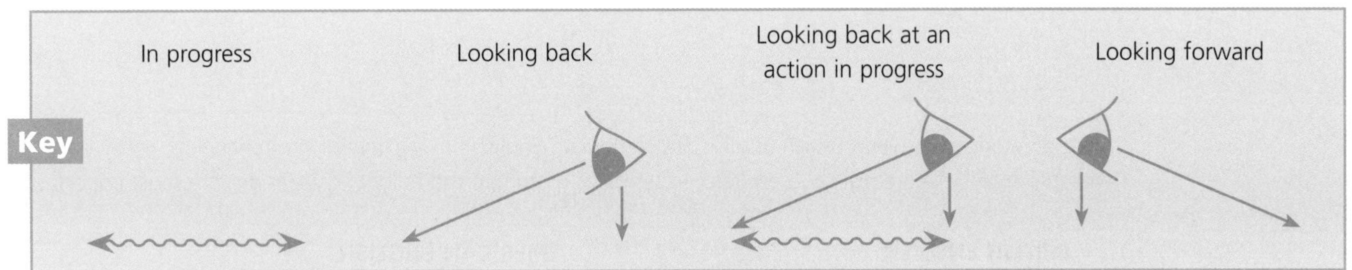

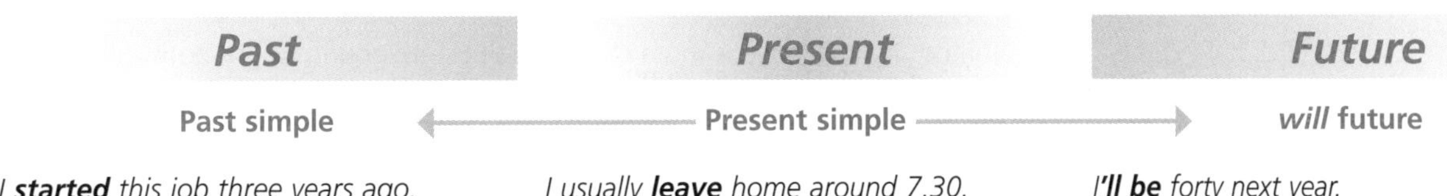

Past | Present | Future

Past simple ← **Present simple** → ***will* future**

*I **started** this job three years ago.*

*I usually **leave** home around 7.30.*

*I**'ll be** forty next year.*
*Inflation **will** probably **rise** in the long term.*

Past continuous

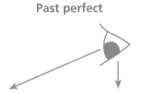

*While I **was working** at ABC I moved from Sales to Marketing.*

Present continuous

*We**'re developing** two new products at the moment.*

Future continuous

*I**'ll be working** at our Paris office next year.*

Past perfect

*The merger **had** already **happened** when I joined the company.*

Present perfect

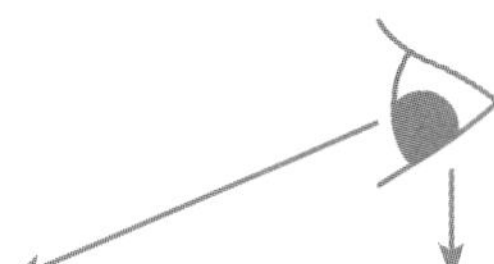

*I**'ve been** in this job for three years.*
*I**'ve finished** the report.*

Future perfect

*By the end of the year I expect that sales **will have improved**.*

Past perfect continuous

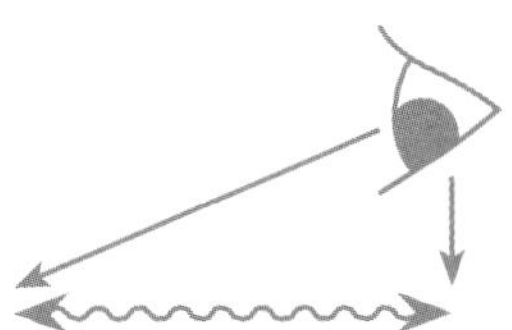

*We**'d been selling** the same product for years before we changed the design.*

Present perfect continuous

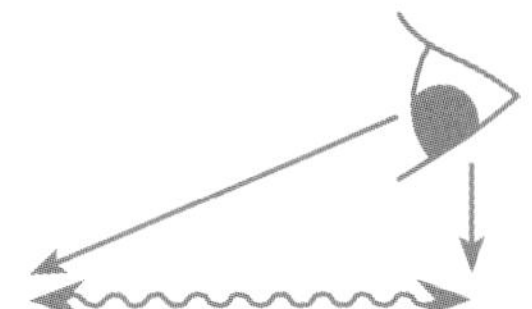

*I**'ve been writing** this report all morning.*

Future perfect continuous

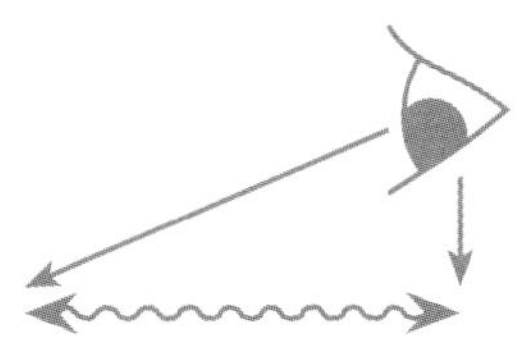

*If I retire when I'm sixty, I**'ll have been working** here for more than twenty years.*

---

was going to

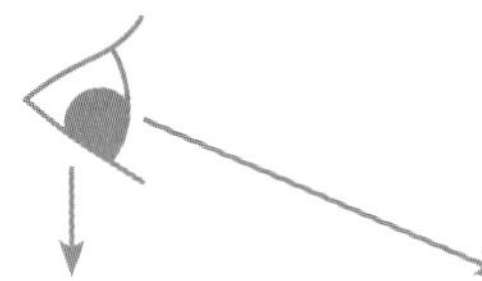

*Sorry, I **was going to call** you, but I completely forgot.*

***be going to* future**

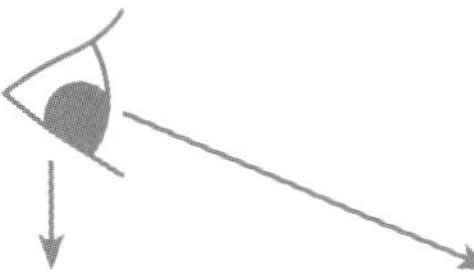

*I**'m going to ask** my boss for a pay rise.*
*That**'s going to be** difficult.*

Appendix 4 British and American English

Most differences between British English and American English are matters of pronunciation, vocabulary and spelling. These are not covered here. In terms of grammar, the following areas are the most important.

BRITISH ENGLISH	AMERICAN ENGLISH

have and *have got*

In BrE *have got* is more common. In AmE *have* is more common. But both countries use both forms.

***Have you got** any children?*	***Do you have** any children?*
***I've got** two children*	***I have** two children.*
***I haven't got** any children.*	***I don't have** any children.*

Present perfect and past simple

In AmE the past simple is often used where the present perfect is used in BrE. This is especially true with *just*, *already*, *yet*, *ever* and *never*. However, the present perfect is still very common in AmE, especially in writing.

*Your taxi **has** just **arrived**.*	*Your taxi **just arrived**.*
*I'**ve** already **spoken** to her about it.*	*I already **spoke** to her about it.*
***Have** you **finished** the report yet?*	***Did** you **finish** the report yet?*
***Have** you ever **eaten** sushi?*	***Did** you ever **eat** sushi?*
*It'**s** never **done** that before.*	*It never **did** that before.*

gotten

In AmE *gotten* is often used as the past participle of the verb *get*.

*It's **got** late. Maybe we should go.*	*It's **gotten** late. Maybe we should go.*
*He's **got** a new job.*	*He's **gotten** a new job.*

shall and *should* for suggestions

In BrE *shall* is used in suggestions, whereas *should* is more common in AmE.

***Shall** we break for coffee now?*	***Should** we break for coffee now?*

Question tags

Question tags are much less common in AmE.

*You can speak French, **can't you**?*	*You can speak French, **right**?*
*I'll call a taxi, **shall I**?*	*I'll call a taxi, **OK**?*

Adverbs

In informal AmE the *-ly* ending to adverbs is often left out. Also, in informal AmE an adjective is sometimes used in place of an adverb.

*It's working **really slowly** at the moment.*	*It's working **real slow** right now.*
*It's working **really well** at the moment.*	*It's working **real good** right now.*

can't and *mustn't*

In BrE *can't* is used to say that something is logically impossible. In AmE *mustn't* is also used.

I called but there's no reply.	*I called but there's no reply.*
*They **can't** be at home.*	*They **can't/mustn't** be home.*

Prepositions

Note the following differences in the use of prepositions.

British English	American English
What did you do ***at*** *the weekend?*	*What did you do* ***on*** *the weekend?*
Pat is ***in*** *the team now.*	*Pat is* ***on*** *the team now.*
It's 10 minutes ***past*** *three.*	*It's 10 minutes* ***past/after*** *three.*
It's twenty ***to*** *three.*	*It's twenty* ***to/of*** *three.*
We're open from Monday ***to/till*** *Saturday.*	*We're open from Monday* ***through*** *Saturday.*
I looked ***out of*** *the window.*	*I looked* ***out*** *the window.*
I stayed ***at home*** *on Saturday.*	*I stayed* ***home*** *Saturday.*
He wrote ***to me*** *about his visit.*	*He wrote* ***me*** *about his visit.*
I ***met*** *an old colleague yesterday.*	*I* ***met with*** *an old colleague yesterday.*
They ***protested against*** *globalization.*	*They* ***protested*** *globalization.*
I looked ***round/around*** *the museum.*	*I looked* ***around*** *the museum.*
She walked ***towards/toward*** *me.*	*She walked* ***toward*** *me.*
I haven't seen him ***for*** *several weeks.*	*I haven't seen him* ***in*** *several weeks.*

Go and ...

In AmE the word *and* is left out from this structure.

I'll ***go and speak*** *to Mary.*	*I'll* ***go speak*** *to Mary.*

somewhere and *someplace*

In informal AmE *someplace*, *anyplace* and *no place* can be used as well as *somewhere*, *anywhere* and *nowhere*.

Let's find ***somewhere*** *to eat.*	*Let's find* ***somewhere/someplace*** *to eat.*

The

Note these differences for musical instruments and the word *hospital*.

My sister plays ***the piano****.*	*My sister plays* ***piano****.*
My mother is ***in hospital****.*	*My mother is* ***in the hospital****.*

Numbers

In AmE there is no *and* after the hundreds when you say numbers.

two hundred ***and*** *fifty*	*two hundred fifty*

On the telephone

Hello, is ***that*** *Paul?*	*Hello, is* ***this*** *Paul?*

The differences above are typical of informal, spoken English. Amongst educated speakers, and in formal written English, the differences are fewer. For example, the present perfect is common in American newspapers and magazines. Often there are greater regional differences within a country than there are between countries.

Note that Canadian English, Australian English, Irish English, etc. are often a mixture of British and American forms. Other varieties of English like Indian English or Philippines English show influences of past historical connections and also have many features of their own.

Listen and Repeat scripts

Track 01 (Unit 1 Task 1)

1 So what exactly do you do?
2 My job involves studying market trends.
3 I don't make any real operational decisions.
4 It doesn't take long to get here.
5 Sarah Kennedy is expecting me.
6 Chinese companies are investing heavily.
7 They're not replying to my emails.
8 Are you enjoying this conference?

Track 02 (Unit 2 Task 1)

1 Where do you work?
2 What project are you working on right now?
3 The production line doesn't work at weekends.
4 The production line isn't working at the moment.
5 We take a sample once a day.
6 We're taking a big risk.
7 I understand that you're expecting a visit.
8 It depends on what you want.

Track 03 (Unit 3 Task 1)

1 What happened after you launched the product?
2 While we were marketing it, our distributor went bust.
3 I didn't see you in the office last week.
4 No, I was working at home for a few days.
5 What did Pat do when she saw the artwork?
6 She called the designers and said it wasn't suitable.
7 Why did Renata take so long to get here?
8 They were doing roadworks and the traffic was moving very slowly.

Track 04 (Unit 4 Task 1)

1 After she'd made a few notes, she started writing the report.
2 I called my husband because the meeting still hadn't finished.
3 I hadn't seen the figures, so it put me at a disadvantage.
4 The rain had stopped by the time I arrived.
5 They'd been producing generators for over ten years.
6 I hadn't been sleeping well.
7 I used to work in marketing.
8 I didn't use to spend so much time on reports.

Track 05 (Unit 5 Task 1)

1 The goods have already left our warehouse.
2 I've just had a brilliant idea!
3 We've known each other for more than twenty years.
4 I've never used my credit card on the Internet.
5 I haven't spoken to Magda yet.
6 I've always worked in insurance.
7 She's been in a meeting since nine.
8 Have you ever been to São Paolo?

Track 06 (Unit 6 Task 1)

1 Last year sales went up by 15%.
2 This year sales have gone up another 12%.
3 Have you seen my laptop?
4 I'm sure I left it here earlier.
5 I've been looking at the contract in detail.
6 I've noticed a lot of potential problems.
7 How long have you been producing cars at this site?
8 We've invested around twenty million dollars.

Track 07 (Unit 7 Task 1)

1 I'll get some more paper.
2 Richard's going to be late.
3 I'm meeting Andrea at the airport at nine.
4 In the future, videoconferences will replace meetings.
5 We're going to test the prototype next week.
6 Would you mind waiting? I won't be long.
7 What are you going to do?
8 I'll see you tomorrow.

Track 08 (Unit 8 Task 1)

1 Tomorrow I'll be interviewing candidates all morning.
2 By the time she arrives you'll have left.
3 As soon as I've finished, I'll tell you.
4 I was going to mention it, but I forgot.
5 We'll have repaid the loan by December.
6 Shall we break for coffee now?
7 Our visitors are due to arrive at 10.30.
8 I can't do it right now – I'm about to have a meeting.

Track 09 (Unit 9 Task 1)

1 The goods were damaged in transit.
2 This ad will be seen by millions of people.
3 The project won't be finished by the end of the month.
4 Twenty retail outlets have been closed.
5 All of our IT systems are being reviewed.
6 Your order can't be shipped until we receive payment.
7 The questionnaire is completed online.
8 A loan has been arranged.

Track 10 (Unit 10 Task 1)

1 The economy is expected to expand next year.
2 They are known to be looking at a merger.
3 The Board is thought to have demanded his resignation.
4 I was given this sample at the trade fair.
5 We were promised delivery within two weeks.
6 I had my car repaired yesterday.
7 We have the components assembled in Vietnam.
8 We're getting the machines cleaned tomorrow.

Track 11 (Unit 11 Task 1)

1 I'm sorry I couldn't come to your talk yesterday.
2 I'm sorry, I can't help you right now.
3 I don't think I'll be able to come to the conference.
4 I managed to speak to him yesterday.
5 I think I'll go home now.
6 I'll give you a hand with your bags.
7 I'll be there at six o'clock.
8 Will you hold the elevator for me, please?

Track 12 (Unit 12 Task 1)

1 You have to fill in this application form.
2 You must try to be more diplomatic.
3 We don't have to decide yet.
4 You're not allowed to park here.
5 I'll have to speak to my boss.
6 We ought to sign the contract.
7 I'd better finish this spreadsheet.
8 We shouldn't have spent so much money.

Track 13 (Unit 13 Task 1)

1 There's no answer. She must be in a meeting.
2 There was no answer. She must've been in a meeting.
3 Lisa should be here soon.
4 Lisa should have arrived by now.
5 Our profits are likely to improve next year.
6 I might have more news for you next week.
7 I may not be able to get there in time.
8 That can't be Dana – she's away at a conference.

Track 14 (Unit 14 Task 1)

1 Could you spell that for me, please?
2 Would you mind giving me a hand?
3 Would you mind if I opened the window?
4 Do you mind if I give you a decision next week?
5 Is it all right if I change my ticket?
6 Would you like me to give you a lift?
7 Shall I make a copy for you?
8 Shall we have a short break now?

Track 15 (Unit 15 Task 1)

1 When do you service the machines?
2 Which project are you working on?
3 Whose car did you use?
4 Where were you working at the time?
5 How much research had you done beforehand?
6 Why have you cut the advertising budget?
7 Who did you meet?
8 Who met you?

Track 16 (Unit 16 Task 1)

1 You went to the conference, didn't you?
2 You didn't go to the conference, did you?
3 You couldn't give me a hand, could you?
4 Let's break for coffee now, shall we?
5 Could you tell me what your terms of payment are?
6 I'd like to know how we can finance this project.
7 Where did you get that information from?
8 What is this piece of equipment for?

Track 17 (Unit 17 Task 1)

1 If sales increase, we make more profit.
2 If sales increase, we'll make more profit.
3 If sales increased, we'd make more profit.
4 If I've made any mistakes, I'll correct them later.
5 If anyone from Head Office calls, say I'm in a meeting.
6 If I was on the Board, I'd argue against the merger.
7 If I were you, I'd wait until tomorrow.
8 Unless he arrives soon, he'll miss the flight.

Track 18 (Unit 18 Task 1)

1 If you'd called me yesterday, I would've told you.
2 If we'd been better prepared, we might've been more successful.
3 If he'd listened more carefully, he wouldn't have made that mistake.
4 Supposing you had a million dollars, how would you invest it?
5 We can start the project next week, as long as everyone agrees.
6 We can start the project next week, unless anyone disagrees.
7 Keep your receipt in case you need to return the goods.
8 I wish we didn't have so many meetings.

Track 19 (Unit 19 Task 1)

1 Have you considered postponing the launch?
2 Do you mind waiting a moment?
3 I got used to waking up early.
4 We're managing to improve our supply chain.
5 We decided to cancel the meeting.
6 We decided we would cancel the meeting.
7 He persuaded the bank to lend him the money.
8 I made them check all the figures again.

Track 20 (Unit 20 Task 1)

1 I remember seeing him before somewhere.
2 I must remember to call her this afternoon.
3 We stopped buying from that supplier.
4 I stopped to buy something for my daughter.
5 I saw her giving the first part of her presentation.
6 I saw her give her whole presentation.
7 We risk being taken over by a larger company.
8 I deserve to be given a pay rise.

Track 21 (Unit 21 Task 1)

1 They promised me a full refund.
2 They offered us a better deal.
3 They offered a better deal to our competitors.
4 I lent my dictionary to Louisa from marketing.
5 I lent Louisa my dictionary.
6 She explained the situation to me.
7 I've prepared a report for the Board meeting.
8 I'll bring some samples for you.

Track 22 (Unit 22 Task 1)

1 Could you fill in this form, please?
2 Could you fill it in, please?
3 Will you back me up in the meeting?
4 Our lawyers will draw up a new contract.
5 We turned down their offer.
6 I couldn't do without my secretary.
7 I've never come across a situation like this.
8 I'm sorry to take up so much of your time.

Track 23 (Unit 23 Task 1)

1 Shall we move on?
2 Shall we move on to the next item on the agenda?
3 Your idea fits in nicely with our existing plans.
4 I try to keep up with developments in my field.
5 Sandra is standing in for Mike.
6 What message do you want to get across?
7 I'd like to bring up the issue of costs.
8 Can I just go over that again?

Track 24 (Unit 24 Task 1)

1 Marketing requires careful planning.
2 We are a small manufacturing company.
3 The meeting was very interesting.
4 I was very interested in your comments.
5 Success in this business depends on having the right contacts.
6 He responds well to working under pressure.
7 I started the job not knowing what to expect.
8 She mentioned having worked in France.

Track 25 (Unit 25 Task 1)

1 make an attempt/do your best
2 make a bid/do business
3 make a complaint/do a course
4 make an investment/do a lot of damage
5 make a mistake/do somebody a favour
6 make a profit/do research
7 make progress/do something about it
8 make a suggestion/do work for somebody

Track 26 (Unit 26 Task 1)

1 He said he'd bring the figures to the meeting.
2 She said she worked for IBM.
3 She said she'd worked for IBM.
4 She said she'd been working for IBM.
5 He said the campaign was a great success.
6 He says the campaign is a great success.
7 She said she'd see me there the next day.
8 He said he'd read my report about the project.

Track 27 (Unit 27 Task 1)

1 I suggested changing the supplier.
2 They refused to lower the price.
3 He advised us to wait until next year.
4 She promised she'd call me today.
5 I thought you'd finished.
6 They asked me when the goods would arrive.
7 She asked me if we'd spent all the budget.
8 He told me not to worry.

Track 28 (Unit 28 Task 1)

1 The train which leaves at 8 am is direct.
2 The train, which leaves at 8 am, is direct.
3 The person who I spoke to on the phone said it was in stock.
4 The items that you wanted were shipped yesterday.
5 The items, which were shipped yesterday, should arrive next week.
6 The customer whose company I visited has placed an order.
7 The technician, who spent over an hour here, said it was working fine.
8 Here's the catalogue we order from.

Track 29 (Unit 29 Task 1)

1 I'm taking a flight that goes via Frankfurt.
2 The flight I'm taking goes via Frankfurt.
3 We introduced a new line that is aimed at the youth market.
4 We introduced a new line aimed at the youth market.
5 The new line we introduced is aimed at the youth market.
6 The hotel where I stayed was quite cheap.
7 The people making the real decisions are all at Head Office.
8 Food sold in supermarkets needs a clearly labeled shelf life.

Track 30 (Unit 30 Task 1)

1 She gave me some information.
2 She gave me a piece of advice.
3 We're making a little progress, but not much.
4 We're making a few sales, but not many.
5 Experience is more important than qualifications.
6 It's an experience I'll remember for a long time.
7 There aren't many spaces in the car park.
8 There isn't much space in my office.

Track 31 (Unit 31 Task 1)

1 Someone is waiting for you – I told them you wouldn't be long.
2 I can bring it to you sometime tomorrow.
3 I can bring it to you anytime tomorrow.
4 There isn't anything we can do.
5 I'd like to say a big 'thank you' to everyone.
6 Every one of our clients is important.
7 Let me introduce myself.
8 Are you doing all the work by yourselves?

Track 32 (Unit 32 Task 1)

1 All we need is a signature.
2 I want to hear everything.
3 I want to hear all your news.
4 None of the machines are faulty.
5 How many people came? None at all!
6 Make sure that each parcel has a label.
7 I believe every word he says.
8 Monday or Tuesday? Either day is fine.

Track 33 (Unit 33 Task 1)

1 This was your suggestion.
2 This suggestion was yours.
3 My own view is that the project is too ambitious.
4 The original idea was Helen's.
5 She's a colleague of mine.
6 lack of funds/level of commitment
7 stroke of luck/waste of time
8 executive search company/stock market launch

Track 34 (Unit 34 Task 1)

1 I read an interesting report last week.
2 I read the report you gave me.
3 Reports are sent out four times a year.
4 We produce an income statement four times a year.
5 Mike is an office worker – he works on the other side of town.
6 The Portuguese are very good negotiators.
7 It's all a question of supply and demand.
8 Product knowledge is very important for a sales consultant.

Track 35 (Unit 35 Task 1)

1 I visited the UK, France and the Netherlands.
2 They wouldn't pay, so we took them to court.
3 My son is in hospital and can't go to school.
4 I'm tired. It's time to go home.
5 I bought this suit from Fifth Avenue when I was back in the States.
6 The Danube is the main river in Central Europe.
7 This article gives advice about buying stocks.
8 Thank you for the advice you gave me last week.

Track 36 (Unit 36 Task 1)

1 Our profits rose slightly in Benelux last year.
2 She's a good negotiator. She negotiates well.
3 There was a slight fall in profits in April.
4 In April profits fell slightly.
5 The talk was quite good.
6 The talk was absolutely excellent.
7 well-made/heavily promoted
8 unexpectedly delayed/completely illegal

Track 37 (Unit 37 Task 1)

1 Model C40 is more powerful than the C30.
2 The most powerful model we make is the C60.
3 The least powerful is the C20 – it's less powerful than the C40.
4 The C60i is just as powerful as the C60.
5 The C60 runs faster than the C40 does.
6 This year has been worse than last year.
7 This is one of the worst years we've ever had.
8 We'll be there soon – it's not much further.

Track 38 (Unit 38 Task 1)

1 A is slightly more expensive than B.
2 A is considerably more expensive than B.
3 A has roughly the same specifications as B.
4 The market is growing bigger and bigger.
5 Investors are becoming more and more sophisticated.
6 The sooner they decide, the better for all of us.
7 It's one of the most rapidly developing countries in the world.
8 This product is more attractively designed than the other.

Track 39 (Unit 39 Task 1)

1 The whole thing was highly professional.
2 Their rates are a little expensive.
3 They replied quite quickly.
4 I marginally prefer option B.
5 Their delivery times are too long for us.
6 Do we have enough chairs for everyone?
7 There are so many people working on this project.
8 There are too many people working on this project.

Track 40 (Unit 40 Task 1)

1 The new offices will be ready in two months' time.
2 I've worked here for two years.
3 I've worked here since January.
4 During the meeting I made a lot of notes.
5 While she was talking I made a lot of notes.
6 I need your report by Friday.
7 He'll be away until Friday.
8 It was a long meeting and we went for a drink afterwards.

Track 41 (Unit 41 Task 1)

1 I want the figures for October and November as well.
2 I want the figures for October as well as November.
3 It's a great idea, although it'll need careful costing.
4 Even though I wasn't feeling well, I still went to work.
5 Korea is a mature market, whereas Vietnam is still growing.
6 While there are still some issues to resolve, I think we should go ahead.
7 Although sales increased, operating profit fell.
8 Despite the increase in sales, operating profit fell.

Track 42 (Unit 42 Task 1)

1 I'm calling to complain because the goods are damaged.
2 I'm calling to complain because of the damaged goods.
3 The goods are damaged, so I'm calling to complain.
4 He called a press conference in order to explain the merger.
5 I'll call a taxi so as not to miss my flight.
6 He runs the company like his father used to.
7 We use this room as a storage area.
8 It looks as if we're going to break even by the end of the year.

Track 43 (Unit 43 Task 1)

1 This process produces less waste, and as a result it's better.
2 Some delays are beyond our control, such as strikes or bad weather.
3 We have plenty in stock. In fact, we could deliver tomorrow.
4 So, overall, things are improving.
5 On the whole, I think you're right, although I disagree on some points.
6 As a rule, we need an upfront payment. However, we can be flexible.
7 Either we could cancel the product launch, or we could postpone it.
8 Can we meet on Friday instead?

Track 44 (Unit 44 Task 1)

1 By the way, how is Claudia? I haven't seen her for ages.
2 As far as Latin America is concerned, we only have a presence in Brazil.
3 Anyway, I really must be going now.
4 Admittedly, option B is a little more expensive.
5 Predictably, Production complained about Sales – again.
6 I waited until ten, and in the end I left.
7 Unless we pay the invoice now, they'll cut our credit line.
8 We should pay the invoice now, otherwise they'll cut our credit line.

Track 45 (Unit 45 Task 1)

1 It's Magda who really does all the work.
2 It was me who spoke to you on the phone last week.
3 The trouble is, it's going to be very expensive.
4 What we need is a bigger budget.
5 What I'm going to do is call them right now.
6 Never before have I received such good customer service.
7 Under no circumstances can we agree to their proposal.
8 Technically speaking, the new machine is very easy to service.

Track 46 (Unit 46 Task 1)

1 I had a hard day at the office.
2 I'll be back in the office at three.
3 You'll see our offices on your left.
4 She'll be here in a few minutes – she's just on the phone.
5 I often work at home in the evening.
6 It was a very well-run meeting. Erika was in the chair.
7 I must've been standing in line for about half an hour.
8 Go down this road, past the church.

Track 47 (Unit 47 Task 1)

1 I've applied for a new job.
2 Does your machinery comply with health and safety regulations?
3 The process consists of four main stages.
4 What did you decide on?
5 We've spent two million euros on advertising this year.
6 Dana reminded me about the appointment.
7 Dana reminds me of my sister.
8 This situation results from bad planning, and it will result in total chaos.

Track 48 (Unit 48 Task 1)

1 It's compatible with your existing IT system.
2 It's important for us to move quickly in these negotiations.
3 I'm so tired. I haven't got used to the time difference yet.
4 Are you interested in any other items from the catalogue?
5 Are you aware of the difficulties you're creating?
6 The starting salary is dependent on previous experience.
7 I'm responsible for all the transport and logistics.
8 The Finance Director is directly responsible to the CEO.

Track 49 (Unit 49 Task 1)

1 The demand for microchips is very cyclical.
2 What exactly is your involvement in this project?
3 I'm not sure about the suitability of this product.
4 There has been a rise in operating profit of 3%.
5 I've called this meeting at short notice.
6 The concert is cancelled due to circumstances beyond our control.
7 We don't have that colour in stock, but we do have more on order.
8 The economy is on track for recovery.

Track 50 (Unit 50 Task 1)

1 Sales grew steadily last month.
2 There was steady growth in sales last month.
3 The economy has got worse, but our market share has improved.
4 Their share price hit a low in May, but it's recovered since then.
5 Their share price peaked in May, but it's fallen back since then.
6 Sales have been flat this year – they stand at around 3000 units a month.
7 Dividends paid to shareholders rose by 6%.
8 We raised dividends paid to shareholders by 6%.

Answer key

Unit 1 Present time 1

1.1
1 Do you often work 2 I don't know 3 do you know
4 doesn't work 5 Yes, I do. 6 I'm writing
7 They're not replying 8 What is happening 9 Are you enjoying
10 Yes, she is.

1.2
1 e 2 c 3 d 4 b 5 a

1.3
1 b 2 a 3 b 4 a 5 a

1.4
1 Do you know 2 works 3 'm 4 do you do 5 work
6 involves 7 don't make 8 supplies 9 're
10 do you often come 11 come 12 doesn't take

1.5
1 is booming 2 are looking 3 are trying 4 is happening
5 are investing 6 are increasing 7 is becoming 8 is moving

Unit 2 Present time 2

2.1
1 do you do 2 are you doing 3 are you working
4 do you work 5 I come 6 I'm coming 7 I'm dealing with
8 I deal with 9 are you going 10 do you usually go

2.2
1 'm looking at 2 look at 3 doesn't work 4 isn't working
5 think 6 'm thinking 7 take 8 're taking 9 aren't/'re not
10 aren't being/'re not being

2.3
1 ✓ 2 do you prefer 3 I don't believe it! 4 ✓ 5 ✓
6 I know 7 contains 8 ✓

2.4
1 'm calling 2 's working 3 think 4 work 5 understand
6 're expecting 7 believe 8 offer 9 depends on 10 want
11 need 12 's dealing

2.5
1 are growing 2 brings 3 are having to (*or* have to)
4 are spending 5 is focusing 6 realize

Unit 3 Past time 1

3.1
1 get/did 2 did you feel/told you 3 tell/did
4 didn't see/got

3.2
1 made 2 didn't take 3 sold 4 weren't 5 Did think
6 didn't have 7 was 8 bought

3.3
1 were marketing/went 2 was working 3 just went
4 called/said 5 were repairing/was moving

3.4
1 supplied 2 grew 3 expanded 4 began 5 built 6 took
7 won 8 made 9 became 10 sold off 11 cut
12 changed 13 transformed 14 was 15 were 16 resigned
17 announced 18 went 19 paid off 20 bought

3.5
1 ate/went 2 was negotiating/decided 3 happened/called
4 was explaining/interrupted 5 were investigating/resigned
6 saw/put 7 was waiting/called 8 was repairing/dropped
9 found/was looking 10 arrived/told

Unit 4 Past time 2

4.1
1 was looking for/had left 2 used to/was
3 had bought/started 4 used to have/changed
5 said/hadn't arrived 6 had turned off/was
7 used to be/used to walk 8 found/had already done
9 knew/had met 10 was having/saw/had grown

4.2
1 had made/started 2 was sure/had set
3 called/still hadn't finished 4 hadn't seen/put
5 had given/felt 6 became/had already been
7 had stopped/arrived 8 was/had already signed

4.3
1 had graduated 2 was just sitting 3 had nearly given up
4 hadn't decided 5 thought 6 was looking 7 told
8 had already taken 9 completed 10 interviewed
11 was working 12 hadn't had 13 started
14 were really exploiting me 15 had become 16 resigned
17 didn't have 18 had 19 had put
20 had always wanted (or always wanted)

4.4
1 had been producing 2 had run out of 3 hadn't been sleeping
4 had already chosen

4.5
1 used to/would 2 used to 3 used to/would 4 used to

Unit 5 Connecting past and present 1

5.1
1 Have you tried 2 've never seen 3 've already spent
4 Have they replied 5 haven't got 6 's just left
7 have gone up 8 Have you ever taken

5.2
1 b 2 a 3 a 4 b 5 a 6 b 7 b 8 a 9 b 10 a

5.3
1 already 2 just 3 for 4 never 5 yet 6 always 7 since
8 ever

5.4
1 c 2 a 3 b

5.5
1 B (since) 2 D (been) 3 A (for) 4 C (just) 5 B (already)
6 D (yet) 7 B (gone) 8 A (so far) 9 C (ever) 10 D (never)

Unit 6 Connecting past and present 2

6.1
1 I phoned 2 I have worked 3 I work 4 I have made
5 I saw 6 We went 7 has been 8 was 9 left 10 has left

6.2
1 went up/have gone up 2 operate/have set up
3 Have you seen/left 4 doesn't look/have come
5 have never spoken/spoke
6 have worked/want/Have you heard

6.3
1 've been looking at/'ve noticed 2 've been calling/'s gone
3 Have you seen/'ve been looking forward
4 have you been producing/'ve invested

6.4
1 haven't seen 2 haven't been 3 left 4 talked 5 's been
6 've never done 7 imagined 8 Have you ever been
9 've often thought 10 has it been 11 had 12 've known
13 've already done 14 put 15 finished 16 've had

6.5
1 have watched 2 began 3 have crashed 4 announced
5 has peaked 6 fell 7 was 8 released 9 have risen
10 has become 11 has also led 12 has improved

Unit 7 Future 1

7.1
1 d 2 c 3 a 4 f 5 b 6 e

7.2
1 I'm having 2 We're going to open 3 it'll probably do well
4 I'll see you 5 what are you going to do
6 Are you doing anything

7.3
1 is going to buy 2 am meeting 3 'll get 4 is going to be
5 will be 6 is going to have 7 will probably replace
8 are going to test (*or* are testing) 9 won't be
10 is going to rain

7.4
1 'll have 2 'll tell 3 are going to be 4 're going to restructure
5 will be 6 're going to offer 7 will the new job involve
8 're going to expand 9 'll be 10 'll have 11 will be
12 're going to move 13 'll have to 14 'll talk

7.5
1 're leaving 2 'll arrive 3 will be 4 're meeting
5 'll probably take 6 aren't doing/'re not doing 7 'll have
8 're staying 9 'll ask 10 'll have

Unit 8 Future 2

8.1
1 you leave 2 I'll be interviewing 3 will have finished
4 due to arrive 5 she comes back 6 I was going to mention it
7 I hope 8 will have repaid 9 is 10 Shall we
11 we've received 12 I'm about to have

8.2
1 c 2 d 3 a 4 b 5 e 6 f 7 h 8 g

8.3
1 will have passed 2 leaves/arrives 3 see 4 'll be seeing
5 will have finished 6 'll be doing 7 hear 8 will have started
9 will you have learned 10 Will you be using

8.4
1 C (would like to) 2 B (expect) 3 D (will fall)
4 B (will probably) 5 A (about to) 6 C (is due to)
7 A (will have begun) 8 B (will be fighting) 9 D (is planning to)
10 C (happens)

8.5
1 is 2 was going to be 3 'll have collected
4 'll be discussing 5 'll have agreed 6 happens 7 meet
8 'll be talking 9 have

Unit 9 Passive 1

9.1
1 were damaged 2 is seen 3 will not be finished
4 have been closed 5 are being reviewed 6 cannot be shipped

9.2
1 ~~by people~~ 2 ✓ 3 ✓ 4 ~~by a technician~~ 5 ✓
6 ~~by someone~~

9.3
1 A promising new drug has been discovered by our R&D department
2 ✗
3 This line was created by one of our best young designers.
4 I'm sorry, that can't be done
5 ✗
6 This payment may not be authorized by the Accounts Department.
7 ✗
8 I was being asked all sorts of highly technical questions.

9.4
1 are designed 2 are put 3 is completed 4 is printed out
5 is offered 6 is analyzed 7 is outsourced

9.5
1 has been arranged 2 will be needed 3 should be finished
4 is being ordered 5 have been offered 6 might be needed

Unit 10 Passive 2

10.1
1 b 2 a 3 b 4 a

10.2
1 repaired 2 to grow 3 was born 4 cleaned
5 to have demanded 6 assembled 7 were you born
8 to be looking.

10.3
1 I was lent 2 I was given 3 We were promised
4 This fabric was made 5 We were sent 6 The flight was booked

10.4
1 has been transformed 2 has happened 3 has privatized
4 have also invested 5 has been brought 6 has been encouraged
7 have been solved

10.5
1 was made 2 is being dealt with 3 will be delivered
4 is attached 5 cannot be opened 6 are guaranteed

10.6
1 is known to have made 2 is said to be
3 is reported to have replied 4 is believed to be trying

Unit 11 Modals, etc. 1

11.1
1 Can you come 2 I can come 3 I couldn't come 4 can we do
5 to be able to 6 I must speak 7 I managed to speak
8 I could hear

11.2
1 can't 2 be able to 3 couldn't 4 could 5 can/be able to
6 can/can't 7 can't/be able to 8 couldn't 9 could

11.3
1 b 2 h 3 f 4 c 5 e 6 a 7 g 8 d

11.4
1 Could I speak to someone 2 I'll put you through
3 I'll just go and have a look 4 Could you repeat that, please
5 I'll be on this number 6 I'll get back to you

11.5
1 d 2 c 3 b 4 a 5 f 6 e 7 h 8 g 9 l 10 j
11 k 12 i 13 o 14 p 15 m 16 n

Unit 12 Modals, etc. 2

12.1
1 c 2 d 3 b 4 a 5 h 6 f 7 e 8 g 9 l 10 k
11 j 12 i

12.2
1 must 2 have to 3 must 4 have to

12.3
1 S 2 S 3 S 4 D 5 S 6 S 7 S 8 D 9 S
10 S 11 S 12 D

12.4
1 don't have to 2 can't 3 have to 4 should 5 shouldn't
6 can

12.5
1 should have 2 had to 3 couldn't 4 had to 5 couldn't
6 should have 7 shouldn't have 8 didn't have to
9 shouldn't have 10 didn't have to

Unit 13 Modals, etc. 3

13.1
1 might 2 can't be 3 must be 4 may not be 5 can't be
6 must be 7 should be 8 might be 9 could be 10 must be

13.2
1 c 2 d 3 b 4 a 5 f 6 g 7 e

13.3
1 should 2 might 3 can't 4 must 5 might 6 should
7 can't 8 must

13.4
1 d 2 a 3 d 4 c 5 c 6 b 7 a 8 d

13.5
1 is likely to 2 will definitely 3 might 4 is almost certain to
5 are unlikely to 6 definitely won't

13.6
1 must 2 might have 3 can't have 4 might 5 can't
6 must have

Unit 14 Modals, etc. 4

14.1
1 giving 2 talking 3 Shall I 4 Would you 5 May I
6 you should 7 could you 8 Would you like 9 Could I
10 we could 11 I give 12 I gave

14.2
1 b 2 c 3 a

14.3
1 d+iii 2 f+i 3 b+vi 4 a+ii 5 c+v 6 e+iv

14.4
1 Would you like 2 I don't mind 3 Do you mind
4 Of course not 5 Would you like me to
6 Thanks, that sounds great 7 shall we 8 Would you mind
9 Would you like to 10 Of course

14.5
Line 1 May I have your name, please?
Line 3 Could you spell that for me, please?
Line 5 Would you mind leaving your passport?
Line 6 Do you think I could have an early morning call?
Line 8 Would you mind if I left a message for a colleague?
Line 9 Would you like me to lend you a pen?
Line 13 I don't think you ought to do that

Unit 15 Questions 1

15.1
1 Did you speak 2 did Lara say 3 Yes, I do.
4 does this machine work 5 started the company
6 did the company start 7 called me 8 did you call

15.2
1 Have you seen the news today? 2 Do you work from home?
3 Can you understand German? 4 Have you already had lunch?
5 Will you be back in time for lunch?
6 Are you enjoying the conference? 7 Did you agree with her?
8 Have you ever spoken to Pierre?

15.3
1 do you know Jim? 2 have you invited? 3 are you going?
4 did you park? 5 are you here? 6 will you have?

15.4
1 When do you get to work? 2 What have you done?
3 Where did you put the report? 4 Why do you stay here?
5 How were you feeling yesterday? 6 Where are you staying?
7 Who do you report to? 8 Whose is this bag?/Whose bag is this?

15.5
1 Are you here on business? 2 What do you do?
3 How long have you been doing that? 4 What did you do before?
5 Does your job involve much traveling?
6 Is this your first visit to Lyon? 7 When did you arrive?
8 How long are you staying for? 9 Where are you staying?
10 What's it like?

15.6
1 What kind of 2 How many 3 how much 4 How far
5 How long 6 Whose 7 Which (limited number of models)
8 what (large number of colours)

Unit 16 Questions 2

16.1
1 what your terms of payment are
2 where the marketing seminar is 3 how we can 4 why you left
5 whether you could

16.2
1 aren't we 2 don't you 3 didn't you 4 have you 5 has she
6 will you 7 is he 8 didn't we 9 aren't I 10 shall we

16.3
1 b 2 b 3 a 4 b 5 a 6 b

16.4
1 Where are you going to?
2 Where did you get the information from?
3 Which funds do you invest in? 4 What does it depend on?
5 Where are you traveling to on Friday?
6 Who did you go on the sales trip with?
7 What is this piece of equipment for?
8 What was the weather like in Sweden?

16.5
1 didn't send the invoice, did you? 2 sent the invoice, didn't you?
3 isn't Mr Peters, is it? 4 is Mr Peters, isn't it?
5 have canceled their order, haven't they?
6 haven't canceled their order, have they?

16.6
1 wasn't it 2 doesn't it 3 shouldn't we 4 do you
5 should it 6 shall we

Unit 17 Conditionals 1

17.1
1 we're/they'll start 2 we took/we'd arrive 3 goes up/is
4 we don't act/we'll miss 5 you change/give me
6 you click/it won't work 7 you order/send
8 you signed/we'd ship 9 you hear/let me
10 I wouldn't/I were

17.2
1 follow/'ll come 2 was/'d argue 3 have/'ll deal
4 knew/'d tell 5 leave/'ll catch 6 wait/'ll give
7 had/'d be

17.3
1 a/d 2 b/c 3 b/d 4 a/b

17.4
1 will 2 won't 3 don't 4 will 5 is 6 unless
7 is going to be 8 be 9 Unless 10 won't 11 would
12 wouldn't 13 didn't 14 would

17.5
1 work/get 2 do/'ll give 3 worked/wouldn't be
4 would happen/reoccurred 5 miss/don't seem 6 fancy/give

Unit 18 Conditionals 2

18.1
1 had called/would have told 2 took/might feel
3 had listened/wouldn't have made
4 we'd found/we'd have moved 5 kept/might present
6 I'd known/wouldn't have invested
7 had been/could have succeeded 8 went/must know

18.2
1 when 2 in case 3 as long as 4 unless 5 as long as
6 in case 7 when 8 unless

18.3
1 hadn't drunk 2 had 3 could stay 4 knew 5 had taken
6 didn't interrupt 7 had 8 could do 9 have
10 hadn't bought

18.4
1 if 2 as long as 3 'd have 4 'd 5 wouldn't've 6 'd
7 've 8 in case 9 Unless 10 'll

18.5
1 b 2 a 3 d 4 c 5 g 6 h 7 e 8 f

Unit 19 Verb + *-ing* or infinitive 1

19.1
1 to miss 2 spending 3 to close down 4 to deliver
5 calling 6 losing 7 to prepare 8 waiting 9 postponing
10 to sign

19.2
1 to give 2 advertising 3 employing 4 to receive 5 writing
6 to speak 7 making 8 thinking 9 to fly 10 to help

19.3
1 advised me to 2 persuade him to 3 remind me to
4 expect her to 5 encouraged me to 6 forced us to
7 prefers me to 8 invite you to

19.4
1 to meet 2 wondering 3 to be 4 asking 5 to raise
6 to wait 7 to use 8 trying 9 to use 10 losing
11 to crash 12 to take 13 to persuade 14 to send

19.5
1 to interview 2 talking 3 to pay 4 worrying 5 pretending
6 using 7 to be 8 to show 9 to take 10 receiving

Unit 20 Verb + *-ing* or infinitive 2

20.1
1 to meet 2 meeting 3 being 4 to make 5 to speak
6 saying 7 to open 8 opening 9 giving 10 to look at
11 to announce 12 quitting 13 selling 14 to describe

20.2
1 a 2 b 3 d 4 c 5 e 6 f

20.3
1 being 2 being 3 to be 4 to be 5 being 6 being

20.4
1 to speak 2 to book 3 to start 4 to go 5 missing
6 to give 7 working 8 to have 9 working
10 to get (*or* getting) 11 missing out 12 to have 13 being
14 taking 15 to finish

20.5
1 to trade in 2 doing 3 losing 4 to accept 5 to bring
6 thinking 7 doing 8 to go back 9 to move 10 to do

Unit 21 Verbs and objects

21.1
1 ✗ 2 ✓ 3 ✗ 4 ✓ 5 ✗ 6 ✓ 7 ✓ 8 ✗ 9 ✗
10 ✓ 11 ✓ 12 ✗ 13 ✗ 14 ✓ 15 ✗ 16 ✓

21.2
1 ~~it~~ 2 ✓ 3 ~~it~~ 4 ✓ 5 ~~it~~ 6 ✓ 7 ~~it~~ 8 ✓

21.3
1 ✓ 2 ✓ 3 ✗ 4 ✗ 5 ✓ 6 ✓ 7 ✗ 8 ✓ 9 ✓
10 ✗ 11 ✓ 12 ✗ 13 ✓ 14 ✓ 15 ✗ 16 ✗

21.4
1 lent me 2 suggest to them 3 promised me
4 announce the news to the journalists 5 explained to them
6 causing us problems 7 the fish to me
8 the whole situation to them 9 cost us
10 the fault to the technician

21.5
1 I lent my Macmillan dictionary to Louisa from marketing.
2 I lent Louisa from marketing my Macmillan dictionary.
3 I sent them an email yesterday.
4 I sent an email to their customer services yesterday.
5 I reported the fault to the technician.
6 I reported the fault to him.
7 I sold him the display model that's been in the showroom.
8 I sold the display model to a man who came in this morning.

21.6
1 to/for 2 to/for 3 for/to 4 to/for 5 for/to
6 to/for 7 to/for 8 to/for

Unit 22 Phrasal verbs 1

22.1
1 C 2 B 3 D 4 A 5 B 6 D 7 C 8 A

22.2
1 find 2 hold/hang 3 look 4 fill 5 deal 6 give
7 take 8 head 9 look 10 take

22.3
1 deal with this/deal with it
2 look up the information/look the information up/look it up
3 keep down our costs/keep our costs down/keep them down
4 do without my BlackBerry/do without it

22.4
1 pick up 2 drop off 3 checking in 4 turn up 5 sort out
6 draw up 7 looking through 8 call on 9 bring out
10 hold up 11 call off 12 get into

22.5
1 off 2 down 3 in 4 on

Unit 23 Phrasal verbs 2

23.1
1 in with 2 along with 3 out of 4 back on 5 up with
6 in for 7 back to 8 up to 9 along with 10 down on
11 up with 12 through to

23.2
1 e 2 c 3 a 4 b 5 f 6 d

23.3
1 down 2 up 3 on 4 behind 5 back 6 in

23.4
1 put through 2 get through 3 hold on 4 go ahead
5 look into 6 get back to 7 breaking up 8 cut off
9 sort out 10 go over

Unit 24 The *-ing* form

24.1
1 c 2 a 3 b 4 e 5 f 6 d

24.2
Noun: 1c, 4e, 6d
Adjective: 2a, 3b, 5f

24.3
1 tiring 2 meeting 3 confusing 4 wearing/lasting
5 welcoming 6 selling/cutting

24.4
1 meet 2 meeting 3 take 4 taking 5 work 6 working

24.5
1 After leaving 2 of being 3 by taking over 4 Before going
5 instead of using 6 without raising

24.6
1 ~~which are~~ 2 ~~While I was~~ 3 ~~who is~~ 4 ~~that is~~ 5 ~~As I was~~
6 ~~who are~~

24.7
1 expecting 2 Not being used to 3 hoping 4 Not being
5 Assuming 6 not knowing 7 reviewing/having reviewed
8 Having lost 9 starting 10 Having heard

Unit 25 *make & do, have, get*

25.1
1 make 2 did 3 make 4 do/make 5 do 6 do/make
7 make 8 made/do 9 did/made 10 did/making
11 make/do 12 do

25.2
1 ✓ 2 ✗ 3 ✗ 4 ✓

25.3
1 b 2 d 3 a 4 f 5 c 6 e 7 h 8 k 9 l 10 i
11 j 12 g

25.4
1 meeting 2 holiday 3 chance/look 4 time
5 discussion/break 6 appointment 7 the fish 8 doubt
9 difficulty 10 fever/day off 11 word 12 go

25.5
1 doing 2 get 3 doing 4 make 5 doing 6 got
7 made 8 done 9 make 10 do 11 did 12 got
13 got 14 made 15 makes 16 do 17 do 18 got
19 got 20 made

Unit 26 Reported speech 1

26.1
1 I've already finished the three tasks 2 I'll be back after lunch
3 Paula's going to contact the printers 4 I want to call Head Office
5 I'm meeting the bank manager at 11 am
6 I found out about the problem a long time ago
7 I have to be back in the office by 3.30

26.2
1 she/following 2 there/me 3 they'd/our/before
4 she/right then

26.3
1 he wouldn't put it in the January Sales, because it was selling very well
2 (that) she'd read the report and (that) she didn't understand section four
3 he finished his presentation he was going to have a drink
4 (that) she was preparing the figures but (that) she wouldn't be long
5 (that) he liked tennis but (that) he didn't play very often
6 (that) she was going to visit their Polish subsidiary but (that) she wasn't sure when

26.4
1 ✓ 2 ✓ 3 ✗ 4 ✓ 5 ✓ 6 ✗ 7 ✓ 8 ✓

26.5
1 hoped 2 his 3 he'd sent 4 the day before 5 the 6 me
7 there 8 was 9 before 10 had gone 11 was meeting
12 that

Unit 27 Reported speech 2

27.1
1 told me 2 said 3 say 4 tell 5 told/said
6 said to/tell me

27.2
1 f 2 d 3 b 4 a 5 e 6 c 7 j 8 k 9 h 10 l
11 i 12 g

27.3
1 if/whether I was on holiday for the whole of August
2 what the letters 'URL' meant
3 if/whether I had prepared the figures 4 when her talk was
5 if/whether he had remembered (*or* he remembered) to back up the file
6 why I had turned off the air conditioning
7 if/whether I spoke German
8 how much she had paid (*or* she paid) for her car

27.4
1 estimated 2 suggested 3 agreed 4 decided

27.5
1 us to give 2 told them 3 to listen 4 said 5 it would
6 reminded them that 7 setting up 8 not to say 9 to chair
10 to meet

Unit 28 Relative clauses 1

28.1
1 b 2 a 3 c 4 d

28.2
1 whose 2 that 3 which 4 who 5 whose 6 who
7 that 8 whose

28.3
1 (that) 2 ✓ 3 (which) 4 ✓ 5 (that) 6 ✓ 7 ✓
8 (who) 9 ✓ 10 (that)

28.4
1 I went to the conference with 2 we order from
3 I'm responsible for 4 we've been waiting for 5 I stayed at
6 I usually deal with

28.5
1 we received the complaint from 2 we're depending on
3 I've been thinking about 4 I most enjoyed listening to
5 we've been hoping for 6 we need to focus on
7 I'm interested in 8 we get the most profits from

28.6
1a T 1b F 1c T 1d F
2a T 2b F 2c T 2d F
3a T 3b F 3c F 3d F

Unit 29 Relative clauses 2

29.1
1 that we introduced last year
2 who could be a useful contact for you
3 whose CV is on your desk 4 who is coming next week
5 that Tom took me to 6 whose presentation I heard
7 where they're going to build the new factory
8 the mobile phone that I was telling you about

29.2
1 ✓ 2 ~~their~~ 3 ✓ 4 ~~it~~ 5 ~~they~~ 6 ~~it~~ 7 ✓ 8 ~~it~~

29.3
1 who 2 whose 3 whom 4 that 5 What 6 that
7 where 8 that

29.4
1 ✓ 2 what 3 ✓ 4 who 5 what 6 which 7 ✓
8 which 9 ✓ 10 What 11 ✓ 12 what

29.5
1 which has become a standard case study in business schools all over the world
2 which was run by Domenico De Sole
3 which would decide the future of the industry
4 which Gucci had been looking for
5 who was the head of a retail group called PPR
6 which LVMH owned

Unit 30 Countable and uncountable nouns

30.1
1 Is/much 2 Are/many 3 How much 4 some advice/was
5 equipment 6 machines 7 a piece of equipment 8 many
9 much 10 a little/much 11 a few/many 12 a lot of demand

30.2
1 a 2 some 3 much 4 many 5 an 6 some 7 many
8 much 9 much 10 many 11 many 12 much

30.3
1a G 1b S 2a G 2b S 3a S 3b G 4a S 4b G

30.4
1 j 2 b 3 g 4 a 5 c 6 d 7 k 8 f 9 i 10 e
11 l 12 h

30.5
1 is 2 some 3 A piece of 4 much 5 some 6 a
7 much 8 experience 9 little 10 some 11 knowledge
12 progress 13 is 14 a lot of 15 information 16 a few
17 much 18 work

Unit 31 Pronouns

31.1
1 something 2 no one 3 anything 4 anyone 5 everything
6 someone 7 everyone 8 anything 9 something
10 nothing

31.2
1 nothing 2 anything 3 anyone 4 Someone 5 anywhere
6 something 7 someone 8 anything 9 anything

31.3
1 asking myself 2 blame yourself 3 taught himself
4 hurt yourself 5 enjoyed ourselves 6 prepare yourself
7 introduce myself 8 make yourselves

31.4
1 anytime, anywhere 2 felt/relaxed 3 every one 4 has/their
5 anywhere 6 somewhere 7 themselves 8 each other

31.5
1 everywhere 2 somewhere 3 anywhere 4 someone
5 Everyone 6 Anyone 7 something 8 everything
9 anything

31.6
1 enjoy yourself 2 Remember 3 help yourself 4 met
5 introduce yourself 6 change 7 ask myself 8 relax

Unit 32 Determiners

32.1
1 none of them 2 a few of them 3 some of them
4 many of them 5 most of them 6 all of them

32.2
1 no 2 Not one 3 Some 4 either 5 Our clients each
6 both days 7 All of 8 any 9 Everything
10 a mobile phone each 11 Every option has been 12 everything

32.3
1 not one 2 no/either 3 neither 4 All 5 every/all 6 each
7 every 8 none 9 any 10 both 11 either 12 each

32.4
1 Neither idea 2 All we have left is 3 Every participant
4 not a single person 5 Some of the audience didn't
6 None of my colleagues speak 7 The only thing we want is
8 weren't any documents 9 Neither hotel was 10 at all

32.5
1 B (Both of them have) 2 C (neither company)
3 A (all its revenue) 4 C (Both are famous) 5 C (every person)
6 A (each) 7 C (anything)

Unit 33 Possessives and compound nouns

33.1
1 My 2 her 3 its 4 your 5 yours 6 our own
7 ourselves 8 yours

33.2
1 waste of 2 lack of 3 error of 4 range of 5 level of
6 piece of 7 stroke of 8 flood of 9 method of
10 success of

33.3
1 company profits/training course 2 staff meeting/sales forecast
3 credit card/department store 4 Internet access/summer sale
5 inflation figures/price range 6 market survey/rush hour
7 information technology/car keys 8 shop assistant/power failure
9 shopfloor worker/working lunch
10 insurance contract/bank loan
11 product features/production costs
12 market leader/marketing budget
13 profit margin/capital expenditure
14 quality control/balance sheet

33.4
1 Ingrid knows that it's Mary's area of work, not hers.
2 When it's Christmas, all our competitors' sales go up more than ours.
3 Alice's friend's called Bill. He's one of Morgan Stanley's top analysts.
4 My boss's PA reads all the customers' emails
5 I went to my doctor's and he's computerized all the patients' records
6 Look at those two Mercedes. One's our director's and the other's a visitor's.

33.5
1 in the meeting 2 my pen 3 mine 4 James's documents
5 colleague of hers 6 's your boss's 7 expert in company
8 shows the sales 9 customer of ours 10 a management training

33.6
1 ~~trade~~ 2 ~~check~~ 3 ~~offer~~ 4 ~~process~~ 5 ~~output~~ 6 ~~share~~
7 ~~line~~ 8 ~~market~~ 9 ~~trade~~ 10 ~~decision~~

Unit 34 Articles 1

34.1
1 the 2 an/the 3 a/The 4 a 5 the/the 6 The/a
7 a 8 an/the 9 an/the other 10 the/the 11 the
12 The Portuguese

34.2
1 ~ 2 a/~/~ 3 an/~ 4 ~/~ 5 a/~ 6 ~ 7 a/a
8 ~/a 9 an/~ 10 an/a

34.3
1 The/a/~ 2 ~/a 3 a/~/the 4 ~/the 5 ~/the/a
6 ~ 7 a/the 8 the/a/the 9 ~/~ 10 A/an/a
11 ~/the 12 ~

34.4
1 a 2 the 3 ~ 4 an 5 ~ 6 ~ 7 ~ 8 the 9 a
10 ~ 11 ~ 12 an 13 the 14 ~ 15 ~ 16 the
17 ~ 18 a 19 the 20 ~ 21 a 22 a 23 the 24 the
25 ~

34.5
1 the 2 the 3 ~ 4 ~ 5 a 6 a 7 ~ 8 the
9 the 10 an 11 the 12 the 13 ~ 14 a 15 ~
16 the

Unit 35 Articles 2

35.1
1 Pisa/car/the Leaning Tower 2 to court 3 Crete
4 the Chancellor/Germany 5 in hospital/school
6 the Alps/Mont Blanc 7 the UK/Canterbury Cathedral
8 the past 9 go home 10 Deutsche Bank
11 university 12 Fifth Avenue/the States
13 Lake Windermere/the Lake District/the north-west/England
14 the rich 15 at work/lunch 16 The Danube/Central Europe

35.2
1a ~ 1b The 2a The 2b ~ 3a ~ 3b The 4a ~ 4b the 5a The 5b ~ 6a The 6b ~ 7a ~ 7b The 8a ~ 8b The

35.3
1 at 2 in 3 at 4 station on 5 still at 6 at 7 the/at 8 to/by

35.4
1 ~ 2 ~ 3 ~ 4 the 5 the 6 the 7 the 8 the 9 the 10 ~ 11 the 12 the 13 the 14 ~ 15 the 16 the 17 the 18 the 19 ~ 20 ~ 21 ~ 22 the 23 the 24 The 25 the 26 ~ 27 the 28 the 29 ~ 30 ~

Unit 36 Adjectives and adverbs

36.1
1 fell slightly 2 improved dramatically 3 dropped significantly 4 recovered slowly 5 has risen gradually 6 grew steadily

36.2
1 tired 2 bored 3 boring 4 exciting 5 big 6 enormous 7 bad 8 freezing

36.3
1 well made 2 heavily promoted 3 badly designed 4 extremely helpful 5 easily recognizable 6 unexpectedly delayed 7 completely illegal 8 quite late

36.4
1 an amazing new software package
2 a large old-fashioned cutting machine
3 two square wooden cartons
4 a difficult three-month transition period
5 high-quality Taiwanese computer chips
6 a well-planned investment strategy
7 a revolutionary new handheld device
8 awful cheap plastic souvenirs

36.5
1 monthly – adj. 2 late – adv. 3 late – adj. 4 well – adv. 5 good – adj. 6 hardly – adv. 7 hard – adj. 8 hard – adv. 9 fast – adv. 10 fast – adj.

36.6
1 strange 2 large 3 properly 4 good 5 regularly 6 invisibly 7 easy 8 quickly 9 right 10 well

Unit 37 Comparing 1

37.1
1 as profitable as 2 the most profitable 3 the most recent 4 than 5 worse 6 the best 7 not as bad as 8 worse 9 longer than 10 further

37.2
1 the biggest 2 smaller than 3 less interesting than 4 the hottest 5 better than 6 as good as 7 more difficult 8 as large as 9 worse than (*or* as bad as) 10 the worst

37.3
1 than/the 2 as/as 3 than/does 4 least 5 best 6 most 7 than/had 8 as/as 9 just/as 10 not

37.4
1 as good an analyst as
2 more sections of the report than me (*or* than I have)
3 as long as I 4 bigger than ours
5 most important presentation I've ever given 6 as interesting as
7 the best communication skills
8 the most interesting people I have ever met

37.5
1 safest 2 lower 3 best 4 cheaper 5 better 6 more attractive 7 riskiest 8 greater 9 worst 10 larger 11 nearer 12 most sensible

Unit 38 Comparing 2

38.1
1 considerably 2 as 3 the better 4 more and more 5 the second largest 6 slightly less 7 fastest 8 more carefully 9 more careful 10 much better 11 the same as 12 the best-

38.2
1 roughly/more or less 2 virtually/nearly 3 exactly/just 4 a bit/a little 5 much/far 6 comparatively/relatively

38.3
1 the most widely accepted 2 the fastest growing 3 the most cleverly designed 4 best-selling 5 the least known 6 the most rapidly changing

38.4
1 slightly 2 as many 3 as much 4 considerably less 5 more than twice 6 roughly the same 7 slightly less 8 not nearly

38.5
1 in comparison with 2 by far the largest 3 considerably more 4 the fastest growing 5 roughly the same 6 half as much as

Unit 39 Adverbs of degree

39.1
1 b 2 a 3 d 4 c 5 g 6 f 7 h 8 e

39.2
1 so few 2 too much 3 such a 4 so 5 too high 6 so much 7 so many 8 so little 9 too good 10 too short 11 tall enough 12 enough money

39.3
1 too 2 so much 3 so many 4 so little 5 so few 6 too 7 such 8 enough 9 so 10 too 11 so 12 such

39.4
1a such a big drop in their share price that 1b so big that
2a such large debts that 2b so large that
3a so well that 3b such a good order fulfilment system that
4a so successful that 4b such a success that

39.5
1 the screen wasn't large enough 2 was such a difficult problem
3 were too few copies 4 too little space
5 presentation was so good 6 didn't sell enough units
7 so many brochures that 8 too little time

Unit 40 Time adverbs

40.1
1 in 2 at 3 at 4 on 5 in 6 at 7 on 8 in 9 in 10 on 11 on 12 in 13 at 14 at 15 on 16 at

40.2
1 g 2 a 3 k 4 m 5 f 6 j 7 e 8 i 9 b 10 l 11 n 12 h 13 d 14 c

40.3
1 this morning 2 the day after tomorrow 3 at night 4 on time 5 in time 6 for 7 during 8 two years ago 9 before 10 During 11 While 12 while 13 during 14 by 15 until 16 then 17 afterwards 18 After lunch

40.4
1 How long have you worked here?/For about six months.
2 How long have you had a subsidiary in Poland?/Since 2009.
3 How long has Peter Middelhoff been CEO?/Since the start of last year.
4 How long has your company had the same logo?/For about twenty years.
5 How long have you known Lei Huang?/For a long time.
6 How long have you had this particular job?/Since the company was restructured.
7 How long have you been interested in antiques?/For ages and ages.
8 How long have you lived in this town?/Since I was born.

40.5
1 Afterwards 2 ago 3 for 4 during 5 after 6 before
7 for 8 for 9 while 10 since 11 ago 12 while
13 afterwards 14 after

Unit 41 Linking words 1

41.1
1 Although 2 despite 3 Although 4 while 5 Whereas
6 though 7 but 8 whereas 9 anyway 10 In spite of
11 although 12 Although

41.2
1a We can handle the transport arrangements and also the insurance.
1b We can handle both the transport arrangements and the insurance.
1c We can handle the transport arrangements and the insurance too.
2a I want the sales figures for October and November as well.
2b I want the sales figures for October as well as November.
2c I want the sales figures for October and also November.

41.3
1 although 2 but 3 still 4 though 5 In spite of
6 whereas 7 anyway

41.4
1a Although it was snowing, the flight left on time.
1b Despite the snow, the flight left on time.
2a In spite of my headache, I still went to the meeting.
2b I had a headache, but I still went to the meeting.
3a Some analysts think that stocks will fall in value, whereas others disagree.
3b Although some analysts think that stocks will fall in value, others disagree.
4a Despite the difficulties in the negotiations, we won the contract.
4b Even though there were difficulties in the negotiations, we won the contract.
5a Whereas oil prices rose slightly last year, this year they have gone down.
5b Oil prices rose slightly last year, although this year they have gone down.
6a They've never been successful, yet they keep on trying.
6b Despite never being successful, they keep on trying.

41.5
1 as well 2 Even though 3 as well as 4 Whereas 5 despite
6 both 7 yet

Unit 42 Linking words 2

42.1
1 so I sent her a copy of the minutes
2 she doesn't know, I'll ask someone else
3 so I have to go now
4 because I had a lot of paperwork to do
5 because of all the paperwork

42.2
1 to make 2 so 3 so that 4 in order to 5 for 6 can
7 could 8 wouldn't 9 won't 10 to see

42.3
1 b 2 a 3 a 4 b 5 a 6 b 7 b 8 a 9 b
10 a 11 a 12 b

42.4
1 ✓ 2 ✗ 3 ✓ 4 ✗ 5 ✓ 6 ✗ 7 ✓ 8 ✓ 9 ✗
10 ✓

42.5
1 as 2 as/like 3 as/like 4 like 5 as/like 6 like 7 as
8 like

42.6
1 as if 2 like 3 so 4 so as not to 5 since 6 as
7 like 8 as 9 so 10 so 11 like 12 to

Unit 43 Developing an argument 1

43.1
1 instead 2 hand 3 As a rule 4 except 5 either
6 As a matter of fact 7 On the whole 8 On the other hand
9 Besides 10 such as 11 for example 12 except for

43.2
1 actually 2 except 3 therefore 4 instead 5 In general
6 such as 7 Either 8 Moreover 9 Nevertheless 10 So

43.3
In general, taking an MBA is a good idea for an ambitious young professional. However, you do have to make some sacrifices. You miss out on two years' valuable experience at work, for example, and it can be very expensive.

43.4
1 B (First of all) 2 A (Besides) 3 D (finally) 4 C (as a result)
5 A (However) 6 B (In addition) 7 D (for example)
8 A (such as) 9 B (in conclusion)

43.5
1 first of all 2 In addition 3 In fact 4 Therefore 5 As a rule
6 However 7 In conclusion 8 instead of

Unit 44 Developing an argument 2

44.1
1 in particular 2 In relation to 3 It seems that 4 Fortunately
5 Actually 6 With regard to 7 in the end 8 at last 9 Unless
10 otherwise 11 e.g. 12 i.e.

44.2
1 Personally 2 Of course 3 Unfortunately 4 By the way
5 Frankly 6 Apparently 7 Anyway 8 Above all
9 Or rather

44.3
1 in particular 2 Clearly 3 as a result
4 On the other hand 5 or rather 6 In fact
7 except for 8 In general 9 although 10 such as
11 as far as start-up companies are concerned 12 Furthermore
13 in the end 14 to sum up

44.4
1 in general 2 except for 3 as a result 4 In fact
5 as far as ... is/are concerned 6 although 7 furthermore
8 on the other hand 9 to sum up 10 in the end
11 in particular 12 or rather 13 such as 14 clearly

Unit 45 Developing an argument 3

45.1
1 It's dollars that we get paid in, not euros.
2 It's brand image that really differentiates products.
3 It was Nouriel Roubini who gave the best analysis of the recession in 2008.
4 It was my ideas that they implemented.
5 It's emerging markets that we should invest in, not our domestic market.
6 It was me who negotiated that deal.

45.2
1 The idea is 2 The answer is 3 The truth is 4 The question is
5 The trouble is 6 What worries me is 7 What we can't do is
8 What happened was 9 What we need is
10 What I'm going to do is

45.3
1 Never before have I seen such incompetence.
2 Under no circumstances will he sell his shares in the company.
3 On no account must you talk to the press about this.
4 At no time did I authorize this payment.
5 Not only did they offer me a promotion, they're also upgrading my car to a Lexus.

45.4
In 1972, five former IBM employees launched a company to develop some software for processing real-time business information. *One year later,* the first component was complete: a financial accounting package. *By the middle of the 1980s*, 50 of the 100 largest German companies were SAP customers, and revenues had reached around $50 million.

45.5
1 Yes, I do understand what you're saying
2 I did order the spare parts 3 Do have a seat
4 I did do everything I could, but it just wasn't enough.

45.6
1 technical 2 Technically 3 Financially 4 financial
5 Commercially 6 commercial

Unit 46 Prepositions of place

46.1
1 at 2 on 3 above/below 4 in 5 on 6 on 7 on
8 by 9 next to 10 over 11 near 12 at 13 on
14 out of 15 near 16 by 17 at 18 in

46.2
1 at 2 on 3 on 4 in 5 on 6 at/in 7 at 8 in
9 on 10 on 11 in 12 At 13 in 14 in/on 15 in/at
16 in 17 at 18 in 19 at 20 in

46.3
1 near 2 on 3 towards 4 at 5 past 6 on 7 across
8 at 9 in front of 10 underneath 11 next to 12 backwards

46.4
1 on 2 at 3 in 4 on 5 next 6 in 7 in
8 opposite 9 in 10 at

Unit 47 Verb + preposition

47.1
1 believe in 2 wait for 3 lead to 4 depend on
5 know about 6 suffer from 7 approve of 8 comply with

47.2
1 for 2 with 3 of 4 about 5 for 6 into 7 on
8 from 9 in 10 on

47.3
1 to/about 2 from 3 of 4 with/about 5 from 6 in
7 for 8 to/about 9 at 10 for

47.4
1 pay for 2 wasted on 3 listen to 4 agreed with
5 apply for 6 involve in 7 rely on 8 apologized for
9 remind about 10 insist on

47.5
1 at 2 with 3 from 4 for 5 in 6 for 7 against
8 for 9 on 10 on 11 to 12 of 13 of 14 in
15 from 16 of

Unit 48 Adjective + preposition

48.1
1 g 2 h 3 d 4 b 5 j 6 a 7 i 8 c 9 f 10 e

48.2
1 popular with 2 safe from 3 attached to 4 dependent on
5 serious about 6 involved in 7 tired of 8 suitable for

48.3
1 about 2 with 3 with 4 for 5 for 6 for 7 with
8 at 9 to 10 for

48.4
1 with the old models 2 to Adrian 3 to driving on the left
4 interested in archaeology 5 at mathematics
6 about the advertising campaign 7 of people 8 on her idea

48.5
1 aware 2 attached 3 dependent 4 prepared 5 capable
6 useful 7 similar 8 involved 9 right 10 opposed
11 compatible 12 lacking 13 late 14 covered

Unit 49 Noun + preposition

49.1
1 to 2 for 3 between 4 with 5 with 6 in/of
7 between 8 to 9 in/of 10 for

49.2
1 trouble with 2 price of 3 advantage of 4 division into
5 payment for 6 objection to 7 involvement in
8 suitability for

49.3
1 At/in 2 for/up to 3 in/by 4 for/on 5 in 6 in
7 on/for 8 on/by 9 In/in 10 on/on/on

49.4
1 a 2 f 3 e 4 c 5 i 6 d 7 h 8 j 9 b 10 g

49.5
1 about 2 In 3 for 4 of 5 with 6 at (*or* in) 7 of
8 out 9 in 10 in 11 on 12 for 13 in 14 for 15 at
16 at

Unit 50 Trends, graphs and figures

50.1
1 slight 2 increased 3 in 4 by 5 improved
6 hit/low/recovered/at 7 peaked 8 slowly/by 9 slow/of
10 to 11 rose/fell 12 raised/cut

50.2
1 one thousand two hundred and thirty
2 twelve thousand three hundred
3 twelve thousand and thirty
4 one hundred and twenty thousand, three hundred
5 one hundred and twenty-three thousand
6 one hundred and twenty-three thousand, three hundred and thirty
7 one million, two hundred and thirty thousand

50.3
1 In addition 2 However 3 although 4 in spite of
5 Therefore 6 so 7 because of 8 because

50.4
1 c 2 f 3 a 4 b 5 e 6 d

50.5
1 much less than 2 almost/a little under 3 around/about
4 exactly/precisely 5 a little over/slightly more than
6 considerably more than

50.6
1 graph 2 figures 3 flat 4 although 5 because
6 recovery 7 up 8 by 9 million 10 euros 11 cut
12 However 13 half 14 rose 15 significantly 16 to
17 over 18 in

Test 1

Test 1.1
1 do you do 2 are you doing 3 don't understand
4 'm talking 5 isn't selling 6 know 7 're staying
8 's just leaving 9 makes 10 do you usually get
11 are the auditors coming 12 comes

Test 1.2
a PS b PC c PC d PS e PS f PC g PS h PC
1 b 2 f 3 a 4 e 5 h 6 d 7 c 8 g

Test 1.3
Present simple: after, always, as soon as, before, every day, hardly ever, most of the time, never, next time, normally, occasionally, often, sometimes, twice a year, until, usually, when
Present continuous: at the moment, currently, nowadays, right now, these days

Test 1.4

1 I usually have lunch at about 1 o'clock.
2 Lunch is often just a sandwich.
3 I visit Head Office in Paris from time to time.
4 I am hardly ever late in the morning.
5 I hardly ever take the train to work.
6 I prepare a sales report once a month.
7 I never miss a Board meeting.
8 I am never late for a Board meeting.

Test 1.5

1 ✓ 2 I agree 3 contain 4 ✓ 5 ✓ 6 We own
7 I know 8 ✓ 9 it seems 10 ✓ 11 ✓ 12 we have

Test 1.6

1 goes up/demand
2 is falling/means
3 Are you waiting/don't think
4 do our customers want/seems
5 hope/knows/'s doing
6 do you mean/don't understand
7 are you saying/Do you want
8 Does your chicken taste/depends/is working
9 aren't being/imagine/have/'re having
10 agree/'re wasting

Test 2

Test 2.1

1 became 2 began 3 broke 4 brought 5 bought
6 chose 7 ate 8 fell 9 found 10 forgot 11 grew
12 kept 13 led 14 lent 15 met 16 rose 17 sent
18 shut 19 spent 20 understood

Test 2.2

1 got/heard 2 used to claim 3 went down/was printing out
4 was/used to dream 5 was descending/started
6 wanted/chose 7 used to have/combined
8 arrived/was waiting 9 knocked/went
10 lost/were discussing 11 was/visited
12 was feeling/decided

Test 2.3

1 Michael had made 2 didn't use to 3 hadn't forgotten
4 used to produce 5 I had read (*or* seen) 6 had already left
7 used to go skiing 8 I had left the window

Test 2.4

1 while/when 2 When 3 at 4 in 5 on 6 When
7 While/When 8 in 9 at 10 when 11 at 12 in
13 while/when 14 when

Test 2.5

1 realized/had seen 2 got/had stopped
3 did you find out/had got 4 joined/had worked
5 sent/had already spoken 6 had always suspected/wasn't
7 left/had gained 8 was/had known

Test 2.6

1 had decided 2 had been thinking 3 had been waiting
4 had already heard 5 had been rising 6 hadn't finished
7 had never met 8 had been looking 9 had seen
10 had been losing

Test 3

Test 3.1

1 I've been waiting 2 I'm waiting 3 had 4 have had
5 I've left 6 I left 7 have you been working 8 are you working
9 haven't paid 10 didn't pay 11 did you last see
12 Have you seen

Test 3.2

1 ~~is~~ has been 2 ~~have started~~ started 3 ~~written~~ writing
4 ~~have you arrived~~ did you arrive
5 ~~You have~~ Have you
6 ~~been~~ has organized 7 ~~since~~ for
8 ~~live~~ have lived 9 ~~wait~~ have been waiting
10 ~~didn't give~~ haven't given 11 ~~'m~~ 've been
12 ~~do you work~~ have you worked

Test 3.3

1 since 2 always 3 already 4 ever 5 just 6 yet
7 for 8 never 9 often 10 So far

Test 3.4

1 has left 2 've never been 3 of *Business Grammar Builder* has
4 've just seen 5 haven't finished 6 working here for
7 (ever) been to Serbia 8 haven't spoken 9 Anna come
10 gone 11 haven't seen David 12 living here for
13 've left 14 haven't finished 15 just left 16 ever been
17 learning (*or* studying) 18 haven't had 19 never eaten
20 playing tennis for 21 forgotten 22 seen Marguerite since

Test 4

Test 4.1

1 I'll be 2 recovers 3 Shall I 4 will be 5 It's going to fall
6 I'll do 7 come back 8 She'll be working 9 we're going to
10 They'll probably

Test 4.2

1 I'm going to get 2 will be here 3 will probably get
4 is going to lend me 5 I'll see you 6 I won't be (*or* I can't be)
7 What exactly are you going 8 will probably

Test 4.3

a *will* b present continuous c *will* (contracted to *'ll*)
d *be going to* e *be going to* f *will* g future perfect
h future continuous
1 d 2 c 3 f 4 e 5 b 6 h 7 a 8 g

Test 4.4

1 I'll call 2 Shall I 3 conference ends (*or* finishes)
4 will you be 5 won't 6 you doing 7 I'll 8 'll be
9 Shall 10 will be launching

Test 4.5

1 Sarah isn't going to get 2 Shall we have 3 I'm going to study
4 I'll be back 5 I'm going to see 6 I won't forget
7 I'm going to do 8 Shall I help you 9 We'll come
10 I'm going to ask 11 I'll have 12 I'm going to have

Test 5

Test 5.1

1 ~~offer~~ offered 2 ~~was been posted~~ was posted
3 ~~be~~ being (*or* to be) 4 ~~ate~~ eaten 5 ~~produce~~ produced
6 ~~being~~ be 7 ~~giving~~ being given 8 ~~is~~ has 9 ~~writing~~ written
10 ~~losing~~ lost (*or* being lost)

Test 5.2

1 The casino has been closed.
2 Our house was broken into last week.
3 Nowadays English is spoken everywhere.
4 The new motorway has finally been opened (*or* has finally opened).
5 This bag was left in reception.
6 All traffic will be banned from the city center.
7 The liquid is left for 24 hours after adding the ingredients.
8 The meeting is being postponed.

Test 5.3

1 have just had all our machines serviced
2 are having the carpet cleaned tomorrow
3 had some business cards printed with the new logo
4 am getting my car repaired
5 have just had my request for credit refused
6 just got fined for illegal parking

Test 5.4

1 starting 2 mean 3 be taken 4 will bring 5 was addressed
6 highlighted 7 be ignored 8 is considered 9 is expected
10 will start 11 will be funded 12 to be found 13 to be done
14 be looked at 15 be given 16 be provided

Test 5.5

1 had these figures checked
2 much less coffee is grown in Columbia
3 was delivered this morning 4 is being redeveloped
5 have been put up 6 will be discussed in the meeting
7 had some new software installed 8 was born 9 were you
10 had his car 11 Alex told 12 a backup copy of this file been

Test 6

Test 6.1

1 can't 2 must 3 need to 4 must have 5 we'd better
6 might 7 should 8 must 9 can't have 10 have to
11 don't need to 12 can't

Test 6.2

1 don't have to 2 mustn't 3 might have 4 have to 5 must
6 could 7 had to 8 must have 9 should 10 didn't have to

Test 6.3

1 c 2 e 3 b 4 d 5 a 6 i 7 f 8 j 9 g 10 h

Test 6.4

1 should 2 don't have to 3 can't be 4 must be
5 should be 6 might be 7 can't 8 might 9 have to
10 ought to

Test 6.5

1 might have 2 must have 3 can't have 4 should have
5 might not have 6 should have 7 shouldn't have
8 could have

Test 7

Test 7.1

1 Have you finished yet?
2 Will I see you tomorrow?
3 Did you have a nice holiday?
4 Do you know what I mean?
5 Are you coming out for a drink later?
6 Have you been waiting long?
7 Are you enjoying yourself?
8 Have you heard the latest?

Test 7.2

1 what the time is 2 what this means 3 how much this costs
4 what time the bank opens 5 I'm in the right seat
6 where the Opera House is 7 this is the way to the station
8 who the speaker at the next session is (*or* who the speaker is at the next session)

Test 7.3

1 c 2 b 3 a 4 ✗ 5 ✗ 6 ✓ 7 ✓ 8 ✓ 9 ✗ 10 ✓

Test 7.4

1 I do/I don't 2 she does/she doesn't 3 they do/they don't
4 I have/I haven't 5 she has/she hasn't 6 I am/I'm not
7 she is/she isn't 8 I can/I can't 9 I will/I won't
10 I did/I didn't 11 it is/it isn't 12 it is/it isn't

Test 7.5

1 You have got 2 won't they 3 aren't leaving 4 haven't they
5 can't you 6 do you 7 didn't you 8 didn't forget
9 couldn't give 10 weren't 11 shall we 12 aren't I

Test 7.6

1 Do you take Visa?
2 Can I see the menu, please?
3 Excuse me, is anyone sitting here?
4 Which country do you come from?
5 Which route did you come by?
6 Who were you talking to just now?
7 What exactly do you mean by that?
8 Could you be a little more specific?
9 What time is the next train to Brussels?
10 Can you tell me what time the next train to Brussels is?
11 Do you need any help with your suitcase?
12 Who does this BlackBerry belong to?
13 Could I ask you something?
14 Do you think I could ask you something?
15 Where is the station?
16 Could you tell me where the station is?

Test 8

Test 8.1

1 would be 2 promote 3 had left 4 stay 5 I'd call 6 had
7 breaks down 8 could phone 9 doesn't recognize
10 we'd been 11 I'd've become 12 goes
13 backed up/wouldn't risk 14 hadn't acted/we'd be
15 had 16 was

Test 8.2

1 'd lose 2 'll be 3 'd've asked 4 'll get 5 'd get
6 'd've missed 7 'll leave 8 'd've sorted out 9 would you do
10 would you have done 11 wouldn't see 12 wouldn't've got

Test 8.3

1 unless 2 if 3 Unless 4 Otherwise 5 If 6 if
7 otherwise 8 unless

Test 8.4

1 had left early/wouldn't have missed
2 had made more copies/would have had
3 had brought your map/wouldn't have gone
4 had invested in new technology/would have survived
5 had waited/wouldn't have happened
6 had realized you were so busy/wouldn't have asked you
7 had collapsed/would have been
8 had brought out their new model on time/wouldn't have lost

Test 8.5

1 b 2 b 3 a 4 a 5 b 6 b 7 b 8 a

Test 8.6

1 were 2 had done 3 hadn't said 4 could speak
5 had ordered 6 had 7 could be 8 had given

Test 9

Test 9.1

1 to eat 2 coming 3 to come 4 giving 5 making
6 Remind 7 visiting 8 to be 9 to be 10 trying
11 to recruit 12 to believe 13 to get 14 interrupting
15 going 16 to meet 17 to deliver 18 winning 19 to see
20 to pack 21 arriving 22 to lift 23 getting away
24 to get away 25 to listen 26 being 27 losing 28 thinking
29 to order 30 to meet

Test 9.2

1 making 2 to rise 3 coming 4 to get through/getting
5 waiting 6 to give 7 causing 8 to compromise
9 unpacking 10 being

Test 10

Test 10.1

1 c 2 g 3 l 4 a 5 d 6 j 7 h 8 e 9 i 10 k
11 b 12 f

Test 10.2

1 I'm looking forward to 2 takes up
3 to put back the meeting to 4 to deal with 5 to sort it out
6 pick me up 7 to go over 8 get through
9 you come across it 10 run out of time

Test 10.3

1 on 2 over 3 through 4 out 5 down 6 by 7 up
8 off 9 into/back 10 away

Test 10.4

1 fall back on 2 get along with 3 cut down on 4 run out of
5 get around to 6 catch up with 7 sit in on 8 face up to
9 move on to 10 get back to

Test 10.5
1 c 2 g 3 f 4 i 5 d 6 b 7 a 8 k 9 l 10 j
11 h 12 e

Test 11

Test 11.1
1 doing 2 having 3 make 4 do 5 make/have/do
6 do/make 7 made/doing 8 makes/do 9 having/making
10 Have/make 11 made/do/do 12 doing/make/having
13 have/have/make 14 doing/have 15 doing/making/do
16 make 17 doing/made 18 have/do/making

Test 11.2
1 d 2 h 3 a 4 f 5 g 6 c 7 b 8 e
9 f 10 c 11 a 12 b 13 e 14 d

Test 12

Test 12.1
1 if (whether) I was going out
2 what I did (*or* had done)
3 if (whether) we often went to Germany
4 how many interviews I'd done
5 if (whether) she was going to change jobs
6 who I talked to (*or* had talked to)
7 if (whether) I would be
8 where our new offices were
9 if (whether) I had seen Anton
10 if (whether) I'd be seeing Masumi

Test 12.2
1 he'd see me there the next day (*or* the day after *or* the following day)
2 they received (*or* they'd received) our email update about the issue the previous week (*or* the week before)

Test 12.3
1 promised to meet Ekaterina
2 invited Jean to come to
3 advised Todd not to sign
4 suggested getting
5 apologized for arriving
6 offered to give
7 congratulated/on winning
8 refused to accept

Test 13

Test 13.1
1 that/which 2 whose 3 who 4 who/that 5 whose
6 which 7 that/which 8 which 9 whose 10 who
11 who/that 12 who/that

Test 13.2
1 (that/which) 2 ✓ 3 ✓ 4 (who/that) 5 ✓ 6 ✓
7 (that/which) 8 ✓ 9 ✓ 10 ✓ 11 ✓ 12 (who/that)

Test 13.3
1 who 2 that

Test 13.4
1 showed me a magazine article which was
2 that we went to yesterday was
3 presentation yesterday that was
4 whose laptop I borrowed wants it
5 who came yesterday gave me
6 that the Japanese visitors who came yesterday
7 who runs our office is
8 a woman whose sister works for
9 who is waiting in reception wants to

Test 14

Test 14.1
1 some time 2 a doctor 3 yours 4 they say that wine
5 every time 6 some advice 7 neither one
8 some information 9 none of us (*or* not one of us)
10 go by taxi 11 was very busy 12 so many 13 None at all
14 Jane's colleague 15 either 16 too little 17 each one
18 Ministry's 19 enough chairs 20 no spare parts 21 is
22 at the end of the report 23 both 24 everyone (or each one)
25 hers 26 some information 27 anything 28 both
29 there wasn't a single question 30 isn't anyone 31 its
32 the boss's son

Test 14.2
Countable nouns: an apartment, a desk, a bag, a job, a trip, a problem, a chance, a litre, a machine, a dollar, an email, a fact, a suggestion, an hour, a course, a law, a step forward, an idea, a policy
Uncountable nouns: some accommodation, some furniture, some luggage, some work, some travel, some trouble, some luck, some wine, some equipment, some money, some correspondence, some information, some advice, some time, some training, some legislation, some progress, some brainstorming, some insurance

Test 14.3
1 There's something in 2 some advice 3 by train
4 Something is worrying 5 on foot 6 one of my boss's friends
7 a tax advisor 8 Nobody knows this business 9 got nothing to
10 Everybody here drinks 11 someone/somebody driving
12 The unemployed need 13 redesigning 14 is nothing we can
15 How much did 16 isn't much 17 an accountant
18 Everybody was late 19 couldn't do anything
20 Not a single person 21 There is no 22 was not in
23 the customer's copy 24 There isn't anything

Test 15

Test 15.1
1 interested 2 by the end 3 very hard 4 lovely blue
5 so friendly 6 extremely good 7 very well 8 tired
9 We never give 10 interested 11 so much
12 such a risky project 13 not experienced enough
14 enough time 15 larger than 16 as large as
17 the best price 18 for three months 19 so tense
20 When I get back 21 before 22 than they do 23 too high
24 less useful 24 as swimming 25 until six

Test 15.2
1 on 2 ago 3 for 4 since 5 on/at/in 6 in 7 on
8 afterwards 9 then 10 After 11 for 12 at 13 at
14 for 15 since 16 During 17 While 18 In/During

Test 15.3

1 spoke really well
2 've been working on this project since January
3 is more profitable than retail banking
4 works very carefully
5 the worst service I have ever seen
6 stayed in Paris until
7 you interested in opera
8 finished positively
9 worked hard
10 plays golf badly
11 plays golf well
12 talk more slowly
13 is not as big as the Chinese market
14 just as many products as Thierry
15 is the least experienced member of the team
16 During the interview
17 've been doing this job since 2008
18 away on holiday until
19 on time
20 in time to save the negotiations
21 your report by
22 in the end we gave up
23 started building this prototype four months ago
24 for two

Test 16

Test 16.1

1 at 2 in 3 at/in 4 over 5 in/in 6 on 7 at
8 to 9 on 10 on 11 at 12 over 13 under 14 at
15 in/at 16 in 17 at 18 to/in 19 on 20 on
21 in/at 22 on

Test 16.2

1 for 2 to 3 to 4 against 5 on/for 6 of 7 into
8 from 9 for 10 with 11 in 12 about 13 on 14 of
15 about 16 with 17 to 18 on 19 in 20 from

Test 16.3

1 about 2 on 3 with 4 in 5 in 6 of 7 in
8 with/for 9 to 10 from 11 for 12 for 13 at
14 for 15 for 16 to

Test 16.4

1 price of 2 reason for 3 advantage of 4 trouble with
5 matter with 6 reply to 7 lack of 8 solution to
9 substitute for 10 investment in 11 advice on
12 pessimism about 13 compliance with 14 increase in

Test 16.5

1 on 2 inside 3 next to 4 to 5 at 6 near 7 across
8 down 9 on 10 at 11 on 12 opposite 13 at 14 off

Index

B

C

D

E

F

G

H

I

J

K

L

M

Q

R